Five Comedies from the Italian Renaissance

Five Comedies
from the Italian Renaissance

Translated and Edited by

LAURA GIANNETTI

&

GUIDO RUGGIERO

THE JOHNS HOPKINS UNIVERSITY PRESS
Baltimore

The Johns Hopkins University Press
2715 North Charles Street
Baltimore, Maryland 21218-4363
www.press.jhu.edu

Library of Congress Cataloging-in-Publication Data
Five comedies from the Italian renaissance /
translated and edited by Laura Giannetti and Guido Ruggiero.
    p.   cm.
Includes bibliographical references.
ISBN 0-8018-7257-X (hbk. : alk. paper)
ISBN 0-8018-7258-8 (pbk. : alk. paper)
1. Italian drama—To 1700—Translations into English. 2. Italian drama (Comedy)—
Translations into English. I. Giannetti, Laura. II. Ruggiero, Guido, 1944—
PQ4244.E6 G534 2003
852'.05230802—dc21
2002009446

A catalog record for this book is available from the British Library.

Per Delma

Contents

Acknowledgments

This project began as a pleasant diversion from other scholarly projects. We were reading Renaissance comedies out loud in Italian and in their English translations for pleasure when we decided that it would be fun to translate for ourselves and our classes Aretino's playful and irreverent *Il marescalco.* The challenges and satisfactions of that translation slowly pulled us into the larger and more demanding project of translating these five comedies. As the project grew, the satisfactions and fun remained, but it engendered a great deal more work than originally anticipated. Fortunately, we were aided and supported in that work by a large group of colleagues and friends whom we would like to thank here not only for their efforts in behalf of this project but also for the way in which they helped to keep it a pleasure.

First and most notably we want to thank those who have read all or part of these translations against the Italian originals: Deanna Shemek, Valeria Finucci, and Dennis Looney. Without their careful and thoughtful readings and their ready collaboration these translations would be much less successful than they are. A large number of other colleagues have contributed to this project, including the Italianists Konrad Eisenbichler, Albert Russell Ascoli, Jane Tylus, Tita Rosenthal, Pier Mario Vescovo, Daria Perocco, Carmela Pesca Cupolo, Elissa Weaver, Maria Galli Stampino, Eugenio Giusti, and the late Robert Dombroski; and other scholars of the period including Edward Muir, Lauro Martines, Joanne Ferraro, Claudio Povolo, Gherardo Ortalli, Marion Kuntz, Mary Lindemann, Ian Frederick Moulton, Peter Stallybrass, Ann Rosalind Jones, Martin Elsky, and Patricia Labalme. Special thanks are also in order for Henry Tom, our editor at Johns Hopkins, and Mary Yates, our hardworking and long-suffering copy editor.

Colleagues at Penn State have also furnished much-appreciated assistance, most notably Linda Woodbridge, Roland Anderson, Robert Lima, A. Gregg Roeber, Londa Schiebinger, Robert Proctor, Amy Greenberg, Susan Squier, Joan Landes, Ted Norton, Nan Woodruff, Matthew Restall, R. Po-chia Hsia, and Sophie De Schaepdrijver. Without the generous support of Josephine Berry Weiss and the Weiss Chair she endowed at Penn State, this project would have been much more difficult to complete. Special thanks are also in order for the staff of the History Department there, always ready to tackle the most bothersome tasks at a moment's notice and with a forgiving smile for our strange jokes and questionable irony.

Along with the scholars noted above, many in Italy have helped with this project. Patrizia Bravetti and Annalisa Bruni at the Marciana library and Michela Dal Borgo at the Venetian Archivio di Stato, as usual, have been particularly helpful both in their official capacities and as friends and scholars. Numerous other friends there have weathered accounts of our ongoing saga of arcane translation woes and triumphs and offered both much-appreciated advice and support; they merit special thanks, especially Sandro Bosato, Virna Pozzobon, Roberto Zambon, Alberta Avila, Rita Giannetti, Valentino Gastini, and Antonietta Mattioni, as well as Mike Torresan and Mauro Zilio who also provided much-needed technical help. Delma Peruch has been a most appreciated and prized friend, supporter, and mother; to her we dedicate these translations.

Introduction: Playing the Renaissance

At the turn of the sixteenth century, with the Italian Renaissance at its cultural high point, Italians discovered a new/old art form: ancient Latin comedies updated and rewritten in Italian. These plays, with their humor, sex, and playful exploration of what we would today call gender roles and social stereotypes, along with their snappy plots and lively wordplay, quickly captured the imagination of Renaissance society and particularly the upper classes. As a result, in the early decades of the century there was a flowering of Italian comedies that loosely imitated ancient Roman models, hence the slightly misleading name given the genre, "erudite comedy." These comedies were written by some of the leading intellectual figures of the age, including Niccolò Machiavelli, Pietro Aretino, and Cardinal Bernardo Dovizi da Bibbiena, all of whom are represented in this volume. These authors and their peers purloined plots from the ancient Roman tradition; from the popular Renaissance short-story form, the *novella,* made popular in the fourteenth century by Boccaccio in *The Decameron;* and from a lively oral culture that delighted in tales of cunning tricksters, sexual escapades, mistaken identity, and young love triumphing over patriarchal wisdom.

Fittingly, these comedies that often turned the everyday world upside down—with women characters playing men and men playing women, with servants ruling masters, with old husbands unknowingly putting their young wives into bed with their lovers, with love triumphing over family marital goals, with wise men acting like fools and fools in love gaining miraculous cunning—were usually performed during carnival, as part of the "anything goes" atmosphere of that special time of the year. In turn, carnival—a festive time of license preceding Lent—found in the comedies of the Italian Renaissance an explosion of playfulness that suited it perfectly. At the same time, however, the play of these comedies was at once fun and social work of the highest order, for in them their authors, actors, and audiences tested the social boundaries of the everyday world and moved beyond those boundaries in ways that were at once titillating, tantalizing, and exploratory.

Now, in theory, in both carnival and comedy such playfulness always came to an end—in carnival with the beginning of Lent, and in the comedy at the end of the last act with a happy ending that returned things to normal. But this is too easy and comfortable a reading. It is the premise of this collection that like carnival, Renaissance comedies did not end with the last act, just as they did not begin with the prologue. They were so popular, so quickly, so deeply embedded in Renaissance culture, that they literally played out some of its deepest themes in the imagination of the time long after carnival and comedy ended. They lived on in the imagination of the upper-class audiences who saw them, because they were so deeply rooted in the everyday realities, humor, and tensions of their world. They also lived on in that they were not merely played out on the stage, they were replayed as literature in published form—often reworked, embellished with yet cleverer wordplay and more complex humor—and were read widely thanks to new, cheaper forms of printing that made such material widely available. And they lived on in the form of endlessly retold tales and jokes, converted back to the oral tradition from which many of them had originally come. Beyond theater, beyond literature, beyond the distinctions between high and low, elite and common, licit and illicit, many of these comedies played out of stage and played imaginatively with the Renaissance itself. With this volume we hope not only to make five of the most intriguing of these comedies available in lively new translations, but also to allow readers to enter the rich and playful world of the Renaissance imagination.

One of the hardest problems we faced was deciding which comedies to include. Essentially we were guided by three closely related criteria. First, we wanted our selections to reflect the historical development of the genre so that readers would come away with a good sense of how Renaissance comedy worked and how it developed. Second, we wanted to select comedies that dealt with the major themes of the genre as a whole—sex, gender, and play—and that brought a carnivalesque perspective to the Renaissance understanding of these aspects of life. And finally, we wanted to select plays that could be simply enjoyed by modern readers for their imagination, humor, and swift-moving plots.

The Comedies

The volume begins with *La calandra* (The Comedy of Calandro) by Bernardo Dovizi da Bibbiena (1470–1520), a noted humanist and an official of the papal court when he wrote the comedy who shortly after became a cardinal. It was one of the earliest Renaissance comedies, first performed in 1513, and as such it became one of the most important exemplars of the genre. It deals with two of the most common themes of the genre: characters dressing to pass as the opposite sex (in a revealing and imaginative exploration of gender roles) and humorous complications caused by cases of mistaken identity (again, in a revealing and imaginative exploration of the way in which identity was marked during the Renaissance). It is difficult to summarize the twists and turns of the plot, which involves a brother and sister, Lidio and Santilla, each masquerading as a member of the opposite sex; a randy old patriarch, Calandro, falling for an attractive youth who is in fact Lidio dressed as a woman as part of a scheme to make love to Calandro's own wife, Fulvia; a series of servants anxious to clear the path for young love; and a charlatan necromancer claiming that he can make people fall madly in love, for a price. The convoluted plot creates a comedic world in which much of the fun for the audience lies in trying to anticipate what turn the action will take next. But with characters exchanging gender roles, the game takes on greater imaginative tension, for the audience now must anticipate the actions of individuals who have transgressed sexual mores and the accepted boundaries of gender. In the end, as is often the case, the patriarch is exposed as the fool that he is (in a series of slapstick gags illustrating Renaissance broad humor at its best); youthful passion wins out; and two marriages in the final act appear to provide the traditional happy ending, giving closure to the transgressive play of the comedy.

The marriages, however, leave some interesting and troubling loose ends that suggest that the closure is merely an illusion. The first marriage involves the main female character, Santilla, who has appeared throughout most of the play passing very successfully as a young man—something that would in itself have been troubling to a contemporary audience, given the Renaissance assurance that women were naturally inferior to men. She marries Fulvia's son Flaminio, a young man whom she has never met, and does so not out of some suddenly discovered love for him—the typical excuse for such marriages—but rather for access to his family's wealth and to provide a cover for his mother's adulterous affair with Santilla's own brother, Lidio. The second marriage, between Lidio and the daughter of Perillo, does seem to tie up some loose ends but then creates a host of new ones. Lidio too has never met his bride, and he is actually in love with the mother of his sister's new husband and deeply committed to that adulterous relationship. Moreover, he enters into the marriage under what can only be called false pretenses, passing himself off to his new wife and her family as the same young man whom his sister had so successfully impersonated in Perillo's household. "Twisted webs" indeed!

In both these marriages, the celebration of young love that is supposedly at the heart of happy endings takes a back seat to financial considerations and illicit sexual pleasure—not unheard of in the Renaissance, but the extreme nature of the deception would have been virtually as troubling to a Renaissance audience as to a modern one. In a sense, of course, young love does triumph, for the marriages mask and allow to continue, for the foreseeable future at least, the adulterous affair between Lidio and Fulvia. But this arrangement—an ongoing adulterous relationship between a newlywed man of about eighteen and his own sister's mother-in-law, a married woman old enough to be his mother—hardly provides the return to normal life that is supposed to characterize the end of a comedy and of the carnival season. This sexually explicit comedy of trickery and adultery written by a powerful future cardinal of the church—who came close to winning the papacy before he died under suspicious circumstances, perhaps poisoned to eliminate him from the competition—is a suggestive warning about how different Renaissance attitudes toward sex and gender were. And it also reveals how playful and troubling even a future cardinal's imagination could be when it came to matters of illicit sex and financial intrigue in the Renaissance.

THE SECOND COMEDY in the volume, Niccolò Machiavelli's *La mandragola* (The Mandrake Root), is another of the earliest and most popular Renaissance comedies; in fact, it has often been called the greatest Italian comedy of the age. It is also one of the best known and most frequently translated, for it was written by the famed political thinker Machiavelli (1469–1527), most noted for *The Prince* and *The Discourses*, his classic works on politics and power. And it suggests a different side of the supposedly dour, hard-headed, Machiavellian Machiavelli who in fact spent many years of his adult life experimenting with comedy as a literary form and wrote two major comedies that survive. This quick and flashy play, about an old lawyer, Messer Nicia, who is tricked into putting his own wife into bed with her would-be lover, shows a humorous and sexual side of Machiavelli that is largely absent from his political writings.

But the clever and cruel trick that leads Messer Nicia to crown himself with cuckold's horns is in many ways more Machiavellian than anything described in *The Prince*, and the key to the trick is the same as the key to the prince's success: *virtù*. *Virtù* in the Renaissance was that combination of cleverness and skill, reason and cunning, that made one man superior to another, and many a Renaissance joke hinged on the way in which possessing this quality allowed one man to triumph over another, whether as a prince or as a lover. Machiavelli's humor also turns on the conflict between the young and old—a classic theme in societies in which wealth, power, and women are controlled by patriarchs, but here colored by a decidedly Renaissance and Machiavellian context, with youthful passion grabbing fortune from the hands of complacent and ultimately foolish "wisdom." This is a play that can be understood on many levels, but even at the most basic level of a joke it reads well and exemplifies the Renaissance fascination with the *beffa* or *burla:* the clever joke that usually victimizes a fool and shows who society's real winners are.

La mandragola is Machiavelli at his most seductive and subversive and provides an excellent introduction to the sex, gender, and play of Renaissance comedies. And again, it is a comedy that does not seem really to end at the end. For although Machiavelli may have cleverly—dare we suggest Machiavellianly—hidden a marriage scene at the end, there is no formal marriage to provide a happy ending for young love; rather, young love is rewarded with a perfect cover under which it can continue as an adulterous relationship aided by the foolish and endlessly cuckolded Messer Nicia.

THE THIRD COMEDY provides a different perspective on Renaissance sex and happiness with yet another clever joke at its core. Pietro Aretino (1492–1556) wrote *Il marescalco* (The Master of the Horse) in the late 1520s after being forced to flee Rome, reportedly because of the obscene poems he had written to accompany Giulio Romano's famous engravings of sexual positions, which apparently scandalized even that jaded city. After wandering for a time, he settled in Venice, writing controversial and risqué works as well as saints' lives and religious tracts; it seems that he never quite gave up the idea of a career in the church, even as he gained international fame for his sexually explicit works and literary attacks on the rich and powerful.

Il marescalco is Aretino at his playfully perverse and subversive best. In a society that often burned male sodomites (at least the active partners) and officially recognized male/male sex as a heinous crime and a sin capable of literally calling down the wrath of God, as on Sodom and Gomorrah, Aretino made his hero, the Marescalco, an open and practicing sodomite who as the comedy opens is being pressed by his lord, the tyrant *(signore)* of Mantua, to take an as yet unseen bride with a handsome dowry as a "reward" for his service. As the Marescalco voices his objections to the plan, we get an extended comic reprise of the Renaissance debate for and against marriage. More interesting still is the clever way in which Aretino guides us through life in a city dominated by a Renaissance prince and court and brings us to the marriage of his hero / victim. Along the way we come to identify with this sympathetically portrayed misogynistic "sodomite" (a most surprising leap to contemplate in the context of Renaissance culture) and in a scene of classic theater follow him through a comic wedding, watching him discover what we already know: that the joke is on him, but to his advantage, for the bride is none other than the young page Carlo, convincingly disguised as a girl—once again the happy ending required of all comedies, but with a decidedly Renaissance twist, for the Marescalco marries a partner exactly to his taste and everyone leaves the stage in laughter.

THE FOURTH PLAY, *Gl'ingannati* (The Deceived), is a classic that was widely imitated during the Renaissance, most notably by Shakespeare in *Twelfth Night.* Like a number of other Renaissance comedies, it was written by the members of an academic society—in this case, the Intronati (the Dazed)[1] of Siena—and was first performed in that city during carnival of 1532. Officially written as an apology to the women of Siena for a previous slight by the group, it is a prototypical Renaissance comedy of cross-dressing, mistaken identity, and youth versus old age.

The main character is a young woman, Lelia, who, dressed as a man, has escaped the convent where her father had left her for safekeeping. In this disguise and going by the name Fabio, she returns to Modena and finds employment as the manservant of the man she loves, who in her absence has fallen in love with another woman, Isabella. Lelia is a considerable success as a young man, so much so that Isabella herself falls in love with her. The resulting complications are both comic and subversive: passing as a man, Lelia exchanges passionate kisses with another woman, she lives as a man with the man she loves, and she flirts with the danger of being sexually assaulted, as either a man or a woman, by the aggressive young men of Modena. The situations in which she

---

1. Many Renaissance academic societies took playfully humorous names that seemed in part to mock their intellectual pretensions but that also suggested the pleasure and play that they saw as crucial attributes of intellectual life. During the Renaissance serious scholarly activity and play were still seen as going together, as such names imply.

finds herself reveal and also challenge Renaissance assumptions about sex and gender for both young men and women.

Things come quickly to a head, however, when Lelia's father returns and concludes plans to marry her to an "old" man roughly his own age. Such arranged marriages were the norm in upper-class circles, and there was frequently a substantial age differential between the young wife and her older husband. But as the play makes clear, large age disparities in arranged marriage were unlikely to result in sexual happiness or a satisfying married life for the young woman. And to give the plot one more suggestive twist, the old man whom Lelia is doomed to marry is none other than the father of Isabella, the woman who has fallen in love with her in her guise as Fabio.

Fortunately for young love, these marriage plans are thwarted in the end, with the return of Lelia's long-lost lookalike brother, Fabrizio. A case of mistaken identity cleverly resolves this apparently hopelessly tangled web of human desires. Mistaken for Lelia in her Fabio disguise, Fabrizio is locked in a bedroom with Isabella for safekeeping. Believing that this is the Fabio she is in love with, Isabella takes full advantage of the situation and at last enjoys the more aggressive expressions of love that she has all along been attempting to get from Lelia—a scene that we do not see but that is reported to us, or at least to the women in the audience, by a servant who accidentally walks in on the young couple in the act. The result is two potential disasters for Renaissance family honor: one young woman, Isabella, who has lost both her virginity and her honor, and another, Lelia, who has merely lost her honor, for dressing as a man (and perhaps for seducing a woman). But both disasters are remedied by a series of weddings that reward young love, thwart patriarchal discipline, and seem to end the play happily.

With the wayward women safely wedded and bedded and family honor restored, it would appear that the transgressions of the play have been successfully resolved. Finally, a comedy that returns life to normal, as the genre supposedly requires. But those who subscribe to this reading of *Gl'ingannati* may be just further victims of its deceptions. For both modern and Renaissance audiences and readers have been exposed to Renaissance women who have successfully penetrated far beyond the boundaries of acceptable sexual and gender behavior—making the play not just humorous but a delicious and dangerous adventure in imagining other possible ways of behaving and living.

THE LAST COMEDY in the volume is both the least typical and the least known. Discovered only in the twentieth century, *La veniexiana* (The Venetian Comedy), written primarily in Venetian dialect, is thought by most scholars to date from the mid-1530s, although a later date may be implied by the heavy emphasis on aristocratic manners and courteous forms of address. The fact that it apparently was never performed and was unknown during the Renaissance also suggests that it may have been written later in the century, when, as a consequence of religious reform, risqué comedies had become less performable, at least in upper-class circles, and more difficult to publish as well. It is profoundly different from other comedies that survive from the period, also perhaps implying a later date of composition.

The main characters are two Venetian women in competition for the same young male lover—on the surface a fairly common theme. But these women are less interested in love than in sex, and the limited plot unfolds from a decidedly feminine point of view, with the sex object of the comedy being clearly the young man, whom both women pursue aggressively within the constraints placed upon them by Renaissance gender norms. Rather than taking place in the streets and squares of a city—the quintessentially masculine domain of the period, and the setting of most Renaissance comedies—the action of this play is largely confined to the bedrooms and halls of private homes, the classic space of women. And in the end there is not even a nod at marriage, resolution, or closure. There is a vaguely happy ending in the sense that both the women will have finally made love to young Giulio. But given the jealous nature of the older lover, Angela, the imperious ways of the younger Valiera, and the fickle Giulio's inexperience, the comedy seems to end not with real closure but poised in the proverbial calm before the storm.

The contrast with other Renaissance comedies is striking—so striking, in fact, that some have been tempted to suggest that this little-known play may have been written by a Venetian woman. Its strongly misogynistic tone might seem to be evidence to the contrary, although, of course, in the Renaissance (as today) misogyny was not limited to men, and the author of this comedy has a good eye for the complexities and power dynamics of life as a Renaissance wife and widow, a world not likely to have been familiar or of interest to most male writers of the period. Whether written by a woman or not, the play, with its open emphasis on sex—including an onstage depiction of sex between women—and its lack of any attempt at a resolution that restores the female characters to their "normal" roles as wives and mothers under the control of men, is a suggestive contrast to the other plays in this volume. Yet like the others, it provides an ending that invites a rethinking of the playful world of the comedy and of Renaissance comedies in general.

Some Reflections on the Social and Cultural World of Renaissance Comedy

At the beginning of the second book of his major work on political theory, *The Discourses*, Machiavelli writes poignantly about the way in which older men—such as he considered himself to be when he wrote this work, in his mid-forties—look on the present and the past, arguing that older men tend to see the present always in a negative light because they have lost the optimism of youth and tend to remember only the positives in their past, overlooking its many negatives. From such an introduction one might expect Machiavelli to go on to argue that the present is not really as bad as it seems, but instead he laments, "Today there is nothing to make more palatable the extreme misery, infamy, and back biting of our times; there is no respect for religion, law, military virtues, rather everything is stained with filth."[2] What moved Machiavelli to reject his own insight and to opt for a negative vision of his own day was that in many ways he and his contemporaries did view their present—the last years of the fifteenth and the first half of the sixteenth century—as the worst of times, and perhaps even the end of time.

Most people, like Machiavelli, saw this period of crisis as having begun with the invasion of Italy by the armies of the French king, Charles VIII, in 1494. This initiated a half-century of war that saw the major powers of Europe fighting out dynastic battles, primarily in the Italian peninsula—a period of turmoil that ended with most of the once proudly independent Italian city-states under the control of the Hapsburg emperors, their Spanish minions, or the French. In fact, these troubling times were so much a part of the mental world of the period that they regularly serve as the source of background events that set in motion the plots of our comedies. For example, in Machiavelli's own *La mandragola* the youthful lover Callimaco refers to the fact that he has just returned to Florence from France, where he had been living peacefully avoiding the wars in Italy. And in *Gl'ingannati* the young heroine, Lelia, and her father, Virginio, have had their lives overturned by the sack of Rome, carried out by troops of the emperor Charles V in 1527, and have lost much of their wealth (and Lelia's twin brother, Fabrizio, as well). At a seemingly much less significant level, these comedies are filled with humor that demeans foreigners, especially the Germans, the Spanish, and the French—those very foreigners who were seen

---

2. Nicolò Machiavelli, *Tutte le opere*, ed. Mario Martelli (Florence: Sansoni, 1971), 145; *Discorsi*, book 2, introd.

as having brought on this period of war and upheaval that ended what many believed was a golden age. In sum, in a time when crisis haunted the imagination of people living in Italian Renaissance cities, that same sense of crisis lies just beneath the surface of the action of their comedies.

BUT MACHIAVELLI DID NOT BLAME these worst of times entirely or even primarily on the foreign invasions of Italy, for he saw the success of the invaders as not so much a result of their merits as a result of the demerits of Italians, as the rather moralizing tone of the passage quoted earlier suggests. For him the Italians of the age lacked those strengths of character that had once made the city-states of Italy superior to the rest of Europe and that had allowed Italians to dominate the rest of Europe culturally, economically, and even to a degree politically. Those strengths were nicely summed up in one word that was a favorite of the time and central to Machiavelli's political and social theories: *virtù*. And not surprisingly, given its importance in the Renaissance, *virtù* plays a central role in our comedies as well. At one level, *virtù* meant something quite simple: an approach to life and a set of behaviors that made one person superior to another. Thus throughout our comedies certain characters are constantly alerting us that they deserve our empathy and are superior (presumably like us) because they have *virtù*, while others are constantly demonstrating that they deserve to be laughed at or be made victims of cruel jokes or even to be despised because they lack this quality. In fact, these comedies offer a better illustration of the complexities and nuances of *"virtù"* than we could provide with any simple definition.

There are two main reasons why defining the term is so difficult. First, it was quite socially sensitive. In other words, it could have quite different meanings at different social levels: what made one servant or artisan better than another was not what made one noble or gentleman better than another.

Second, the meaning of the term changed as social perceptions changed over time. Broadly speaking, however, for the upper classes we can chart three general shifts across the Renaissance. At the end of the Middle Ages and the beginning of the Renaissance (roughly 1200–1325), in most of northern Italy *virtù* was still associated with a warrior ethos that had set a rural warrior nobility above the rest of society: *virtù* placed a premium on direct, often violent action and implied a distrust of overly reasoned behavior; it prized camaraderie between male warriors and a set of behaviors that were direct, brusque, and violent. With the shift to a more urban focus and the increasing domination of the upper classes by merchants, bankers, and lawyers, the meaning of *virtù* changed, and in some ways that change marks the beginning of the Renaissance. The older values of a warrior society were slowly displaced by the values of this new elite, and by the opening of the fifteenth century, if not earlier, *virtù* had become a set of characteristics that included a more reasoned and calculated approach to life that placed a premium on being able to control the future through planning, discipline, and indirect action using moderate behavior that stressed self-control. Perhaps the one exception to this more controlled and moderate vision of correct behavior was in the realm of love, and this tension between *virtù* and love lies at the heart of virtually all of our comedies, as will be discussed below.

Finally, what Machiavelli at the beginning of the sixteenth century viewed as a lack of *virtù* in his times might be more correctly viewed as yet another shift in the vision of that quality. As the now old merchant-banker elites of the earlier Renaissance became more aristocratic—the most notable example being perhaps the Medici family of Florence, who had started out as bankers (and probably pawnbrokers) and during the sixteenth century gradually became nobles and dukes—the ideal of *virtù* continued to evolve. Especially important in this newer vision of *virtù* were the manners and courtly ways that suited a new, more aristocratic upper class who now, rather than investing in trade and competing to rule their city-states, more and more preferred to invest in land, live off their revenues, and socialize at court—a newer reality that Aretino bitterly satirizes in *Il marescalco* and that is deeply integrated into the extreme courtesies and careful dissimulations of *La veniexiana*.

As it evolved across the Renaissance, however, *virtù* was constantly evaluated by society in terms of honor—another crucial concept in our plays. People who displayed *virtù* were deemed to be honorable; those who did not lacked honor, and they not only were shameful but often were publicly shamed. The full implications of this in Renaissance society and in our comedies are hard to understand today because the honor/shame dynamic is less strong in modern society and less closely evaluated in the public arena, at least in most areas of life today. If one were to imagine the types of pressures that teenagers today feel to wear certain brand-name products playing a significant role in virtually all social interactions, one would begin to have some sense of the power of the honor/shame evaluation in the Renaissance. Of course, even that analogy is misleading, but at the heart of this public evaluation of honor was a crucial performative aspect of life in the Renaissance. As Machiavelli himself was quick to point out, it was less what you actually were that mattered and much more how you displayed yourself in a public situation. Honor, shame, and in a way even self were much more publicly evaluated phenomena, and the fascination with all these issues in our comedies and the way in which they are played out on stage suggest a great deal about how these things worked in the Renaissance.

ONE THING THAT OFTEN DISTURBS READERS of these comedies is that much of the humor is so cruel that it hardly seems funny. This humor has sometimes been explained as a type of universal human behavior that distinguishes outsiders from insiders or defines certain people as society's scapegoats, but the *virtù*-honor-shame dynamic of the Renaissance provides a much more culturally specific explanation. People who publicly display their lack of *virtù* are people without honor, and not only do they deserve to be mistreated, they *must* be mistreated—publicly—in order both to be forced back to *virtù* and the correct ways of behaving and to serve as a lesson for others. This was done in many ways during the Renaissance, but one popular way was through the *beffa* or *burla:* a cruel joke that humorously demonstrated to all, including the butt of the joke, the lack of honor and *virtù* in certain forms of behavior.

Aretino's *Il marescalco* can be read in part as one long cruel joke that turns on the main character's incorrect sexual preference for young boys and his determination to stick with that preference over what society and *virtù* required: leaving young boys behind when one reached adulthood to take on a wife and all the responsibilities of adult male life, especially the continuing of a family line through fathering and raising children. Time and again the Marescalco is warned about the dishonorableness of his behavior, and eventually the duke of Mantua does as he has threatened to do throughout the play and forces him to marry. Threatened with death and thoroughly humiliated, the Marescalco submits, in a comically brutal travesty of the usual happy weddings that supposedly end Renaissance comedies. But Aretino irreverently turns the traditional *burla* on its head—calling into question the *virtù* of the courtiers who witness the whole event and perhaps traditional Renaissance sexual mores as well—by revealing in the end that the bride is none other than a comely young boy disguised as a girl. The intended victim leaves the stage laughing happily with his perfect "bride" as one of the courtiers ruefully remarks, "I guess we've been had." In the end the *burla* is on the other characters of the play, especially the courtiers of Mantua.

Machiavelli's *La mandragola* offers another classic *burla,* this time in a noncourtly setting and with an apparently more traditional sense of *virtù.* The butt of the cruel joke here is the old lawyer Messer Nicia, a man so blinded by his desire to have children and so deluded in his belief in his own wisdom that he never realizes that he is being dishonored. Led by the cunning Ligurio and the unscrupulous Fra Timoteo—each a slightly different twist on the Machiavellian view of men of *virtù*—Messer Nicia eventually puts his own wife to bed with Callimaco, the man who wants to become her lover, makes sure with his own hands that he is being well and truly cuckolded, and lives happily ever after, the oblivious victim of adulterous young love.

In a similar fashion poor old Calandro, the cuckolded husband of Bibbiena's *La calandra*, finds himself the butt of a series of pratfall-type jokes. All turn on his lack of *virtù* and the cleverness of the servant Fessenio, who claims to be able to teach him how to "drink" a woman and to kill and resurrect himself, and convinces him that he must be dismembered and put into a trunk. And, of course, in the end Calandro too suffers the typical fate of dishonored husbands lacking *virtù* in Renaissance comedies: he is cuckolded, and the comedy ends with the assurance that he will continue to be so.

ANOTHER IMPORTANT FORM OF HUMOR in these comedies also turns on the *virtù*-honor-shame dynamic: the comic reversals of the normal order of things that were broadly associated with Renaissance humor and carnival. At the simplest level, such humor could be as basic as the quip by Giannicco in *Il marescalco* about a wall urinating on a man—a reversal of the ordinary practice of men urinating on walls. But reversal-type humor went much deeper into the imaginative world of the Renaissance, playing with and testing the very boundaries and givens of that world in ways that made these comedies at once transgressive, funny, and fun to imagine. Perhaps the best examples are the female characters who skate on the edge of what honor allows (and beyond) by dressing as men, a major theme in two of our plays, *La calandra* and *Gl'ingannati*, and in many other Renaissance comedies. These women reverse normal gender roles by passing as men and in the process reflect as women on what it means to be a man, often quite consciously enjoying the reversal of the normal order. That such behavior was considered to be dishonorable and dangerous adds spice to the humor of, for example, the scene in which we see Lelia kissing Isabella and discussing what an enjoyable game it is to do so. Later she worries, as do we, about what it will lead to, but the delicious reversal of the scene calls for laughter, a laughter perhaps strengthened by the dangerous way in which that kiss turns the world on its head. Adding another twist to these gender reversals is the fact that until the 1560s in Italy all the actors in these comedies would have been male. Watching the scene in which Lelia disguised as a man kisses Isabella, a Renaissance audience would have known that it was "actually" a woman kissing a woman, and also that it was even more "actually" a man playing a woman kissing another man playing a woman. How deliciously transgressive to have one apparently simple kiss on stage that can be imagined as female/female sex, as male/male sex, or as a simple case of a treacherous servant kissing his master's mistress; such humor really does turn the world on its head.

RETURNING TO *VIRTÙ:* In *La calandra,* in *La mandragola,* and to a degree in *Gl'ingannati,* the characters who display the most *virtù* are, suggestively, not male members of the upper classes but servants like Fessenio, men of lesser standing on the make like Ligurio, and women like Lelia or Santilla. This may be simply because *virtù* was expected of upper-class men and thus was funnier and more interesting to imagine in its lack than in its presence among such individuals. In turn, the power of *virtù* is clearly more visible and telling when we see it working where one would normally not expect it: in servants, men of lesser standing, and young women (reversals of the normal order of things again). Of course, the plot lines of these plays were often drawn from ancient comedies or Renaissance popular stories, both of which genres typically featured clever servants and the weak triumphing over the strong. But from their central role in these comedies it is clear that these themes had special resonances in the sixteenth century as well. The centrality of these themes in Renaissance comedy may also reflect deeper tensions in the period such as an increasing sense of powerlessness in the upper classes related to political and social changes associated with foreign domination and the rise of a more courtly society. But *virtù* figures in these comedies largely as an attribute of those normally seen as powerless, and that may reveal ultimately how deeply the faith in its powers was ingrained in the Renaissance imagination: acting with *virtù* gave power to the powerless and allowed them to help young love win out against all the things that were stacked against it.

But love and *virtù* did not work together easily in the Renaissance: most of the protagonists of these plays are young upper-class people in love, and to put it simply, their love gets in the way of their *virtù*, especially when *virtù* is understood as rational, calculating behavior. The Renaissance was acutely aware that love, especially young love, was not a reasonable or moderate emotion. It was a strong, often violent emotion that overwhelmed people with passion and robbed them of their senses and peace. Callimaco in *La mandragola* is a classic example: he is so madly in love with Lucrezia, a woman whom he has barely seen, that he cannot sleep or eat or find any rest, let alone reason. He wanders the city lost in bleak thoughts, breaks out into emotional soliloquies, and even contemplates suicide. And when it becomes clear that the plot to unite him with Lucrezia is going to work, he bursts out with "Good God! What did I do to deserve to be so lucky? I'm going to die of happiness!" As Ligurio quips to the audience, "What a character! Whether for happiness or for sadness, he seems to be bent on dying." In the throes of love, Callimaco clearly does not exhibit much in the way of *virtù*. The older lovers in these comedies are even more foolish when they succumb to this powerful emotion, underlining the message that the passions of young love are not for the old and offer little opportunity to exhibit *virtù*.

Perhaps the character who comes closest to exhibiting *virtù* while in love is Lelia in *Gl'ingannati*. Having escaped the convent where her father had put her, she moves through the streets of Modena disguised as a male servant. She must be clever and quick-witted to pass successfully as a man, and she does so with considerable *virtù*. Moreover, serving the man she loves as his manservant and becoming involved in his plans to win the love of another woman, Lelia constructs complex schemes to undermine his plans and win him back as her lover. Clearly she is a woman who demonstrates much in the way of *virtù*. But even for her, love is a mad passion that leads her to risk her honor and reputation and chart a dangerous course that has her hovering always on the brink of dishonor and shame. But Fortune, that most fickle of Renaissance goddesses, reveals her enduring fondness for young lovers by having Lelia's brother return at a critical moment to bed and wed her rival, creating the swift resolution that removes all obstacles to her own marriage and allows her to live happily ever after with her honor unsullied.

Outside of comedy—a realm in which everything ends well and everyone at least theoretically lives happily ever after because the genre requires it—the passion of young love struck most people in the Renaissance, perhaps even many young lovers, as being the wrong kind of emotion on which to build a marriage. Marriages were practical affairs arranged by families to continue a family line and to keep young people and their passions safely under control, as the supporters of marriage in *Il marescalco* repeatedly point out. And marriages ideally were arranged not by people in the throes of passion but by those deemed capable of judging, coolly and with *virtù*, what the best interests were of all involved: mature, practical adults such as parents, male relatives, or even at times rulers, as in the Marescalco's case.

Arranged marriages were the norm, and it was expected that they would be successful because they were based not on dangerous and unstable passions like young love but on rational calculations. Scholars once believed that this meant that there was little affection in Renaissance marriages and that love played no part in the ideal of matrimony. Recently, however, that view has softened somewhat, and it has been argued cogently that the Renaissance ideal of arranged marriages included the faith that over time, couples who had been well matched in terms of background and prospects would develop a form of cooler love or affection that would last the duration of the marriage. And while Renaissance comedies tend to present most marriages—aside from the ones that conclude their plots—as unhappy, with wives saddled with foolish, cruel, or jealous husbands and husbands with foolish, vain, or nagging wives, even in such relationships this ideal occasionally peeks through. For example, in *Il marescalco*, even as Aretino mocks the idea, his pro-marriage characters stress the sweetness and affectionate supportiveness of the ideal marital relationship.

One danger for arranged marriages that surfaces regularly in these comedies was that marriages were relatively easy to initiate during the Renaissance, thus allowing young lovers to marry on their own, thwarting the best-laid plans of their elders. Until the middle of the sixteenth century, the only actual requirement was a formal exchange of consent between the two individuals to be married. Thus in *Gl'ingannati*, when Flamminio finally decides to marry Lelia, the couple simply exchange expressions of consent—essentially saying "I do"—and then are allowed to kiss and head off to bed to enjoy their new state of matrimony. In *Il marescalco*, even the more elaborate ceremony of the title character's marriage to the page Carlo actually involves no more than an exchange of consent (achieved, given the Marescalco's extreme reluctance to marry, amid much hemming and hawing and with the help of a death threat).

The easy initiation of marriage, of course, did nothing to help restrain the passions of the young, and it was yet another reason why young women of marriageable age had to be married off quickly, before they could act on their own, and were kept locked up until they could be safely married off in accordance with the interests of their parents and larger families. It also created quite a bit of uncertainty about when one actually was married—something that doesn't enter into the comedies presented here but is one reason why, for example, Virginio and Gherardo in *Gl'ingannati* often refer to Lelia as if she were already married to Gherardo; they, and other characters as well, assume that because her father has consented to marry her to Gherardo and she is a dutiful daughter who will concur, she has all but consented. With Gherardo clearly wanting the marriage, consent was virtually established, and the two old men regularly refer to Lelia as Gherardo's wife.

Ceremonies of marriage could be also quite simple. During the Renaissance there were a host of reasons why one had to be careful about giving one's hand to another person, for it was a gesture implying many things, but between a man and woman it had to be done with particular care so as not to be construed as a sign of consent to marriage. In *La mandragola*, when Messer Nicia asks his wife to offer her hand to her lover on the front steps of the local church the night after they had initiated their affair, to a Renaissance audience the scene would have strongly suggested a wedding, even though the woman was already married. The bedroom scene in *La veniexiana* between the widow Angela and young Giulio might seem to have similar implications, although suggestively, both characters express their devotion to each other in a language of courtship that stresses service and devotion but carefully avoids any mention of marriage or consent to marry. Giulio may offer to be Angela's eternal servant and she may give him an emerald and a gold chain, but marriage is never mentioned; theirs is only an affair.

But to return to arranged marriages: In addition to their supposed stability, during the Renaissance such marriages offered another practical advantage to the bridegroom, a dowry; and just as in life off the stage, in life on the stage the dowry plays a crucial role. When the Marescalco's friends try to talk him into getting married, some of them mention the joys of marriage but virtually all of them smack their lips at the handsome dowry of four thousand scudi that the duke is offering with the bride. This would have been a considerable fortune, and when such sums were involved they made marriage a very important economic move for a man. In fact, in the sixteenth century dowries had become very expensive for the upper classes; dowry inflation had driven the price through the ceiling, and many families had real problems raising the sums required.

Not surprisingly, we see this problem at work in our comedies as well, most directly in *Gl'ingannati,* in which Virginio has worked out a way to minimize his dowry costs by marrying his daughter Lelia to a man who would be satisfied with a relatively modest dowry, the old widower Gherardo. He defends his decision by pointing out that he lost most of his fortune in the sack of Rome and wants to retain some wealth to leave to his long-lost son Fabrizio if he should ever be found alive. Virginio plans to give his daughter a dowry of one thousand florins, which is more than enough to get her married to an old man eager for a young bride anyway. And in addition to taking advantage of Gherardo's desire, Virginio has made the agreement contingent upon his son's not returning within four years; if he should return, eight hundred florins will be returned to Virginio to help his son get set up in life, and Gherardo will have to credit Lelia with the eight hundred florins subtracted from the dowry. This last complication reveals another crucial aspect of dowries: while husbands had the use of dowries, in most Renaissance cities when the husband died the dowry was to be returned to the wife to serve as the economic base for her life as a widow or as a new dowry to allow her to remarry. By working out this deal with Gherardo,

Virginio has made sure that Lelia would have a one-thousand-florin dowry to her credit if she should become a widow, whether her brother returned or not. And given the significant age differential between her and Gherardo—it is implied that he is in his fifties and she is about eighteen—it was very likely that she would become a widow and this proviso would come into play. Dowries often were complex contractual relationships of this sort, and given the investment of family resources and the wealth to be gained, it is no wonder that there was so little room in marriage arrangements for the passions of young love.

Lelia's plight suggests in passing another aspect of the impact of the cost of dowries on upper-class marriages during the Renaissance: Virginio fears that the nuns with whom he has left Lelia while he was away on business want to persuade her to become a nun, and he sees their motivation as less spiritual than economic. Many upper-class women became nuns because in their early teens, when it came time to marry, their families could not or would not raise the large sums necessary to dower them appropriately. It also took a dowry to become a nun, but usually the sum was more modest than that required for a marriage dowry (even though exclusive nunneries could be expensive to enter and very luxurious, especially before the reforms of the Council of Trent began to tighten things up at the end of the sixteenth century). Another economic advantage of having a daughter become a nun was that the family could continue to contribute to her support over time, or at least they could contemplate doing so. Of course, that was also the case with marriage, but the problem remained that a family had to be prepared to make a much larger economic sacrifice immediately; to marry a daughter honorably required a major outlay of wealth at the outset via the dowry.

The humorous picture of the rather free and licentious life of nuns that we see at Lelia's convent reflects what many people at the time believed to be true of convents. There were, of course, many nuns who were deeply committed to their calling and the monastic way of life, but with so many women becoming nuns for purely financial and familial reasons, some convents were very worldly indeed. In *La veniexiana*, for example, it is mentioned in passing that it was at a party at a convent that Giulio first saw Valiera and fell in love with her. In fact, in Venice the cultural life at a number of convents was so brilliant, with music and parties, discussions, and even the performance of plays (one of the rare places where women in the early sixteenth century acted on stage), that foreign nobles were regularly taken to visit them as one of the local attractions that refined visitors should not miss. This alternative to marriage for upper-class women, then, was not quite as gloomy as sometimes depicted, and for some it seemed a very positive alternative, more attractive than marriage to a much older man for both economic and family reasons.

BUT TO RETURN TO "YOUNG LOVE," that dangerous passion unfit for building marriages: A word needs to be said about the other half of that phrase, "young." In the cast of characters of *La calandra*, Lidio is described as an "adolescent," and we modern readers may think we are on familiar ground with this term until we find out that he is living on his own and has been doing so for a while, and that he has a married mistress, Fulvia, who has a son more or less his own age. This begins to suggest that terms like "adolescent" and "young" may not be as clear and familiar as they at first appear. Perhaps the most significantly different aspect of the Renaissance concept of youth is that it was gender-specific and socially sensitive. As far as gender is concerned, "youth" was a decidedly different span of time for males and females. Upper-class girls were considered children until about age twelve to fourteen or fifteen, when they reached puberty. Until the end of this period of childhood they were relatively free to play in the streets and were considered socially and sexually innocent. Once they hit puberty, however, they were deemed ready for marriage and in fact had to be married off within a rather narrow time range or they would be in danger of being considered not marriageable at all. This contributed mightily to the dowry pressure that families felt and made it that much more attractive to put daughters in convents before they became *zitelle* (the Renaissance equivalent of old maids).

The reasons for this rush to marry daughters early and quickly were myriad, but perhaps the most significant were sexual and social. As far as sex was concerned, the purpose of marriage was to produce heirs—especially male heirs—to continue a family line. One much-feared danger that our comedies refer to again and again was that those heirs would not be true sons of their fathers, that somehow other men would have fathered the sons that a man believed to be his. One way to avoid that danger was to marry young women off as soon as they reached childbearing age—at puberty—and have them begin producing children immediately. Closely intertwined with this fear was a concern about how difficult it was actually to control daughters once they reached puberty. With a rapid marriage, a young girl was sexually engaged immediately by her husband (in theory, at least), and that new husband and his larger family could monitor her behavior and contacts to their satisfaction. Virginio in *Gl'ingannati* again provides a fine example of the dangers of not following this scenario. Clearly he was concerned about his daughter and her reputation as well as his own, but nonetheless Lelia had managed to get out on her own and into what had the potential to be a lot of trouble, running around town dressed as a man and even living with the man she loved. Better to marry young women off before such dangers had a chance to be realized.

Social factors also put pressure on upper-class families to see their daughters married quickly after they reached puberty. Marriage was a unique moment that allowed a family to proclaim its wealth and power, not just through a large dowry but also through elaborate celebrations and public displays of wealth, and families who were able to do so were eager to do so and not leave any room for doubt about their ability to do so. In a way this is the flip side of the dowry-raising problems discussed earlier. Those who had the means, or who could at least put on a convincing show of having the means, were eager to prove it. Among upper-class families of this sort, waiting too long to marry off a daughter was a definite social faux pas.

In the case of Virginio in *Gl'ingannati*, in another time and in a different social setting it would probably have made more sense for him to wait to marry off his eighteen-year-old daughter until he knew whether his son was alive or dead and until he had reestablished a stronger economic base. But the factor that was driving him to marry his daughter off, easily overlooked by modern readers, was that by Renaissance standards she was getting decidedly old for a first marriage. Literally her youth was passing her by, as youth for young women was limited to that very short period of time between reaching puberty and being married. Once teenagers were married, they became adult women with the responsibilities of child rearing and running a household. This meant that most upper-class women of the Italian Renaissance were adults at fourteen or fifteen, like the young wife Lucrezia in *La mandragola*, who was probably still in her late teens but was treated as a full adult by all the characters in the play (and a woman to be reckoned with at that).

For lower-class women this picture was rather different. Marriage usually came later, in the late teens or early twenties. One significant reason for this was that dowries were much lower for lower-class women, although they were necessary for marriage at virtually every social level. Because dowries were lower, potential husbands and their families looked for other things that a wife could bring to a marital alliance like a skill, maturity, intelligence, or the ability to run a household and raise children well. All these things were easier to judge when a woman was older and more accomplished. In turn, because it was difficult for many lower-class families to raise a dowry, women often had to work for a while to earn one before they could marry. In fact, that situation was undoubtedly the source of a number of the unmarried lower-class women whom we see in these comedies working as servants, many of whom are promised dowries for special services rendered. Suggestively, however, many of these servants do not seem to be chastely waiting out these years of youthful servitude so as to marry as virgins. Samia, for example, in *La calandra,* claiming to have been encouraged by her mistress Fulvia's adulterous example, says, "One would be mad not to seize these pleasures when one has the chance, for there's plenty of trouble and aggravation just waiting for us behind the door," then rushes off to enjoy some of those pleasures with the butler. In a poignant and rather brutal scene in *Il marescalco,* Giorgina, the Count's maidservant, meets her lover, the Duke's footman, and says she wishes that he could give her one of the marriage rings that the Marescalco so loathes. After much billing and cooing he leaves her, promising to meet her later for another tryst, then confides to the audience that he has decided to drop her. Her hopes for marriage in return for sexual favors, it seems clear, are going to be dashed, as was probably often the case. Yet it appears that at lower social levels, pregnancy followed by marriage was a frequent option, especially in more tightly knit communities in which neighborhood and family pressures could force young men to "do the right thing." In larger cities where community and family ties were often less strong, or when a woman was on her own, away from home and family support, premarital pregnancy could be much more difficult.

Nena's scene in bed with her mistress in *La veniexiana* points in an unusual way to another danger that woman servants faced: being used sexually by their masters or members of their families. Nena doesn't seem to object much, beyond complaining that her mistress's attentions are interfering with her sleep, and their sex play would have had the decided advantage of not posing the risk of pregnancy. Sex with the males of a household was a decidedly more dangerous business, as there was little hope of marriage if one became pregnant, although some masters actually did marry off their pregnant servants to retainers or lower-class clients or raised the children of such relationships as bastards. But in many cases pregnant servants were cast out to fend for themselves, and without dowries (and often without the support of their natal families) the results could be very unhappy indeed—opening up a darker side of the Renaissance that our comedies seldom hint at. Behind all this stand two crucial and often cruel realities: lower-class women were less likely to arrive at marriage as virgins (and often lived out their lives in a series of unstable relationships without ever being married), and they were more exposed to the decidedly predatory sexuality of those above them on the social scale.

ONE POTENTIALLY POSITIVE ASPECT of the situation for lower-class women during the Renaissance—and one that is so ubiquitous in our comedies that it is easy to overlook—is the fact that they had more freedom to move about outside the home. (Of course, the obverse side of this freedom is that it left them exposed to the sexual predations of men.) Upper-class women, in contrast, were kept under close control and were seldom allowed to go out of the house alone once they reached puberty. That explains why the upper-class women in these comedies have to operate from their doorsteps or windows, sending their servants and supporters out to run their errands and to summon lovers and helpers to their homes. The upper-class female protagonists of *La veniexiana* are able to play such active roles in that comedy precisely because the action takes place largely inside their palaces. It is much harder for the upper-class women of the other comedies to be so active, in part for a simple technical reason: the action takes place in the streets of a city, and upper-class women were not supposed to be out in those streets alone. This fact is highlighted in *La calandra* when Fulvia decides that she absolutely must visit Lidio to find out if he still loves her and, if not, to see if she can reignite his passion. The only way she can see to do this without risking dishonor or discovery is to dress as a man, an exploit that is clearly traumatic for her and is viewed as heroic by her servant. The play's depiction of the courage it took for her to overcome her fear for the sake of love inadvertently reveals how much the ideal of keeping upper-class women locked in the home was respected, even in Renaissance comedies.

Women dressing as men to wander the streets is a regular feature of these plays. Cross-dressing plays a major role in *Gl'ingannati,* in which we learn that the nuns in Lelia's convent kept men's clothing on hand to wear when they wanted to go to the city on personal business. And, of course, Lelia takes this ploy much further, dressing as a boy to serve as her lover's manservant and wandering the streets acting as a major protagonist in what is largely her comedy. But with Lelia, the cross-dressing that is in one sense only a technical necessity, a way to get her more involved in the action of the comedy, has a host of deeper implications as well. Perhaps what strikes a modern audience first is how easily she passes as a young man. People do notice a certain femininity about her, but they write it off to her being a young man without a beard. This may say something about what it meant during the Renaissance to be a young man, and we will discuss that further below, but it also implies deeper things about Renaissance ways of regarding gender and identity. In many ways gender and identity, like honor, were seen as being external and performative, not internal or connected with a deeper sense of self. Thus Lelia could put on the clothes and manners of a young man and for all intents and purposes essentially *become* a young man, even to the extent of advancing quite far in a love affair with another woman. Santilla in *La calandra* is such a success as a man that her patron, Perillo, wants to marry her to his own daughter. And in fact she participates successfully in the male world of the streets, with male friends and enjoying the joking banter of that world with ease and success. Even better, she does all this with the awareness that passing as a man gives her a wide range of opportunities unavailable to her as a woman. On one level the cross-dressing of these plays is just another instance of the comic reversals typical of Renaissance humor, but this imaginative toying with the boundaries of gender and selfhood also sheds light on the Renaissance understanding of those concepts.

MALES FOLLOWED A VERY DIFFERENT PATH through youth. As with girls, childhood ended with puberty or perhaps even a bit before, but with puberty, upper-class males began a long period of *gioventù* (youth), during which they were generally referred to as *giovani* (youths)—a period that could last from about age twelve until they married, usually in their late twenties or early thirties. In fact, it is not unusual to run across never-married men in their mid-thirties still being referred to as *giovani* too immature for the responsibilities of adult male status. All the sympathetic male lovers of our comedies fall into this category; older men who fall in love are usually depicted as fools at best.

But even in the world of comedy, life is not easy for these young men. They are usually short of both money and the kind of real power that upper-class male adults would have wielded, and the lack of both suggests a third telling lack that again it might be easy to miss from a modern perspective: most of them lack a strong parental authority figure. Fathers and mothers alike are tellingly missing from the central moments of these comedies. In *La calandra*, the young twins Santilla and Lidio have lost their parents. In *La mandragola*, Callimaco's parents died more than ten years earlier, and the relatives who sent him off to Paris to study remain unseen. In *Il marescalco*, the title character's parents go unmentioned aside from a brief reference to the fact that they produced him and that he should likewise marry and produce children of his own. In *Gl'ingannati* we do have one parent who plays a significant role, Virginio, Lelia's father, but he is neutralized for most of the play, first because he is off on business and then because he is unaware of where his daughter really is and what is actually happening. Finally, in *La veniexiana*, young Giulio is off on his own in Venice, well dressed but lacking funds or any visible family support.

Where have these parents disappeared to? Most likely they have been banished to the land of potentially difficult characters who don't belong in a tale because they would wreck the plot or make everyone else in it uncomfortable. Fathers are simply much too powerful to be allowed a place in Renaissance comedies, and when they do appear, as in *Gl'ingannati* (or other comedies like Machiavelli's *La Clizia* and Donato Giannotti's *Il vecchio amoroso*), they tend to warp the plot because they are too powerful and controlling to be ignored. Virginio has Lelia's life totally in his hands, and even the characters most unhappy with his decisions about her future ruefully accept that this is his right as a father. She succeeds as a protagonist only via a series of deceptions that allow her to escape her father's control and that crucially keep him out of the real action of the comedy, leaving him largely a dark threat on the horizon.

The situation was much the same for Renaissance sons, with the crucial exception that their period of powerlessness in the face of their fathers' authority lasted much longer, at least until their fathers were willing to set them up on their own with some financial independence and allow them to marry and gain a dowry. Often that moment did not arrive until their fathers actually died—yet another reason for the convenient demise of so many parents before our comedies begin. But as long as fathers ruled, young males were under their thumbs economically and practically, and that means quite simply that for the youthful independence of these comedies to have room for full play, these youths have to be largely father-free. Offstage, where fathers were not so easily disposed of, generational conflict was frequently the name of the game, with troubled elders ruing the unruly and dangerously emotional ways of youth and equally troubled youth ruing their overly strict and controlling elders. Onstage, that generational conflict was resolved in the sense that, after many tantalizing brushes with disaster and dishonor, the youthful folly that the fathers had so feared ended in laughter, love rewarded, and all the young people, at least, living happily ever after. The flirting with dangerous situations that no right-thinking father would ever condone is at the very heart of most plots, and thus fathers are very much a part of these comedies, even in their absence.

Mothers are, if anything, even more absent, which at first glance might seem strange, for mothers in the Renaissance were theoretically not authority figures, so why banish them from the action of the comedy? Moreover, given the typical age differential between partners in marriage and the young age at which women married and began to bear children, it might be assumed that mothers would be much closer to their youthful sons than their fathers would be. One of our young lovers at, say, eighteen could have had a mother in her early thirties, and in his formative years his mother could easily have been in her teens, a close and perhaps supportive friend locked up in the home with her children.

So where are the mothers? In *La mandragola*, Sostrata, one of the few mothers to appear in these comedies, seems to be mainly a tool for helping Callimaco get her daughter Lucrezia into bed, although she does deliver some perceptive lines on the realities of being a wife (she warns her daughter that she must produce children in order to secure her financial future). Suggestively, the kind of maternal affection that might be expected of mothers is reserved for another character: the *balia*, or wetnurse. A common character in many Renaissance comedies, the *balia* figures prominently in two of the comedies here, *Il marescalco* and *Gl'ingannati* (the wetnurse in *La calandra* has only a minor, nonspeaking part), and in both she plays the affectionate role one might expect of a mother concerned about the welfare of her child and full of advice on how to navigate the tricky waters of the last days of youth. The Marescalco's *balia* affectionately urges him to accept marriage and adult status, leaving his youthful ways behind, and Clemenzia, Lelia's *balia* in *Gl'ingannati*, seeks to protect her both from the marriage her father has arranged for her and from the dishonor she risks by going about dressed as a man—and most tellingly, each *balia* regularly refers to her ex-nursling as "my son" or "my daughter."

In fact, these two *balie* are among the most sympathetic adults in these comedies, even when their advice is actually counterproductive and they are being as harping as any of the other adult characters. During the Renaissance most upper-class children spent their first years being nursed by a *balia*, either at the child's home or more regularly at the *balia*'s home, often in the countryside, and so their first and perhaps strongest maternal figure was their *balia* and not their mother. This would certainly help to explain the lack of mothers in these comedies, although their absence may be a product of deeper fears.

Unfortunately, that very lack of mention that attracts attention means that these comedies provide almost no strong evidence to explain it. The older upper-class women who appear in our comedies may shed some light on the question. Virtually all of them are sexual beings, and sexually promiscuous. Even Sostrata, Lucrezia's mother in *La mandragola*, is introduced to us as a woman once noted for her easy virtue. Fulvia, the mother in *La calandra* who is old enough to be her lover's mother, and Angela, the widow in *La veniexiana*, are sexually active women who literally take their youthful lovers in hand. If we recall that a Renaissance mother was often close in age to her sons, such scenes may have had troubling overtones of incestuous attachments in families where young mothers and sons may have felt some natural alliances against a dominating older father. Such speculations must be very tentative, but fears of incest do seem to haunt the psyche of societies in which mothers and sons are close in age, and it may well be that another factor in the strange absence of mothers from these works is that such fears are the stuff of tragedy, not comedy.

NOT ONLY ARE THE FATHERS AND MOTHERS generally missing from these comedies, there are hardly any other characters who might be in a position to effectively oppose young love. The only exception to this is a telling one. Tutors and teachers, sometimes referred to as pedants, are surprisingly prevalent in these plays, and for young upper-class males they may well have been more significant authority figures on a day-to-day level than fathers or mothers. In a nicely ironic touch, however, these supposedly wise characters are consistently represented as learned fools (and fools whose learning is often dubious at that). Does this mean, as some students might suspect, that people who earn their living as teachers are actually quite foolish, for all their supposed learning? Perhaps. Certainly, too much learning was seen during the Renaissance as a handicap in worldly affairs, whether at court, where grace, ease, and wide general knowledge were preferred over deep and arcane scholarship, or in the merchant-banker world, where *virtù* meant the practical ability to make money and get things done. And the pedant/tutor characters of these comedies definitely lack either a practical sense of how to apply their learning effectively or a courtly sense of how to demonstrate it with grace and ease.

These characters seem to be entirely lacking in *virtù*. They throw Latin sayings around to show off their learning but frequently misquote or misapply them; they speak sententiously to impress those around them, but no one is impressed; they defend reason over youthful emotion but demonstrate just how foolish reason can sometimes be. These learned fools are a classic example of the comic reversal, with reversals sometimes being piled upon reversals when the blissfully unaware pedant offers an apparently foolish observation that turns out to be quite accurate. Like the other sources of reversal humor in these comedies, they provide not just laughs but an opportunity to reimagine the givens of Renaissance life. They also offer an excellent chance to poke fun at authority without openly attacking other perhaps less attackable authority figures such as fathers, lords, and princes. Behind the laughter, however, one thing is clear: the youths of these comedies are amazingly free from authority figures, whether they are demoted from that role by being ridiculous like pedant/tutors or largely absent like mothers and fathers—and this permits them the freedom of action that allows these comedies to play with a scary but ultimately happy world without authority getting in the way.

IL MARESCALCO ADDS SOME COMPLEXITY to our picture of youth and young love in the Renaissance by openly acknowledging something that is hinted at in all these comedies: that heterosexuality did not rule the sex life of the period, especially for youths. The affectionate sexual relationship between the Marescalco and his young servant Giannicco seems close to a modern homosexual relationship, and the Marescalco's exclusive interest in other males also seems to fit modern stereotypes of homosexuals as people taking sexual interest only in those of their own gender. Stereotyping of this sort is questionable even for modern sexual practice and certainly does not fit the Renaissance. While the Marescalco may have no interest in women and clearly wishes to remain in his happy world of male/male sex, he is interested only in younger males who play the passive role in sex to his active role, as the language of the comedy makes absolutely clear. He shows no interest in males his own age or older. And while the other characters who are his friends and companions may not approve of his sexual preferences, they assume that he will leave them behind when he takes on the role of an adult man, marries, and begins to produce children. Although he insists that he cannot and will not do that, no one takes his protest particularly seriously, and his unwillingness is universally discounted as mere stubbornness. Behind this lies the assumption that male/male sex was more a practice than a matter of sexual identity. And as a practice it was interchangeable with any number of other sexual practices. One might prefer one sexual practice over another but not have any problem practicing a wide range of them, just as one might prefer steak but be willing to eat fish.

During the Renaissance, male/male sexual relationships were categorized under the general rubric of sodomy—a catchall term for any sexual activity that was considered "not natural" (meaning, basically, without the potential to produce offspring), but the term was used most regularly for male/male sex. Sexual activity between males followed a fairly strict customary ideal: Young males as they reached puberty were seen as largely passive in their sexual orientation, and if they participated in sex at all, it was usually as passive partners in relationships with older male youths or women. (In relationships with older women, they would have been expected to be more passive partners than older males would have been, as is hinted at in the bedroom scene in *La veniexiana* in which Giulio claims to have dozed off while Angela made love to him.) As they became older they slowly made the transition to active sexuality, and their range of sex objects could include younger male youths, prostitutes, older women, and women of marriageable age (the last two being more dangerous and less acceptable in terms of contemporary mores, although theoretically all were forms of illicit sex). Finally, much to the relief of worried parents and a concerned society, in their late twenties or early thirties upper-class male youths ideally settled down to the correct adult male role of husband, father, and safe heterosexual. Occasional escapes to prostitutes or concubines were frowned upon, but since the actual policing of mores was in the hands of families ruled by husbands and fathers, such transgressions were largely ignored, unless they became too disruptive. Any return to male/male relationships, however, was more troubling, and if discovered it was usually punished severely.

The situation in *Il marescalco* illustrates two aspects of this vision of male sexuality particularly well. First, and most clearly, the Marescalco himself is resisting the crucial transition from youth to adult status and marriage. In fact, his resistance is so strong and his antiwoman stance so adamant that his sexual preference begins to seem not merely a practice but something much closer to a Renaissance sense of sexual identity. Second, and less clearly, the Marescalco's young lover Giannicco seems to be outgrowing his passive stage and making the expected transition to active sexuality, expressing an increasingly strong desire to spread his wings and take an active role in sex himself, whether it be with the Marescalco's future (and presumably to be neglected) wife or with the many women that the songs he is constantly singing suggest are out there waiting for him and his newfound active lust.

This transition for young males from a passive role that was often seen as quite feminine to a more aggressive masculine role towards the end of their teens is also reflected in the comedies that focus on male/female sexual relationships. The theme is particularly strong in *La veniexiana* and *Gl'ingannati*. In the former, although the young love object Giulio goes about dressed up as a soldier, he is regularly characterized as quite feminine and even unsuited for the role of being the lover of the two adult women who are chasing him. (It should be noted, however, that the younger of these "adult" women, the high-handed bride Valiera, would probably have been actually his own age or younger.) In *Gl'ingannati*, Lelia dressed as a young man is often put down for being too young and feminine looking to be attractive to women, although she manages to win the affections of Isabella in competition with the older male who just happens to be the man she herself loves. Another character in the play, Giglio the Spaniard, comments ruefully on the success of this apparent young boy by suggesting that he looks more as if he should be on the receiving end of sex than on the giving end.

This sexual ambiguity in part turns on the assumption that for most of a young male's teenage years (at least until he grew a beard), he could be seen as being as much feminine as masculine. And this in turn meant that onstage, young male actors could play women and also that young male and female characters could cross-dress and pass easily for one another. Offstage as well, young males could take female roles in sexual relationships with males or more passive than usual roles with older women, and although it might be formally considered wrong, as long as they followed the "correct" path of maturation, becoming aggressive male lovers and eventually husbands, fathers, and patriarchs, all was well that ended well. Much of the action and real tension of these comedies, as well as their humor, hinges upon these two tricky transitions in the Renaissance vision of male development: the transition from male youth to male adult, and the earlier transition from passive boy more feminine than not to aggressive youth more masculine than not.

YOUNG LOVE AND YOUNG LUST, then, are decidedly different in these comedies, but still close enough to our own experiences perhaps that we can laugh at them along with their Renaissance audiences and readers. But laughing is the key, because after all these are comedies and meant to be laughed at, and laughter today still allows us to turn the world on its head, to think the unthinkable and cross all kinds of boundaries in imaginative and empathetic ways, and to imagine putting at risk everything that we would never actually dare to put at risk. Certainly we hope that this historical introduction will help you to enjoy these comedies in terms of their Renaissance meanings as well. Yet even we do not always understand the humor of these comedies, and that, in fact, is one of the most stimulating things about them. At times the humor we don't understand or can't laugh about, upon consideration, tells us more about the Renaissance and about ourselves than the jokes that work. For critical thinking, the lack of fit, the lack of perfect understanding, the joke that doesn't work, can be as revealing as those that do. But like the authors of these comedies, we hope that your laughter will predominate and that your understanding will often be a smiling one. So laugh and be well, dear readers.

The Translations

Our aim in these translations has been to render these comedies in clear, rich, and playful English prose that is as faithful as possible to the playful Italian that is such an important element of their humor. We have tried to find a middle ground between a too-free style of translation that would misrepresent the original texts by imparting a modern colloquial flavor, and a too literal, philological style that would obscure the humor and rich wordplay. Moreover, in providing a reading that reasserts these comedies' irreverent and insistent interest in sex, the cultural differences between men and women (gender), and the centrality of play, pleasure, and passion in Renaissance life, we have sought to highlight a crucial set of themes that many modern translations overlook but that were central to these comedies' success in the Renaissance. We have tried to bring these comedies to life for modern readers in the same way that they came to life on the Renaissance stage and in the imaginations of their original audiences, though in the end, of course, this is an impossible task, as our imaginations today are decidedly different from those of the Renaissance, and readers will take these translations and hopefully make them interesting and fun as they see fit.

In these translations, fools sound like fools, people who are confused or madly in love talk nonsense, and characters who are playing with words to convey double meanings or just to be funny and clever will at first sound strange. But wordplay is a significant part of the playful fun of these comedies, and when the language takes an unexpected turn, watch for the joke, the sexual innuendo, the clever pun, or merely the foolishness. In the most difficult or significant cases we have used notes to alert the reader to what is going on, but part of the fun of these comedies is letting one's imagination flow with the clever language that is designed to challenge assumptions and expectations.

For each comedy we designated one modern critical edition as primary, usually the one most widely recognized by scholars as authoritative, and based our translations on that edition. But we also consulted other significant editions, to get the best reading possible. When we were satisfied with our translations, we compared them with a limited number of modern English translations, where such exist. The editions we consulted are listed below. For each play, the primary critical edition is listed first, and the English translations are listed last.

La calandra

Bibbiena, Bernardo Dovizi da. *La calandra, commedia elegantissima per messer Bernardo Dovizi da Bibbiena*. Edited by Giorgio Padoan. Padua: Editrice Antenore, 1985.

——. *La calandria*. In *Il teatro italiano, II, la commedia del Cinquecento*, 2d ed., edited by Guido Davico Bonino, with notes by Paolo Fossati, vol. 1, 3–87. Turin: Einaudi, 1977.

——. *La calandria*. Edited by Paolo Fossati. Turin: Einaudi, 1967.

——. *The Follies of Calandro (1513)*. Translated by Oliver Evans. In *The Genius of Italian Theater*, edited by Eric Bentley, 31–100. New York: Mentor Books, 1964. [This is only a partial translation.]

La mandragola

Machiavelli, Niccolò. *Mandragola*. Edited by Pietro Gibellini. Milan: Garzanti, 1997.

——. *Mandragola*. Edited by Giorgio Inglese. Bologna: Il Mulino, 1997.

——. *Mandragola; Clizia*. Edited by Ezio Raimondi and Gian Mario Anselmi. Milan: Mursia, 1984.

——. *La mandragola*. In *Il teatro italiano, II, la commedia del Cinquecento*, 2d ed., edited by Guido Davico Bonino, vol. 1, 89–150. Turin: Einaudi, 1977.

——. *The Mandragola*. Translated by Bruce Penman. In *Five Italian Renaissance Comedies*, edited by Bruce Penman, 11–58. Harmondsworth: Penguin Books, 1978.

——. *Mandragola*. Translated by Mera J. Flaumenhaft. Prospect Heights, Ill.: Waveland Press, 1981.

——. *The Mandrake Root*. Translated by Peter Bondanella and Mark Musa. In *The Portable Machiavelli*, edited and translated by Peter Bondanella and Mark Musa, 430–79. Harmondsworth: Penguin Books, 1979.

——. *The Mandrake*. Translated by Kenneth and Laura Richards. In *Ariosto's The Supposes, Machiavelli's The Mandrake, Intronati's The Deceived: Three Italian Renaissance Comedies*, edited by Christopher Cairns, 133–75. Lewiston, N.Y.: Edwin Mellen Press, 1996.

Il marescalco

Aretino, Pietro. *Il marescalco*. In *Pietro Aretino: teatro*, edited by Giorgio Petrocchi, 1–91 and 760–77. Milan: Arnoldo Mondadori, 1971.

——. *Il marescalco*. In *Pietro Aretino: tutte le commedie*, edited by G. B. de Sanctis, 31–92. Milan: Mursia, 1968.

——. *The Stablemaster*. Translated by George Bull. In *Five Italian Renaissance Comedies*, edited by Bruce Penman, 113–91. Harmondsworth: Penguin Books, 1978.

——. *The Marescalco*. Translated and edited by Leonard G. Sbrocchi and J. Douglas Campbell. Ottawa: Dovehouse Editions, 1986.

Gl'ingannati

Accademici Intronati di Siena. *La commedia degli ingannati*. Edited by Florindo Cerreta. Florence: Olschki, 1980.

Anonimo. *Gl'ingannati*. In *Il teatro italiano, II, la commedia del Cinquecento*, 2d ed., edited by Guido Davico Bonino with notes by Roberto Alonge, vol. 2, 87–183. Turin: Einaudi, 1977.

Accademici Intronati di Siena. *Gl'ingannati*. In *Commedie del Cinquecento*, edited by Nino Borsellino, vol. 1, 201–89. Milan: Feltrinelli, 1962.

Gl'Intronati. *The Deceived*. Translated by Bruce Penman. In *Five Italian Renaissance Comedies*, edited by Bruce Penman, 193–278. Harmondsworth: Penguin Books, 1978.

Accademia degli Intronati. *The Deceived*. Translated by Nerida Newbigin. In *Ariosto's The Supposes, Machiavelli's The Mandrake, Intronati's The Deceived: Three Italian Renaissance Comedies*, edited by Christopher Cairns, 251–92. Lewiston, N.Y.: Edwin Mellen Press, 1996.

Anonymous. *The Deceived*. Translated (partially) by Thomas Love Peacock. In *The Genius of Italian Theater*, edited by Eric Bentley, 99–142. New York: Mentor Books, 1964.

La veniexiana

La veniexiana. Edited by Giorgio Padoan. Venice: Marsilio Editore, 1994.

Ignoto Veneto del Cinquecento. *La venexiana*. Edited by Ludovico Zorzi. Turin: Einaudi, 1965.

Anonimo. *La venexiana*. In *Il teatro italiano, II, la commedia del Cinquecento*, 2d ed., edited by Guido Davico Bonino with notes by Ludovico Zorzi, vol. 1, 323–402. Turin: Einaudi, 1977.

La Venexiana: A Sixteenth Century Venetian Comedy. Edited and translated by Matilde Valenti Pfeiffer. New York: S. F. Vanni, 1950.

La Veniexiana (1535). Edited and translated by Carolyn Feleppa Balducci. Ottawa: Dovehouse Editions, 2000.

Five Comedies from the Italian Renaissance

❦

La calandra

(The Comedy of Calandro) [1]

By Bernardo Dovizi da Bibbiena (1470–1520)

CHARACTERS:

FESSENIO: a servant—ostensibly to CALANDRO, but actually to LIDIO

POLINICO: a tutor

LIDIO: an adolescent

CALANDRO

SAMIA: FULVIA's servant

RUFFO: a necromancer

SANTILLA: LIDIO's sister

FANNIO: SANTILLA's servant

FULVIA: CALANDRO's wife

A WHORE

A PORTER

Some TAX OFFICERS

The WETNURSE of LIDIO and SANTILLA

The BROTHERS of FULVIA

1. First performed at the court of Urbino on 6 February 1513. Giorgio Padoan in his critical edition of 1985 corrected the traditional title *La calandria* to *La calandra*.

Prologue [2]

Today you will see a new comedy entitled *Calandra*—in prose, not in verse; modern, not ancient; Italian, not Latin. It is called *Calandra*, which comes from the name of Calandro, a character whom you'll find so foolish that it's hard to imagine Nature ever creating such a man. But if you have seen or heard of someone much like him, and particularly of that Martino da Amelia [3] (who believed that the star of Diana [4] was his wife, that he was the Amen, and that when he wanted to he could become in turn a woman, a god, a fish, and a bush), then you won't be surprised that Calandro believes and does the foolish things that you will see.

The author didn't want to present this comedy in verse because it treats of everyday things and uses everyday language, and especially because we speak freely in ordinary prose, not in meter. That this comedy is not ancient should upset no one of good taste, for modern things and the new are always more enjoyable than the old or the ancient. The latter, from long use, often seem musty. It's not in Latin, because it is being played before large numbers of people who are not all learned, and the author—wanting to give you greater pleasure— decided to use Italian so that everyone could understand and enjoy the comedy equally. Moreover, given that Italian is the language that God and Nature have given us, it shouldn't be less appreciated or enjoyed than Latin, Greek, or Hebrew. Our language wouldn't be inferior if we praised, practiced, and polished it with the same diligence that the Greeks and the others did theirs. For those who appreciate other languages over their own are their own enemies. I know that as far as I'm concerned I hold my own language more dear than any other, and I believe the same is true for you. So I hope you'll be pleased to hear this comedy in your own language. But I've made a mistake: you will hear this

2. This prologue—often attributed to Baldesar Castiglione (1478–1529), author of *The Book of the Courtier*, although Padoan argues for its having been written by Bibbiena—accompanied the play's first performance and was regularly used in later performances. A second prologue attributed to Bibbiena, but rejected by Padoan, is occasionally printed with the comedy; see Bibbiena, *La calandria*, ed. Paolo Fossati (Turin: Einaudi, 1967), 17–21. This second prologue makes no reference to the comedy, and Padoan argues that it is not even a prologue to a comedy.

3. A proverbial fool portrayed by Ludovico Ariosto (1474–1533) in his comedy *La lena*. Many commentators have argued that Calandro is also based on the fool Calandrino from Boccaccio's *Decameron*. While there are clearly many echoes of Calandrino in Calandro, Calandrino is quite different from Calandro: he is younger, with a wife closer to him in age (and closer emotionally), much less well to do (an artisan), a victim of jokes played on him by good friends rather than by a false servant, and ultimately more lovable.

4. The planet Venus.

comedy in our language, not yours, for after all we are the ones who are speaking and you listening.

If there are those among you who will say that the author has stolen this shamelessly from Plautus,[5] let them complain, for Plautus—that big lunkhead!—deserves to be robbed because he left everything unlocked and unguarded. But the author swears on the holy cross that he hasn't stolen even this much [*snapping his fingers*] and is willing to see the two comedies compared. And so, he says, if you have doubts, you should look through Plautus's comedies yourself, and you'll see that nothing is missing that one usually finds there. That being the case, then, nothing has been stolen from Plautus, so don't call the author a thief. And if nonetheless someone isn't able to give up on this, at least we beg him not to bring the matter to the attention of the local police chief—instead, go whisper it quietly in the ear of Plautus. But now here comes someone to tell you the plot of the comedy. Get ready to listen closely; keep your ears wide open.

The Argument

Demetrio, a citizen of Modon,[6] had a son named Lidio and a daughter called Santilla, born as twins. They were so similar in shape and manners that if they weren't dressed differently, no one could tell them apart. This you should believe because, leaving aside all the other possible examples, it's enough to mention those two most noble Romans (noble in terms of both family and deeds), Antonio and Valerio Porcari, who are so similar that they're always being mistaken for each other all over Rome.

Returning to these two children, however: They lost their father when they were six. Then the Turks took Modon and burned it, killing everyone they found there. Their wetnurse and a servant named Fannio, to save Santilla, dressed her as a boy and, believing that her brother had been killed, called her Lidio. They fled Modon, but along the road they were taken prisoner and carried off to Constantinople. The Florentine merchant Perillo ransomed all three and brought them with him to Rome, where they lived in his house. Staying with him for a long time and living very comfortably, they learned the language and the customs of the place. Today Perillo has decided to give his daughter in marriage to Santilla, called by everyone Lidio and believed by everyone to be a man.

---

5. Ancient Roman playwright (ca. 250–184 B.C.) and author of *The Menaechmi*, from which the plot of this comedy was borrowed, with some significant variations. Most notably, the twins who drive the plot here are a boy and a girl, rather than two boys, which allows Bibbiena to play with issues of sex and gender absent from Plautus's comedy.

6. Greek city controlled by Venice as part of its maritime trading empire. As an important port city for Venetian war fleets, it was a regular bone of contention between Venice and the Turks.

Meanwhile, the male Lidio escaped from Modon with the servant Fessenio and went to Tuscany in Italy, where he adopted the ways of living, dressing, and speaking of that place. When he was seventeen going on eighteen he moved to Rome, where he fell in love with Fulvia. She loved him as well, and he went to her several times disguised as a woman so that they could enjoy their love together.

After being mistaken for one another many times, Lidio and Santilla finally happily recognize each other. Now watch them carefully, keeping your eyes wide open so that you don't mistake one for the other. I must warn you, however, that they are both of the same height and manner, both are called Lidio, both dress, speak, and laugh the same way, and both are today in Rome, where in a moment you will see them. Don't believe, however, that they've come here from Rome by means of necromancy, for the city that you see here before you is Rome. That city, once so large, spacious, and great that with all its triumphs it encompassed many cities, countries, and rivers, now has become so small that, as you see, it can be easily contained in your city. That's the way the world turns.

Act I

⁀ SCENE I ᔖ

FESSENIO, alone

FESSENIO: It's certainly true that when one works out a plan, Fortune always works out another. So it was that when we decided to live peacefully in Bologna, Lidio, my master, learned that his sister Santilla was alive and had come to Italy. And immediately the love that he had always felt for her—greater than the love of any other brother for his sister—was rekindled. This was because they were born twins, and Nature made them so similar in looks and shape and speech that in Modon, if Lidio dressed as a girl and Santilla as a boy, not only foreigners but their mother and even their own wetnurse couldn't tell which was Lidio and which was Santilla. And just as the gods couldn't have made them more alike, they couldn't have loved one another more. Lidio, however, had thought his sister was dead, but when he learned that she was alive, he began to search for her.

So we came to Rome four months ago, and looking for his sister, he found instead Fulvia, a Roman woman. Falling madly in love with her, he had me hired by Calandro, her husband, as a servant, in the hopes that in that position I could help him satisfy his desires. And they were satisfied virtually immediately with her consent, because she, burning with desire for him, had him come to make love to her disguised as a woman called Santilla, right in the middle of the day.

But lately, fearing that their passion would be discovered, Lidio has begun to avoid her, pretending that he wants to leave Rome. As a result, Fulvia is so inflamed and enraged that she can find no peace and has begun to go to enchantresses, magicians, and necromancers to help her win back her lost lover. And using first me, then her servant Samia, who's also in on everything, she sends him pleas and gifts as well as the promise that she'll marry her son to Santilla if she's ever found.[7] All this she's done in such a way that if her husband weren't such a muttonhead, he'd have already caught on. And then the whole problem would fall onto my shoulders, so I need to know how to be quick on my feet.

All by myself, I'm doing the impossible. Really, no one can ever serve two masters at once, and I'm servant to three: to the husband, to the wife, and to my own master. This means I never have a moment's peace. Actually, I'm not complaining, because one who has too much peace in this world lives a living death. And if it's true that a good servant should never have it easy, I must be better than most, because I never have time to even pick my nose. Well, as if that were not enough, another amorous adventure has come along, and I'm really eager to talk with Lidio about it. And—oh! Oh my, there he is with that Momo[8] di Polinico, his tutor. When you hear that tutor's thunder, the storm can't be far behind. I'll stand over here out of the way a bit and see what they're talking about.

ʿᴅ SCENE II ᕣᵓ

POLINICO, LIDIO, and FESSENIO

POLINICO: Certainly, Lidio, I would have never thought that you would come to this and become someone who chases after vain love and despises all that is worthy.[9] But I attribute all this to that fine fellow Fessenio.

---

7. Women of the upper classes usually married quite young, at around fourteen, with brides as young as twelve being not unusual. Upper-class men tended to marry at a much later age, usually in their late twenties or early thirties. Occasionally for family reasons, however, as would have been the case here, they could be married at eighteen or even younger. Thus Fulvia could be in her early thirties and easily have a son of eighteen, more or less the same age as her lover Lidio. In the Renaissance it was often assumed that older women made excellent mistresses for younger men.

8. Momo is a figure from ancient mythology, son of Night, known particularly as someone who took the names of the gods in vain. He was a popular character during the Renaissance, and a work named after him was written by Leon Battista Alberti (1404–72). The name suggests that Polinico will be one of the learned fools so popular in Renaissance comedy.

9. *Virtù*. This is often not "virtue," as it is frequently translated, but that set of qualities that

FESSENIO: [*In hiding, aside*] By God . . .

LIDIO: Don't talk like that, Polinico.

POLINICO: But Lidio, I see everything more clearly than you and that filthy servant of yours, Fessenio.

FESSENIO: [*Aside*] To hell with— . . . I'll give him—. . .

POLINICO: The wise man always considers the negatives.

FESSENIO: [*Aside*] Now we're in for some of his highfalutin pedantries.

POLINICO: If this affair of yours becomes known, aside from your being in great danger, everyone will consider you a rogue.

FESSENIO: [*Aside*] Lazy pedant!

POLINICO: Doesn't everyone disdain and hate those who are vain and frivolous? How is it possible that you, a foreigner, have become involved in such an affair? And with whom? One of the most noble women of this city. Flee, I say! This love puts you in great danger.

LIDIO: Polinico, I'm young, and youth is an age totally ruled by Love. Serious matters are for the more mature. I'm not capable of seeking anything except what Love desires, and Love demands that I love this noble woman more than myself. And if this should become known, I believe that many will hold me in higher esteem for it. For while a woman should avoid falling in love above her station, a man ought to love a woman of higher rank.

FESSENIO: [*Aside*] Great reply!

POLINICO: [*Aside*] These are ideas that that evil Fessenio has put into his head in order to gain control over him.

FESSENIO: [*Coming forward and speaking to* POLINICO *angrily*] You're the evil one!

POLINICO: I am surprised you did not get here sooner to ruin good advice.

FESSENIO: Well, I won't have to ruin yours.[10]

POLINICO: Nothing is worse than to see the lives of wise men in the hands of fools.

FESSENIO: I've always given him wiser advice than you.

POLINICO: He who is inferior in manners cannot be superior in advice. I did not know how you really were earlier, Fessenio, otherwise I would not have recommended you highly to Lidio.

FESSENIO: Do you think I need your compliments?

made one person better than another in the Renaissance. These qualities varied with the social status, occupation, and gender of the individual and could often be quite contrary to virtue as a moral attribute. See our introductory essay.

10. I.e., because you have none to give.

POLINICO: It is true, I see now, that when one speaks well of someone, one is often wrong; but when one speaks badly of him, that is never the case.

FESSENIO: You reveal your foolishness in trying to speak well of someone you don't know. I know very well that when I talk about you, I've never been wrong.

POLINICO: In other words, you have defamed me?

FESSENIO: You said it.

POLINICO: Well, I am not about to argue with you; it would be about as useful as shouting against thunder.

FESSENIO: You act this way because you're completely wrong about me.

POLINICO: I act this way so as not to use more than words against you.

FESSENIO: And what could you do to me, even in a hundred years?

POLINICO: [*Making threatening gestures*] You'll see: like this and this—

FESSENIO: Don't play with fire.

POLINICO: Enough! Enough! With a servant I don't want to—

LIDIO: Come on, Fessenio, that's enough.

FESSENIO: He better not threaten me. I may be a poor servant, but even a fly has his limits, and even the smallest hair has its shadow. Do you hear me?

LIDIO: Be quiet, Fessenio.

POLINICO: Let me continue my conversation with Lidio, if you please.

FESSENIO: And say something that makes sense, for a change.

POLINICO: Listen, Lidio. You know that God has given us two ears so that we can hear clearly what we need to hear.

FESSENIO: And only one mouth so as to talk only a little.

POLINICO: [*To* FESSENIO] I am not talking to you. [*To* LIDIO] Every evil is easy to deal with early on, but with time they become more difficult to overcome. I say overcome this love of yours now.

LIDIO: Why?

POLINICO: You are never going to get anything out of it but trouble.

LIDIO: Why?

POLINICO: For heaven's sake! Don't you realize that the companions of love in the souls of mortals are anger, hate, hostility, conflict, ruin, poverty, suspicion, doubt, and foul disease? Flee love. Flee!

LIDIO: For heaven's sake! I can't, Polinico.

POLINICO: Why not?

FESSENIO: Why not go to hell, Tutor?

LIDIO: Everything is subject to love's power. Why, there's no greater pleasure than to have one's love, and without that there isn't anything that's perfect, virtuous, or refined.

FESSENIO: Exactly. Perfect!

POLINICO: There is no greater vice in a servant than flattery. And you listen to him? My dear Lidio, listen to me.

FESSENIO: Yeah, he's so refined!

POLINICO: Love is like a fire: when you throw sulfur on it or other foul things, it makes men sick.

LIDIO: But when you throw on incense, aloe, or amber, it makes a perfume that will revive the dead.

FESSENIO: [*Laughing*] You've turned the tables on Polinico!

POLINICO: Come back, Lidio, to praiseworthy things.

FESSENIO: It's praiseworthy to adjust to the times.

POLINICO: What is good and honest is praiseworthy. I warn you, things will turn out badly.

FESSENIO: The prophet has spoken!

POLINICO: Remember that the virtuous soul is not moved by desire.

FESSENIO: Nor does it flee out of fear.

POLINICO: [*To* FESSENIO] You are doing real harm. And you know that it is a great arrogance to make fun of the counsels of the wise.

FESSENIO: While you give yourself the title of wise man, you christen yourself a fool, because even you ought to know that there isn't a greater foolishness than to seek what's impossible.

POLINICO: It is better to fail telling the truth than to win with lies.

FESSENIO: I'm telling the truth as much as you are. But I'm not a Doctor Damn-Everything like you. Just because you can say four words in Latin, you think you're brilliant and everyone else is an idiot. Well, you're no Solomon yourself. You don't even realize that the advice must be different for a young man and for an old one, for people living a quiet life and for people leading a dangerous one. As an old man you lead the life that you are advising him to lead. But Lidio, who is young, should be allowed to do the things that young men do. And you should adapt yourself to his age and desires.

POLINICO: It is evident that the more servants a master has, the more enemies he has. This man will lead you to the gallows. And even if nothing goes wrong you will always be sorry, because there is nothing more devastating than the memory of the errors one has committed. So please leave her, Lidio.

LIDIO: I can no more leave her than my body can leave its shadow.

POLINICO: Actually, it would be better if you hated her than if you merely left her.

FESSENIO: Oh my! Poor Lidio can't lift a calf, and he wants him to carry an ox.

POLINICO: She will drop you soon enough for another. Women are fickle.

LIDIO: Oh, oh, oh! All women are not the same.

POLINICO: They do not all look the same, but they all have the same nature.

LIDIO: You're making a great mistake.

POLINICO: Oh, Lidio, face the facts, do not be fooled by their faces; there is not one in the whole world who is different. You should know that you cannot have faith in women, even after they are dead.

FESSENIO: This guy is more right than he realizes.

POLINICO: What?

FESSENIO: You're adjusting perfectly to the times.

POLINICO: Actually, I am telling Lidio the perfect truth.

FESSENIO: There's nothing more to say!

POLINICO: But what are you trying to say?

FESSENIO: I'm saying that you really do adjust to the times.

POLINICO: How?

FESSENIO: In that you're an enemy of women, just like almost everyone else at this court.[11] Still, you're wrong, and you slander them unfairly.

LIDIO: What Fessenio says is true, because one can't accept what you've said about women. Why, they are what makes the world good and happy, and without them we men would be useless, inept, harsh, and like beasts.

FESSENIO: Why bother with all that? Don't we know that women are so worthy that there isn't a man today who doesn't imitate them or who wouldn't willingly—body and soul—become one?

POLINICO: I will not reply to that.

FESSENIO: You have no way to contradict it.

POLINICO: Just remember, Lidio, that it is always wise to avoid evil, and thus once again I tell you for your own good, shake off these vain infatuations.

LIDIO: Polinico, there isn't a thing in the world that it's more useless to attack or counsel against than love, for by its very nature it's more easily overcome by

---

11. Padoan suggests that this is an allusion to the popularity of sodomy at the Roman court. Perhaps, but this reading assumes that men who practiced sodomy were more misogynistic than other men.

exhaustion than by the advice of others. So if you think you can persuade me to give up this love, you are trying to catch shadows or the wind with a net.

POLINICO: This really troubles me. There was a time when you were more malleable than wax, but now you are harder than an old oak. Do you really believe that you know her? Give it some thought. And get it through your head that things are going to turn out badly.

LIDIO: I don't think so. And even if it were true, haven't you taught me that it's more laudable to die for love and better to die loving?

POLINICO: Enough! Go ahead and do as you and this fool here wish. You will learn to your regret soon enough the power of love.

FESSENIO: Wait a second, my dear Polinico. Do you know what powers love has?

POLINICO: What are you talking about, idiot?

FESSENIO: Just like truffles! They both make young men's affairs come to a head and old men fart.

LIDIO: Ha, ha, ha!

POLINICO: Oh, Lidio! Are you mocking and laughing at my advice? I have nothing more to say to you. I will leave you to your own devices and go. [*He leaves*]

FESSENIO: Go to hell! See how he pretends to be the good one? As if we didn't know him for the vile hypocrite he is! Still, he has created such a stir over your love for Fulvia that I haven't had a chance to tell you a really good story about Calandro.

LIDIO: Tell me, tell me! With this sweet tidbit we'll overcome the bitter taste Polinico left us with.

ᚱᚢ SCENE III ᚷᚹ

LIDIO and FESSENIO

LIDIO: All right, tell me.

FESSENIO: Calandro, the husband of your mistress, Fulvia, and my supposed master—that blockhead whom you are giving horns—saw you yesterday dressed as Santilla when you came to visit Fulvia and when you left. And thinking that you were a woman, he fell so madly in love with you that he enlisted me to win that woman's love—that is, yours. I pretended to give it my best, and I've given him hope that I'll bring this Santilla to him—today, even.

LIDIO: [*Laughing*] What a joke! And now that you mention it, I remember that yesterday, as I was leaving Fulvia dressed as a woman, he followed me for a bit. But I never imagined that it was out of love. Let's see where this game takes us!

FESSENIO: I'll take care of it, leave it to me. I'll tell him again that I've accomplished miracles for him. And you can be sure, Lidio, that he believes me capable of even more than I claim. I regularly tell him the most ridiculous things in the world, for he's the greatest simpleton you'll ever find. I could list thousands of his stupidities, but to make a long story short, just let me say that he's so full of foolish ideas that if just one of them were to enter the mind of Solomon or Aristotle or Seneca, it would be strong enough to destroy all their wisdom and learning. And what's even funnier is that he thinks he's so handsome and attractive that any woman who sees him falls immediately in love with him, as if he were the most handsome young man in town. In the end, he who eats hay is an ox, as people say, and he's hardly any better than Martino da Amelia and Giovan Manente.[12] So it'll be easy to lead him by the nose, what with this silly love of his.

LIDIO: [*Laughing*] I'm going to die laughing! But tell me, since he thinks I'm a woman and I am a man, when he's with me, what'll happen?

FESSENIO: You can leave that to me as well, and everything will turn out just fine. But uh-oh! Here he comes now. Go away, he mustn't see me with you. [LIDIO *leaves*]

⁊ SCENE IV ⁊

CALANDRO, FESSENIO

CALANDRO: Fessenio!

FESSENIO: Who's calling me? Oh, Master!

CALANDRO: All right, tell me what's on with my dear Santilla?

FESSENIO: Do you want me to tell you what's on with Santilla?

CALANDRO: Yes.

FESSENIO: I'm not exactly sure. Still, I think she has on a jacket, a blouse, an apron, gloves, and slippers.

CALANDRO: What slippers, what gloves? Drunkard! I didn't ask you what she has on but what's on with her?

FESSENIO: Ohhh, you wanted to know what's on with her?

CALANDRO: Exactly, my good man.

12. For Martino da Amelia, see n. 3. Giovan Manente was another proverbial fool.

FESSENIO: When I saw her a little while ago, she was—you won't believe this!—she was sitting there with her chin in her hand like this, and I was telling her about you, and she was listening to me with her eyes and her mouth wide open, with a little of that sweet tongue of hers hanging out of her mouth, like this.

CALANDRO: Now you've replied just as I wanted. But let me ask, did she listen to you willingly?

FESSENIO: Listen willingly? Why, I've already so charmed her that within a few hours you'll have your desire. Could you ask for anything more?

CALANDRO: My dear Fessenio, I'll reward you.

FESSENIO: I hope so.

CALANDRO: Certainly. Oh, help me, Fessenio, I feel sick.

FESSENIO: O my master, do you have a fever? Let me see.

CALANDRO: No! Oh, what fever? Muttonhead! This Santilla has hit me hard.

FESSENIO: She hit you?

CALANDRO: Oh, you're so slow! I'm saying that I've really fallen for her.

FESSENIO: Well, you'll soon be with her.

CALANDRO: Let's go right now, then.

FESSENIO: There are still a few little problems to work out.

CALANDRO: Don't waste any time, then.

FESSENIO: I won't rest until it's all set up.

CALANDRO: Do it.

FESSENIO: You'll see, I'll be back with her reply shortly. Goodbye. [*Aside as* CALANDRO *leaves*] What a fine lover! What a case! [*Laughing*] Both the husband and the wife are madly in love with the same person! Oh, I see Samia, Fulvia's servant, coming out of the house. She seems preoccupied, and that means something important may be happening, because she knows everything. I'll find out from her what's going on in the house.

SCENE V

FESSENIO and SAMIA

FESSENIO: Samia! Oh, Samia! Wait a second, Samia.

SAMIA: Oh! Oh, Fessenio!

FESSENIO: What's going on in the house?

SAMIA: Actually, things aren't going well for my mistress.

FESSENIO: What's wrong?

SAMIA: She's all upset.

FESSENIO: Why?

SAMIA: Don't ask me.

FESSENIO: What?

SAMIA: She's too . . .

FESSENIO: Too what?

SAMIA: . . . worked up about . . .

FESSENIO: Worked up about what?

SAMIA: . . . about her love for your Lidio. Do you understand now?

FESSENIO: Oh! I knew that already.

SAMIA: But there's another thing that you don't know.

FESSENIO: What?

SAMIA: That she's sending me to someone who'll make Lidio do what she wants.

FESSENIO: How?

SAMIA: By means of chants.[13]

FESSENIO: Chants?

SAMIA: Yes, sir.

FESSENIO: And who will this chanter be?

SAMIA: What chanter? I said I'm going to someone who'll either make him love her or destroy him if he doesn't.

FESSENIO: Who?

SAMIA: Ruffo, the necromancer, who makes people do what he wants.

FESSENIO: How?

SAMIA: He has a fabulistic spirit.

FESSENIO: You mean a familiar spirit.[14]

SAMIA: I don't know how to say all those magical words. But I do know enough to tell him to come to my mistress. Be well. And be sure not to tell anyone about this.

FESSENIO: Don't worry. Goodbye.

---

13. Samia has mispronounced *incanti* (enchantments, spells) as *canti* (chants, songs).

14. Again Samia has misspoken, calling Ruffo's spirit *favellario* (fabulistic, or fool of stories) when the correct term is *familiare* (familiar). Such spirits were used for a wide range of magic in the Renaissance, both learned and popular. In this case Fulvia is seeking a punishing form of love magic that will make Lidio suffer until he returns to her.

ᵀᴼ SCENE VI ᴼᵀ

SAMIA and RUFFO

SAMIA: It's so early that Ruffo won't have returned yet to eat. I'd better go look for him in the piazza. Oh my, what luck! I see him coming this way. Oh, Ruffo! Ruffo! Don't you hear me, Ruffo?

RUFFO: [*Looking around*] I don't see who's calling me.

SAMIA: Wait up!

RUFFO: Who are you?

SAMIA: You've got me all in a sweat!

RUFFO: Well, what do you want?

SAMIA: My mistress asks that you come right now to speak with her.

RUFFO: Who is your mistress?

SAMIA: Fulvia.

RUFFO: The wife of Calandro?

SAMIA: Yes, her.

RUFFO: What does she want with me?

SAMIA: She'll tell you.

RUFFO: Doesn't she live just over there on the edge of the piazza?

SAMIA: Yes, it's just a couple of steps. Come along.

RUFFO: Go on ahead, and I'll follow in a moment. [SAMIA *leaves*] Will this woman be another one of those simpletons who believe that I'm a necromancer and that I have a spirit, as so many foolish women are saying? Well, I'll figure out soon enough what she's after. [FESSENIO *enters*] I'll go into her house before this person coming along sees me.

ᵀᴼ SCENE VII ᴼᵀ

FESSENIO and CALANDRO

FESSENIO: [*Alone*] Now I see that the gods have their pranksters just like mortals. Here is Love, who usually makes only noble hearts fall; now he's taken hold of that muttonhead Calandro, and he's not letting go. This proves that Cupid doesn't have enough to do, if he's willing to get involved with such an absolute beanbrain. But he did this because Calandro as a lover is like a lamb among wolves. And certainly, putting him in that company, Cupid has set him up well to be skinned alive—the featherweight is well netted. [CALANDRO *enters*]

CALANDRO: Oh, Fessenio! Fessenio!

FESSENIO: Who's calling me? Oh, Master!

CALANDRO: Have you seen Santilla?

FESSENIO: Yep.

CALANDRO: How does it look?

FESSENIO: You have real taste. When all is said and done, I think you've found the most attractive thing that could be found in all of the Maremma.[15] Do everything you can to have her.

CALANDRO: I will, even if I have to go barefoot and naked.

FESSENIO: [*To the audience*] Learn these fine words by heart, you lovers.

CALANDRO: If I ever have her, why, I'll eat her up.

FESSENIO: Eat her up? Ah, Calandro, have pity on her! Wild beasts eat each other; men don't eat women. Actually, it's true that one may drink a woman, but one shouldn't eat her.

CALANDRO: What! You drink a woman?

FESSENIO: Yes, you drink them.

CALANDRO: Oh. How do you do that?

FESSENIO: Don't you know?

CALANDRO: Really, I don't.

FESSENIO: Oh, how sad that a real man like you doesn't know how to drink women!

CALANDRO: Well, teach me!

FESSENIO: I'll tell you. When you kiss a woman, don't you suck her?

CALANDRO: Yes.

FESSENIO: And when you drink, don't you suck?

CALANDRO: Yes.

FESSENIO: All right, so, kissing a woman when you suck her, you're drinking her.

CALANDRO: That makes sense to me. Heavens! But I've never drunk my Fulvia, and still I've kissed her many times.

FESSENIO: Ohhh! Well, you haven't drunk her because she also kissed you,

---

15. Padoan suggests that Maremma is a deformation of *mare* (sea) implying "no place." We prefer the simpler reading that Fessenio is referring to the Tuscan region known as the Maremma notorious for being rustic and backward (the term is used in this sense in *Gl'ingannati*, act I, scene v). In either case the remark seems to be ironic.

and as much as you sucked from her, she sucked from you; thus, you drank no more of her than she of you.

CALANDRO: I see now, Fessenio, that you're more learned than Orlando,[16] because you're exactly right: there was never a time when I kissed her that she didn't kiss me back.

FESSENIO: Ah! See how I'm telling you the truth?

CALANDRO: But tell me this, there was this Spanish woman who always kissed my hand. Does this mean that she wanted to drink me?

FESSENIO: That's a big secret! Spanish women kiss hands, not because of love or because they want to drink you. No, they do it because they want to suck the rings off your fingers.[17]

CALANDRO: Oh, Fessenio, you know more secrets of women . . .

FESSENIO: [*Aside*] Especially when it comes to your woman!

CALANDRO: . . . than an archi-tit![18]

FESSENIO: Really! An archi-tit, eh?

CALANDRO: Why, that Spanish woman drank up two of my rings. From now on, I swear to God, I'm going to be careful not to let any woman drink me ever again.

FESSENIO: You are wise.

CALANDRO: No one is going to kiss me unless I kiss them back.

FESSENIO: Calandro, be careful, because if some woman were to drink your nose, your cheek, or your eye, you would become the ugliest man in the world.

CALANDRO: I'll be very careful. But do something so that I can hold my Santilla in my arms.

FESSENIO: Leave it to me. I'm going to go take care of the last little details right now.

CALANDRO: Good, but be quick!

FESSENIO: I just have to go there, and then I'll return in a little while with everything set up. [*They leave, going in different directions*]

---

16. One of the heroes of the chivalric epics that drew upon the deeds of the knights of the French king Charlemagne. Orlando was known for his intelligence and learning, especially in relation to his peers.

17. The stereotyping of Spaniards as greedy and grasping is a regular feature of Renaissance comedies.

18. *Architetto.* Calandro has mispronounced *architetta* (architect), substituting *-tetto* (tit) for *-tetta.* Padoan suggests a possible double meaning, with *architetto* implying a gynecologist. As gynecologists were virtually unheard of in the Renaissance—women healers dealt with such matters—this reading seems unlikely.

❧ SCENE VIII ☙

RUFFO, alone

RUFFO: A man should never lose hope, because often one gets lucky when one least expects it. Just as I figured, this woman thinks I have a spirit. And she's madly in love with a young man. Having found no other way to get what she wants, she has come to me to ask that I make him come to her as a woman during the day and promising me a good deal of money if I can make her happy. I think I can do this, for the man she loves is a certain Lidio,[19] a Greek who is an acquaintance and friend of mine. We come from the same town, and his servant Fannio is also my friend. So I should be able to carry this off. Still, I won't promise her anything until I get a chance to talk with this Lidio. Fortune has given us a great opportunity, if Lidio is ready to go after it like me.[20] Let's get on with it, then! I'm off to the house of the Florentine merchant Perillo, where Lidio lives. And it's lunchtime, so maybe I'll find him at home.

Act II

❧ SCENE I ☙

The FEMALE LIDIO,[21] FANNIO, and the WETNURSE

FEMALE LIDIO: It's very clear how much more fortunate men are than women. And I more than others have found this to be true, because ever since that day when our homeland of Modon was burned by the Turks, I've always gone about dressed as a man called Lidio (which was the name of my most noble brother), and with everyone believing me to be a man I've had enough good luck to make everything work out well for us. On the other hand, if I'd dressed as and taken the name of a woman (which of course I am), the Turk who held us as slaves wouldn't have sold us, and Perillo wouldn't have bought our freedom either, so we would

---

19. The Lidio he knows, however, is not the Lidio who goes to Fulvia dressed as a woman, but his twin sister Santilla, who, as will become clear in the next scene, goes about dressed as a man and uses the name Lidio.

20. Because the referents of Italian pronouns are sometimes ambiguous, this sentence could also be read as "Fortune has given us a great opportunity, if Lidio has her and I have her [money] as well."

21. *Lidio femina*, in other words, Santilla dressed as a man. It seems suggestive that Lidio dressed as a woman remains "Lidio" in the stage directions of the comedy, whereas Santilla dressed as a man becomes "the Female Lidio."

have been left in miserable slavery. And you know that if I were really a man instead of a woman, life would be easy for us—in fact, since Perillo believes me to be a man (as you know) and has found me always absolutely trustworthy in his business concerns, he has become so fond of me that he wants to give his only daughter, Virginia, to me as my wife along with all his goods, which will be hers when he dies. The moment I heard from Perillo's nephew that he wanted to marry me to her tomorrow or the day after, I left home to discuss this with you two, my wetnurse and Fannio, my servant. I'm really worried, as I'm sure you can understand. I don't know what to—

FANNIO. [*Interrupting*] Be quiet! For heaven's sake, be quiet! We don't want this woman who's coming up to us all worked up to hear what we're talking about.

❧ SCENE II ☙

SAMIA, the FEMALE LIDIO, FANNIO, and the WETNURSE

SAMIA: [*Aside*] I can tell you, she's madly in love with him. She said that she saw her Lidio from the window and she sent me to speak with him. I'll take him aside to have a word with him. [*To the* FEMALE LIDIO] Good day, sir.

FEMALE LIDIO: Welcome.

SAMIA: A couple of words.

FEMALE LIDIO: Who are you?

SAMIA: You're asking me who I am?

FEMALE LIDIO: I'm just trying to find out what I don't know.

SAMIA: You'll find out soon enough.

FEMALE LIDIO: What do you want?

SAMIA: My mistress asks that you love her as she loves you and that you come to her when you wish.

FEMALE LIDIO: I don't understand. Who is your mistress?

SAMIA: What? Lidio! You're kidding, right?

FEMALE LIDIO: You're the one kidding me.

SAMIA: If you don't know Fulvia or me, it's a miracle. Come on, now, what do you want me to tell her?

FEMALE LIDIO: My good woman, if you can't explain this to me any better, I can't reply any better.

SAMIA: Are you pretending that you don't understand?

FEMALE LIDIO: I don't understand you, I don't know you, and furthermore I don't have any desire to know you or understand you! Go in peace.

SAMIA: You are certainly discreet! By the holy cross, I'm going to tell her about this.

FEMALE LIDIO: Tell her anything you want, just as long as you get out of my life, both you and she.

SAMIA: Go to hell! [*Aside as she walks off*] You'll change your tune whether you want to or not, you stingy Greek, because my mistress is sending me to the necromancer. And if his spirit does his job, Fulvia will win in the end.

FEMALE LIDIO: How wretched and sad is the fortune of us women! When I see these things I realize with tears in my eyes even more how very difficult it is for me to be a woman.

FANNIO: I would have liked to find out what she was really talking about. That wouldn't have been bad.

FEMALE LIDIO: My bigger problem overwhelms everything else. Still, if she speaks to me again, I'll try to treat her more civilly.

FANNIO: I know that woman.

FEMALE LIDIO: Who is she?

FANNIO: Samia, the servant of Fulvia, a Roman noblewoman.

FEMALE LIDIO: Oh, oh, oh! Now I remember her too. Oh well, never mind! It's true, she did mention Fulvia.

☜ SCENE III ☞

The FEMALE LIDIO, FANNIO, RUFFO, and the WETNURSE

RUFFO: Hey there! Hello!

FEMALE LIDIO: Whose voice is that?

RUFFO: I've been looking for you for a while.

FANNIO: Hello, Ruffo. What's up?

RUFFO: Good things!

FANNIO: What?

RUFFO: I'll tell you.

FEMALE LIDIO: Wait a second, Ruffo. [*To the* WETNURSE] Listen, Tiresia, go home and see what our master Perillo is doing about this marriage of mine, and when Fannio gets there send him back to tell me what's going on because I don't want to be found there today. Then maybe I'll be able to find out if the popular saying is true: "He who still has time, still has hope." Now run along. [*The* WETNURSE *leaves*] Now, Ruffo, tell me your good news.

RUFFO: Even though I've known you just a short time, I'm really fond of you two, since we're fellow countrymen, and the heavens have given us a chance to work together.

FEMALE LIDIO: We're certainly fond of you too, and we're willing to work with you. But what's this all about?

RUFFO: I'll tell you quickly. Listen. A woman has fallen in love with you, Lidio, and wants you to love her as much as she loves you. And having found no other way to get her wish, she came to me. The reason she did is because I do magic by drawing figures and points and use chiromancy as well. Thus, among women, who are so credulous, I have the reputation of being a great necromancer. And they believe absolutely that I have a spirit that helps me do and undo things as I wish. All this I willingly allow them to believe, as it's often very profitable and not without its occasional sweet rewards from these simple women—as in this case with this one, if you handle her cleverly. She wants me to force you to go to her, and I've given her some hope, hoping that you'll help me with this. If you're willing, we can get rich from this affair, and you can have some fun with her as well.

FEMALE LIDIO: Ruffo, such things would seem to require quite a bit of deception, and as I'm inexperienced, I could easily end up the fool. But I do have faith in you as a wheeler-dealer, and if I decide to play, I'll give the game my best shot. Let Fannio and me think it over. But tell me, who is she?

RUFFO: A certain Fulvia, rich, noble, and beautiful.

FANNIO: Oh, oh, oh! The mistress of the woman who was just here!

FEMALE LIDIO: That's right.

RUFFO: What, her servant spoke with you?

FEMALE LIDIO: Just now.

RUFFO: What did you say?

FEMALE LIDIO: I told her pretty bluntly to get lost.

RUFFO: That's not all bad. Still, if she speaks to you again, you'll have to be more friendly if we're to make this work.

FEMALE LIDIO: All right.

FANNIO: Tell me, Ruffo, when would Lidio need to be with her?

RUFFO: The sooner, the better.

FANNIO: When?

RUFFO: During the day.

FEMALE LIDIO: But I'd be seen!

RUFFO: Right. But she wants the spirit to force you to go to her in the form of a woman.[22]

FANNIO: And what will she be able to do with him if the spirit gives him the form of a woman?

RUFFO: I imagine that she means that he should come dressed as a woman, not really as a woman, even if that's what she said.

FEMALE LIDIO: Isn't this a neat plot, Fannio?

FANNIO: Really neat. I like it a lot!

RUFFO: Well, do you want to give it a try?

FEMALE LIDIO: I'll let you know in a bit.

RUFFO: Where will I find you?

FANNIO: Here.

FEMALE LIDIO: Whoever arrives here first, waits for the others.

RUFFO: Good. Goodbye, then. [*He leaves*]

᷈᷈ SCENE IV ᷈᷈

FANNIO and the FEMALE LIDIO

FANNIO: This is a heaven-sent chance for you to get your wish to disappear for the day, because if you go to this woman, not even Jove would be able to find you. And moreover, once she reveals to you that she's a whore, you'll be able to hit her up regularly for money to keep you quiet. But best of all, the whole thing is enough to make one die laughing. She's asked you—a woman—to come to her disguised as a woman! You should go to her: trying out just what she asked for, she'll find just what she doesn't want.

FEMALE LIDIO: Shall we go for it?

FANNIO: That and nothing else!

FEMALE LIDIO: Well . . . go on home, find out what's going on there, and get the clothes we'll need. Then meet me at Franzino's shop, and we'll give Ruffo our yes.

FANNIO: Get going, because this man I see coming could be someone Perillo has sent for you.

FEMALE LIDIO: He's not one of our people, but still, you're right. [*Both leave, going in opposite directions*]

---

22. I.e., so that no one would notice.

❦ SCENE V ❧

FESSENIO and FULVIA

FESSENIO: There's Fulvia at her door. I'll go talk with her a bit and tell her that Lidio wants to leave, to see what she'll say.

FULVIA: Welcome, my dear Fessenio. What news do you have about my Lidio?

FESSENIO: I'm afraid he's quite changed.

FULVIA: Oh dear! Tell me, what's going on?

FESSENIO: He's really thinking about leaving to find his sister, Santilla.

FULVIA: Oh, poor me! He wants to leave?

FESSENIO: He's thinking about it, at least.

FULVIA: My Fessenio, if you wish to help yourself, if you want what is good for Lidio, if you value my health, find him, persuade him, beg him, press him, implore him not to leave for this reason. I'll have all of Italy searched for her. And if she's found, my Fessenio, right now, as I said earlier, I give you my word, I'll marry her to Flaminio, my only son.

FESSENIO: Do you really want me to tell him that?

FULVIA: That's what I'm pledging, and I'll keep my word.

FESSENIO: I'm sure he'll be glad to learn this. It will make him happy.

FULVIA: I'll be ruined if you can't help me with him. Beg him to save my life, which is his.

FESSENIO: I'll do what you ask. And in order to serve you, I need to go back home, where he is now.

FULVIA: My dear Fessenio, you will be doing as much for yourself as for me. Goodbye. [*She enters her house*]

FESSENIO: This woman is barely hanging on, and by God, I'm beginning to feel sorry for her. It would be good if Lidio would come to her dressed as a woman today, as he used to do. And he'll do it because he wants it just as much as she does. But first I must take care of Calandro's business. And here he is now, coming back. I'll tell him that I've arranged his affair.

❧ SCENE VI ❧

FESSENIO and CALANDRO

FESSENIO: Good health to you, Master. May you be even healthier because I'm saluting your health! Give me your hand.

CALANDRO: You can take all of me—my hand and my feet.

FESSENIO: [*Aside*] Don't these quick replies just drip from his mouth?

CALANDRO: What's up?

FESSENIO: What, you ask? The world's in your hands. You're a lucky man.

CALANDRO: What are you talking about?

FESSENIO: I'm talking about your Santilla: she loves you even more than you love her, and she's even more eager to be with you than you are to be with her, because I told her how generous, handsome, and wise you are. [*Aside*] Echhhh! [*To* CALANDRO] What she wants now is exactly what you want. Listen, Master, she had barely even heard your name before she became all aflame with love for you. Now everything's going to be fine, and you'll be happy.

CALANDRO: You're right about that! I can hardly wait to kiss those bright ruby red lips and that face all wine and cheese!

FESSENIO: Good! [*Aside*] He meant that face all milk and honey, I hope.

CALANDRO: Oh, Fessenio, I'll make you emperor!

FESSENIO: [*Aside*] With what gentle behavior my friend here seeks favor!

CALANDRO: Let's go to her.

FESSENIO: What do you mean, go to her? What are you thinking? Do you think she's a whore? I need to carefully arrange your going to her.

CALANDRO: Well, how does one go to her, then?

FESSENIO: On one's feet.

CALANDRO: I know that. But I'm asking, how?

FESSENIO: You must realize that if you just go walking up to her place, you'll be seen. And therefore I arranged it with her that you'll go to her in a trunk so that no one will know about you and she won't lose her honor. And once the trunk is in her room, you can take all the pleasure together you want.

CALANDRO: Well, then, I'm not going to go on my feet as you said.

FESSENIO: [*Laughing*] What a clever lover you are, and in the end you're right.

CALANDRO: This isn't going to be hard on me, is it, Fessenio?

FESSENIO: Not at all, you old devil, you. Not at all.

CALANDRO: But tell me, will the trunk be big enough that I can get all of me in?

FESSENIO: Who cares? If we can't get you in in one piece, we'll cut you up into pieces and get you in.

CALANDRO: What? In pieces, really?

FESSENIO: Of course, in pieces!

CALANDRO: Oh my. How?

FESSENIO: Very nicely.

CALANDRO: Tell me.

FESSENIO: Don't you know?

CALANDRO: No, in the name of the holy cross.

FESSENIO: If you'd ever been aboard ship you'd know, because you would have regularly seen that when they need to fit hundreds of people into a little boat, they can't do it unless they disconnect from one person first a hand or an arm, then from another the legs and so on until they've stowed them all away like the other cargo. That way they get them all aboard using the least amount of space.

CALANDRO: But then what happens?

FESSENIO: Well, then when they arrive in port, those who want to, reattach their members. And it often happens that by mistake or perversity someone takes the member of someone else and puts it where they wish. And sometimes this doesn't turn out well because someone takes a larger member than he needs or a leg that's shorter than his own so that he becomes lame or malformed. Does that make sense?

CALANDRO: Of course. I can tell you that when I'm in that chest, I'm going to be very careful not to lose my member!

FESSENIO: If you don't lose it yourself, then certainly no one else will take it, considering that you'll be alone in the trunk. If you don't fit and we have to do like they do with those who go on board ship, I can tell you that we'll probably just disconnect your legs. And since you're going to be carried, you won't need them anyway.

CALANDRO: And where do you disconnect a man?

FESSENIO: In all the places where things stick out, like here and here and here. . . . Do you want to know how?

CALANDRO: Yes, please.

FESSENIO: I can show you in a second, because it's simple. It just takes a little spell. Say it like I do, but quietly, because you have a tendency to shout, and that would wreck everything.

CALANDRO: Don't worry about me.

FESSENIO: Let's try a hand for now. Give it to me [*taking* CALANDRO's *hand*] and say this: "Ambracullàc."[23]

CALANDRO: Anculabràc.

FESSENIO: You got it wrong. Say: "Ambracullàc."

CALANDRO: Alabracùc.

FESSENIO: Worse yet! "Ambracullàc."

CALANDRO: Alucambràc.

FESSENIO: Oh my, oh my! All right, repeat after me: Am . . .

CALANDRO: Am . . .

FESSENIO: . . . bra . . .

CALANDRO: . . . bra . . .

FESSENIO: . . . cul . . .

CALANDRO: . . . cul . . .

FESSENIO: . . . lac . . .

CALANDRO: . . . lac . . .

FESSENIO: Buff . . .

CALANDRO: Buff . . .

FESSENIO: . . . a . . .

CALANDRO: . . . a . . .

FESSENIO: . . . lo . . .

CALANDRO: . . . lo . . .

FESSENIO: . . . brain . . .

CALANDRO: . . . brain . . .

FESSENIO: I'll . . .

CALANDRO: I'll . . .

FESSENIO: . . . givit . . .

CALANDRO: . . . givit . . .

FESSENIO: [*Yanking hard on his arm*] . . . to you!

CALANDRO: Ouch! Oh! Ow! Good God!

FESSENIO: You'd wreck anything. Damn, you have so little memory and so little patience! In the name of heaven's pussy, didn't I tell you just now that you shouldn't shout? You've broken the spell.

CALANDRO: And you've broken my arm!

FESSENIO: Do you realize that now you can't be disconnected anymore?

CALANDRO: What are we going to do, then?

23. The word evokes "abracadabra" but can also be read as "big brown bottom."

FESSENIO: Well, I'll just have to find a trunk big enough to fit you into all in one piece.

CALANDRO: Oh, that sounds good. Go find one so that I won't have to be disconnected, for the love of God, because my arm is killing me!

FESSENIO: I'll take care of it right away.

CALANDRO: Meanwhile I'll go to the market and return shortly. [*He leaves*]

FESSENIO: Good idea. Goodbye. [*Aside*] Now I need to find Lidio and arrange things. We'll be laughing about this all year! But I need to get away without talking with Samia, whom I see over there in her doorway babbling to herself. [*He leaves*]

❧ SCENE VII ❧

SAMIA and FULVIA

SAMIA: Things change so quickly! Not even a month has passed since Lidio was so in love with my mistress that he wanted to be with her every minute. And now that he sees her so in love with him, she's mud to him. If a remedy isn't found quickly, she'll do something so foolish that the whole city will find out. And I'm beginning to worry that Calandro's brothers[24] are already beginning to suspect something, because she doesn't care about anything, think about anything, or speak about anything except Lidio. It's true that those who find love in their heart feel spurs in their flanks. I just hope to heaven that she comes out of this all right.

FULVIA: [*Calling from inside*] Samia!

SAMIA: I hear her calling me from upstairs. She must have seen Lidio from the window, as I see him over there speaking with someone I don't know. Or maybe she wants to send me back to Ruffo.

FULVIA: Saaaamia!

SAMIA: Cooooming! [*She goes in*]

---

24. Calandro's brothers are a significant worry because honor was a family concern. If Fulvia's affair became public knowledge, not only would she lose her honor but all those males in her husband's family—the family that was responsible for her correct behavior—would be dishonored as well. Brothers were often significant players in Renaissance affairs of honor.

✥ SCENE VIII ❧

The FEMALE LIDIO and FANNIO

FEMALE LIDIO: Tiresia told you this?

FANNIO: That's right.

FEMALE LIDIO: And at home they're talking about my marriage as a sure thing?

FANNIO: Exactly.

FEMALE LIDIO: And Virginia is happy with this?

FANNIO: She's ecstatic.

FEMALE LIDIO: And they're preparing the wedding?

FANNIO: The whole house is in an uproar.

FEMALE LIDIO: And do they think I'll be happy?

FANNIO: They're certain of it.

FEMALE LIDIO: Oh, poor Santilla! What makes everyone else happy makes me only sad. The warm feelings of Perillo and his wife are like a knife in my heart, because I can't do what they want and what would be in my own best interest. Damn! God has given me, instead of light, darkness; instead of life, death; instead of the cradle, the grave; from the moment I was born. Why, the moment I was born, my luck died. O my sweet brother, you're infinitely blessed if you lie dead and buried in our homeland, as I believe! What will I do now, miserable Santilla? Now I can call myself Santilla, if I can't be Lidio anymore. I'm a woman, and it seems that I'm to be a husband! But if I marry this woman, it will immediately become clear that I'm a woman and not a man. And for that offense, father, mother, and daughter will all want to kill me. I can't refuse to marry her, and yet if I do, they will curse me and throw me out. If I reveal that I'm a woman, I'll just cause the same thing to happen. I can't stand this any longer! Woe is me! As they say, "One path leads over the cliff, and on the other the wolves are waiting."

FANNIO: Don't give up, for it may well be that the heavens haven't abandoned you. It seems to me that we should follow your plan to not let Perillo find you today. And if we do, going to that woman is a perfect opportunity, and I have the clothes ready for you to dress as a woman. Remember the old saying, "The person who escapes from one bind slides by a thousand more."

FEMALE LIDIO: I'll try anything. But where is that Ruffo?

FANNIO: We left it that whoever arrived first would wait.

FEMALE LIDIO: It'd be better if Ruffo were waiting for us. Let's leave so that

that man over there doesn't see us, just in case it's someone Perillo has sent looking for me, even though it doesn't seem to be one of his people. [*They both leave*]

❧ SCENE IX ❧

FESSENIO and CALANDRO

FESSENIO: [*Alone*] Things couldn't be going better. Lidio is going to dress as a woman and wait for Calandro in his ground-floor room so that when he arrives, he'll seem to him to be a beautiful young woman. Then, when the moment comes to go to bed, in the dark after he has closed the shutters, he'll have a cheap whore take his place with Calandro. Being such a thick-headed clod that he doesn't know his ass from a hole in the ground, he'll never figure it out. But here he comes now, all happy. [CALANDRO *enters*] May the heavens bless you, Master!

CALANDRO: And you, my dear Fessenio. Have you taken care of the trunk?

FESSENIO: All taken care of. And you'll fit in without having to disconnect even a hair, as long as you get in carefully.

CALANDRO: Wonderful! But explain something to me that I've been wondering about.

FESSENIO: What's that?

CALANDRO: When I'm in the trunk, do I need to be asleep or awake?

FESSENIO: Oh, that's a very clever question! Asleep or awake, eh? Well, don't you know that on horseback one stays up in the saddle, in the street one walks, at the table one eats, on the bench one sits, on the bed one sleeps, and in the trunk one dies?

CALANDRO: One dies!?

FESSENIO: Yes, one dies. Why the fuss?

CALANDRO: Shit! That doesn't sound like a good idea.

FESSENIO: Haven't you ever died before?

CALANDRO: No, not that I know of.

FESSENIO: Well, then, how do you know it's not a good idea, if you've never tried it?

CALANDRO: And you, have you ever died?

FESSENIO: No problem! Tons of times, tons and tons of times.

CALANDRO: Does it hurt much?

FESSENIO: It's just like sleeping.

CALANDRO: Do I have to die, then?

FESSENIO: Right, when you're in the trunk.

CALANDRO: And who's going to kill me?

FESSENIO: You'll have to kill yourself.

CALANDRO: And how do I kill myself?

FESSENIO: It's as easy as falling off a log. And since you don't know how, I'll be glad to explain it to you.

CALANDRO: Great, tell me.

FESSENIO: You close your eyes and, twisting your arms, fold your hands together on your chest. Then you stay real, real still and very, very quiet, and you don't look at anyone or listen to what they say to you.

CALANDRO: I've got it. But then the problem is, how does one come alive again?

FESSENIO: This is one of the most secret secrets in the whole world, and almost no one knows it. Even though you can be sure I wouldn't tell anyone else, I'm willing to tell you. But look, Calandro, you must give me your word that you won't tell anyone else, ever.

CALANDRO: I give you my word that I won't tell anyone, and if you want, I won't even tell myself.

FESSENIO: [*Laughing*] It's fine with me if you tell yourself, but only in one ear, not in the other, at least for the moment.

CALANDRO: All right, teach me.

FESSENIO: You know, Calandro, that there's no difference between a live person and a dead one except for the fact that when a person is dead, he never moves. Nonetheless, if you follow my directions, you'll always be resurrected.

CALANDRO: Tell me how.

FESSENIO: With your face turned towards the sky, you spit straight up. Then you give your whole body a shake, like this. Then you open your eyes, speak, and move all your members. When that's done, Death flies off and the person returns to life. And you can believe me, my dear Calandro, that the person who does this never, never dies. Now you can say that you have the most wonderful secret in the whole universe and even the Maremma.[25]

CALANDRO: This is certainly a great gift! Now I know how to die and to be reborn whenever I want.

FESSENIO: Exactly! [*Aside*] Master Blockhead.

CALANDRO: And I'll do it all perfectly.

FESSENIO: I'm sure.

25. See n. 15.

CALANDRO: Do you want to try it out a bit, to see if I've got it right?

FESSENIO: Ah, what a good idea! But be sure to do it right.

CALANDRO: You'll see. Now, watch. [*Lying down*] Here I am.

FESSENIO: Screw up your mouth. More. Screw it up good . . . a little bit the other way . . . a little lower. Ah! Now, go ahead and die right there. Oh, that's very good! It's just wonderful to work with wise men! Who else could have learned to die as perfectly as this fine man? From the outside he seems perfectly dead. If he's that dead inside, he won't feel a thing. [*Hitting him*] Take that! Good. And *that!* Very good. Take this! Impressive indeed. Calandro! Oh, Calandro! Calandro!

CALANDRO: I'm dead—really dead.

FESSENIO: Come alive. Come alive. Come on! Come on, now! My word, you are really great at dying. Spit straight up.

CALANDRO: Psssht! [*Spitting*] Ugh! Psssht! [*Spitting again*] Ugh! Ugh! Well, you certainly did a bad thing in bringing me back to life.

FESSENIO: Why?

CALANDRO: I was just beginning to see the other world.

FESSENIO: You'll have plenty of time to see it when you're in the trunk.

CALANDRO: I can't wait!

FESSENIO: Let's get going. Now that you know how to die and be resurrected so well, there's no time to waste.

CALANDRO: Let's go! I'm hot to trot!

FESSENIO: No, no, no! We want to do everything in an orderly manner so that Fulvia doesn't find out. You tell her that you're going to your country home and then come to Menicuccio's house, where you'll find me with everything we need to carry this off.

CALANDRO: Excellent. I'll do it immediately, as my beast is ready to go.

FESSENIO: Let me see. [*Bending over and looking closely at* CALANDRO'S *crotch*] Is he ready?

CALANDRO: [*Laughing*] I would say that the mule is all saddled up and ready to go!

FESSENIO: [*Laughing*] I meant that thing!

CALANDRO: Me, I can't wait to be in the saddle—but in the saddle of that sweet angel from paradise. [*He leaves*]

FESSENIO: Sweet angel, eh? Dream on. If things go according to my plan, that muttonhead will couple today with the sewer, not heaven. And now he's ready to ride. I need to get going and tell that old whore that everything's ready and to wait for me. Oh, oh, oh! I can already see Calandro in the saddle! It's going to take a wonderfully heroic little mule to carry that broken-down elephant!

⟡ SCENE X ⟡

CALANDRO and FULVIA

CALANDRO: Fulvia! Oh, Fulvia!

FULVIA: Sir, what do you want?

CALANDRO: Come to the window.

FULVIA: What do you want?

CALANDRO: Is everything all right? I'm going out to our country house to check on our son Flaminio to make sure he's not wasting all his time hunting.

FULVIA: Good idea. When will you return?

CALANDRO: Perhaps this evening. Goodbye. [*He leaves*]

FULVIA: Goodbye. [*Aside as* CALANDRO *leaves*] And good riddance. What a distinguished husband my brothers stuck me with! It depresses me just to look at him.

Act III

⟡ SCENE I ⟡

FESSENIO, alone

FESSENIO: [*Showing the audience the clothes that* CALANDRO *has taken off to enter the trunk*] Here, O spectators, are the remains of love. If you're looking for good manners, wisdom, and understanding, buy these and wear them for a while. For these are the clothes of that foolish Calandro, who is so wise that he believes the young man he has fallen in love with is a girl. Why, this Calandro's a man who's so godlike that he can die and be resurrected whenever he wants. Whoever wants to buy these clothes, just put your money down—I can sell them because he has just passed away. Just now he put himself to death when he climbed into the trunk. [*Laughing*] So now Lidio, elegantly dressed as a woman, is happily awaiting this distinguished lover, who to tell you the truth is more disgusting than Bramante.[26] I've run on ahead in order to find the old whore I hired for this affair. And here she comes now. And over there I see the porter bringing the trunk. He thinks he's carrying precious merchandise, not realizing that it's some

---

26. This Bramante has been identified with the Saracen king Bramante in the chivalric epics of the Renaissance and also with the architect Donato Bramante, whom Bibbiena may have known in Rome.

of the cheapest stuff in the city. Doesn't anyone want to buy these clothes of love? No? Well, goodbye, then. I'm off to couple a muttonhead with an old whore. Goodbye.

ᴥ SCENE II ᴥ

The WHORE, FESSENIO, the PORTER, the TAX OFFICERS, and CALANDRO

WHORE: Here I am, Fessenio. Let's go.

FESSENIO: [*To the* PORTER] Take this trunk of ours ahead first. No, not that way, Porter. Go straight ahead.

WHORE: What's in it?

FESSENIO: Things worthy of you, my dear.

WHORE: What?

FESSENIO: Silk and cloth.

WHORE: Whose are they?

FESSENIO: They belong to the man you have to make it with, pretty one.

WHORE: Oh! And will he give some of them to me?

FESSENIO: Of course, if you do exactly as I told you.

WHORE: No problem.

FESSENIO: Make sure, above everything else, that you remember, absolutely, to call yourself Santilla, and then all the other things I told you.

WHORE: I won't leave out a thing.

FESSENIO: Otherwise you won't get a thing.

WHORE: I'll play my part perfectly. But uh-oh! What are those tax officers trying to do to the porter?

FESSENIO: Oh no! Hold on, be quiet! Listen.

TAX OFFICER: [*To the* PORTER] Hey you, what have you got in there?

PORTER: Huh? How should I know?

TAX OFFICER: Have you been to the tax office?

PORTER: Not me.

TAX OFFICER: What's in there? Speak up.

PORTER: Me, I haven't seen it open.

TAX OFFICER: Tell me, you rogue!

PORTER: They told me it was silk and cloth.

TAX OFFICER: Silk?

PORTER: Uh-huh.

TAX OFFICER: Is it locked?

PORTER: Nah, don't think so.

TAX OFFICER: Then you've lost it.[27] Put it down.

PORTER: No way! [*Calling to* FESSENIO] Oh, sir!

TAX OFFICER: Put it down, you crook. Or do you want me to give you one upside the head, maybe?

FESSENIO: Oh no! Damn. This is going all wrong. Our plot is wrecked, everything's a mess, it's all going to come out and we're ruined!

WHORE: What's going on?

FESSENIO: The plan is ruined.

WHORE: Tell me, Fessenio. What's going on?

FESSENIO: Help me, Sofilla!

WHORE: What do you want?

FESSENIO: Ummm . . . I've got it! Cry, moan, scream, tear out your hair.

WHORE: Why?

FESSENIO: Just do it, and you'll find out soon enough.

WHORE: All right. Oh, oh, oh! Boo-hoo-hoo!

TAX OFFICER: [*Opening the chest*] Ohhh my! This is a dead man!

FESSENIO: [*Hurrying up to the* TAX OFFICER] Hey there! What are you doing? What are you after?

TAX OFFICER: This porter here told me that there were taxable goods in here, and instead we found a dead man.

FESSENIO: Yeah, he's dead.

TAX OFFICER: Who is it?

FESSENIO: The husband of this poor woman. Don't you see how she's suffering?

TAX OFFICER: Well, why is he being carried around in this trunk?

FESSENIO: To tell you the truth, in order to fool the crowd.

TAX OFFICER: Why's that?

FESSENIO: Because otherwise everyone would gang up on us and kick us out.

TAX OFFICER: And why's that?

FESSENIO: He died of the plague.

TAX OFFICER: The plague?! Oh, God! And I touched him!

FESSENIO: That's your problem.

TAX OFFICER: Where are you taking him?

FESSENIO: To bury him in some ditch, or perhaps dump him and the trunk in some river.

27. I.e., I'm confiscating it for duty that hasn't been paid on it.

CALANDRO: Psssht! [*Spitting*] Ugh! Psssht! [*Spitting again*] Ugh! Drown me, eh? I'm not dead! No way, you bastards! [*Everyone flees except* CALANDRO *and* FESSENIO]

FESSENIO: Oh, look at them all run! Wait, Sofilla! Porter! Wait, Sofilla! Porter! All right, then, keep running! The devil himself wouldn't be able to make them come back. Go on! This is what happens when one gets involved with madmen. Go on!

⁓ SCENE III ⁓

CALANDRO and FESSENIO

CALANDRO: [*Getting out of the trunk and hitting* FESSENIO *with his fists*] You traitor, Fessenio! So you planned to drown me, eh?

FESSENIO: Ouch! Ow! Master, why are you hitting me?

CALANDRO: You ask me why, you villain?

FESSENIO: Yes, why?

CALANDRO: You deserve it, you dirty crook.

FESSENIO: As they say, sir, "The person who does a good deed always is mistreated in return." So you're beating me because I rescued you, right?

CALANDRO: What kind of rescue is this?

FESSENIO: What kind? I said all that so you wouldn't be carried off to the tax offices.

CALANDRO: And what would have happened if they had taken me there?

FESSENIO: What would have happened? Why, I should have let them carry you off, and you'd have found out.

CALANDRO: What the devil would they have done?

FESSENIO: Well, you certainly seem to have been born yesterday. You were caught being smuggled without having paid the import taxes. Smuggled goods, caught in the act. Why, they would have sold you just like all the other smuggled goods.

CALANDRO: But . . . well, you did very well, then. Forgive me, Fessenio.

FESSENIO: Next time, wait till things are worked out before you get all excited. [*Aside*] I'll be damned if I don't pay you back.

CALANDRO: I'll do as you say. But tell me, who was that really ugly woman who ran off?

FESSENIO: Who was she? Didn't you recognize her?

CALANDRO: No.

FESSENIO: That was Death,[28] who was with you in the trunk.

CALANDRO: With me?

FESSENIO: With you. Exactly.

CALANDRO: Oh, oh! I never saw her in there with me.

FESSENIO: Oh, sure! Look, you don't see Sleep when you sleep, either; or, when you drink, Thirst; or Hunger, when you eat. And what's more, if you're willing to be honest with me, while you're alive right now you don't even see Life, yet clearly she's with you.

CALANDRO: [*Looking around*] Right, I don't see her at all.

FESSENIO: Well, in the same way, you don't see Death when you die.

CALANDRO: Why did the porter run off?

FESSENIO: Because he was afraid of Death. So I'm afraid you're not going to be able to go to Santilla today.

CALANDRO: Death is going to have me, if I don't have Santilla today.

FESSENIO: I don't know what to do . . . unless you're willing to face a bit of hardship.

CALANDRO: Fessenio, to have her I'm willing to face anything. Why, I'm even ready to go to bed without my socks on.

FESSENIO: Oh my! Naked feet in bed, eh? That would be too much. God would be displeased.

CALANDRO: Tell me what I need to do, then. Go ahead.

FESSENIO: You'll have to play the role of the porter. You've already changed your clothes, and since you've just been dead for a while, your face is changed enough that no one will recognize you. I'll claim to be the woodworker who made the trunk. Santilla will immediately understand the new plan, because she's wiser than a sibyl. And then you two can take care of things on your own.

CALANDRO: Oh, your plan is excellent. For her love I'd even carry very large chests.

FESSENIO: [*Aside*] Wow! This guy is really on fire. [*To* CALANDRO] All right, pick it up. [CALANDRO *struggles to lift the chest*] Get it up! Oh, hell. Steady, man. Hold on. Have you got it?

CALANDRO: [*Breathlessly*] No problem.

FESSENIO: All right. Go ahead, stop at the door, and I'll be right behind you. [CALANDRO *moves off as* FESSENIO *turns to the audience*] This ox certainly looks good under his load! Silly muttonhead! While I'm rounding up that old whore and getting her in through the back door, Lidio will have to let this guy give him

---

28. In Italian, death (*morte*) is feminine and thus easily personified as a woman.

a kiss. Well, it will be heavy going for him for a bit, but it'll make Fulvia's kisses seem all the sweeter. But here comes Samia. She hasn't seen Calandro. I'll speak to her for a moment. And the muttonhead will be all the more charged up for the wait!

❧ SCENE IV ☙

FESSENIO and SAMIA

FESSENIO: Where have you been?

SAMIA: To that necromancer she sent me to see, just down the street that way.

FESSENIO: What did he say?

SAMIA: That he'll visit her shortly.

FESSENIO: [*Laughing*] Who knows what pretty lies he'll bring? I'll go find Lidio and do what Fulvia asked me to do earlier.

SAMIA: Is he at home?

FESSENIO: Yes.

SAMIA: What do you think he'll do?

FESSENIO: To tell you the truth, I'm not all that hopeful. But I don't really know.

SAMIA: Enough said. Things don't look good for us.

FESSENIO: Goodbye.

❧ SCENE V ☙

SAMIA and FULVIA

SAMIA: [*Alone*] I can hardly say that things are going well. The news isn't good from either Lidio or the spirit. Fulvia is going to be desperate when she hears. There she is at the door.

FULVIA: It's taken you long enough to get back!

SAMIA: I couldn't find Ruffo until just now.

FULVIA: What did he say?

SAMIA: Not much, I'm afraid.

FULVIA: What?

SAMIA: That the spirit told him—oh, how did he put it? I don't remember exactly.

FULVIA: Damn you, you birdbrain!

SAMIA: Ummm . . . oh! I remember. He said that the spirit answered ambushiously.

FULVIA: You mean ambiguously?

SAMIA: Yeah, something like that.

FULVIA: He didn't say anything else?

SAMIA: That he would ask the spirit again.

FULVIA: Anything else?

SAMIA: That if he decides to help you, he'll come by right away.

FULVIA: Alas! It looks like this isn't going to work. What about Lidio?

SAMIA: He seems about as interested in you as in an old shoe.

FULVIA: Did you find him?

SAMIA: And I spoke with him.

FULVIA: Tell me, tell me, what did he say?

SAMIA: You aren't going to be happy.

FULVIA: Oh, for heaven's sake! What happened? Spit it out.

SAMIA: To make a long story short, it seemed that he had never heard of you.

FULVIA: What are you saying?

SAMIA: Just that.

FULVIA: How did you get that idea?

SAMIA: He answered me so strangely that I was afraid.

FULVIA: Maybe he was playing a joke on you?

SAMIA: He wouldn't have insulted me like that.

FULVIA: Maybe you didn't know what to say?

SAMIA: You couldn't have prepared me better.

FULVIA: Maybe it was because there was someone with him?

SAMIA: I took him aside.

FULVIA: Maybe you were talking too loud?

SAMIA: I was practically whispering in his ear.

FULVIA: Well, then, what did he say?

SAMIA: He told me to get lost.

FULVIA: So he doesn't love me anymore?

SAMIA: He doesn't love you, and he doesn't respect you.

FULVIA: Do you really think so?

SAMIA: I'm sure of it.

FULVIA: Alas! What am I hearing?

SAMIA: You heard what I said.

FULVIA: And he didn't even ask about me?

SAMIA: Worse—he claimed not to even know who you are.

FULVIA: So he's forgotten me!

SAMIA: You're lucky if he doesn't hate you as well.

FULVIA: O cruel heavens! Now I see clearly just how cruel he is and how miserable I am. Oh, how unhappy is the fate of women! And how badly we are repaid for the love we give our lovers! How wretched I am for having loved too much! Alas, I've given so much of myself to another that I'm no longer my own. O cruel heavens, why won't you make Lidio love me as I love him? Or make me shun him as he has shunned me? So cruel!

But what am I asking for? To stop loving and reject my Lidio? Ah, surely I could neither do this nor desire it. Instead, I need to speak with him myself. And why wouldn't it be all right for me to dress myself as a man to go to him, just as he has so often dressed himself as a woman to come to me? It makes sense. And he's so good that he warrants this. Why, I'd take on even greater risks for him.

Why shouldn't I do it? Why don't I go? Why should I waste my youth? There's no greater sadness than when a woman has wasted her youth without enjoying it. Those who think they'll make up for their lost youth when they're old are sadly mistaken. When will I find another lover so fine? And when will there be a better time to go find him than right now, considering that he's at home and my husband is away? Who's going to stop me, hold me back?

Yes, I'll do it, since it's clear that Ruffo isn't really ready to commit his spirit to my cause. Go-betweens never do things as well as the person who's directly concerned; they don't pick the right time; they can't really show a lover's love. If I go to him, he'll see my tears, he'll hear my lamentations, my prayers. I'll either throw myself at his feet, or pretend to die, or embrace him. And how could he ever be so cruel as not to pity me? Loving words whispered in an ear and heard by the heart have almost infinite power, and for lovers they make almost everything possible. That's what I hope. That's what I'll do. Now I'll go get dressed as a man. You, Samia, stay by the door and make sure no one stops here so that when I leave I won't be recognized. I'm going to do it all right now.

ꙮ SCENE VI ꙮ

SAMIA and FULVIA

SAMIA: [*To the women in the audience*] O poor, unhappy women! How many trials we must suffer when we put ourselves in the hands of Love. Look at Fulvia, who was once so prudent; now she's so inflamed by this man that she doesn't know what she's doing. Not able to have her Lidio, she's going to look for him dressed as a man, without a thought to the trouble it could cause if it ever became known. Hasn't she been treated unfairly? She has given this man her possessions, her honor, and her flesh, and as far as he's concerned she's no better than mud. Well, we women, we're all victims of fortune. Here she comes already, dressed as a man. She certainly is quick, isn't she?

FULVIA: You understand, I'm off to find Lidio. Stay here and keep the door locked until I come back.

SAMIA: All right. [FULVIA *leaves;* SAMIA *watching her with admiration says to the audience*] Look at that!

ᘒ SCENE VII ᘓ

FULVIA, alone

FULVIA: Love can make one do the most unlikely things. There was a time when I was hardly willing to leave my room without a chaperon. Now, moved by Love and dressed as a man, I'm outside my house alone. Still, if that was a form of timid slavery, this is a bold freedom.[29] I'm going straight to his house, even though it's quite a way off from here, for I know exactly where it is. And I'll make him hear me out, which I know I can do because there won't be anyone else there besides his old servant woman and perhaps Fessenio, who knows everything anyway. No one will recognize me, so no one will ever know. And if it should come out, all I can say is that it's better to have tried and be sorry than to be sorry for not having tried.

ᘒ SCENE VIII ᘓ

SAMIA, alone

SAMIA: She's off to seek her pleasure. And where once I would have condemned her, now I excuse and commend her, because the person who hasn't tasted love doesn't understand how sweet the world can be and is a sorry creature. I, for one, know that I'm never happier than when I'm with my lover Lusco, our butler. Now we're alone in the house, and he's just over there in the

---

29. During the Renaissance upper-class women did not go out into the streets alone, a restriction that plays a significant role in many comedies. Dressing as a man was a ploy frequently used in comedies to overcome such restrictions, although it was a dangerous ruse that would have put a woman's honor at risk.

courtyard. Better still, we can lock the door and enjoy ourselves a bit. My mistress has taught me that even I should go after my good times. One would be mad not to seize these pleasures when one has the chance, for there's plenty of trouble and aggravation just waiting for us behind the door. [*She goes in, locking the door*] Oh, Luuusco!

⁀ SCENE IX ⁀

FESSENIO, alone

FESSENIO: [*Coming down the street as* SAMIA *shuts the door*] Wait, don't close the door. Hey there! Don't you hear me? Well, it'll be opened for me in a bit. [*He stops to address the audience*] And now that Calandro is with the beautiful old bag that I brought to him through the back door, I want to tell Fulvia the whole story. I know she'll die laughing! Really, the whole thing is enough to make the dead laugh. What strange holy mysteries those two must be enjoying! But now let's see if I can get in to see Fulvia. [*He walks up to the door*]

⁀ SCENE X ⁀

FESSENIO and SAMIA

FESSENIO: [*Knocking*] Are you deaf in there? Hey! Hey! [*Knocking again*] Open up. Hey! Hey! [*Knocking harder*] Don't you hear me?
SAMIA: [*After a moment*] Who's knocking?
FESSENIO: Your Fessenio. Open up, Samia.
SAMIA: Right away.
FESSENIO: Why don't you open up?
SAMIA: I'm getting up to put the key in the lock.[30]
FESSENIO: Hurry up, please.
SAMIA: The key can't seem to find the hole.
FESSENIO: Come, now, come on.
SAMIA: Oh! Ohhh! Mmmm. I can't yet.
FESSENIO: Why not?
SAMIA: The hole's all plugged up.
FESSENIO: Blow on the keyhole.

---

30. The sexual overtones of keys and locks are in play throughout the scene.

SAMIA: Ohhhh! I can do better than that.

FESSENIO: What?

SAMIA: I'm going as fast as I can.

FESSENIO: What's gotten into you?

SAMIA: Oh! Ohhh! Ohhhhhh! Blessed be the shovel handle! Fessenio, I've taken care of the problem, and I've lubricated the key so well that it should open the door just fine now.

FESSENIO: So open it.

SAMIA: There, it's done. Don't you hear me pulling back the bolt? [*Peeking breathlessly from behind the door*] You can come in, if you want.

FESSENIO: What's up with all these locks and keys?

SAMIA: Today Fulvia wanted me to be sure to put the key in the lock.

FESSENIO: Why?

SAMIA: I can tell you everything. She went out dressed as a man to find Lidio

FESSENIO: Oh my! Samia, what are you saying?

SAMIA: You heard me. I was supposed to stay here with the door locked and open it only when she returned. Now, goodbye. [*She closes the door*]

❧ SCENE XI ☙

FESSENIO, alone

FESSENIO: Now I see that it's really true that those who are madly in love are willing to try anything, no matter how dangerous or unlikely—just like Fulvia, who's gone to Lidio's house not realizing that she'll find her husband there. And he, even as stupid as he is, isn't going to be able to avoid being suspicious, seeing her dressed up like a man, alone in that place. He might get so worked up that he would tell her relatives.[31] I'd better hurry there to see if there's anything I can do to undo the damage. But oh, oh, oh, what's this? Ohhhh! Why, Fulvia! Oh, she's dragging Calandro along like a prisoner. What the hell is this? Let me hide over here a minute to see what's going on.

---

31. Another reference to the Renaissance sense of honor and of male responsibility for female behavior. When a wife seriously misbehaved, her relatives from her natal family, especially her father and brothers, were often called upon to confer on punishment, as if their honor was still compromised by her behavior.

❧ SCENE XII ❧

FULVIA and CALANDRO

FULVIA: Oh, what a fine husband! So that's the "country house" you said you were going to! So that's what you were up to, eh? So there's not enough for you at home? You have to go searching for it elsewhere? Oh! Is this the man to whom I've given so much love? Whom I've served so faithfully? Now I understand why you haven't tried anything for the last several nights: you've been planning to discharge your load somewhere else and want to come to the battle like a fresh knight. I swear I don't know how to keep myself from gouging your eyes out! Did you really think you could pull the wool over my eyes and get away with it? My word, you're no cleverer than anyone else. So at this hour, and dressed like this, because I couldn't trust anyone else to do it, I had to come get you. And now I'm dragging you along, you dirty dog, just like you deserve, so that you will be shamed and everyone will pity me for all the awful treatment I've had to suffer from you, you ingrate! Think for a second, you louse, if I were as foul a woman as you are a foul man, how easy it would have been for me to find satisfaction with others as you have done. Right? Why, I'm not so old or ugly that I would have been refused, if I hadn't had more respect for myself than for your stupidity. You can be sure that I'll have my revenge on that woman I found you with. But that's hardly enough: I'll not rest until I pay you back for this and have my revenge on her as well.

CALANDRO: Are you finished?

FULVIA: Yes.

CALANDRO: Damn it, you disrespectful woman, let me drag myself along by myself! You've hauled me out of the earthly paradise and ruined all my pleasure. What a nuisance you are! You're not even worth a pair of her old shoes. She gave me more and better caresses than you ever did. Why, I like her better than honeyed wine. She shines more brightly than the star of Venus. She's more magnificent than the full moon and wiser than the fairy Morgana.[32] Of course you couldn't let me get away with it—no way, you being the pain in the ass that you are! And if you ever do her any harm, you'll regret it!

FULVIA: Get going! That's enough! Get in the house. In the house! Open up! Hey there, open up! [*The door opens, and she pushes him in, then stops a moment in the doorway*]

32. The fairy of the Arthurian cycle of tales popular in Europe during the Renaissance.

〘 SCENE XIII 〙

FESSENIO, alone

FESSENIO: O Fessenio, what have you just seen? O Love, how great is your power! What poet, what doctor, what philosopher could ever be so clever, so wise as one of your followers? All learning, all theory from anyone else falls far short of yours. What other woman, without the help of Love, would have been able to escape so cleverly from such great danger? I've never seen such clever wickedness. She has stopped there in the doorway. I'll go over and give her some hope as far as Lidio is concerned, for the poor woman deserves some compassion.

〘 SCENE XIV 〙

FULVIA, FESSENIO, and SAMIA

FULVIA: Look, my dear Fessenio, how unfortunate I am! Instead of finding Lidio, I found that muttonhead, my husband. Still, I managed to avoid getting into trouble.

FESSENIO: I saw everything. Move inside a bit so that no one else sees you dressed like that.

FULVIA: Good thinking. [*She moves inside the doorway a bit*] My great desire to be with Lidio has so blinded me that I've forgotten the need to be careful. But tell me, dear Fessenio, have you talked with my Lidio?

FESSENIO: [*Aside*] As they say, "The blood always flows to the point where one is wounded." [*To* FULVIA] Yes, I spoke with him.

FULVIA: Yes?

FESSENIO: Yes.

FULVIA: Well, my dear Fessenio, tell me what he said.

FESSENIO: He's not going to leave so soon.

FULVIA: Oh, God! When can I talk with him?

FESSENIO: Maybe even today. When I saw you with Calandro I was on my way to persuade him to visit you.

FULVIA: Arrange it, my dear Fessenio; it'll be worth your while! My life is in your hands.

FESSENIO: I'll do all I can. But now I'd better go find him. Stay calm.

FULVIA: Calm? I'm afraid I'm stuck with strife and complaints. You're going to what will bring me calm: you're going to Lidio.

FESSENIO: Goodbye.

FULVIA: My dear Fessenio, come back soon.

FESSENIO: I will. [*He leaves as* SAMIA *comes to the door to join her mistress*]

FULVIA: Oh, poor Fulvia! If I have to go on like this for very long, I'm sure I'll die. Woe is me, what am I to do?

SAMIA: Maybe Ruffo's spirit will do the trick.

FULVIA: Well, maybe. But Samia, since that necromancer doesn't seem to be beating a path to our door, why don't you go speak to him again?

SAMIA: That's a good idea. I'll get right on it.

FULVIA: Encourage him to help. And come back quickly!

SAMIA: As soon as I've spoken with him. [*She leaves*]

❧ SCENE XV ☙

SAMIA and RUFFO

SAMIA: Oh, oh, oh! What good luck! Here's Ruffo. May the heavens reward you, sir.

RUFFO: What are you looking for, Samia?

SAMIA: My mistress is eager to know what you've done for her.

RUFFO: I think everything is going to work out fine.

SAMIA: But when?

RUFFO: I'll come by to tell Fulvia everything.

SAMIA: Unfortunately, you're working very slowly.

RUFFO: Samia, these are operations that can't be done in the blink of an eye. One needs to bring together stars, words, liquids, herbs, stones, and so many strange things that it takes time.

SAMIA: Still, if you carry it off, rewards . . .

RUFFO: I certainly hope so. [SANTILLA *dressed as* LIDIO *and* FANNIO *enter*]

SAMIA: [*Seeing them*] Ohhh! Do you know the lover?

RUFFO: I'm sure I don't.

SAMIA: That's him over there.

RUFFO: Do you know him well?

SAMIA: Why, I talked to him not more than a couple of hours ago.

RUFFO: What did he say to you?

SAMIA: He seemed pricklier than a briar patch.

RUFFO: Go talk with him now to see if the spirit has made him sweeter.

SAMIA: Do you think I should?

RUFFO: Please, go ahead.

SAMIA: I'll go.

RUFFO: Wait a second! Afterwards, go back to Fulvia's house by the back way. I'll go there right now.

SAMIA: It's as good as done. [*She walks over to the* FEMALE LIDIO]

RUFFO: [*Aside*] While she's talking with Lidio, I'll stay here out of sight and listen.

﹖ SCENE XVI ﹗

FANNIO, the FEMALE LIDIO, and SAMIA

FANNIO: Oh, Lidio, here comes Fulvia's servant. Remember, she's called Samia. Treat her nicely.

FEMALE LIDIO: That's what I was planning to do.

SAMIA: Are you still upset?

FEMALE LIDIO: No, God no. My dear Samia, forgive me, but earlier I was worried about another matter and wasn't myself—so much so that I don't even know what I said to you. But tell me, how's my dear Fulvia?

SAMIA: Do you want to know?

FEMALE LIDIO: That's exactly why I'm asking you.

SAMIA: Ask your own heart.

FEMALE LIDIO: I can't.

SAMIA: Why not?

FEMALE LIDIO: Oh, don't you know that my whole heart is with her?

SAMIA: God makes you lovers as honest as He makes things easy for you. [*Aside*] Just a little while ago this fellow couldn't even remember her, and now he wants me to believe that he has no other desire. [*To* FEMALE LIDIO] As if I didn't know that you hate her and don't want to be near her!

FEMALE LIDIO: Really, I can't endure another minute without her.

SAMIA: [*Aside*] By the holy cross, that spirit has really done the trick. [*To* FEMALE LIDIO] You'll come, then, just like you used to?

FEMALE LIDIO: What do you mean, just like I used to?

SAMIA: Why, dressed as a woman.

FEMALE LIDIO: Well, sure . . . just like the other times.

SAMIA: Oh, what great news I have for Fulvia! I mustn't stay here any longer. I'll go home the back way so that no one will see me coming from you. Goodbye.

FEMALE LIDIO: Goodbye. [SAMIA *rushes off*]

⁓ SCENE XVII ⁓

The FEMALE LIDIO, FANNIO, and RUFFO

FEMALE LIDIO: Did you hear that, Fannio?

FANNIO: Yes, and I picked up on that "just like you used to," also. Clearly she has mistaken you for someone else.

FEMALE LIDIO: Clearly.

FANNIO: We should tell Ruffo, whom in fact I see coming along now.

RUFFO: [*Coming up to them*] Well, have you decided what you want to do?

FEMALE LIDIO: How could we possibly pass this one up?

RUFFO: [*Laughing*] Now that's the friend I remember! And you're absolutely right, Lidio, she's as pretty as a picture.

FEMALE LIDIO: I know her and where she lives.

FANNIO: It'll be fun.

RUFFO: And profitable!

FANNIO: Ruffo, if I understood what you said earlier, this woman came to you because all other means had failed her, which I take it means that she has tried this before. But obviously no one has ever spoken to us about any of this. So it seems likely that Lidio here has been mistaken for someone else, the way he was by her servant today. So it seems that, just to be sure, you should tell Fulvia that your spirit says she shouldn't speak of the past with Lidio anymore. That way our trick won't be discovered, and we'll avoid the great scandal that would follow.

RUFFO: Yes, a wise idea. I'll take care of it. Come on, then, there's nothing more to discuss here! Let's get to it. I'll go to her. You two get ready.

FEMALE LIDIO: Go, and then come back here and we'll be ready and waiting.

FANNIO: Lidio, go on and get ready. I'll be along shortly. I just want to speak for a moment with Ruffo. [*The* FEMALE LIDIO *leaves*]

RUFFO: What's up?

FANNIO: I want to tell you a secret about this affair that you couldn't possibly guess. But you must be sure not to tell anyone.

RUFFO: May God deny me every pleasure if I ever tell anyone.

FANNIO: Look, Ruffo you'll ruin me and lose your own profits from this affair if you talk.

RUFFO: Don't worry. Tell me.

FANNIO: Have you realized that my master, Lidio, is a hermaphrodite?

RUFFO: What does worms-at-night mean, anyway?

FANNIO: I said hermaphrodite, not worms-at-night. Hell, you're thickheaded!

RUFFO: Well, what does it mean?

FANNIO: You don't know?

RUFFO: That's why I'm asking you.

FANNIO: Hermaphrodites are people who are both sexes at once.

RUFFO: And Lidio is one of those?

FANNIO: Yes, that's what I'm telling you.

RUFFO: In other words, he has the sex of a woman and the root of a man?

FANNIO: Yes sirree!

RUFFO: I swear on the Holy Bible that your Lidio always seemed to me to have something a bit feminine about his voice and manner.

FANNIO: So you should know that this time, because Fulvia asked her to come as a woman, she'll find her to be a woman and have relations with her as a woman, and she'll believe in your spirit even more and adore you as well.

RUFFO: This is one of the best plots I've ever heard of! And I can tell you, we're going to make bushels of money.

FANNIO: You're right. Do you think Fulvia will be openhanded?

RUFFO: Openhanded? Why, lovers can't keep their purses closed anyway, and for this kind of love they will give ducats, cloth, animals, offices, their possessions, and their lives.

FANNIO: All this makes me feel better.

RUFFO: You've made me feel much better with this herms-after-night business.

FANNIO: I'm glad you can't say it, because you wouldn't be able to tell anyone even if you wanted to.

RUFFO: Catch up with Lidio and get changed. I'll go tell Fulvia that she's going to get what she wants.

FANNIO: All right, I'll be her woman servant.

RUFFO: That's fine. Be ready when I get back.

FANNIO: It'll just take a second. [*Aside*] I did well to find those clothes for me as well.

❧ SCENE XVIII ❧

RUFFO and SAMIA

RUFFO: So far everything is going better than if the heavens themselves had arranged it. If Samia has already gotten home by the back way, Fulvia will be expecting me. I'll explain to her that the spirit has done everything she wanted and that she must say some words and do some things with this image so that she thinks she's working a spell. And I'll remind her that she's not to tell anyone besides her servant about what happened or happens in this affair of hers or my role in it. I'll do this quickly and then return to the others. I see Samia there in the doorway.

SAMIA: Come in, Ruffo, and hurry to Fulvia, who's waiting in that downstairs room, because Calandro, that muttonhead, is upstairs.

ᴖ SCENE XIX ᴖ

SAMIA and FESSENIO

SAMIA: [*Still standing in the doorway as* FESSENIO *comes up*] Where are you headed, Fessenio?

FESSENIO: I've come to see your mistress.

SAMIA: You can't talk with her now.

FESSENIO: Why not?

SAMIA: She's with the necromancer.

FESSENIO: Oh. Well, let me in, anyway.

SAMIA: Really, I can't.

FESSENIO: What foolishness!

SAMIA: You're the fool.

FESSENIO: I am—well, better that we leave that alone. All right, I'll take a little walk and come back to see Fulvia later.

SAMIA: That's a good idea.

FESSENIO: [*Aside, leaving*] If Fulvia knew what I know, she wouldn't be bothering with spirits, because Lidio wants to be with her even more than she wants to be with him. And he wants to visit her today. But I want to tell her myself, because I know she'll give me some reward. So I didn't tell Samia. But I'd better get out of here, because if Fulvia sees me she'll think I've come to see her necromancer. That must be him coming out of the house.

ᴖ SCENE XX ᴖ

RUFFO, alone

RUFFO: Everything's going well. I hope to overcome my poverty and get rid of these rags, because she has already paid me well. I couldn't have a better game to play. This woman is rich and, from what I can tell, more in love than wise. If I'm not mistaken, I think she'll pay even more, a lot more, and I really need some big-time good luck like this. My, my, it does seem like every now and then dreams actually come true. This is the bird for plucking that last night I dreamed I'd find. I dreamed that I pulled a bunch of feathers from its tail and stuck them in my hat. If she lets me get my hands on her, as it looks like she already has, I'll pluck her so clean that I'll be well off for a while. By God, even I will be able to have some fun and enjoy the good life. Oh, what luck! [FANNIO *dressed as a woman signals to him*] But who is that woman calling me? I don't know her. I'll just go over and see what she wants.

ᔓ SCENE XXI ᔒ

RUFFO and FANNIO (dressed as a woman)

RUFFO: Ohhh! Fannio, you look so different in that getup that I didn't recognize you!

FANNIO: Aren't I a doll?

RUFFO: You sure are! Go make that poor woman happy.

FANNIO: I'm afraid she may not be all that happy this time.

RUFFO: Yes, yes, you're right, because Lidio can only make love to her as a woman!

FANNIO: That's it. Oh well, what do you say, shall we go?

RUFFO: Sure. Is Lidio all dressed?

FANNIO: He's waiting for me nearby. And he looks so good, there isn't anyone who wouldn't believe him a woman.

RUFFO: Oh, this really is rich! But Fulvia's waiting for you. Go get Lidio and go to her. I'll hang around to see how things work out. Oh, oh, oh! There's Fulvia already at the door. She was quick about doing what I told her.

ᔓ SCENE XXII ᔒ

FESSENIO and FULVIA

FESSENIO: You can stop suffering now, my lady.

FULVIA: Why?

FESSENIO: Lidio is more inflamed by love for you than you are for him. As soon as I told him what you wanted, he got ready and he's coming.

FULVIA: My dear Fessenio, your news is worth more than a new pair of tights,[33] and you can be sure you will be rewarded. Listen, that's Calandro, upstairs calling for clothes to go out. Hide over there so that he doesn't see me with you. Oh, how perfect! Oh, how happy I am! Everything finally seems to be going right. I'll just go throw that meathead out so that I'll be free. [*Going into the house*]

FESSENIO: I'm sure these lovers are ready to make up for lost time. And if Lidio is wise he'll have her confirm her promises about his sister just in case she ever turns up. Calandro won't be at home, so they'll be free to enjoy themselves for a good long time. I can roam about on my own. But oh, oh, oh! There's Calandro coming out. I'd better get out of here, for if he sees me and stops to talk, he might see Lidio, who should be arriving any minute. [*He leaves*]

✺ SCENE XXIII ✺

CALANDRO, the MALE LIDIO (dressed as a woman), FESSENIO (dressed as a woman), the FEMALE LIDIO (dressed as a woman), and FANNIO (dressed as a woman)

CALANDRO: [*Having just come out the door and seeing the* MALE LIDIO *coming towards him*] Oh, this is my lucky day! Just out the door, and I see my sweet sun coming towards me. But heavens, how shall I greet her? Should I say, "Good morning"? But it's not morning. "Good afternoon"? It's not that late. "God be with you"? Sounds like a coachman. I'll say, "My pretty soul." No, that's not a greeting. "Heart of my body"? Surgeons say that. "Angel face"? Sounds too common. "Divine spirit"? Sounds like a drink. "Thief of my eyes"? Not a good choice of words. Oh my, she's already here. [*To the* MALE LIDIO] Soul . . . ah, heart . . . oh, er, face . . . um, eye . . . may you catch the pox! Oh, what a muttonhead I am! I've ruined everything! [*The* FEMALE LIDIO *enters well behind the* MALE LIDIO, *and neither sees the other*] Well, actually, I did well to swear at that woman because this one over here is my Santilla, not that one. [*He rushes up to the* FEMALE LIDIO] Good morning . . . uh, I mean good afternoon. Wait! By God, this isn't her. I was fooled. [*Turning back to the* MALE LIDIO, *who has walked along a bit with his back to them*] This one here is mine. But no. [*Beginning to turn around*] She's that one, I'll go over to her. But actually she's really this one. My word! Yes, this one is my life. No, actually that one is. I'll go over to her. [*The* FEMALE LIDIO *runs towards* FULVIA'*s house and hides*]

---

33. During the Renaissance, tights were a highly prized gift for servants; see n. 22 in *La veniexiana*.

MALE LIDIO: [*To* FESSENIO] Darn it, this madman thinks I'm a woman, and he's fallen in love with me. He'll follow me all the way to his house. Let's go home. I'll change and come back to Fulvia later. [*They leave*]

CALANDRO: Rats! That's not her. So it must be the one who went down that street. I'll try to find her. [*He runs off in the wrong direction*]

FEMALE LIDIO: [*Coming out of hiding and speaking to* FANNIO] Now that I've escaped that beast, let's get into the house quickly. There's Fulvia in the doorway signaling to us. Quick, let's go in.

Act IV

⟡ SCENE I ⟡

FULVIA and SAMIA

FULVIA: Samia! Oh, Samia!

SAMIA: My laaady?

FULVIA: Come down here immediately.

SAMIA: Coooming!

FULVIA: Hurry up, you little reprobate. Move it!

SAMIA: Here I am. What do you want?

FULVIA: Go find the spirit man, Ruffo, right away, and tell him to come here right now. Right now!

SAMIA: I'll go get my veil.

FULVIA: Your veil? You fool! Get going, now, fly!

SAMIA: [*Aside as she rushes off*] What the devil is she all worked up about? It's like she's got a demon in her. I would have thought Lidio would have worked that all out, and in, by now.

FULVIA: O deceitful spirits! O foolish human minds! O deceived and un-happy Fulvia, you've not only injured yourself, you've injured the person you love more than yourself! Alas, I've found what I was searching for, and I find that it's not what I wanted! If the spirit can't fix this, I'm prepared to kill myself, for a willing death would be less bitter than this life of suffering. But here's Ruffo. I'll know soon if I should have hopes or be in despair. There's no one around. It's best to talk out here because inside, the benches, the chairs, the chests, the windows all seem to have ears.

☙ SCENE II ❧

RUFFO and FULVIA

RUFFO: What's wrong, madam?

FULVIA: [*Sobbing*] My tears show better than any words what I'm feeling.

RUFFO: Tell me what the problem is. Fulvia, don't cry. What's wrong, my lady?

FULVIA: I don't know whether I'm forced to suffer because of my ignorance or your trickery, Ruffo.

RUFFO: Ah, madam! What are you saying?

FULVIA: It's either fate or my sins or the evilness of your spirit, I don't know which, but you've suddenly changed my Lidio from a man into a woman. I felt him all over and touched him, and I didn't find any of his normal things, except for the fact that he looks the same. And it's not so much the loss of my pleasure that I'm crying for as the damage to him. For it seems to me he no longer has what made him most desirable. Now you understand my tears, and you'll understand why I've called you.

RUFFO: If it weren't for your tears, Fulvia, which would be hard to fake, I would have great trouble believing what you're saying. But because I believe you're telling the truth, I think you'd better blame yourself, because I remember you asked for Lidio in the form of a woman. So I imagine that the spirit, in order to serve you exactly as you wished, sent your lover to you both dressed as a woman and *as* a woman. But don't worry: the spirit who turned him into a woman can turn him back into a man.

FULVIA: Now that I see how this happened, I feel better. But if you give me back my Lidio complete, I'll give you all the money and property I have.

RUFFO: Well, since I know the spirit likes you, I can promise you that your lover will return to you as a man immediately. But in order to avoid misunderstandings, tell me exactly what you want.

FULVIA: The first thing is that you must give him back his sword to put in my scabbard. Do you understand?

RUFFO: Perfectly.

FULVIA: And then he should return to me dressed as a woman, but not sexually a woman.

RUFFO: If you had told me this this morning, we could have avoided this mistake. But it's not all bad, because this way I can show you the power of my spirit.

FULVIA: Free me quickly of this anguish, for until I see him I can't be happy.

RUFFO: You will not only see him, you will be able to touch him with your hands.

FULVIA: Will he return to me today?

RUFFO: It's already two in the afternoon, and he'll be able to stay with you for only a little while.

FULVIA: I don't care how long he stays, as long as I can see that he is a man again.

RUFFO: But how will you be able to avoid drinking the glass down, if you have it in front of you?

FULVIA: Will he come today?

RUFFO: The spirit will make him come immediately, if you wish. Be ready for him here in the doorway.

FULVIA: That's not really necessary, because coming as a woman, he can be seen by everyone, and he won't be recognized as a man.

RUFFO: All right.

FULVIA: My dear Ruffo, be happy, because you'll never again be poor.

RUFFO: And you, never again unhappy.

FULVIA: How long must I wait?

RUFFO: As soon as I get home, it will be done.

FULVIA: I'll send Samia along so that you can let me know what the spirit tells you.

RUFFO: Do that. But remember, your lover should get presents as well.

FULVIA: Oh, don't worry, he'll be awash in money and jewels.

RUFFO: Be well. [FULVIA *goes in*] It is with good reason that Love is depicted as blind, because those who are in love never see the truth. This woman is so blind that she believes that a spirit can change a man into a woman and back again, as if nothing more was required than to cut off the member of a man and make a hole there and then you have a woman. Or then sew up that lower mouth and stick on an instrument and you've made a man. Ohhh, the foolishness of lovers! Oh, oh! Here come Lidio and Fannio already changed back and dressed as men.

ᵀᶟ SCENE III ᵍᵀ

RUFFO, the FEMALE LIDIO, and FANNIO

RUFFO: I would like you to be still dressed as women.

FEMALE LIDIO: Why?

RUFFO: [*Laughing*] To return to her.

FANNIO: Why are you laughing so hard?

RUFFO: Ha, ha, ha, ha!

FEMALE LIDIO: Speak up. What's so funny?

RUFFO: [*Still laughing*] Fulvia believes that the spirit has changed Lidio into a woman, and she's begging me to turn you back into a man and return you to her.

FEMALE LIDIO: Well, what did you say?

RUFFO: That I would do it at once.

FANNIO: Good.

RUFFO: When will you go back to her?

FEMALE LIDIO: I don't know.

RUFFO: You don't seem very enthusiastic. Don't you want to go back?

FANNIO: It'll happen.

RUFFO: It better, because I told her the spirit said that she should give out a lot of presents for this, and she's promised to do so.

FANNIO: We'll do it, don't worry.

RUFFO: But when?

FANNIO: Once we've taken care of a little matter, we'll get dressed up again and return to her immediately.

RUFFO: Don't let me down, Lidio. From here I seem to see her servant in the doorway. I don't want her to see me with you. Goodbye. But listen, Fannio, I want to tell you something privately. [*To* FANNIO] See to it that the worms-in-the-night here uses the pestle with Fulvia and not the mortar this time. Got it?

FANNIO: Right. Goodbye. [RUFFO *leaves*]

❧ SCENE IV ❧

FANNIO, the FEMALE LIDIO, and SAMIA

FANNIO: Samia's coming out of her house. Hide over here until she passes us.

FEMALE LIDIO: What is she saying to herself?

FANNIO: Be quiet and listen.

SAMIA: [*To herself*] This is what you get for getting involved with spirits, silly! Look at the mess they've made of your Lidio.

FANNIO: [*To* FEMALE LIDIO] She's talking about you.

SAMIA: They turned him into a woman, and now they need to turn him back into a man. Today has been hard on him, and it meant hard work for me. But if it all works out, everything will be fine. And I'll know soon, because she has sent me to find out from the necromancer. She's ready to give to her lover plenty of cash, as soon as she learns that he's got the right stuff back.

FANNIO: Did you hear that about cash?

FEMALE LIDIO: Yes.

FANNIO: All right, let's get dressed up to return to her.

FEMALE LIDIO: You're clearly out of your mind, Fannio. You've promised Ruffo that we'd return, but I don't know how you think we're going to carry this off.

FANNIO: What do you mean?

FEMALE LIDIO: You're asking me? Simpleton! As if you didn't know that I am a woman!

FANNIO: So what?

FEMALE LIDIO: So what, he says! Don't you realize, you fool, that if I try to satisfy her, I won't have the right stuff, and I'll be dishonored, Ruffo will lose his credibility, and she'll remain without a lover? How do you plan for me to carry this one off?

FANNIO: How, eh?

FEMALE LIDIO: Right, how?

FANNIO: Where there are men, there are ways.

FEMALE LIDIO: But where there are only women, and it will only be her and me, there simply is no way.

FANNIO: You're joking, aren't you?

FEMALE LIDIO: You're the joker. I'm all too serious, unfortunately.

FANNIO: When I promised that you'd return, I'd already thought of everything.

FEMALE LIDIO: Well, tell me. What?

FANNIO: Didn't you tell me that you were in a dark room with her?

FEMALE LIDIO: Yes.

FANNIO: And that she spoke with you only with her hands?

FEMALE LIDIO: That's right.

FANNIO: Well, I'll be with you like I was earlier.

FEMALE LIDIO: Oh my! What are you planning to do?

FANNIO: Listen. As your servant . . .

FEMALE LIDIO: I know.

FANNIO: Dressed like you . . .

FEMALE LIDIO: And?

FANNIO: When you're alone with her in the room, pretend that you need to tell me something and leave. Then you stay outside as me, and I'll go back into the room in your place. Since I don't have a beard, in the dark she won't be able to tell me from you. And so she'll believe that you've returned to being a man, and she'll credit the spirit! Then there will be plenty of money for us all, and I'll enjoy her as well.

FEMALE LIDIO: My word, Fannio, I've never heard a more clever plan.

FANNIO: So I wasn't wrong when I told Ruffo that we'd return.

FEMALE LIDIO: Certainly not. But in the meantime it would be a good idea to find out what's going on at my house with my impending marriage.

FANNIO: That's a future problem, and our plan was to try to avoid the last act.

FEMALE LIDIO: Unfortunately, postponing things doesn't make them disappear. Tomorrow we'll be right back in the mess we're in today.

RUFFO: Who knows? And as they say, "The person who escapes from one bind slides by a thousand more." Our plan to return to Fulvia can work, and it certainly can't hurt.

FEMALE LIDIO: All right. But first, out of love for me, go home and find out from Tiresia what's happening. Then hurry back and we'll go right on to Fulvia's.

RUFFO: Well said. I'll do it.

❧ SCENE V ☙

The FEMALE LIDIO, alone

FEMALE LIDIO: Oh, we poor women, we're oppressed not only in deeds but even in thought! It's not just that there are so many things I can't do as a woman; I can't even imagine how I might do them as a woman. Oh, poor me! What should I do? Wherever I turn, I'm so surrounded by tribulations that I don't know where to look for a way out. But here comes Fulvia's servant, and she's speaking with someone. I'll hide until they've passed.

❧ SCENE VI ☙

FESSENIO and SAMIA

FESSENIO: What are all these problems? Tell me.

SAMIA: My God! The devil's right in the middle of everything.

FESSENIO: What?

SAMIA: The necromancer has converted Lidio into a woman.

FESSENIO: Ha, ha, ha, ha!

SAMIA: You're laughing?

FESSENIO: Right, I am.

SAMIA: It's true. I swear on the Gospels.

FESSENIO: [*Laughing*] Have you lost your mind?

SAMIA: You oaf! It's true whether you like it or not. Fulvia touched him all over, and he was a she and there was nothing left of his normal self except the look.

FESSENIO: [*Still laughing*] So what's she going to do, then?

SAMIA: You don't believe me, so I'm not going to tell you.

FESSENIO: No, tell me, in the name of the cross. [*He crosses himself*] Go on, what are you going to do now?

SAMIA: The spirit is going to turn him back into a man. I'm coming from the necromancer, who has given me this special letter for Fulvia.

FESSENIO: Let me see it.

SAMIA: Oh no! Don't touch it. It might harm you.

FESSENIO: Even if it makes me fall down dead, I want to see it.

SAMIA: Be careful what you do with it, Fessenio. These are demonic things.

FESSENIO: Don't give me a hard time. Show it to me.

SAMIA: Leave it alone. At least make the sign of the cross before you touch it, Fessenio.

FESSENIO: Bah, give it here.

SAMIA: All right, but look, you have to be quieter than a fish about this, because if it ever gets out, we're all in deep trouble.

FESSENIO: Don't worry. Give it to me. [*He takes it*]

SAMIA: Read it out loud so that I can hear it, too.

FESSENIO: [*Reading*] "Ruffo sends his greetings to Fulvia. The spirit knew that your Lidio was changed from a man to a woman. He had a good laugh with me about it. You yourself were the cause of his loss and your unhappiness. But rest assured that he will reattach to your lover his branch—"

SAMIA: [*Interrupting*] What does he mean, his branch?

FESSENIO: He'll have his third leg back, do you understand? [*Again reading*] "—and he'll come to you immediately. The spirit says also that he'll desire you more than ever, that he'll never love another, or desire another, or have sex with another, or think of another. You must not speak of this to anyone, because if you do there will be great scandal. Send your lover money often, and send it to the spirit as well to make him grateful to you and to make me happy. Be happy and remember me, your faithful servant."

SAMIA: Now do you believe that spirits are all-powerful and all-knowing?

FESSENIO: There's not a man in the whole world who's more amazed than I.

SAMIA: I must take this good news to Fulvia at once.

FESSENIO: Go with God's grace. [SAMIA *leaves*] Oh, the power of heaven! Must I believe, then, that Lidio was changed from a man into a woman by means of spells and that now he can't love or have sex with anyone except Fulvia? Only the power of heaven could do such a thing. Yet Samia says that Fulvia touched him with her hands. I want to see this miracle before he returns to being a man, and then I'll worship this necromancer, if I find it's true. I'll go this way to find Lidio. Maybe he's at home. [*He leaves*]

Act V

ꙮ SCENE I ꙮ

SAMIA, the FEMALE LIDIO (dressed as a man), and
the MALE LIDIO (dressed as a man)

SAMIA: [*Alone*] Indeed, women shine on money like the sun shines on ice: both seem to continually make it melt away. The moment she read that letter from the necromancer, she gave me this bag of ducats to take to Lidio. [*The two* LIDIOs *enter from opposite directions, at first not seeing one another*] And there he is now. [*To* FEMALE LIDIO, *holding out the bag to her*] Oh, Lidio, look how your lover does her duty! Don't you hear me, Lidio? What are you waiting for? Go ahead, take it.

FEMALE LIDIO: I'm ready.

MALE LIDIO: Give it to me.

SAMIA: [*To* FEMALE LIDIO] Uh-oh! Poor me, I've fouled up. Excuse me, sir. I wanted this one here, not you. Goodbye. [*To* MALE LIDIO] You, listen.

FEMALE LIDIO: Now you're making the mistake. Speak with me; send him away.

SAMIA: [*To* FEMALE LIDIO] You're right. I'm so silly, I was making a mistake. [*To* MALE LIDIO] Goodbye. [*To* FEMALE LIDIO] You, come over here.

MALE LIDIO: What's this "goodbye"? Come back to me.

SAMIA: [*To* MALE LIDIO] Oh, oh, oh! To you, yes. [*To* FEMALE LIDIO] I want this one, not you. [*To* MALE LIDIO] You, listen. [*To* FEMALE LIDIO] You, goodbye.

FEMALE LIDIO: "Goodbye"? Aren't you talking to me? Aren't I Lidio?

SAMIA: [*To* FEMALE LIDIO] Of course! Now you're you. [*To* MALE LIDIO] You, no. [*To* FEMALE LIDIO] I've been looking for you. [*To* MALE LIDIO] You can go on about your business.

MALE LIDIO: You're out of your mind. Take a good look at me. Aren't I Lidio?

SAMIA: [*To* MALE LIDIO] Oh, oh, oh! Now I know you. You are Lidio. I want you. [*To* FEMALE LIDIO] Not you. You get lost. [*To* MALE LIDIO, *offering him the bag of money*] You take this.

FEMALE LIDIO: What do you mean, "you take this"? You fool, I am me, not him.

SAMIA: [*To* FEMALE LIDIO] Right. I was making a mistake. You're right. [*To* MALE LIDIO] You're wrong. You run along. [*Offering the money to* FEMALE LIDIO] Take it.

MALE LIDIO: What are you doing, you imbecile? You seem to be giving the money to him, but you know it's ours.

FEMALE LIDIO: What do you mean, "ours"? Give it to me.

MALE LIDIO: No, to me!

FEMALE LIDIO: What do you mean, to you? I'm Lidio, not you!

MALE LIDIO: Give it here.

FEMALE LIDIO: Not *that* "here." Give it here to me.

SAMIA: Oh, oh! I don't want either of you to take it from me by force, so I'm just going to start screaming. But hold on a second. Let me take a good look at you and figure out which one is really Lidio. Good God! Oh, what a miraculous miracle! They are as alike as two peas in a pod, as like as snow to snow, as one egg to another—in fact, I can't tell you apart because you seem to be Lidio, and you as well. You are Lidio, and you are too. But I have an idea. Tell me, is either of you in love?

MALE LIDIO: Yes.

FEMALE LIDIO: Yes.

SAMIA: Which one?

MALE LIDIO: Me.

FEMALE LIDIO: Me.

SAMIA: Where does this money come from?

MALE LIDIO: From her.

FEMALE LIDIO: From my love.

SAMIA: Great, what luck! It's still not clear. Tell me, who is this lover?

MALE LIDIO: Fulvia.

FEMALE LIDIO: Fulvia.

SAMIA: Who is her dear lover?

MALE LIDIO: Me.

FEMALE LIDIO: Me.

MALE LIDIO: [*To* FEMALE LIDIO] You?

FEMALE LIDIO: Yes, me.

MALE LIDIO: No, me.

SAMIA: Oh, oh, oh! Damn, what's going on here? Wait! Which Fulvia are you talking about?

MALE LIDIO: Calandro's wife.

FEMALE LIDIO: Your mistress.

SAMIA: They're one in the same. Clearly I've gone mad, or these two are possessed by demons. But wait a second, I have another idea. Tell me, how are you dressed when you go to visit her?

MALE LIDIO: As a woman.

FEMALE LIDIO: As a young woman.

SAMIA: Oh, this would be funny if it weren't so terrible! But oh, oh! This will tell. What time did she want her lover to visit?

MALE LIDIO: During the day.

FEMALE LIDIO: At midday.

SAMIA: Even the devil couldn't tell them apart. Clearly this is a fiendish plot devised by that damn spirit. It would be better to take the money back to Fulvia, and she can give it to whichever of the two she likes. You know how she is. I don't know which of you two to give it to. But Fulvia should be able to tell her real lover. So whichever of you two is him, go to her and you'll get the money from her. Goodbye.

MALE LIDIO: [*Aside*] I've never seen anyone who looks as much like me as he does, not even in the mirror. When I have time, I'll find out who he is. But since such opportunities don't come along every day and Fulvia might even have second thoughts, I think it would be best if I went to her right away dressed as usual, as a woman. That's a pile of money. That's exactly what I'm going to do, by God. [*He rushes off*]

FEMALE LIDIO: So that's the lover I've been mistaken for. What's taking Fannio so long? If he were here now as planned, we could return to Fulvia and maybe we could grab that money. Still, I need to give some thought to my own problems.

ꙮ SCENE II ꙮ

FESSENIO, the FEMALE LIDIO, and FANNIO

FESSENIO: [*Entering and not seeing the* FEMALE LIDIO] I haven't found Lidio at home or in the streets.

FEMALE LIDIO: [*To herself*] What should I do now?

FESSENIO: Until I find out if it's true that he has been turned into a woman, I can't relax. But oh, oh, oh! Is that him? No. Yes. No, it's not. But yes, it is. He seems deep in thought.

FEMALE LIDIO: Oh, what luck!

FESSENIO: He's talking to himself.

FEMALE LIDIO: I'm in a terrible bind!

FESSENIO: What can it be?

FEMALE LIDIO: Am I to be so quickly ruined?

FESSENIO: Oh my! What ruin?

FEMALE LIDIO: Just for being too much loved . . .

FESSENIO: What does he mean?

FEMALE LIDIO: . . . must I give up these clothes?

FESSENIO: Oh no! That's it. And his voice does seem to have become more feminine.

FEMALE LIDIO: And give up this freedom?

FESSENIO: Can this really be true?

FEMALE LIDIO: Am I now going to be known as a woman and no longer as a man?

FESSENIO: The cat's out of the bag, as they say.

FEMALE LIDIO: From now on I'll be correctly called Santilla and no longer Lidio.

FESSENIO: Dear me! It really is true.

FEMALE LIDIO: I wish I'd died the day that Modon was taken.

FESSENIO: O cruel heavens! How can this have happened? If I hadn't heard it with my own ears, I'd never have believed it. But I need to talk with him. Oh, Lidio!

FEMALE LIDIO: Who is this ass?

FESSENIO: [*Aside*] Could it be true that Lidio can't remember anyone except his Fulvia, as the spirit promised? [*To* FEMALE LIDIO] So you call me an ass, eh? As if you didn't know me!

FEMALE LIDIO: I've never known you, and I have no desire to do so.

FESSENIO: You don't know your own servant, then?

FEMALE LIDIO: You, my servant?

FESSENIO: If you don't want me anymore, I can find plenty of others.

FEMALE LIDIO: Goodbye, go on. I have no intention of speaking with drunks.

FESSENIO: You're not speaking with a drunk—rather, I'm speaking with someone who has become forgetful. Still, you can't hide from me. I know your problems as well as you.

FEMALE LIDIO: What problems do I have?

FESSENIO: You have been magically changed into a woman.

FEMALE LIDIO: I, a woman?

FESSENIO: Yes, a woman.

FEMALE LIDIO: You're badly mistaken.

FESSENIO: I'd like to be sure, however.

FEMALE LIDIO: Ah, you rogue, what do you want to do?

FESSENIO: I'd be sure if I could see for myself.

FEMALE LIDIO: You ribald, so that's what you have in mind, is it?

FESSENIO: I'll touch him here with my hand, even if he kills me. [*He tries to touch her as she dodges away*]

FEMALE LIDIO: Oh, what presumption! Get away. [*Seeing* FANNIO *as he enters*] Oh, Fannio! Oh, Fannio! You're just in time. Hurry, run!

FANNIO: What's going on?

FEMALE LIDIO: This vile man says that I'm a woman, and he wants to dishonor me by touching me.

FANNIO: [*To* FESSENIO] What strange notion has brought you to this?

FESSENIO: What madness has brought you between my master and me?

FANNIO: This is your master?

FESSENIO: Mine, yes. Why do you ask?

FANNIO: My good man, you're mistaken. I know well that you don't serve him and that he's never been your master. In fact, he's very much my master, and I've always been his servant.

FESSENIO: You've never been his servant, and he's never been your master. I'm certainly your servant, and you're certainly my master. I'm the only one who is telling the truth here, and you two are lying.

FEMALE LIDIO: It's not surprising that you speak so arrogantly, for your actions are equally presumptuous.

FESSENIO: It's not surprising that you've forgotten me without even realizing it, for you've lost your memory and don't even know yourself.

FANNIO: [*To* FESSENIO] Watch what you say to him.[34]

FEMALE LIDIO: I don't know myself?

FESSENIO: Sir—no, I should say, my lady: if you knew yourself, you'd still know me.

FEMALE LIDIO: I know myself well enough. You're the one I don't know.

FESSENIO: It would be more accurate to say that you've found others and lost yourself.

FEMALE LIDIO: And whom have I found?

FESSENIO: Your sister Santilla, who's now a part of you, for you've become a woman. You've lost yourself because you are no longer a man, no longer Lidio.

FEMALE LIDIO: Which Lidio?

FESSENIO: [*Aside*] Oh, poor thing. She doesn't remember a thing! [*To* FEMALE LIDIO] For heaven's sake! Master, don't you realize that you used to be Lidio from Modon, son of Demetrio, brother of Santilla, student of Polinico, master of Fessenio, and lover of Fulvia?

FEMALE LIDIO: [*Aside to* FANNIO] Watch, Fannio, watch. [*To* FESSENIO] Fulvia is indeed in my soul and memory.

FESSENIO: I know that you remember only Fulvia and nothing else. That's because you've been placed under a spell.

❧ SCENE III ❧

The MALE LIDIO, FESSENIO, the FEMALE LIDIO, and FANNIO

MALE LIDIO: [*Entering*] Fessenio! Oh, Fessenio!

FESSENIO: Who is that woman calling me? Wait here for me a moment, and I'll be right back.

FEMALE LIDIO: Fannio, if I thought my brother was alive, I would be full of hope now. I'd like to think that the person he has mistaken me for is my brother.

FANNIO: You don't know for sure that he's dead.

FEMALE LIDIO: You're right.

FANNIO: And it's clear that he's talking about our Lidio and that he's alive and that he's here, and I'd almost, almost say that that's Fessenio.

---

34. Padoan suggests that this remark is addressed to Santilla, but considering the way the argument develops and the probability that Fannio would defend his mistress, this injunction to calm down is more likely addressed to Fessenio.

FEMALE LIDIO: Oh, God! I think I'm going to faint from the tenderness and happiness that I feel.

FESSENIO: [*To* MALE LIDIO] I'm still not entirely sure if you are Lidio or if that one is. Let me have a better look at you. [*He looks him over and begins to touch him*]

MALE LIDIO: What are you, drunk?

FESSENIO: Yes, I see now that you're you and that you're a man.

MALE LIDIO: Right now I want to go where you know I want to go.

FESSENIO: Go on! Go to Fulvia, go like a traveling salesman—give her pleasure and take her money. [MALE LIDIO *leaves;* FESSENIO *returns to* FEMALE LIDIO *and* FANNIO]

FEMALE LIDIO: All right, what do you have to say for yourself?

FESSENIO: If I did or said anything that displeased you, forgive me. It's now clear to me that I mistook you for my master.

FEMALE LIDIO: Who's your master?

FESSENIO: One Lidio from Modon, who looks so much like you that I thought you were he.

FEMALE LIDIO: [*To* FANNIO] My dear Fannio, ohhh, it's obvious! [*To* FESSENIO] What's your name?

FESSENIO: Fessenio, at your service.

FEMALE LIDIO: We're so pleased! There's no room for doubt. Oh, my dear Fessenio! My dear Fessenio! You are mine. [*She embraces and kisses him*]

FESSENIO: What do all these hugs and kisses mean? No, no! Now you want me for your servant, is that it? Look, when I said before that you were my master, I was really lying. I'm not your servant, and you're not my master. I have another master, and you'll have to find another servant.

FEMALE LIDIO: You are mine, and I am yours!

FANNIO: Oh, my dear Fessenio. [*He embraces him*]

FESSENIO: What is it with all these hugs? Oh, there's something strange going on here!

FANNIO: Come over here out of the way a bit, and we'll explain everything. It's Santilla, the sister of Lidio, your master.

FESSENIO: [*To* FANNIO] *You* are our Santilla?

FANNIO: Don't shout. *She* is. I'm Fannio.

FESSENIO: Oh, my dear Fannio!

FANNIO: Don't get all excited out here in public. Calm down and be quiet.

❦ SCENE IV ❦

SAMIA, FESSENIO, the FEMALE LIDIO, and FANNIO

SAMIA: [*Rushing up*] Oh dear! Oh, oh, oh! Oh no! Oh, my poor mistress, who has been dishonored and ruined in one stroke!

FESSENIO: What's wrong, Samia?

SAMIA: Oh, unlucky Fulvia!

FESSENIO: What's going on?

SAMIA: Oh, my Fessenio, we're ruined.

FESSENIO: What's wrong? Tell me.

SAMIA: Horrible news.

FESSENIO: What?

SAMIA: Calandro's brothers caught your Lidio with Fulvia and have sent for him and her brothers. They're all coming to the house to shame her and maybe even kill Lidio.

FESSENIO: Oh no! This is terrible. My poor master! Have they captured him?

SAMIA: Not yet.

FESSENIO: Why didn't he flee?

SAMIA: Fulvia thought that if the necromancer could turn him into a woman again before they found Calandro and her brothers and they all got home, then both her honor and Lidio would be saved. On the other hand, if he had fled, he would have been saved, but her honor would have been lost. So she has sent me flying to the necromancer. Goodbye.

FESSENIO: Listen, wait a second. Where in the house is Lidio?

SAMIA: He and Fulvia are in the downstairs room.

FESSENIO: Doesn't that room have a low window in back?

SAMIA: Yes, maybe he could escape that way if he wanted to.

FESSENIO: No, that's not the reason I asked. Tell me, is there anyone there who could stop someone from getting into the room that way?

SAMIA: Virtually no one. In all the excitement everyone rushed to the door of the room.

FESSENIO: Samia, all this business about the necromancer is just foolishness. If you want to save your mistress, go back to the house and politely make sure no one is near that door.

SAMIA: I'll do what you say. But watch out, because this could really be a disaster.

FESSENIO: Don't worry. Hurry up.

FEMALE LIDIO: Oh dear, my Fessenio, it seems that the heavens have willed that I should find my brother and lose him at the same time, and that today he'll lose his life and I mine.

FESSENIO: There's no time for such talk now. This situation needs a solution that's as intelligent as it is quick. No one can see us here. Change clothes with Fannio. Hurry, go! . . . Ah, that's it! Take this. Put that on. . . . It's perfect. Don't worry, come with me. You, Fannio, wait here. I'll explain to you, Santilla, what you have to do. [*They rush off, leaving* FANNIO *alone*]

FANNIO: What trials Fortune has given these two, brother and sister! Today will bring them either their greatest grief or their greatest happiness ever, depending on how this works out. Heaven has certainly made them alike not just in looks but also in luck. They're in it together now, and they'll share the good and bad that comes their way. But until I see how things turn out, I really don't know if I should be happy or sad, or if I should be worried or hopeful. Now it's up to heaven to decide whether Lidio and Santilla will escape from all their trials and dangers. I'll wait to see what the future brings, hiding here.

❧ SCENE V ❧

The MALE LIDIO, alone

MALE LIDIO: I've escaped a very grave danger, and much to my chagrin I don't understand how. I was in a manner of speaking a prisoner and bewailing my bad luck and Fulvia's when all of a sudden someone brought by Fessenio jumped into the room through the back window and immediately exchanged clothes with me.[35] And Fessenio brought me out the same way, being careful that no one saw me and saying "Everything's all right, be happy." So now I find myself instead of very unhappy, very content. Fessenio stayed behind to talk with Fulvia at the window. I'll stick around to see how things turn out. And oh, it looks good! Fulvia has come to the door looking all happy.

35. I.e., so that he is now dressed as a man.

❧ SCENE VI ☙

FULVIA, alone

FULVIA: This has certainly been a perilous day for me, but thank heavens, all these dangers have been happily overcome. And the end of this present danger has brought me incredible happiness, because not only has my honor been saved and Lidio's life, but now we have a way to be together more often and more easily. Only a god could be happier than I!

❧ SCENE VII ☙

CALANDRO and the BROTHERS of FULVIA

CALANDRO: . . . and I've brought you here so that you could see the dishonor she has brought to me and to you. And then when I've finished beating her, you can send her to the devil, because I don't want this shame in my house. Look at how brazen she is! There she is standing in the doorway, as if she were both good and beautiful!

❧ SCENE VIII ☙

CALANDRO, FULVIA, and the BROTHERS of FULVIA

CALANDRO: What are you doing out here, you corrupt woman? And you have the nerve to wait for me here, knowing that you've cuckolded me! I don't know how to keep myself from wringing your neck. But first I want you to watch while I kill that man that you have in your room, you slut! Then I'll tear your eyes out with my own hands.

FULVIA: O my dear husband! What has caused you to call me an evil wife when I'm not one, and to become a cruel man when up until now you've never been one?

CALANDRO: Shame on you! You still have the audacity to speak? As if we didn't know that you have in that room your lover dressed as a woman!

FULVIA: My dear brothers, this man is trying to reveal to you what I have always tried to hide: that is, my own patience and his outrageous behavior, which every day is a tribulation to me. There's not a wife who is more faithful or worse treated than I. And he's not even ashamed to claim that I've cuckolded him!

CALANDRO: It's absolutely true, you evil woman! And now I want to show your brothers.

FULVIA: Go on in, all of you, and take a look at the person I have in my room, and watch this fierce baboon carry out his murder. Go on, hurry up! [*They all enter the house*]

ᴥ SCENE IX ᘒ

The MALE LIDIO, alone

MALE LIDIO: Fessenio assured me that everything was all right, but I can't see anything, and I'm worried. I don't know that fellow Fessenio had me change clothes with. Fessenio hasn't come out. Calandro went in threatening Fulvia. He's so blind with rage that he may well do her some harm. But if I hear any shouts inside the house, I'm going to go in there and save her, even if it costs me my life. A true lover is nothing if not courageous.

ᴥ SCENE X ᘒ

FANNIO and the MALE LIDIO

FANNIO: [*Entering*] There's Lidio, or actually Santilla. She didn't do a thing.[36] [*To* MALE LIDIO] Let's change back. Take off your clothes and give them back.

MALE LIDIO: What change are you talking about?

FANNIO: It was only a little while ago that Fessenio had us change clothes; you ought to still remember. Here, take yours and give me mine.

MALE LIDIO: Yes, I remember that I changed clothes, but these aren't the ones I gave you.

FANNIO: You seem a little out of it. Do you think I sold the old ones?

MALE LIDIO: Don't make trouble. Here comes Fessenio.

---

36. Mistaking the male Lidio for Santilla and seeing him standing outside dressed in Fannio's clothes, Fannio assumes that "she" did not do whatever Fessenio had planned for "her" to do and suggests that they re-exchange their clothes.

✺ SCENE XI ✺

FESSENIO, alone

FESSENIO: Oh, oh, oh! It was perfect! They thought they would find under those women's clothes a young man whom Fulvia had taken as a lover, and they were going to kill her and shame her. But when they found that it was a young woman, everyone calmed down and decided that Fulvia was the most chaste woman in the world. So now she is highly honored, and I'm very happy. Santilla came out of the house all content, after they released her. And there's Lidio over there.

✺ SCENE XII ✺

SANTILLA, FESSENIO, LIDIO, and FANNIO

SANTILLA: Well, Fessenio, where's my brother?

FESSENIO: That's him over there, still wearing the clothes you gave him. Let's go to him. [*They approach* LIDIO] Lidio, do you know who this woman is?

LIDIO: Certainly not. Tell me who she is.

FESSENIO: She's the one you left with Fulvia in your place. And she's the woman you've been searching for so long.

LIDIO: Who?

FESSENIO: Your Santilla.

LIDIO: My sister?

SANTILLA: I'm your sister, and you're my brother.

LIDIO: You're my dear Santilla? Yes, now I recognize you; it's you. O my dear sister, how long I've been searching for you and longing for you! Now I am content. Now I have fulfilled my desire. Now I no longer suffer.

SANTILLA: O my sweet brother, I'm truly seeing and hearing you! I can hardly believe it's you here alive before me, for I've been weeping for so long at the thought of your death. And now, having had so little hope, I'm all the happier to see you so well.

LIDIO: And you, sister, are all the dearer to me for having saved my life on the very day that I found you, for if you hadn't been here, I might well have been killed.

SANTILLA: Now my sighs and tears are at an end. This is Fannio, our servant, who has served me faithfully.

LIDIO: Ohhh, my Fannio, I remember you clearly now. Having served one person, you've made two happy, and you'll definitely be rewarded.

FANNIO: Nothing could make me happier than to see you alive and with Santilla.

SANTILLA: What are you looking at so intently, my dear Fessenio?

FESSENIO: I've never seen two people so alike as you two. Now I understand why there have been so many delightful confusions today.

SANTILLA: That's the truth.

LIDIO: Delightful for sure, and more so than you realize.

FESSENIO: We can talk about all that later at our leisure. Right now let's focus on what's most important. I told Fulvia when she was inside that this was Santilla, your sister, and she was very happy, and we all agreed that Santilla will marry Flaminio, her son.

SANTILLA: Now I understand why she kissed me so tenderly there in the room and said, "Which of us should be more happy, I can't say. Lidio has found his sister, I a daughter, and you a husband."

LIDIO: It's as good as done.

FANNIO: There's another thing perhaps better yet.

LIDIO: What?

FANNIO: As Fessenio said, you two are so alike that no one can tell you apart.

SANTILLA: I know what you're going to say: that Lidio with our help can take my place and marry Perillo's daughter, whom he wanted to give to me.

LIDIO: Is that likely?

SANTILLA: It's as likely as the sun coming up in the morning and truer than true.

LIDIO: Oh, how lucky we are! After a great storm, everything becomes very calm and clear. We'll be better off than in Modon.

FESSENIO: As much better as Italy is better than Greece, as Rome is more worthy than Modon, and as two fortunes are worth more than one. We've all won out in the end.

LIDIO: Let's get to it! Let's go arrange everything.

FESSENIO: Spectators, the marriages will be celebrated tomorrow. Those who want to see them can wait around. Those who don't want to waste the time waiting can go home. Here, for the moment, there's nothing left to do. Be well, and applaud.

La mandragola

(The Mandrake Root) [1]

By Niccolò Machiavelli (1469–1527)

CHARACTERS:

CALLIMACO: a young man

SIRO: CALLIMACO's servant

MESSER [2] NICIA: a lawyer

LIGURIO: a parasite

SOSTRATA: LUCREZIA's mother

FRA TIMOTEO: LUCREZIA's confessor

A WOMAN

LUCREZIA: MESSER NICIA's wife

1. The date of the play's first performance is uncertain, although most scholars lean towards carnival of 1518, when it was presumably performed to honor the marriage of Lorenzo de'Medici (son of Piero the Gouty) to the French princess Maddalena de la Tour d'Auvergne. Machiavelli was experimenting with comedy as early as 1504 and worked actively with the form from 1512 on. The first printed edition was published in 1518, and a nonautograph manuscript from 1519 exists in the Laurentian library.

2. Messer was a polite form of address that denoted a certain status. Once largely reserved for the nobility, by the sixteenth century, with the rapid growth in the use of honorifics, it had lost much of its weight. In the case of Messer Nicia it has a rather ironic valence, for although he emphasizes his own status throughout, his foolishness constantly calls his worthiness into question.

Song[3]

Because life is brief
And the trials are many
That, living and striving, each person suffers,
    We go seeking our desires,
As the years slip by and are consumed.
For the person who renounces pleasure
To live with anxiety and worries
Doesn't recognize the deceptions
Of the world; or by what evils
And by what strange events
All mortals are often oppressed.
    To escape this misery,
We have chosen the solitary life,
And ever in merrymaking and gaiety
We live like joyful youths and happy nymphs.
Now we have come here
With our song
Solely to honor this
Happy celebration and sweet company.
    And then again we have been brought here
In the name of him who governs you,[4]
In whom one sees all
Good, as if in God Himself.
For such heavenly grace,
For such a happy state,
You can live happily.
Enjoy, and thank the person who has given you all this.[5]

3. To be performed before the comedy, sung by nymphs and shepherds. Machiavelli wrote this and the songs between the acts for a performance planned for carnival of 1526 for his good friend Francesco Guicciardini (1483–1540), the Florentine historian, political thinker, and statesman. The performance was to have taken place in Faenza, one of the main cities of the Romagna, which Guicciardini ruled as papal governor at the time, but he was recalled to Rome before the comedy was actually performed. Machiavelli's great love at the time, Barbara Salutati, a noted singer and courtesan, was slated to sing the songs and, according to some accounts, aided Machiavelli with their composition.

4. Francesco Guicciardini (see n. 3).

5. Usually assumed to refer to the Medici pope Clement VII (1478–1543), though possibly a reference to Guicciardini. This ambiguity may have allowed both Guicciardini and the pope to feel complimented.

Prologue[6]

God save you, kind spectators, because we hope your kindly manner means that this comedy will please you. If you will keep quiet, we will tell you about a strange thing that happened in this city not long ago. Take a look at this scene that we have just displayed, which will give you plenty to laugh at: this is your Florence. Another time it might become Rome or Pisa. That doorway over there on my right is the house of a lawyer who learned quite a lot of law from Bogusius.[7] That street over there in that corner is the street of Love, where the person who falls[8] never stands up straight again. Next, if you don't leave first, you will recognize, in the habit of a friar, the prior or abbot who lives in that church there on the opposite side.

A young man, Callimaco Guadagnio, just come from Paris, lives over there in that house on the left. Above all other good men, he exhibits the signs and ways of a gentleman worthy of honor. He greatly loved a well-mannered young woman, and because of this he deceived her, as you will learn—and I wish that you, my ladies in the audience, might be deceived as she was.

This tale is called *Mandragola*. The reason for this you will learn as the play unfolds, I predict. The author is not very famous, but if you don't find the comedy funny he is prepared to buy the wine afterwards. A poor lost lover, a rather dim lawyer, a friar of questionable morals, a parasite who enjoys deception—today they will bring you some light diversion.

And if this seems too frivolous to be worthy of a man who wants to seem wise and grave, please forgive the author, because in doing this he is trying to make the best of these bad times, when he has little else to turn to. For he has been forbidden to demonstrate his abilities[9] in other ways, and there is no reward for his work.

The reward he expects is that everyone will sit on the sidelines and laugh sarcastically while speaking ill of all that they see or hear. This undoubtedly explains why ancient virtue[10] has been entirely lost today. Seeing that everything is debased, people aren't prepared to work or strive to accomplish through a

6. The original prologue is in verse, but we have rendered it in prose to make it easier to follow in English.

7. Actually "Buezio," which seems to humorously suggest the Roman philosopher and educator Boethius (ca. 480–524) but is a play on *bue* (ox), implying that this lawyer is both a fool (bogus) and a cuckold (wearing horns).

8. I.e., falls to Love's temptations. The play on lost erections and lost morality is clear.

9. *Virtù.*

10. *Virtù.*

thousand hardships a thing that will be blown away by the first breeze or quickly obscured by fog.

If anyone believes, however, that he can daunt this author by maligning him and hopes in this way to frighten him off or get him to give up, let me warn that person that the author also knows how to malign others, and actually this is his greatest skill. In fact, wherever Italian is spoken he fears no one, even though he may play the servant to those who are more powerful than he.

But let's leave the badmouthing of others to those who wish to do so and return to our comedy, before the hour gets too late. Don't worry about mere words anyway or respecting some old fool who hardly knows whether he is dead or alive. But here comes Callimaco, and he has with him Siro, his servant. He'll tell you everything. Everyone listen carefully, and don't expect to hear any further explanations from me.

Act I

SCENE I

CALLIMACO and SIRO

CALLIMACO: Siro, don't leave. I need you for a moment.

SIRO: At your service.

CALLIMACO: I imagine that earlier you wondered about my hurried departure from Paris, and now[11] you're wondering why a month has passed without my doing anything.

SIRO: That's true.

CALLIMACO: I haven't said anything until now—not because I lacked faith in you, but because I judged that if one doesn't want his affairs known, it's better to keep them secret until one must reveal them. But now I need your help, so I've decided to tell you everything.

SIRO: I'm your servant, and servants must never pry or ask about their master's business. But when a master speaks, a servant must serve him faithfully. That's the way I've always done it and always will.

CALLIMACO: Yes, I know. I imagine you've heard me tell this story a thousand times, but it won't hurt you to hear it a thousand and one times: When I was ten, after my parents died, those who were responsible for me sent me to Paris, where

---

11. I.e., now that I've returned to Florence.

I lived for twenty years.[12] Ten years ago, when the wars and the ruin of Italy began with the invasion of King Charles,[13] I decided to stay on in Paris and not return to my homeland, judging that it was safer to live there than here.

SIRO: Yes.

CALLIMACO: And having ordered that everything be sold off here except my house, I lived there very happily for another ten years—

SIRO: Right.

CALLIMACO: —having divided up my time between study, pleasure, and business in such a way that I was successful in each without any one interfering with the other. As a result, as you know, I lived very moderately, trying to treat everyone correctly and not offend anyone. And so, I believe, I was well liked by everyone, burghers and gentlemen, foreigners and countrymen, poor and rich.

SIRO: That's right.

CALLIMACO: But it seemed to Lady Fortune that I was too well off, so she made Cammillo Calfucci come to Paris.

SIRO: Now I begin to understand your problem.

CALLIMACO: He, like the other Florentines, was often invited to dine with me, and in our conversations one day we began to discuss where one could find the most beautiful women—in Italy or in France. And because I couldn't speak about the Italians—as I was so young when I left—Cammillo defended them, and some other Florentines who were there took the part of the French. After much discussion from all sides, Cammillo became rather irate and insisted that even if all the other women of Italy were monsters, he had a relative who would still make them the winners.

SIRO: Now I see clearly where you're headed.

CALLIMACO: He named Madonna Lucrezia, wife of Messer Nicia Calfucci, whom he praised so highly for both her beauty and her manners that all of us were amazed. And in my case this provoked such a great desire to see her that, casting aside all caution, not caring whether there was war or peace in Italy, I set out to return home. When I got here I found that the reputation of Madonna

---

12. This means that Callimaco is about thirty. As an upper-class Florentine, he would thus be in the last years of his *gioventù*, or youth, a period that stretched from about age twelve to the late twenties or early thirties. Within a few years he would ideally marry and be recognized as a fully adult male.

13. The invasions of King Charles VIII of France (1470–98) having begun in 1494, the events of the comedy must have been set in 1504.

Lucrezia fell far short of the reality, which is very seldom the case. And I'm aflame with so great a desire to be with her that I can't find any peace.[14]

SIRO: If you'd spoken to me in Paris, I'd have known how to advise you. But now I don't know what to say.

CALLIMACO: I'm not confiding in you to ask your advice, but to get it off my chest a bit and so that you'll be ready to help me when the time comes.

SIRO: You can count on me. But what hope can you have?

CALLIMACO: Poor me! None.

SIRO: Why?

CALLIMACO: Listen. First, her very nature blocks my desire, for she's very virtuous and totally against the games of love. Then, she has a very rich husband who is completely under her control, and even if he's not young, he's not as old as he looks. Moreover, she doesn't have relatives or neighbors with whom she spends evenings out, and she doesn't go to parties or the other entertainments that young women usually enjoy. No artisans work in her home. There are no women or male servants who aren't afraid of her. All of which means that there's no one to corrupt.[15]

SIRO: What do you think you can do, then?

CALLIMACO: There's nothing so impossible that there's not some reason for hope, and even if that hope is small and vain, both a man's longing and his desire to succeed make him keep trying.

SIRO: In the end, then, what gives you hope?

CALLIMACO: A couple of things. First, there's the stupidity of Messer Nicia, who, even if he is a doctor of law, is the simplest and most foolish man in Florence. Second, there's the longing that he and she share to have children. After being married six years without having any and being extremely rich, they're dying to have them. There's a third point as well: her mother was an easy woman in her day, but she's so rich now that I'm not quite sure how to work on her.

SIRO: Have you tried anything yet?

CALLIMACO: Yes, but only a small move.

SIRO: What?

---

14. A classic representation of the sudden and mad passion associated with youthful love during the Renaissance. Callimaco will repeatedly demonstrate the dangerous qualities of such love, revealing obliquely why few people thought it a good criterion for selecting a marital partner.

15. Machiavelli provides here a good list of the ways a Renaissance would-be lover could make contact with a married woman (of the upper classes, at least). Literature and the records of adultery trials concur on this.

CALLIMACO: You know Ligurio who comes regularly to eat with me. He was a matchmaker[16] before he went over to cadging dinners and meals. And because he's an amusing fellow, Messer Nicia is very close to him, which Ligurio takes advantage of. And tellingly, even if he doesn't invite Ligurio to eat with him, he lends him money every now and then. I've made this Ligurio my friend and have explained to him about my love. He's promised to help me however he can.

SIRO: Take care that he doesn't make a fool of you—that type of freeloader can't be trusted.

CALLIMACO: You're right. Still, when a plan has something in it for an ally, you have to have faith in him from the moment that you involve him. I've promised him that if he succeeds, I'll give him a goodly sum of money, and if he doesn't, he'll receive a few meals and I, at least, won't eat alone.

SIRO: So what's he promised to do so far?

CALLIMACO: He's promised to persuade Messer Nicia to take his wife to the baths this May.

SIRO: What good will that do you?

CALLIMACO: Me? Well, it could be that such a place will bring out another side of her, because in those places people do nothing but enjoy themselves. And I'll go there and make myself as attractive as possible, being as openhanded and lavish as I can. I'll also make friends with her and her husband . . . who knows? One thing leads to another, and only time will tell.

SIRO: Not bad.

CALLIMACO: When he left me this morning, Ligurio said he'd speak with Messer Nicia about this and let me know.

SIRO: Look, here he comes with Messer Nicia now.

CALLIMACO: I'll wait over here, so that I can speak with Ligurio when he gets rid of the lawyer. Meanwhile, you go on about your business inside, and if I need you to do anything I'll call.

SIRO: I'm off.

---

16. Literally, a marriage broker. Because most marriages were arranged by the families involved, marriage brokers were often engaged to find a partner and work out the details of a suitable match. Some of the less successful slid into more shady professions, acting as go-betweens in love affairs or even as pimps. Ligurio seems to be following this trajectory and displays the characteristic cunning of the go-between. It is interesting to speculate on the relationship between Ligurio's cunning (*virtù*) and the cunning skill (*virtù*) that Machiavelli called for in his ideal ruler in *The Prince*.

ᵜ☉ SCENE II ☉ᵜ

MESSER NICIA and LIGURIO

MESSER NICIA: I believe that your advice is good, and I spoke with the wife about it last night. She said that she'd give me an answer today. But to tell you the truth, I'm not enthusiastic about going.

LIGURIO: Why?

MESSER NICIA: Because I'm a homebody, and I'm also not eager to have to move my wife, manservant, and household. Besides, I spoke last night with several doctors. One said that I ought to go to San Filippo, another to Porretta, a third to Villa, and they all seemed to me a bunch of birdbrains. To tell you the truth, these doctors of medicine don't know what they're talking about.

LIGURIO: But obviously your first reason is the most telling: you clearly aren't comfortable losing sight of the dome of the cathedral.[17]

MESSER NICIA: You're wrong there. Why, when I was younger, I traveled all over the place. I never missed a fair in Prato, and there's not a burg in these parts that I haven't seen. And, in fact, I can tell you that I've even been as far as Pisa and Livorno—really![18]

LIGURIO: Did you see the Carrucola of Pisa?[19]

MESSER NICIA: You mean the Verucola.[20]

LIGURIO: Ah yes, the Verucola. And at Livorno, did you see the sea?

MESSER NICIA: Of course I saw it!

LIGURIO: How much larger is it than the Arno River?[21]

MESSER NICIA: The Arno? Why, it's four times . . . more than six times . . .

---

17. The dome of the cathedral of Florence, built in the fifteenth century, dominated the skyline then as now.

18. Prato is just a few miles from Florence, and Pisa and Livorno, while farther away, are still close even by Renaissance standards.

19. Apparently no such structure existed, but *carrucola* recalls the verb *carrucolare*, to make a fool of someone, which is clearly what Ligurio is doing. Renaissance Florentines were noted for the pleasure they took and the cleverness they showed in making fools of others, a form of joking known as a *beffa* or *burla*.

20. Nicia corrects Ligurio with a mistake of his own: La Verruca was a fortification on the hill of the same name to the southeast of Pisa near the little town of Calci. Machiavelli was probably well aware of this fortress. It was a crucial point of resistance when Pisa was retaken by the Florentines in 1503, and Machiavelli played a major role in that campaign. The term also means "wart."

21. The river that bisects Florence.

why, more than seven times larger. Actually, it's so big I'd have to say that you see nothing but water, water, water.

LIGURIO: Well, seeing as how you've pissed in so many different places, I'm amazed that you're worried about going off to the baths.

MESSER NICIA: How childish you are! Do you think it's easy to turn a whole household upside down? Still, I want so much to have children that I'm ready to do anything. But speak a bit with those doctors and see where they recommend I go, and meanwhile I'll speak with the wife, and then let's get together later here.

LIGURIO: All right.

🏵 SCENE III 🏵

LIGURIO, CALLIMACO

LIGURIO: [*Aside*] I don't believe there's a more foolish man alive than that one. And how Fortune smiles on him! He's rich. He has a beautiful wife, wise, well mannered, and fit to manage a kingdom. Rarely, it seems, is that proverb about marriage true that says, "God makes humans, and they find their matches," because one often sees an excellent man saddled with a beast or a sensible woman married to a madman. But something good can be made to come of his foolishness, so that Callimaco may have his desire. Ah, but here he is. [*To* CALLIMACO] What are you up to, Callimaco?

CALLIMACO: I saw you with the lawyer and waited until you got rid of him in order to hear what you've accomplished.

LIGURIO: You know the quality of the man: limited foresight, even less spirit, and an unwillingness to leave Florence. Nonetheless, I stiffened his backbone, at least, and finally he agreed to everything. I'm confident that when you commit to this plan, we'll get him to go, but I'm not sure that in the end we'll get what we want.

CALLIMACO: Why not?

LIGURIO: Oh, I don't know. You know that there are all kinds of people at these baths. Some man could turn up there who likes Madonna Lucrezia as much as you do, and he could be richer and more attractive, which would mean that we would have arranged all this for someone else's benefit. Or it could happen that all the attention she'll get there will make her even more unwilling. Or perhaps if she relaxed a bit there, she'd turn to another rather than to you.

CALLIMACO: I'm afraid you're right. But what can I do? What other plan can

I try? Where can I turn? I have to try something, however extreme, however dangerous, even if it's ruinous, even if it's dishonorable! I'd rather die than live like this! If only I could sleep at night, if only I could eat or carry on a conversation, if only I could find pleasure in something, I would be more patient and wait for the right moment. But here there's no escape. If I don't have some hope in a plan, I'll die! And if I must die, I'm not about to be put off from doing whatever is necessary to make the plan work, no matter how awful, cruel, or evil.

LIGURIO: Don't get so worked up. Calm down!

CALLIMACO: You know that it's to calm myself that I stiffen my resolve with such thoughts. So either we must continue with the plan to send them to the baths, or we have to find another strategy so that I can have some hope. If not true hope, even false will do, as it fuels the thoughts that ease my suffering a bit.

LIGURIO: I understand, and I'm your man.

CALLIMACO: I believe you, even though I know that people like you live to prey on others. Nonetheless, I don't see myself as one of your marks, because if you were to try to trick me, when I found out about it I'd have my revenge, and you'd lose both the run of my house and the hope of getting what I've promised you.

LIGURIO: Put your trust in me. As if the reward that you've promised and that I hope to earn weren't enough, I feel that you're a kindred spirit, and I want your desires to be satisfied almost as much as you do. But enough of this. The lawyer has ordered me to find a doctor and learn which bath would be best to go to. I want you to follow my instructions: you're to say that you've studied medicine and that you've practiced in Paris. He'll readily believe you because he's a fool and because you have the learning to say a few words in Latin to him.

CALLIMACO: What good will this do?

LIGURIO: It'll allow us to send him to the bath that we want, and . . . hmmm . . . it will allow us to try another scheme I have that will be shorter, surer, and safer than the baths.

CALLIMACO: What are you saying?

LIGURIO: I'm saying that if you're willing, and have faith in me, I'll have this whole affair pulled off for you by this time tomorrow. And even if he had the sense to look into whether or not you're a doctor—which he doesn't—the speed of the plan and the scheme itself will ensure that he won't figure out what's happening or have time to screw things up even if he were capable of it.

CALLIMACO: You restore me to life! But this is too huge a promise, and you're filling me with too much hope. How will you do it?

LIGURIO: You'll see when the time is right. For now it wouldn't be wise for me to tell you because there's hardly enough time to put the plan in motion, never mind talk about it. Go into your house and wait for me there. I'll find the lawyer. And if I bring him to meet you, follow my lead and go along with what I say.

CALLIMACO: All right, but you're filling me with hopes that I fear will go up in smoke.

Song

Love, the person who doesn't try
Your great power, hopes in vain
Ever to truly witness
What may be heaven's highest merit.
Nor will such a person know what it means in the same instant
To live and die, to seek evil and flee the good,
To love themselves less than others.
And they'll never know how often
Fear and hope freeze and burn our hearts,
Or understand how both men and gods
Tremble before the arrows with which you're armed.

Act II

⌇ SCENE I ⌇

LIGURIO, MESSER NICIA, and SIRO

LIGURIO: As I said, I believe that God has sent us this person to fulfill your desires. He has practiced extensively in Paris. And don't be surprised by the fact that he hasn't done so here in Florence, for he has very good reasons: first, he's rich, and second, he's about to return to Paris at any moment.

MESSER NICIA: But this is important, my friend. I don't want him to get me into a pickle and then leave me in the stew.

LIGURIO: Don't worry about that. The only thing you have to worry about is whether or not he'll take your case. But if he takes it, he's not the man to leave you until he has penetrated to the heart of your problem.

MESSER NICIA: All right, I trust you on this. But as far as his learning goes, I'll be able to judge that as soon as I talk with him. He won't be able to fast-talk me.

LIGURIO: Exactly so. Because I know you, I'm sending you to him so that you can talk with him yourself. And afterwards, if he doesn't seem in his manner, learning, and way of speaking to be the type of man you would trust with your very life, why, then, I'm not the man I seem to be!

MESSER NICIA: So be it, in the name of the Holy Spirit! Let's go. But where does he live?

LIGURIO: He lives in this piazza. His door is that one you see right over there.

MESSER NICIA: Go ahead, knock.

LIGURIO: [*Knocking*] There, it's done.

SIRO: [*From inside*] Who is it?

LIGURIO: Is Callimaco in?

SIRO: He's here.

MESSER NICIA: Why don't you call him Doctor Callimaco?

LIGURIO: He doesn't bother with such formalities.

MESSER NICIA: That doesn't matter. Give him his due title, and if he doesn't like it, he can ignore it.

SCENE II

CALLIMACO, MESSER NICIA, and LIGURIO

CALLIMACO: Who's asking for me?

MESSER NICIA: *Bona dies, domine magister.*[22]

CALLIMACO: *Et vobis bona, domine doctor.*[23]

LIGURIO: [*Aside to* NICIA] What do you think?

MESSER NICIA: [*Aside to* LIGURIO] Very good! By the holy book, he's something!

LIGURIO: Gentlemen, if you wish me to remain, speak in a language that I can understand, otherwise we will be following two different paths.[24]

CALLIMACO: What brings you to see me?

MESSER NICIA: How should I explain? I am seeking two things that anyone else would flee—that is, to make problems for myself and for others. I do not

---

22. Latin: "Good day to you, my lord doctor."
23. "And to you, my lord lawyer."
24. Literally, "we will be left with two different hearths" or "two different families."

have children and wish to have them, and in order to acquire this problem I have come to create problems for you.

CALLIMACO: I would never consider it a problem to do you a favor or any good and honorable man like you. Why did I labor so many years to gain wisdom in Paris, if not in order to be able to assist men like you?

MESSER NICIA: Thank you very much. When you have need of my skills, I will willingly help you as well. But let us return *ad rem nostram*.[25] Have you thought about which bath would be best for my wife to get pregnant? For I know that Ligurio has talked with you about this matter.

CALLIMACO: That is correct, but in order to fulfill your wishes it is necessary to learn the reason for your wife's sterility, because there can be several causes. *Nam causa sterilitatis sunt aut in semine, aut in matrice, aut in instrumentis seminariis, aut in virga, aut in causa extrinsica.*[26]

MESSER NICIA: This is the most worthy man in the world!

LIGURIO: In addition, it could be that her sterility is caused by your impotence. When that is the case, there is no remedy.

MESSER NICIA: Impotent, me? Are you joking! I doubt there is another man in Florence as rugged and hard as I am.

CALLIMACO: If that is the case, rest assured that we will find you a solution.

MESSER NICIA: Isn't there some other solution besides the baths? I really do not want the bother, and my wife is not eager to leave Florence.

LIGURIO: Yes, there is. Let me explain; Callimaco is much too modest. Callimaco, didn't you tell me that you knew how to make certain potions that infallibly result in pregnancy?

CALLIMACO: Yes, I did. But I like to be discreet with strangers, because I do not want people to think I am a charlatan.

MESSER NICIA: Do not worry about me. You have so impressed me with your quality that there is nothing I would not believe or do under your instruction.

LIGURIO: I think you'll need to see a urine sample.

CALLIMACO: Yes, of course, one cannot overlook that.

LIGURIO: [*To* CALLIMACO] Call Siro so that he can go with the lawyer to his house for the sample and bring it back. We'll wait here.

---

25. "To our business."

26. "Now the causes of sterility are as follows either in the semen or in the womb or in the seminal vessels or in the phallus or caused by external causes."

CALLIMACO: Siro! [SIRO *enters*] Go with him. [*To* NICIA] And if you please, sir, return as soon as possible, and in the meantime we will work something out.

MESSER NICIA: What do you mean, "if you please"? I will be back in a heartbeat. I have more faith in you than Hungarians have in their swords.[27] [*He leaves with* SIRO]

❧ SCENE III ❧

MESSER NICIA and SIRO

MESSER NICIA: Your master is a man of many talents.

SIRO: More than you think.

MESSER NICIA: The king of France must hold him in great respect.

SIRO: Yes, great.

MESSER NICIA: For that reason he ought to be happy in France.

SIRO: Yes, I imagine so.

MESSER NICIA: And he would do well there. In this land there are only the constipated; no one appreciates ability.[28] If he remains here, no one will give him the time of day. I know what I'm talking about because I've shit bricks to learn some legal jargon, and if I had to live on what I make on that, I'd be out in the cold, I can tell you.

SIRO: Do you earn a hundred ducats a year?

MESSER NICIA: Not even a hundred lire, not even a hundred grossi, by God! In this city, people without status, people like me, can't even find a dog willing to bark at them. And we're only good enough to go to funerals or weddings or pass the day sitting on the proconsul's bench giggling like young girls. But what do I care? I don't need anyone. There are plenty who are worse off than me. But I wouldn't want anyone to hear that I said this, because I could be stuck with some special tax or, even worse, have the words shoved up my ass in retaliation.

SIRO: Don't worry.

MESSER NICIA: This is my house. Wait here; I'll be right back.

SIRO: All right.

---

27. It has been suggested that Machiavelli was referring not to swords (*spade*) but to Spano: Pippo Spano, a Florentine condottiere famous for his service in Hungary. However, references to Hungarians' proverbial faith in their swords were common during the period. See, for example, the 1534 letter of Roberto Strozzi to Benedetto Varchi printed in *Venice: A Documentary History*, ed. David Chambers and Brian Pullan (Oxford: Blackwell, 1992), 383.

28. *Virtù*.

᪥ SCENE IV ᪥

SIRO, alone

SIRO: If other lawyers were like this one, we'd all be going out of our minds. As it is, this false Ligurio and my master, who has lost all reason in his mad love, are taking him down a path that leads straight to his dishonor. Actually, that's no skin off my back, as long as we aren't caught, though if we *are* caught, my life's at risk as well as my master's life, and his possessions. Already he's become a doctor. I don't know where they're headed with this trickery or what their plan is. But here comes the lawyer with a jug of urine in hand. Who wouldn't laugh at this stupid oaf?

᪥ SCENE V ᪥

MESSER NICIA and SIRO

MESSER NICIA: [*To* LUCREZIA, *offstage*] I've done everything you've asked, now I want you to do it my way. If I'd known that we wouldn't have children, I would have rather married a peasant woman capable of bearing them. [*To* SIRO] Here, take it, Siro. And follow me. What a chore it was to get My Lady Birdbrain to give me this sample. And it's not that she doesn't want to have children—she wants them more than I do—but every time I ask her to do something, she makes a tragedy out of it.

SIRO: Be patient. Women can usually be led where you want to take them with smooth talk.

MESSER NICIA: What smooth talk? She's a pain in the neck. Hurry up and tell the doctor and Ligurio that I'm here.

SIRO: Here they come out of the house.

᪥ SCENE VI ᪥

LIGURIO, CALLIMACO and MESSER NICIA

LIGURIO: [*Aside to* CALLIMACO] The lawyer will be easy to persuade. The woman will be the problem, but for her we'll find a way.

CALLIMACO: [*To* NICIA] Do you have the specimen?

MESSER NICIA: Siro has it under his cloak.

CALLIMACO: Give it here. Oh my, this specimen shows a weakness of the kidneys.

MESSER NICIA: Yes, and it seems cloudy, even though she just did it a few minutes ago.

CALLIMACO: That is not surprising. *Nam mulieris urine sunt semper maioris grossitiei et albedinis et minoris pulcritudinis quam virorum. Huius autem inter cetera causa est amplitudo canalium, mixtio eorum que ex matrice exeunt cum urina.*[29]

MESSER NICIA: [*Aside*] Oh my! By Saint Puccio's pussy, this fellow's got me in the palm of his hand.[30] How well he speaks about these things!

CALLIMACO: I am afraid that she is not covered to her satisfaction during the night, and for this reason the urine is cloudy.

MESSER NICIA: She has a quilted cover, but she spends four hours on her knees in the cold, stubbornly stringing together Our Fathers, before she comes to bed.

CALLIMACO: In the end, sir, either you will have faith in me or not; either I will show you a sure remedy or not. As for me, I will give you the remedy. If you have faith in me, you will take it, and if a year from today your wife is not carrying her little boy in her arms, I will give you two thousand ducats.

MESSER NICIA: Tell me, then, for I honor you above all others, and I believe in you more than in my confessor.

CALLIMACO: Listen. There is not a cure more certain to make a woman become pregnant than to give her a potion to drink made from the mandrake root.[31] This is something I have tried several times, and it has always worked. In fact, if it were not for this cure, the queen of France would be sterile, and many other princesses would be in that state[32] as well.

---

29. "For the urine of women always has a greater density and whiteness and is less fine than that of men. Moreover, this is explained by, among other things, the largeness of the urinary channels and the mixture with other substances as the urine exits the womb."

30. Saint Puccio's pussy (a popular expression in Renaissance Florence) appears to be a reference to the story of Friar Puccio and Isabetta in Boccaccio's *Decameron*, III, 4. We thank Dennis Looney for his suggestion that there is a double entendre about masturbation in Nicia's remark about being "in the palm of his hand."

31. *Mandragola.*

32. Some editions capitalize *stato* and take *quello Stato* to mean "that State," i.e., the State of France. Others have read, instead of *quello, questo*—i.e., *questo stato*, which they and we read as referring to the physical state of being sterile. Machiavelli was one of the first political thinkers to conceive of the State as a category of analysis, but this passage hardly seems to be concerned with nuances of political theory and clearly does not need a concept like the State to denote the realm of France.

MESSER NICIA: Is this possible?

CALLIMACO: Yes, just as I have told you. And Fortune has so favored you that I just happen to have brought with me all the ingredients that are necessary for that potion, and you may have them.

MESSER NICIA: When should she take the potion?

CALLIMACO: This evening after dinner, because the moon is favorable and there could not be a better time.

MESSER NICIA: No problem. Mix it up, and I will make her take it.

CALLIMACO: Oh, there is just one other thing: the man who has sex with her the first time after she has taken this potion will die within eight days, and nothing in the world can save him.

MESSER NICIA: Bloody shit! I want nothing to do with that sort of crap! You're not going to do me in! What a mess you've got me into.

CALLIMACO: Calm down, there is a way out.

MESSER NICIA: What?

CALLIMACO: Have her immediately sleep with someone else. That person staying with her for a night will draw to himself all the deadly qualities of the mandrake root. After that, you can enjoy her without danger.

MESSER NICIA: I am not going to do that!

CALLIMACO: Why not?

MESSER NICIA: Because I am not the sort of man to turn my wife into a whore and put horns on my own head.

CALLIMACO: What are you saying, sir? I am afraid you are less discerning than I thought. Are you unwilling to do what the king of France and the most important men of his realm have done?

MESSER NICIA: Who do you think I could find who would be willing to do such a crazy thing? If I were to tell him the truth, he would not do it; if I did not tell him, I would be betraying him, and it would be a matter for the Council of Eight.[33] I do not want to get into trouble.

CALLIMACO: If that is all that is worrying you, leave it to me.

MESSER NICIA: How will you arrange it?

CALLIMACO: Listen. I will give you the potion tonight after supper. You give it to her to drink and immediately put her to bed, by which time it will be about ten in the evening. Then we will all put on disguises, you, Ligurio, Siro, and me,

---

33. One of the chief criminal tribunals of Florence, hearing most of the capital crimes like murder.

and we will go out to find someone to serve our purposes in the Mercato Nuovo or the Mercato Vecchio, or in the area. The first young lout we find alone, we will tie him up and with a few whacks take him to your house and into your bedroom in the dark. There we will put him into the bed, telling him what he is to do, and it will all go smoothly. Afterwards, in the morning, we will throw him out before dawn, then you can have your wife get washed, and you can have her whenever you want without danger.

MESSER NICIA: I am willing to do it, since as you say the king and his princes and gentlemen have all used this method. But remember, above all else, the Council of Eight must not know!

CALLIMACO: Who would tell them?

MESSER NICIA: There is only one last problem, and it is not an easy one.

CALLIMACO: What is that?

MESSER NICIA: Convincing my wife. And I am afraid she will never agree.

CALLIMACO: That is a problem. But I would not want to be a husband if I could not make my wife do what I want.

LIGURIO: I have a solution.

MESSER NICIA: What?

LIGURIO: Her confessor.

CALLIMACO: Who is going to win over her confessor? You?

LIGURIO: Me, money, our wickedness, and that of the clergy.

MESSER NICIA: I am doubtful, if for no other reason than because if I tell her to, she will not want to talk with her confessor.

LIGURIO: There's a solution even for that.

CALLIMACO: Tell me.

LIGURIO: Have her mother take her.

MESSER NICIA: She does trust her.

LIGURIO: And I know that her mother shares our opinion. Let's get going, time flies, and evening is coming. [*Aside to* CALLIMACO] Get lost, Callimaco, but be sure that at five o'clock we find you at home with the potion ready to go. We'll go to her mother's house, the lawyer and I, to bring her in on the plan, as I know her well. Then we'll go to the friar, and later we'll bring you up to date on what we've done.

CALLIMACO: [*Aside to* LIGURIO] Oh, don't leave me alone!

LIGURIO: You look a wreck.

CALLIMACO: Where should I go?

LIGURIO: Here, there, down this street, up another. Florence is big!

CALLIMACO: I'm dying!

Song

Everyone sees how happy is he
Who is born a fool and believes everything!
Ambition does not press him,
Fear does not move him,
Which normally are the seeds
Of suffering and pain.
This lawyer of yours,
Dreaming to have children,
Would believe that an ass can fly,
And everything else of value he has forgotten,
Having pinned all his hopes on this.

Act III

✿ SCENE I ✿

SOSTRATA, MESSER NICIA, and LIGURIO

SOSTRATA: I've always heard that a wise man picks the lesser of two evils. If in order to have children there's no other option, we must do this as long as we all agree that it doesn't weigh on anyone's conscience.

MESSER NICIA: That's the way it is.

LIGURIO: You go and find your daughter, and Messer Nicia and I will go find Fra Timoteo, her confessor, and explain everything to him so that you don't have to. Then you both will hear what he has to say.

SOSTRATA: Good. Your road's in that direction, and I'll go find Lucrezia and bring her to speak with the friar, no matter what.

✿ SCENE II ✿

MESSER NICIA and LIGURIO

MESSER NICIA: I imagine you're wondering, Ligurio, why we have to go through all this to convince my wife, but if you knew the whole story, you wouldn't be surprised.

LIGURIO: I imagine it's because all women are suspicious.

MESSER NICIA: No, it's not that. Once she was the sweetest person in the world and the most easygoing. But when a neighbor told her that she would become pregnant if she made a pledge to hear the first mass of the Servite Friars every morning for forty days, she did so and went for about twenty mornings. And do you know, one of those damn friars began to follow her around in such a way that she didn't want to go back again? It's such a shame when those who are supposed to provide good examples are so evil. Isn't that so?

LIGURIO: I'll be damned if you aren't right!

MESSER NICIA: Ever since, she's been as jumpy as a hare, and the minute I suggest something to her she has a thousand qualms.

LIGURIO: Now I see how it is. But what about her pledge?

MESSER NICIA: She got a dispensation.

LIGURIO: Good. But give me twenty-five ducats, if you have them, for we'll need to spend a bit to make a quick friend out of the friar and give him the hope of gaining more.

MESSER NICIA: Here, take them. It's no big deal, I'll get them back elsewhere.

LIGURIO: These friars are fiendishly clever, sharp, and wise, because they know our sins as well as their own. If one isn't experienced in dealing with them, it's easy to be fooled and fail to win their support. So I don't want you to ruin things while we are negotiating, because a man of your character who stays the whole day in his study and knows all about books is less suited to bargain when it comes to worldly affairs. [*Aside*] This guy is such a fool, I'm afraid he'll ruin everything.

MESSER NICIA: Tell me what you want me to do.

LIGURIO: All right, just leave the talking to me and don't say anything unless I give you a sign.

MESSER NICIA: Fine, but what sign?

LIGURIO: I'll wink, bite my lip—no! Let's do it another way. When was the last time you spoke with the friar?

MESSER NICIA: It's been more than ten years.

LIGURIO: Good. I'll tell him that you've gone deaf. Don't answer, and don't say anything unless we speak very loudly.

MESSER NICIA: All right.

LIGURIO: As far as that goes, don't worry about anything I say that seems not to fit with our plan, because everything will work itself out.

MESSER NICIA: All right.

LIGURIO: But I see the friar, and he's speaking with a woman. Let's wait until they're finished.

SCENE III

FRA TIMOTEO and a WOMAN

FRA TIMOTEO: If you wish to confess, I'll take care of you.

WOMAN: Not today, I'm meeting someone. I'd just like to quickly get a few things off my chest. Have you said those masses for Our Lady?

FRA TIMOTEO: Yes, madam.

WOMAN: Take this florin and say a mass for the dead every Monday for two months for the soul of my husband. Even though he was a beast, still, the flesh calls, and when I remember him I can't help feeling something. Do you really think he's in purgatory?

FRA TIMOTEO: Without doubt.

WOMAN: I'm still not so sure. You know the sorts of things he would do to me sometimes. Oh, how many times I complained to you about him! I tried to discourage him as much as I could, but he was so demanding. Oh, my God!

FRA TIMOTEO: Don't worry, the mercy of God is great. Even if a man cannot escape such desires, he always has plenty of time to repent.

WOMAN: Do you think that the Turks will invade Italy this year?

FRA TIMOTEO: If you don't say your prayers, I'm afraid they will.

WOMAN: Heavens! God help us with those devils! I'm really afraid of that impaling they do. But I see a woman here in the church who has some thread of mine; I'll go and speak to her. Good day!

FRA TIMOTEO: Be well.

SCENE IV

FRA TIMOTEO, LIGURIO, and MESSER NICIA

FRA TIMOTEO: [*Aside*] Women are the most charitable people and the most troublesome. The person who gets rid of them gets rid of all the troubles as well as all the profits; the person who cultivates them gets the troubles with the profits. Of course, it's true that one can't have sugar without flies. [*To* LIGURIO *and* NICIA *as they come up to him*] My good sirs, what brings you here? Is this Messer Nicia?

LIGURIO: Speak loudly. He's virtually deaf and thus hears almost nothing.

FRA TIMOTEO: [*In a loud voice*] Welcome, sir!

LIGURIO: Louder.

FRA TIMOTEO: [*In a louder voice*] Welcome!

MESSER NICIA: Good to see you, Father.

FRA TIMOTEO: [*In a loud voice*] What brings you here?

MESSER NICIA: Fine, thank you.

LIGURIO: It would be best if you spoke with me, Father. You two would have to put this piazza in an uproar in order to talk.

FRA TIMOTEO: What can I do for you?

LIGURIO: Messer Nicia here and another good gentleman, whom you'll learn about later, want to give out several hundred ducats as alms.

MESSER NICIA: Bloody shit!

LIGURIO: [*Aside to* NICIA] Shut up, damn you! It won't be that much. [*To* FRA TIMOTEO] Take no notice, Father, of anything he says. Being deaf, at times he thinks he hears weird things and reacts strangely.

FRA TIMOTEO: Go ahead with this subject, and let him say whatever he wants.

LIGURIO: I've some of that money with me, and it's meant for you to distribute as charity.

FRA TIMOTEO: With pleasure.

LIGURIO: But before we make this donation, we need your help with a strange problem of Messer Nicia's concerning the honor of his house that only you can help with.

FRA TIMOTEO: What is it?

LIGURIO: I don't know if you know Cammillo Calfucci, Messer Nicia's nephew.

FRA TIMOTEO: Yes, I know him.

LIGURIO: A year ago he went to France on business, and because his wife had died, he left his daughter of marriageable age in a convent, which I'll leave unnamed for the moment.

FRA TIMOTEO: What happened?

LIGURIO: It happened that, from either the carelessness of the nuns or the foolishness of the girl, she's now four months pregnant, which means that if the damage isn't put right prudently, Messer Nicia, the nuns, the girl, Cammillo, and the Calfucci family all will suffer dishonor. Messer Nicia is so concerned about this dishonor that if it can be avoided he has pledged to give three hundred ducats for the love of God—

MESSER NICIA: What crap!

LIGURIO: [*Aside to* NICIA] Shut up! [*To* FRA TIMOTEO] —and donate them to you for distribution, as only you and the abbess of the nunnery can solve this problem.

FRA TIMOTEO: How?

LIGURIO: You persuade the abbess to give the girl a potion that will make her abort.

FRA TIMOTEO: This is a matter that requires serious thought.

LIGURIO: Serious thought? Look, it will serve several good ends: you'll save the honor of the convent, the girl, and her relatives, return a daughter to her father, satisfy this gentleman here and all his relatives, and do all the charity that three hundred ducats allows, and on the other hand you'll be offending nothing but a chunk of unborn flesh, without feelings, which could be lost all the same in a thousand ways. I believe that the good is to be found in what does good for the most people and what makes the most people happy.

FRA TIMOTEO: So be it in the name of God. What you wish will be done, everything in the name of God and for charity. Tell me the convent, give me the potion, and, if you wish, the money, so that it can begin to do some good.

LIGURIO: Now you seem to be that man of the church I held you to be. Here, take this part of the money. The convent is—but wait a second, there's a woman in the church who's trying to get my attention. I'll be right back. Stay here with Messer Nicia; I need to have a couple of words with her. [*He leaves*]

SCENE V

FRA TIMOTEO and MESSER NICIA

FRA TIMOTEO: How old is the girl?

MESSER NICIA: I'm flabbergasted!

FRA TIMOTEO: [*In a loud voice*] I said, "How old is the girl?"

MESSER NICIA: God damn him!

FRA TIMOTEO: [*In a loud voice*] Why?

MESSER NICIA: Because he deserves it!

FRA TIMOTEO: What a mess I'm in! I'm dealing with one man who's mad and another who's deaf. One runs away, and the other can't hear me. Still, [*hefting the ducats*] if these aren't counterfeit, I'll make out better than either of them in this affair. But here comes Ligurio.

❧ SCENE VI ❧

LIGURIO, FRA TIMOTEO, and MESSER NICIA

LIGURIO: [*Aside to* NICIA] Be quiet, sir. [*To* FRA TIMOTEO] I have excellent news, Father.

FRA TIMOTEO: What?

LIGURIO: That woman I spoke with told me that the young girl lost the child on her own.

FRA TIMOTEO: Good! [*Aside*] And so this charity is as good as lost.[34]

LIGURIO: [*Half-overhearing him*] What are you saying?

FRA TIMOTEO: Oh, I'm saying that you should now be even more willing to give money for charity.

LIGURIO: The contributions will be made as you wish. But we need you to do another favor for the gentleman.

FRA TIMOTEO: What's that?

LIGURIO: Something less troublesome, less scandalous, more useful for us, and more profitable for you.

FRA TIMOTEO: What is it? I'm on good terms with you, and we've become so close that I don't believe there's anything I wouldn't do to help you.

LIGURIO: I'll tell you privately in church. Messer Nicia can leave the talking to me and wait for us out here. [*To* NICIA] Wait here, sir, we'll be back shortly.

MESSER NICIA: Don't rush back!

FRA TIMOTEO: Let's go. [FRA TIMOTEO *and* LIGURIO *go into the church*]

❧ SCENE VII ❧

MESSER NICIA, alone

MESSER NICIA: Is it day or night? Am I awake or dreaming? Am I drunk, even though I haven't had a drop to drink yet today, chasing around with this foolish drivel? We came here to say one thing to the friar, and he told him something

---

34. *Andrà alla grascia.* If *grascia* is spelled with a capital *g*, like the Florentine tax office of the same name, the phrase could be read literally as meaning that the money will go to the tax office now instead of to Friar Timoteo and his charity (with the ironic implication that the money was now simply lost). But if *grascia* is spelled with a lower-case *g*, as in the manuscript edition of 1519, the phrase could be taken as the idiomatic expression meaning "it will melt away," or in other words, "the charity is as good as lost."

completely different. Then he told me to pretend that I was deaf, but I would have been better off putting wax in my ears like the Dane,[35] so that I wouldn't have heard all the crazy things he said. And God knows to what end! I've lost twenty-five ducats without us having even begun to talk about my problem, and now they've left me here like a bump on a log. But here they come again. To hell with them if they haven't spoken about my problem.

<h2 align="center">⁂ SCENE VIII ⁂</h2>

FRA TIMOTEO, LIGURIO, and MESSER NICIA

FRA TIMOTEO: [*Aside to* LIGURIO] Have the women come. I know what I have to say, and if they'll listen to me we'll complete this coupling this evening.

LIGURIO: Messer Nicia, Fra Timoteo is ready to take care of everything. The women must come to see him.

MESSER NICIA: You give me new life! Will the child be a boy?

LIGURIO: A boy.

MESSER NICIA: I'm crying, I'm so happy!

FRA TIMOTEO: Go on into the church. I'll wait for the women here. Stay to one side so that they don't see you. Once they've left, I'll tell you what they said.

<h2 align="center">⁂ SCENE IX ⁂</h2>

FRA TIMOTEO, alone

FRA TIMOTEO: I'm not sure who's fooling whom. This crook Ligurio came to me with that first story to try me out. If I agreed to it, he knew he could get me to do the second thing. And if I hadn't agreed—to what was, after all, a lie of no importance—he wouldn't have revealed the second thing to me and would thus have avoided needlessly giving away their plans. It's true that I've been tricked, but I'll turn the trick to my advantage. Messer Nicia and Callimaco are rich, and I'll get a goodly sum from each, for different reasons. The thing must remain secret because it's important for them and me that it remain so. Whatever happens, I won't lose. It's true that I'm worried that we'll have problems with Madonna Lucrezia, because she's wise as well as good. But I'll play on her goodness. And in

---

35. Roger the Dane, the popular figure in chivalric romances, who, advised by a fairy, put wax in his ears in order not to hear the bewitching cries of his enemy.

the end, ~~all women are pretty slow~~. If you find one who knows how to say a few words, she seems wise because in the land of the blind, the person with one eye is king. But here she comes now with her mother, who clearly is no saint and will be a great help to me in winning her daughter over to my designs.

✧ SCENE X ✧

SOSTRATA and LUCREZIA

SOSTRATA: I know that you know, my dear daughter, that I value your honor and well-being as much as anyone in the whole world and that I wouldn't advise you to do anything that would harm you. I told you once, and I'll say it again, that if Fra Timoteo tells you that this is not an issue of conscience, you shouldn't give it a thought.

LUCREZIA: I've always been afraid that Messer Nicia's longing to have children would lead to trouble. And so every time he's come up with some scheme, I've become worried and uneasy, especially after what happened to me when I went to the masses of the Servite Friars. But of all his schemes, this one seems the most bizarre. To give up my body to this dishonor and to cause the death of the man who dishonored me—even if I were the last woman on earth and it fell to me to start the human race all over again, I don't think I would be allowed to do it.

SOSTRATA: There are many things I can't explain to you, my child. You talk with the friar, see what he tells you, and then do what he, we, and those who wish you well advise.

LUCREZIA: I'm so upset!

✧ SCENE XI ✧

FRA TIMOTEO, LUCREZIA, and SOSTRATA

FRA TIMOTEO: Welcome. I know what you've come to me to talk about, because Messer Nicia has explained it to me. In fact, I've been looking over my books for more than two hours to study the matter, and after much research I've found many things that in particular and in general are in our favor.

LUCREZIA: Are you serious or joking?

FRA TIMOTEO: Ah, Madonna Lucrezia! Would I joke about something like this? Don't you know me better than that?

LUCREZIA: All right, Father, but this is the strangest thing I've ever heard of.

FRA TIMOTEO: Madonna, I understand, but I don't want you to talk like that anymore. Now, there are many things that from afar seem terrible, unsupportable, strange, but when you actually do them they become familiar, supportable, ordinary. They say that the fear of evil is worse than the evil itself, and this is a case that proves the point.

LUCREZIA: May God make it so!

FRA TIMOTEO: I want to return to what I was saying earlier. As far as your conscience is concerned, you need to follow this general rule: where there is a clear good and an indefinite evil, one must never lose that good for fear of that evil. And in this case there is a clear good: you will become pregnant and gain a soul for God Our Father. And the uncertain evil is that the man who lies with you after you have taken the potion may die, but there are those who do not die. Yet, as it is an uncertain thing, it is better that Messer Nicia not run that risk. As far as the act itself is concerned, don't imagine that it would be a sin. For it is the will that sins, not the body. And the sin in sex comes from not pleasing one's husband or from taking pleasure oneself in the deed, but you will be pleasing him and taking no pleasure. Moreover, one must consider the end of every action: your goal is to fill a seat in paradise and to satisfy your husband.[36] The Bible says that the daughters of Lot, believing that they were the last women alive, slept with their father, and because their intentions were good, they did not sin.

LUCREZIA: What are you trying to persuade me to do?

SOSTRATA: Let yourself be persuaded, my child. Don't you understand that a woman who doesn't have children doesn't have a secure home? If her husband dies, she is left like an animal, abandoned by everyone.[37]

FRA TIMOTEO: I swear to you, madam, as a man of the cloth, that as far as your husband's plan is concerned your conscience should be no more bothered than by eating meat on Wednesdays, a sin that is washed away with a bit of holy water.

36. Machiavelli is restating the often misunderstood maxim from *The Prince* that one must consider the ends or outcome of a course of action in order to judge the means employed. If one overlooks the irony of Fra Timoteo's advice, however, his argument is quite moral and Christian, for will and intention are the keys in sinning and evaluating an action. If Lucrezia is willing to do good in the end and not intending any evil, she is not sinning.

37. Machiavelli again reveals what an acute observer he was of contemporary life. A widow without children was of virtually no value to her marital family and was often left on her own with only what had been provided for her in her husband's will or returned to her from her dowry. The family's desire to protect its next generation, especially male heirs, put women with children in a much stronger position.

LUCREZIA: Where are you leading me, Father?

FRA TIMOTEO: I am leading you to something that will give you reason always to pray for me and that will give you even more satisfaction a year from now.

SOSTRATA: She'll do what you want. I'll put her to bed myself this evening. What are you afraid of, you little crybaby? There are dozens of women in this city who would be happy to be in your place.

LUCREZIA: All right. But I doubt that I'll be alive tomorrow morning.

FRA TIMOTEO: Don't worry, my child: I'll pray for you. I'll say the prayer of the angel Raphael, asking him to be by your side.[38] Go in peace now and prepare yourself for this mystery, for it's getting rather late.

SOSTRATA: Peace be with you, Father.

LUCREZIA: God and Our Lady protect me from evil!

❧ SCENE XII ☙

FRA TIMOTEO, LIGURIO, and MESSER NICIA

FRA TIMOTEO: Ligurio, come on out here!

LIGURIO: How did it go?

FRA TIMOTEO: Fine. They've gone home prepared to do everything. And there won't be any problems because her mother is going to stay with her until she puts her to bed.

MESSER NICIA: Really?

FRA TIMOTEO: Oh my! You're cured of your deafness, eh?

LIGURIO: San Clemente has granted him this grace.

FRA TIMOTEO: It would be good to give an ex voto[39] to attract some attention[40] so that I could profit even more from your good fortune.

MESSER NICIA: Let's not bother with details. Will my wife give me a hard time about doing what I want?

---

38. A reference to a story from the apocryphal book of Tobit (the final form of the Bible had not yet been established, and several books today deemed apocryphal were widely known then). In the story, Tobias, who wishes to marry Sarah, faces a problem: each of the seven previous men who have married her have been murdered on the wedding night by her demon lover. The angel Raphael gives Tobias a magical remedy to drive the demon away, and he succeeds in bedding Sarah. Raphael would seem to be a good bet for a prayer to protect Lucrezia in her impending magical bedding.

39. An object given in thanks for a grace received, usually perceived as some kind of miraculous intervention. Often it was a picture that represented the grace received.

40. I.e., attract some attention to your miraculous cure.

FRA TIMOTEO: As I said, no.

MESSER NICIA: I am the happiest man in the world!

FRA TIMOTEO: I believe you. You're going to have a son, and as they say, "The man who has not, will not."

LIGURIO: Go on now, Father, to say your prayers, and if we need you for something else we'll call you. You, Messer Nicia, go to your wife to keep her from changing her mind. I'll find Doctor Callimaco and have him send you the potion. At seven let's all meet again to organize what we need to do at ten.

MESSER NICIA: That sounds good. Goodbye.

FRA TIMOTEO: Goodbye.

Song

Successfully worked to its desired end,
This scam is so smooth
That it carries off one's worries
And makes every bitterness sweet.
O scam, you are a solution so fine and rare,
You show the right way to lost souls;
You, with your great power
To make others happy, make Love rich;
You overcome with your saintly counsels alone
The power of gems, poisons, and spells.

Act IV

SCENE I

CALLIMACO, alone

CALLIMACO: I wish I knew what they've accomplished. How can it be that I haven't run across Ligurio? And it's not just five, it's already six! I've been so worked up, and I still am! It's true that Nature and Fortune balance things out: one doesn't do a person any good without the other doing some evil. And in this case the greater my hopes have become, the greater my fear has become. Poor me! Can I continue to live with so many worries and tossed so between my fears and hopes? I'm a ship caught between two opposing winds: the closer I come to port, the more in danger I am of losing everything in the storm.

The foolishness of Messer Nicia fills me with hope; the prudence and strength of Lucrezia fills me with fear. Alas, I can't find peace anywhere. Every time I try to get control of myself, my mad passions well up and say to me, "What are you doing? Have you gone mad? Once you've had her, what will you do? You ought to admit your mistake; you'll regret all the effort and worry you've put into this. Don't you realize how much better things are in anticipation than they are when you actually have them? On the other hand, the worst that can happen is that you'll die and go to hell, and plenty of people have died and plenty of good men have gone to hell! Are you ashamed to join them? Face up to fate.[41] Either flee evil or, if you can't, face it like a man. Don't be bowled over by it or laid low like a woman." In this way I lift my spirits, but it only lasts a little while, because from all sides I'm overwhelmed by the desire to be with her just one time—overwhelmed with sighs from my head to my toes and totally shattered. My legs tremble, my insides churn, my heart pounds in my chest, my arms lose their force, my tongue falls mute, my eyes flash, and my head swims.[42] Still, if I can find Ligurio, I can get this off my chest. But here he comes now, hurrying. His report will either let me live happily for a bit or utterly kill me.

🌿 SCENE II 🌿

LIGURIO and CALLIMACO

LIGURIO: [*Aside*] I've never wanted more to find Callimaco, and I've never had more trouble finding him. If I were bringing him bad news, I'd have found him immediately. I've looked for him at home, in the piazza, in the market, at the Pancone delli Spini, at the Loggia de'Tornaquinci, and I still haven't found him. These lovers have quicksilver under their feet and can't stay still.

CALLIMACO: [*Aside*] What's wrong with me that I don't call out to him? He really does seem happy. [*To* LIGURIO] Oh, Ligurio! Ligurio!

LIGURIO: Oh, Callimaco! Where have you been?

CALLIMACO: What news?

LIGURIO: Good.

CALLIMACO: Good, really?

41. Machiavelli uses *sorte* (fate), not *fortuna* (fortune), but the passage recalls the one in *The Prince* where he argues that one must act like a man with (the feminine) *fortuna* and take her by force.

42. This parodic catalog of the emotions that the Renaissance associated with youthful love suggests why most adults of the period (at least in their more sober moments) accepted the idea that arranged marriages were better than those based on such emotions. In another of his comedies, *La Clizia*, Machiavelli seems to poke fun at his own brushes with that mad passion as a supposedly mature older adult.

LIGURIO: Really good.

CALLIMACO: Is Lucrezia willing?[43]

LIGURIO: Yes.

CALLIMACO: The friar did his part?

LIGURIO: Done.

CALLIMACO: What a blessed friar! I'll always pray for him.

LIGURIO: [*Aside*] Oh, sure. As if God blesses those who do evil as well as those who do good! [*To* CALLIMACO] Your friar will want something more than prayers.

CALLIMACO: What?

LIGURIO: Money.

CALLIMACO: He shall have it. How much have you promised him?

LIGURIO: Three hundred ducats.

CALLIMACO: Fine.

LIGURIO: The lawyer has forked over twenty-five.

CALLIMACO: Why?

LIGURIO: It's enough that he paid them.

CALLIMACO: What did Lucrezia's mother do?

LIGURIO: Virtually everything. When she heard that her daughter could have this pleasant night without it being a sin, she never gave up begging, ordering, nagging Lucrezia. Finally she took her to the friar, and there she went on until Lucrezia gave in.

CALLIMACO: Good God! What did I do to deserve to be so lucky? I'm going to die of happiness!

LIGURIO: [*Aside*] What a character! Whether for happiness or for sadness, he seems to be bent on dying. [*To* CALLIMACO] Have you prepared the potion?

CALLIMACO: Yes, I have it.

LIGURIO: What are you going to send?

CALLIMACO: A glass of hippocras tea, which is perfect because it soothes the stomach and cheers the brain—oh, no, no, no! I'm ruined!

LIGURIO: What is it? What's happening?

CALLIMACO: There's no hope!

LIGURIO: What the hell are you talking about?

CALLIMACO: We haven't accomplished a thing. I've boxed myself in!

---

43. The critical edition of Giorgio Inglese inverts, without explanation, this and the next speech by Callimaco and Ligurio's replies. Most other editions follow the more logical order of speeches that we follow here.

LIGURIO: Why? Why won't you say it? Take your hands away from your face.

CALLIMACO: Don't you remember that I told Messer Nicia that you, he, Siro, and I would grab someone to put into bed with his wife?

LIGURIO: So what?

CALLIMACO: So what?! If I'm with you, I can't be the one who's grabbed. If I'm not with you, he'll see through the plot.

LIGURIO: True. But isn't there some way out?

CALLIMACO: I don't think so.

LIGURIO: Yes, it'll work!

CALLIMACO: How?

LIGURIO: Let me think a little.

CALLIMACO: I'm obviously in real trouble, if you have to start thinking now!

LIGURIO: I've found the answer!

CALLIMACO: What?

LIGURIO: Since he's in this up to his neck, I'll have the friar get us out of it.

CALLIMACO: How?

LIGURIO: We'll all have to be disguised. I'll make the friar disguise himself: he'll change his voice, face, and clothes, and I'll tell the lawyer that he's you, and he'll fall for it.

CALLIMACO: I like the idea, but what will I do?

LIGURIO: You should put on a short mantle and come by his house with a lute in hand, singing a little song.

CALLIMACO: Without disguising my face?

LIGURIO: Yes. If you were to wear a mask, he'd be suspicious.

CALLIMACO: Then he'll recognize me!

LIGURIO: No he won't, because I want you to screw up your face and open, twist, or clench your lips, close an eye—try it.

CALLIMACO: [*Making a face*] How about this?

LIGURIO: No.

CALLIMACO: [*Trying again*] This?

LIGURIO: Not enough.

CALLIMACO: [*Trying again*] Like this?

LIGURIO: Yes, yes, remember that. I have a false nose at home that I want you to wear.

CALLIMACO: All right. What happens next?

LIGURIO: When you come along singing, we'll be there. We'll grab you and, throwing away your lute, we'll turn you around a few times. And then we'll take you into the house and put you in bed with Lucrezia. The rest you'll have to figure out on your own!

CALLIMACO: Just getting there is the key.

LIGURIO: You'll get there. But to be able to return there, that's up to you, not us.

CALLIMACO: What do you mean?

LIGURIO: You're going to win her tonight, but before you leave, you have to let her know the truth: explain the plot to her, show her your love, tell her how much you treasure her. And then explain to her that she can be your lover without any dishonor to herself or else be your enemy, but only at the cost of great dishonor. It's impossible that after a night with you she'll want that night to be the last.

CALLIMACO: Do you think so?

LIGURIO: I'm certain. But let's not lose any more time, it's already eight. Call Siro, send the potion to Messer Nicia, and wait for me at home. I'll find the friar, get him disguised, and bring him here. Then we'll find the lawyer and do what remains to be done.

CALLIMACO: Sounds good. Get going. [LIGURIO *leaves*]

SCENE III

CALLIMACO and SIRO

CALLIMACO: Oh, Siro!

SIRO: Master?

CALLIMACO: Come here.

SIRO: Here I am.

CALLIMACO: Go get that silver goblet that's in the cupboard in my room and bring it to me covered with a bit of cloth, and be sure not to spill it along the way.

SIRO: Yes, sir. [*He leaves*]

CALLIMACO: This fellow has been with me for ten years, and he has always served me faithfully. I believe I can trust him in this matter as well. Even though I haven't explained our scheme to him, I imagine he's figured it out. Well, he's just wicked enough to go along with it, and he seems to be doing just that.

SIRO: [*Returning with the cup*] Here it is.

CALLIMACO: Good. Hurry to Messer Nicia's house and tell him that this is the medicine that his wife is to take right after supper. And the sooner she has supper, the better. Tell him also that we'll be in position, ready and on time, and that he should be there as well. Go, now, and make it quick.

SIRO: I'm off.

CALLIMACO: Listen a second. If he wants you to wait, wait and come back with him. If he doesn't, come back after you've given him the cup, all right?

SIRO: Yes, sir. [*He leaves*]

☙ SCENE IV ❧

CALLIMACO, alone

CALLIMACO: I'm waiting here for Ligurio to return with the friar. And those who claim that it's a hard thing to wait are absolutely right. I'm losing ten pounds every hour thinking where I am now and where I could be in two hours, fearing that something could happen to ruin my plans. If that were to happen this would be the last night of my life, because I'll throw myself in the Arno. Or hang myself. Or jump out that window. Or I'll stab myself on her doorstep— anything to end it all. But is that Ligurio I see? Yes, that's him, and he has with him what seems to be a hunchback with a limp. That must be the friar. Ah, those friars—when you know one, you know them all! Who's that other fellow coming up with them? It must be Siro, who's already been to the lawyer's house. That's him. I'll wait for them here to have a word with them.

☙ SCENE V ❧

SIRO, LIGURIO, FRA TIMOTEO (disguised), and CALLIMACO

SIRO: Who is that with you, Ligurio?

LIGURIO: An honorable man.

SIRO: Is he really lame, or is he pretending?

LIGURIO: Mind your own business.

SIRO: My, but he has the face of a great scoundrel!

LIGURIO: Be quiet, and don't mess things up! Where's Callimaco?

CALLIMACO: Here I am. Welcome, all!

LIGURIO: Oh, Callimaco, tell this silly Siro to keep quiet. He's already said a thousand foolish things.

CALLIMACO: Siro, listen up: tonight you must do everything Ligurio tells you as if it were I who were ordering you. And everything that you see, feel, or hear you're to keep absolutely secret if you value my possessions, my honor, and my life as well as your own good.

SIRO: You can count on me.

CALLIMACO: Did you give the goblet to the lawyer?

SIRO: Yes, sir.

CALLIMACO: What did he say?

SIRO: That he'll be here shortly, ready for everything.

FRA TIMOTEO: Is that you, Callimaco?

CALLIMACO: At your service. Our agreement is sealed. I and all my fortune are yours to use as if they were your own.

FRA TIMOTEO: I understand and believe you. So I'm ready to do for you what I wouldn't do for any other person in the world.

CALLIMACO: Your labors will be rewarded.

FRA TIMOTEO: It's enough that you're my friend.

LIGURIO: Enough of these formalities; Siro and I must get disguised. Callimaco, you come with us, as you have matters of your own to attend to. The friar will wait for us here. We'll hurry back and go get Messer Nicia.

CALLIMACO: Sounds good to me. Let's go.

FRA TIMOTEO: I'll wait for you here. [CALLIMACO, SIRO, *and* LIGURIO *leave*]

⸙ SCENE VI ⸙

FRA TIMOTEO (disguised), alone

FRA TIMOTEO: Those who claim that keeping bad company leads men to the gallows are right. And often one ends up in trouble as much for being too friendly and too good as for being too wicked. God knows I didn't intend to harm anyone. There I was in my cell, reciting my prayers, counseling my flock, when along came this devilish Ligurio. He got me to stick a finger into this evil business, and then an arm, and now I'm in up to my neck and I'm not sure where it will all end. Still, I can take comfort in the fact that when a thing is important to many people, they all take care to see that it succeeds. But here come Ligurio and that servant.

⁊ᔆ SCENE VII ᘐᔆ

FRA TIMOTEO (disguised), LIGURIO, and SIRO

FRA TIMOTEO: Welcome back!

LIGURIO: How do we look?

FRA TIMOTEO: Great.

LIGURIO: We're missing the lawyer. Let's head for his house. It's already after nine and time to get going.

SIRO: Who's that opening his door, a servant?

LIGURIO: No, it's him. [*Laughing*] Oh my!

SIRO: Why are you laughing?

LIGURIO: Who wouldn't laugh? He has on a short little cloak that doesn't even cover his ass. And what the hell is that thing he's got on his head? It looks like one of those fur hoods that church canons wear. And he has a puny little sword sticking out between his legs. [*Laughing*] And he's muttering something. Let's hide here a minute and hear his complaints about his wife.

⁊ᔆ SCENE VIII ᘐᔆ

MESSER NICIA (disguised)

MESSER NICIA: What nonsense that crazy wife of mine has been up to! She sent the maid to her mother's and the servant to our country house. Actually, I should commend her for that, though I can't commend her for all her silly antics before we could get her to go to bed: "I don't want to! . . . How can I do this? . . . What are you getting me into? . . . Woe is me! *Mamma mia!*" And if her mother hadn't given her a good goose, she still wouldn't be in bed. A pox on her! I do appreciate women who aren't easily swayed, but she's too much. She's stubborn as a mule, the birdbrain! Yet if someone said, "The most intelligent woman in Florence should be hanged!" she would no doubt reply, "Why me?"

I know that this evening the lance will find its mark, but before I leave the lists I want to check it all out myself so that I can say, like Monna Ghinga, "I have seen it with these very hands."[44]

Actually, I look rather good in this disguise. Who'd recognize me? I seem

---

44. Evidently a reference to a proverb claiming that seeing with one's hands is superior to seeing with one's eyes.

taller, younger, thinner, and there's not a woman in Florence who'd charge me to take her to bed. But where are the others?

🌿 SCENE IX 🌿

LIGURIO, MESSER NICIA, FRA TIMOTEO, and SIRO (all disguised)

LIGURIO: Good evening, sir!

MESSER NICIA: Oh my! Help! Oh!

LIGURIO: Don't be afraid, it's us.

MESSER NICIA: Oh! Are you all here? [*Suddenly belligerent*] Why, if I hadn't recognized you immediately, I would have run you through with this sword; it's hard and penetrates like nothing else I have! Are you Ligurio? And you Siro? And that other one, are you the doctor?

FRA TIMOTEO: [*Disguising his voice*] Yes, sir.

MESSER NICIA: Look at him! My, he's disguised well. I would never have recognized him! Not even the famous Hugo Here[45] would know him!

LIGURIO: I had him put two nuts in his mouth so that his voice wouldn't be recognized.

MESSER NICIA: What a dolt you are!

LIGURIO: Why?

MESSER NICIA: Why didn't you tell me this before? I would have put two in my mouth as well. You know how important it is not to be recognized!

LIGURIO: Here, take this and put it in your mouth.

MESSER NICIA: What is it?

LIGURIO: A ball of wax.

MESSER NICIA: Give it to me. [*He puts it in his mouth, then spits it out, gagging and coughing*] Echh! Ugh! Phew! Damn you, you half-assed rogue!

LIGURIO: Oh, forgive me! I gave you the wrong one by mistake.

MESSER NICIA: [*Gagging and coughing*] Phew, phew! Wha—, wha—, what *was* that?

LIGURIO: Bitter aloe.

MESSER NICIA: God damn you! Phew, phew. . . . Doctor, why don't you say something?

---

45. "Va-qua-tu" was the nickname of a famous jailer in fifteenth-century Florence who supposedly knew everyone in the city—the proverbial person who knows everyone. The nickname means literally "You go here," a jailer's greeting to arriving prisoners.

FRA TIMOTEO: [*Disguising his voice*] Ligurio has made me angry.

MESSER NICIA: Oh my, you disguise your voice so well.

LIGURIO: Let's not lose any more time here. I'll be the general and will order our ranks for the battle. On the right horn I will post Callimaco, I will be on the left, and between the two horns will be the lawyer. Siro, you take up the rear, to give assistance to those who are so inclined. The code word will be Saint Cuckoldeau.

MESSER NICIA: Who is Saint Cuckoldeau?

LIGURIO: He's the most honored saint in France. Let's go, we'll set our ambush here at this corner. . . . Listen! I hear a lute.

MESSER NICIA: Yes, that's what it is. What should we do?

LIGURIO: We need to send a scout on ahead to find out who it is, and we'll take action according to what he reports back.

MESSER NICIA: Who'll we send?

LIGURIO: You go, Siro. You know what you have to do. Check him out, look him over, and return immediately to report.

SIRO: I'm off.

MESSER NICIA: I don't want us to grab some old crab, all broken-down and sick; then we would have to replay this game tomorrow.

LIGURIO: Don't worry, Siro is reliable. Here he is back already. What did you find, Siro?

SIRO: He's the most perfect young lout you'll ever see! He's not more than twenty-five, and he's coming along alone in a cloak playing a lute.

MESSER NICIA: Things are falling into place, if you're telling the truth! But if you're wrong, watch out, for this will come home to roost with you.

SIRO: He's just like I said.

LIGURIO: Let's wait until he comes around the corner, and then we'll jump him.

MESSER NICIA: Pull back a bit, Doctor, you seem awfully hard and stiff this evening. Here he comes.

CALLIMACO: [*Singing*] Let the devil come to your bed, since I'm not allowed to come myself!

LIGURIO: Stop! Give me that lute!

CALLIMACO: Oh, help! What have I done?

MESSER NICIA: You'll see. Cover his head, gag him!

LIGURIO: Turn him around!

MESSER NICIA: Again! One more time! Take him inside!

FRA TIMOTEO: [*Disguising his voice*] Messer Nicia, I'm going to rest because I have a headache that's killing me. If you don't need me, I won't come back until morning.

MESSER NICIA: Fine, Doctor, there's no need to return. We can handle this ourselves. [*All but* FRA TIMOTEO *go into the house*]

❧ SCENE X ☙

FRA TIMOTEO (disguised), alone

FRA TIMOTEO: [*To the audience*] They've gone into the house, and I'm going to return to the monastery. And you spectators, don't worry: no one's going to sleep tonight, and so the acts of the play won't be interrupted.[46] I'll say my offices. Ligurio and Siro will eat, for they haven't eaten today. The lawyer will go from room to room, worrying whether his goose is really being cooked as it should be. Callimaco and Madonna Lucrezia won't sleep, because I know that if I were he and you were she, we wouldn't sleep either.

Song
O sweet night, O holy
Hours, dark and quiet,
Who accompany yearning lovers,
You carry with you such
Happiness wherever you rest
That all alone you make souls blessed.
You give worthy prizes
To bands of lovers
For their long trials;
You make, O happy hours,
Every cold heart burn with love!

---

46. Machiavelli is playfully claiming that he is not breaking the unity of time and action required by the classical rules of theater, which held that the events of a play must be continuous. In fact the night does interrupt the action, but the friar asks the audience to fill in the lost time with their imagination—a clever and risqué strategy worthy of Machiavelli.

Act V

🙦 SCENE I 🙤

FRA TIMOTEO, alone

FRA TIMOTEO: I didn't sleep a wink last night, I was so anxious to learn how things went for Callimaco and the others. I tried to pass the time with various chores: I said matins, I read a life of the Holy Fathers, I fixed a lamp in the church that was broken, I changed the veil on an image of Our Lady that works miracles. How many times have I asked those friars to keep her clean! And then people wonder why devotions have fallen off. I remember when there were five hundred ex votos here, and today we're lucky if there are twenty. It's our own fault, because we haven't been able to keep up Her holy reputation. Once we went in procession every evening after saying the offices, and we sang the lauds for her every Saturday. We ourselves regularly made pledges to her, so that people always saw new ex votos, and we encouraged men and women in confession to make new pledges to her. Now none of these things are done, and people wonder why religious enthusiasm has cooled. Oh, how foolish my brothers are! But I hear an uproar coming from the house of Messer Nicia. There they are. By my faith, they're bringing out their prisoner! I've arrived just in time. Clearly those youngsters drank their cup dry; they've kept at it till daybreak. I want to listen in on what everyone's saying without being seen.

🙦 SCENE II 🙤

MESSER NICIA, CALLIMACO, LIGURIO, and SIRO (all disguised)

MESSER NICIA: Grab him there, and I'll grab him here, and you, Siro, grab him from behind.

CALLIMACO: Don't hurt me!

LIGURIO: Don't worry. Get lost!

MESSER NICIA: Let's not go any further.

LIGURIO: You're right, let's turn him loose here. Spin him around a couple of times so that he doesn't know where he's come from. Spin him, Siro!

SIRO: Done!

MESSER NICIA: Turn him around one more time.

SIRO: Done again!

CALLIMACO: And my lute!

LIGURIO: Move on, you lout, get lost! And if I hear you talking about last night, I'll slit your throat!

MESSER NICIA: Look at him run! Let's go change. We should all be out early this morning so that it doesn't seem like we were up all night.

LIGURIO: You're right.

MESSER NICIA: Ligurio and Siro, go find Doctor Callimaco and let him know that everything went well.

LIGURIO: What can we tell him? We don't know anything. You know that after we brought him to your house, we took off to the wine cellar to drink. You and your mother-in-law stayed with him, and we haven't talked to you until just now, when you called us to throw him out.

MESSER NICIA: That's true. Oh, I have some fine things to tell you! My wife was in bed in the dark. Sostrata was waiting for me by the fire. I brought in that guy, and so that nothing remained in doubt, I took him into a little pantry that I have off that room where there was a small lamp that gives off just a little light, so he couldn't see my face.

LIGURIO: Very wise.

MESSER NICIA: I made him undress. He protested, but I turned on him like a dog, and he got undressed in a flash and stood there naked. He had an ugly face: a great grotesque nose, a misshapen mouth, but you've never seen more handsome flesh—white, soft, comely! And about the rest, don't ask.

LIGURIO: It's best not to speak of the rest. Why did you have to see everything?

MESSER NICIA: Are you joking? Since I'd stuck my hands in the stew, I wanted to get to the bottom of the pot. I wanted to see if he was healthy. If he had syphilis,[47] where would that have left me? It's easy for you to talk.

LIGURIO: You were right to check him out.

MESSER NICIA: When I saw that he was healthy, I dragged him along behind me, and in the dark I took him into the bedroom and put him to bed. And before I left, I decided I should feel to make sure everything was going as it should. I'm not the type of man who takes fireflies for lanterns!

LIGURIO: How wisely you managed everything!

47. Syphilis had appeared in Europe only recently, in the mid-1490s. Contemporaries debated whether it was a new disease or an ancient one that had reappeared, but much like AIDS today, it was seen as being sexually transmitted, and it had a major impact on the imagination of the period.

MESSER NICIA: After I had touched and felt everything, I left the room and locked the door. Then I returned to my mother-in-law by the fire, and we chatted and waited all night.

LIGURIO: What did you talk about?

MESSER NICIA: About Lucrezia's foolishness and how much better it would have been if she had agreed to everything at once, without all that nonsense. We also talked about the baby boy, whom I can practically already feel in my arms, the little brat! Finally I heard the bells strike seven, and worrying that dawn would come, I returned to the bedroom. And can you imagine it? I couldn't get the lout out of bed!

LIGURIO: [*Aside*] I can imagine!

MESSER NICIA: He really liked his sauce! Finally he got up, and I called you and we got rid of him.

LIGURIO: It went well.

MESSER NICIA: What do you think: should I feel bad?

LIGURIO: About what?

MESSER NICIA: About that poor boy, who has to die so soon. Last night is going to cost him dearly.

LIGURIO: Oh, don't give it a thought. Let him worry about it.

MESSER NICIA: You're right. But it seems like a thousand years before I will see Doctor Callimaco and get to celebrate with him.

LIGURIO: He'll be out within the hour. But it's already morning. We'll go change, and what will you do?

MESSER NICIA: I'll go home as well and put on my good clothes. Then I'll have my wife get up and get washed and take her to church so that she can be purified. I'd like you and Callimaco to be there so that we can thank the friar and reward him for his help.

LIGURIO: That sounds good. We'll do it. See you soon. [*All leave except for* FRA TIMOTEO]

❧ SCENE III ☙

FRA TIMOTEO, alone

FRA TIMOTEO: I overheard their conversation and enjoyed it all, especially the foolishness of this lawyer! The conclusion is what I enjoyed most of all, however. And since they're going to come looking for me at home, I mustn't wait here. I'll meet them at the church, where my wares bring more. But who's that coming out of that house? It looks like Ligurio, and that must be Callimaco with him. I don't want them to see me, for the same reasons. In the end if they don't come to find me, there'll always be time to go find them. [*He leaves*]

SCENE IV

CALLIMACO and LIGURIO

CALLIMACO: As I told you, my dear Ligurio, I was uncomfortable until about three in the morning, for even if it was very enjoyable, still it didn't seem right to me. But then I told her who I was and explained to her the love I felt for her and how easily, what with her husband's foolishness, we could continue to enjoy one another without any dishonor and promised her that when God took him to his just reward, I'd marry her.

After considering my arguments and the difference between making love with me and with Nicia, and the difference between the caresses of a young lover and an old husband, she said, after a few sighs, "Considering that your cleverness, the foolishness of my husband, the simplicity of my mother, and the corruptness of my confessor have led me down this path, which I would have never taken on my own, I feel that this was written in the stars and that I'm not capable of resisting what the heavens have ordered me to accept. However, I am taking you as my lord, master, and guide; you are my father, my defender, and I want you to be my every good. What my husband wanted for one night, I want him to have forever. You will become his close friend. So come this morning to the church, and from there come to dine with us. And you'll have the run of our house so that we can be together whenever we want without raising any suspicions."

When I heard these words I almost died at their sweetness. I couldn't begin to reply with all that I wanted to say. So I'm the happiest man who ever lived. And if this happiness isn't interrupted by death or time, I'll be the most blessed of the blessed, more a saint than any saint.

LIGURIO: I'm very pleased by all your good fortune. It went exactly as I said it would. But what should we do now?

CALLIMACO: Let's head for the church, because I promised to be there when she, her mother, and the lawyer arrive.

LIGURIO: I see his door opening. The women are coming out, and the lawyer is following behind.

CALLIMACO: Let's go into the church and wait for them there.

༚ SCENE V ༀ

MESSER NICIA, LUCREZIA, and SOSTRATA

MESSER NICIA: Lucrezia, I believe it would be better to do things with respect for God and not behave like a wild woman.

LUCREZIA: [*With irritation*] All right, what do you want me to do now?

MESSER NICIA: Look at how she replies: she thinks she's a rooster and not a hen this morning.

SOSTRATA: We shouldn't be surprised. She's rather worked up this morning.

LUCREZIA: What are you trying to say?

MESSER NICIA: I'm saying that it would be better if I went ahead to speak with the friar and tell him that he should meet you at the door of the church to purify you, because this morning you seem truly reborn.

LUCREZIA: Well, why don't you hurry yourself along, then?

MESSER NICIA: You sure are fiery this morning! Last night you seemed half dead.

LUCREZIA: That's thanks to you.

SOSTRATA: Go on and get the friar. But there's no need, he's already in front of the church.

MESSER NICIA: So he is.

༚ SCENE VI ༀ

FRA TIMOTEO, MESSER NICIA, LUCREZIA, CALLIMACO, LIGURIO, and SOSTRATA

FRA TIMOTEO: I have come out because Callimaco and Ligurio told me that the lawyer and the women were coming to church. Here they come now.

MESSER NICIA: *Bona dies,*[48] Father.

FRA TIMOTEO: Welcome, and good day to you all. Madam, may God grant you a handsome son.

LUCREZIA: God willing!

FRA TIMOTEO: And He wills it all.[49]

---

48. "Good morning."

49. Fra Timoteo seems to be invoking the laughing, intimate God of Boccaccio's *Decameron*, a God who supports young lovers in defiance of the formal restrictions placed on sex by society and the church.

MESSER NICIA: Is that Ligurio and Doctor Callimaco that I see in the church?

FRA TIMOTEO: Yes, sir.

MESSER NICIA: Call them.

FRA TIMOTEO: Gentlemen, come here!

CALLIMACO: God save you all!

MESSER NICIA: Doctor, give your hand to my wife.[50]

CALLIMACO: Willingly.

MESSER NICIA: Lucrezia, this man is the reason we will have a staff to support us in our old age.

LUCREZIA: I hold him in the highest regard, and I want him to be our close friend.

MESSER NICIA: Now you are truly blessed! I want him and Ligurio to come today and dine with us.

LUCREZIA: Absolutely.

MESSER NICIA: And I want to give them the key to the ground-floor room under the loggia so that they can return there whenever they wish, because without any women in their house, they've been living like beasts.

CALLIMACO: I accept, and I will make use of it whenever my need arises.

FRA TIMOTEO: I could use some money for charity.

MESSER NICIA: You can be sure, sir, that I will send it to you today.

LIGURIO: Is everyone forgetting Siro?

MESSER NICIA: He has only to ask; whatever I have is his. You, Lucrezia, how much money do you need to give the friar to be purified?

LUCREZIA: I don't remember.

MESSER NICIA: How much?

LUCREZIA: Give him ten grossi.[51]

MESSER NICIA: Oh, my heart!

FRA TIMOTEO: And you, Lady Sostrata, seem to be flourishing this morning.

---

50. There is a nice irony in Nicia's asking Callimaco to give his hand to his wife. Until the Council of Trent (1545–47, 1551–52, 1562–63), marriage required only the consent of both parties, and consent was often expressed merely by the couple giving each other their hands and expressing their consent. Adding to the irony, this was often done on the steps of the local church, as in this case. Of course, Lucrezia is already married, but Nicia is unwittingly underlining the fact that things have changed dramatically in their marriage. Renaissance comedies usually ended with a wedding, and this joining of hands might also be seen as Machiavelli's playful fulfillment of that norm.

51. Although not a large amount of money, it is clear from Messer Nicia's response that for a stingy man like him it appeared to be a large sum for the service.

SOSTRATA: Who wouldn't be happy?

FRA TIMOTEO: All of you go into the church so that we may say the regular prayers. Then, after I've said the office, you may go home for dinner. [*To the audience*] You, spectators, don't wait for us to leave: the office takes time, and I'll stay in the church while they leave by the side door and return home. Enjoy yourselves!

꧁ ꧂

Il marescalco

(The Master of the Horse) [1]

By Pietro Aretino (1492–1556)

CHARACTERS:

A STREET-HAWKER[2]

GIANNICCO: a boy servant

The MARESCALCO: the Master of the Horse[3]

MESSER JACOPO

AMBROGIO

The BALIA: the MARESCALCO's wetnurse

The PEDANT

The KNIGHT'S PAGE

The DUKE'S FOOTMAN

The COUNT

The KNIGHT

The JEW

The JEWELER

MESSER JACOPO'S SON

An OLD WOMAN

---

1. Begun in 1527 while Aretino was in Mantua, this comedy was clearly revised after he moved to Venice in that year and was first published in 1533.

2. *Istrione.*

3. Often misleadingly translated as Stablemaster, this term denotes an official responsible for the horses of his lord—an important office in a culture in which horses were such a crucial aspect of noble life. It might be translated as Marshall, though we prefer to avoid the modern associations of that term.

CARLO: the bride
A MATRON
A GENTLEWOMAN
MESSER PHEBUS
The COUNT'S MAIDSERVANT
The COUNT'S SERVANT

Prologue

[*Recited by the* STREET-HAWKER]

If it were not for the fact that I respect those noble manners that made you all come here to ornament and honor this place with your divine presence, just as the great Ippolito de'Medici[4] ornaments and honors the world with his divine magnificence, in the name of God, by this holy cross, I would now, ahem, at this very moment, ah . . . quite shortly, ahhhh . . . soon hide myself in a . . . ahem, so that my companions wouldn't find me present this evening at this their comedy to honor the great Cardinal Giovanni of Lorraine.[5] My reason for this is that those boneheads have given the responsibility for the "Prologue" and "Explanation of the Plot" to a butthead, an ox, a snotnose who doesn't have anywhere near enough brains to come before you here and tell you about how the magnanimous Duke of Mantua, an example of kindness and liberality in our most sad century, having in his service a certain Marescalco—who was as enthusiastic about women as a moneylender is enthusiastic about spending money—organized a practical joke on him, whereby this Marescalco would have to take a wife along with a dowry of four thousand scudi. So, dragging him to the home of the most well-mannered Count Nicola, a place of superior men[6] and a haven for the accomplished and polite, this Marescalco was forced to marry a boy dressed as a girl. When he discovered the trick, the valiant man was happier in finding that his bride was male than he'd formerly been sad in thinking her female. Now, if it isn't a mortal sin not to punish with a wife such a venerable

---

4. Ippolito de'Medici (1511–35) received the cardinal's hat at age eighteen and quickly became a major figure in Roman and Florentine political life—exactly the type of rising star Aretino would have wanted to curry favor with. He died young, either of malaria or of poison administered by those who feared his rapid rise to power.

5. D. 1550.

6. *Virtù.*

faggot who wasn't at all worried about being such a brute,[7] and even less worried about telling you about it to your face,[8] please speak up. Actually, the male witches, oops, I mean the male actors,[9] who gave me this responsibility deserve to be punished in the same way. For you should know, my lords, that it wasn't by chance that I who in a swindle can play every role should all by myself be showing you everything that my companions will present to you this evening. And you can judge on your own, after you've heard me and them, who most merits your praise.

If I had to give you the plot (or the serving up of the story,[10] as Petrarch calls it), there's not a single apothecary or hospital that I wouldn't make seem incompetent by comparison. I'd come before you wearing a toga and a crown of laurel[11] (if it weren't for the fact that all the laurel leaves are hanging on the heads of graduates in cheap bars and thus not available), and I'd show off my gravity, pacing around and then stopping to fix you with a learned gaze, and I'd say, "Spectators, Lightness loves Evermore, and by means of Cleverness attracts to himself here and there Need, in such a way that the sweet ears of summer enjoy the love of Desire, giving succor to Often, who on the fresh sweet grass to the music of liquid crystals sang of the golden, pearly, and crimson coloring of she who slew him."[12]

If I were a procuress (speaking with all respect), I'd dress myself as a mendicant friar, without shoes or a belt, mumbling Our Fathers and inserting Hail Marys, and after I had smelled the backsides of all the churches I'd make sure the master of the house wasn't home, and then coming up to the door of the

---

7. A reference to the fact that the Marescalco is a sodomite. The use of the term "faggot" just before is an attempt to capture the sense of the pejorative *castrone* (literally, a castrated animal).

8. In the critical edition of Giorgio Petrocchi this phrase reads exactly the opposite: "who is afraid to tell you to your face." But the structure of the sentence and the personality of the Marescalco (who throughout the play aggressively defends his sexual preferences) suggest that a *"non"* has been omitted, or at least that this last phrase was meant to be read ironically, because throughout the comedy the Marescalco is an aggressive defender of his sexual preference for young males and his desire not to marry. And, crucially, he is not the least bit shy about voicing these opinions in front of the audience.

9. A suggestive confusion of *stregone* (male witches) and *istrione* (male actors).

10. *Serviziale* has the double meaning of serving up a story and giving an enema.

11. *Laureato* originally meant to be crowned with laurel leaves, like ancient Roman poets laureate, but by the Renaissance the term had also been associated with the actual or metaphorical crowning of university students upon graduation, who were thus also known as laureates.

12. Aretino is making fun of medieval allegorical romances, in which characters like Desire, Need, and Cleverness abounded.

mistress of the house, I would knock very quietly. Once in, before getting down to business, I'd tell her of all my trials, my fasts, and my prayers. Then, with many pleasing little tales, I'd compliment all her beauties, since there's not a woman who doesn't enjoy hearing praise for her beautiful eyes, her pretty hands, her sweet airs. And then, complimenting her smile, her speech, the redness of her lips, the brightness of her teeth, and pulling out an exclamation, I'd gush, "O Madonna, the whole of Italy would be unworthy to pluck a single hair from your eyelashes." And as soon as I'd won her with my weapons of praise, sighing I'd say, "Your graces have put in a bad way the most cultivated, the most handsome, the richest young man of this city." Then, at the right moment, I would place a little letter in her hand. And if perchance her husband were to discover me, I would have plenty of excuses ready, certainly better ones than that I had brought wool to spin or had come to gather eggs.

If I were Little Miss Prissy,[13] eating cherries in two bites and that third male leg in one bite, the minute that same procuress gave me that letter, I'd look at her first this way and then like this, and calling her a whoremonger I'd say as I was gouging her eyes out with my fingers, "I? I?! Do I strike you as being a woman of that sort, eh? You bewitcher of mists, you drinker of babies, you charlatan!"[14] Then I'd rip up the letter and throw her down the stairs. But the minute she was gone I'd collect the pieces and put it back together. Once I had seen what it said, I'd do whatever seemed best. If the offer seemed intriguing, bypassing the procuress who had brought it I'd signal my lover from the balcony myself, smiling like this, and curtsying to him like so, and moving my head like this, with my lips held like this and tightened a little. Then I'd open my lips with certain artful sighs from the heart, and having my tears and laughter all in place I'd outdo even the best of whores. Then I'd make him so jealous that he'd be more eager to bring me presents than to win my love. And there isn't a trickier lawyer in the whole world, better at covering up a scandal, than I'd be in conning my husband if he should catch me with my lover in the house.

Then how well I could play the role of one madly in love with such a lady! Why, there isn't a Spaniard or a Neapolitan who would beat me for deep sighs, torrents of tears, and mannerly words! Elegantly dressed, I'd promenade around the square followed by a page dressed in the colors given me by my goddess,

13. *Madonna schifa il poco:* a reference to the character in Boccaccio's *Decameron* who found everything too crude for her delicate tastes.
14. *Caccia diavoli:* an exorcist—literally, one who kicks out devils—here apparently having the sense of someone who falsely offers such services, a charlatan. Witches were often accused of drinking the blood of babies.

flashing my shoes of velvet and showing my feathers with every step. And in a low voice, walking below the walls of her house, I'd sing over and over again, "Every place saddens me where I do not see my love."[15]

I would have madrigals composed in her honor and have Tromboncino[16] write songs about her. On my hat I'd wear a medal composed of a fishhook, a dolphin, and a heart, signifying that I'm hooked with a pure heart to the end.[17]

What fool who fears that his wife will be carried off by every fly and mosquito would be able to play the jealous husband better than I? Why, I'd even lock up the toilet so that the lovers couldn't get in, all sweet smelling, to make a cornucopia of me.[18] I wouldn't be drawn into going to dances, parties, comedies, or weddings, nor would I accept the invitations of friends or relatives, because dances, parties, comedies, and weddings were created by the god Cupid so that lovers could arrange times and places for their little you-know-whats.

God could tell you how I'd play the part of a miser, a perfect pennypincher and tightwad. By myself and with my own hand I'd water the wine and weigh the bread and measure out the soup, and no one would be able to wrest a penny from my hands, not even with hooks. And I'd spend two hours arguing down the price of a few pounds of meat, which I'd then slice thin enough to serve ten people, and I'd have five or six meetings with myself before I'd pay the salary of my servant.

And if you'd allow me, real man that I am, I'd imitate the he-man warrior-hero of literature.[19] I'd tilt my hat like this, hang my sword at my side at this fearsome angle, and letting my socks fall down a bit I'd stride out as if I were moving to the sound of the drums of war—like this—and with a fierce glare I'd look every passerby threateningly in the eye, stroking my beard with one hand. Unhappy would be the stone that touched my foot, and the first person who

---

15. A verse from Petrarch's *Canzoniere*, xxxvii, 33, here used to caricature the Petrarchan conceits of love poetry.

16. Bartolomeo Tromboncino was a musician from Verona who worked at the court of Mantua, where this play is set. He wrote several songs based on Petrarch's sonnets, including one that used the lines just quoted.

17. The wordplay turns on the meanings of *amo*, which as a noun means "fishhook" but as a verb means "I love," and *delfino*, "dolphin," which when divided into two words as *del fino* means "to the end" when modifying "I'm hooked" (to render the double meaning of *amo*) or "pure" when modifying "heart." The wordplay imitates the poetic language of love and at the same time renders it ridiculous.

18. A play on the fact that a cornucopia is a horn (literally, a richness of horns) and that men who were cuckolded were said to wear horns. It may be significant as well that the cornucopia was filled with food and fruit that others feasted upon.

19. The *miles gloriosus*, or braggart soldier, was a stock character of ancient Roman comedy.

crossed my path I would cut in two and hang back to front and send the result on the road as a marvel. O unforgiving Mother of Grace, O dear God, O paradise of the Stradiot warriors,[20] tear me away from this mirror, for my reflection frightens me! Am I a scary sight, or what?

Now we come to the parasite. Oh, I would be so polite! However many silly boasts my master made, I would agree to everything. If he asked me, "Am I handsome?" I'd reply, "Extremely handsome." And if he asked, "Am I courageous?" I'd reply, "Extremely courageous." "Am I generous?" "Extremely generous." "Don't I have ten Arabian stallions in my stall?" "Of course." "Don't I have expensive clothes brocaded with gold and silver?" "Yes." "Don't I have a hundred thousand ducats at home?" "Exactly." "Don't all the beautiful women love me?" "All of them." "Don't I enjoy the love of a noblewoman?" "Yes, sir." "The king loves me, right?" "He adores you." "And didn't the emperor give me a thousand foot soldiers?" "Sure." "Don't I sing well?" "Singingly." "How well do I play?" "Like Messer Marco da la Aquila."[21] "How's my tumbling?" "Miraculous." "My jumping?" "Phenomenal." "My fencing?" "Flourishing." "My running?" "Extraordinary." In sum, I'd confirm all his boasts so that I'd make my living robbing the life from his soul as well as his money from his hands and his shirt off his back. And constantly feeding his vanity, in eight days I'd become his brother.

I'd make an excellent tough old trooper. I'd say, "In my time the duke Borso d'Este held a joust with real men at arms, who wore full battle armor." "In my time the Bentivoglio family at a wedding had a test of arms, the quintana,[22] where I broke with just six blows a heavy vessel filled with birds and pictures." "In my time I danced at the party of the famous condottiere with the bad name[23] with a woman whose hand I held with a handkerchief because in those days it was bad manners to touch the bare hand of a woman when dancing.

---

20. Stradiot warriors were Venetian mercenaries from the Balkans notorious for their brutality. That the invocations are so mismatched adds to the humor of the passage.

21. A famous lutist and composer.

22. The *inguintana* or *quintana* was a medieval tournament competition involving a target mounted on a swinging arm that was counterweighted by a massive weight. Knights would try to hit the target with their lances without being knocked off their horses by the weight, which would swing around at them when they hit the target. Borso d'Este (1413–71) was duke of Ferrara and a condottiere (professional soldier) noted for his peaceful rule of his city. The Bentivoglio were an old Bolognese family famous as condottieri and tyrants of Bologna, most notably Giovanni II Bentivoglio (1443–1508).

23. Perhaps a reference to Bartolomeo Colleoni, whose last name suggests testicles (*coglioni*) and who was often referred to in comic literature in passages playing on that double meaning.

Nowadays, when dancing, men hold a woman's hand under their cloaks using a thousand little tricks, and it's all very dishonest and lascivious." Enough said!

I must confess, however, that I'd be hard pressed to act like a lord.[24] For if I were a lord (may God protect me from such a fate), I'd never be able to ignore the faithfulness of a follower, the help of a friend, or the ties of flesh and blood like they do. Nor would I be able, even with all my muttonheadedness, to match their—I hate to say it—ignorance. But here comes Giannicco. Oh, what a clever little crook! Oh, what a great wanton! Listen to what he has to say, for I must say goodbye to Your Lordships.

Act I

SCENE I

GIANNICCO, and the MARESCALCO

GIANNICCO: [*Singing*]

My master takes a wife,
My master takes a wife in this city,
In this city.
He will take her, he will not,
He will have her, and he will not, this evening,
This evening.

MARESCALCO: [*With his back to* GIANNICCO] Where the devil is that little pain in the butt? Why is it[25] that I can never find him when I want him?

GIANNICCO: [*Still singing*] She makes me ache between my legs.

MARESCALCO: [*Turning and seeing* GIANNICCO] So where have you been?

GIANNICCO: I didn't hear you, Master. Good luck to you!

MARESCALCO: What's this good luck bit?

GIANNICCO: Haven't you heard?

MARESCALCO: What do you mean, haven't I heard?

24. *Signore*, here denoting a local lord or ruler of a city. In Renaissance Italy most cities were ruled by a *signore*, and a number of them had important courts that set the standards for court society in Italy and beyond. The term can also be used like "sir" as a term of respect for those who are not actually rulers. At times Aretino also plays with the fact that term can refer to God as well, just as it does in English (Our Lord, the Lord).

25. Literally, "how can nature allow that." Here "nature" is used in that Renaissance sense of "that which exists" and as a result is correct and what should be.

GIANNICCO: I mean haven't you heard about the wife that the Lord is going to give you?

MARESCALCO: [*Laughing*] Courtier's jokes!

GIANNICCO: Time will tell.

MARESCALCO: Who told you this garbage?

GIANNICCO: Gentlemen, pages, staff, falconers, doormen, the tablecloth.

MARESCALCO: Court tales.

GIANNICCO: Words.

MARESCALCO: Oh, shut up!

GIANNICCO: Well, I'm excited.

MARESCALCO: Why?

GIANNICCO: Why, because of this news, of course.

MARESCALCO: You're crazy.

GIANNICCO: In God's name, Master, everyone's talking about what you'll do and say.

MARESCALCO: Will you shut up?

GIANNICCO: As you wish, Your Lordship.

MARESCALCO: Look who's here. [*To* MESSER JACOPO, *who enters*] What's up, Messer Jacopo?

⁊ SCENE II ℰ

MESSER JACOPO, the MARESCALCO, and GIANNICCO

JACOPO: I always find you here with your young sweetheart.[26]

MARESCALCO: May God punish him.

GIANNICCO: *A vobis.*[27]

MARESCALCO: [*Angrily*] What did you say?

GIANNICCO: That you're wrong.

JACOPO: [*Laughing*] Well, this is a comedy!

MARESCALCO: You'd better talk about something besides wives, otherwise . . .

GIANNICCO: What do you want me to talk about? Husbands? And if the whole world is saying that the Lord is going to give you a wife, why can't I say it, too?

MARESCALCO: Right, right.

26. *Pivo:* in the extensive jargon of illicit sex, a common term for a young male lover, passive partner to an older male; literally, "flute."

27. "You, instead." The first of much Latin (and pseudo-Latin) in this play.

JACOPO: Surely what Giannicco is telling you could hardly be news to you. I came to congratulate you, because I understand that in addition to being beautiful, well mannered, and well born, she'll bring you a dowry of four thousand scudi.[28]

MARESCALCO: It would be extremely bizarre if I had to take a wife this evening without ever having heard anything about it.

JACOPO: Good lords, like ours, do good things for us before we even think to wish for them. And ours does this so that those who serve him may be secure in the knowledge that they'll be rewarded for their services even when they least expect it.

MARESCALCO: Our Lord has the best reign of any lord alive, God save him. But whatever happens, he won't nail me with this wife.

GIANNICCO: Take her, take her, sweet Master.

MARESCALCO: I'll take her, all right—to throw her down a well!

JACOPO: Down a well, huh?

MARESCALCO: You heard me, down a well.

JACOPO: Why, even the greatest of our courtiers would feel blessed to have her.

MARESCALCO: Goodbye.

JACOPO: Wait just a moment.

MARESCALCO: Leave me alone, for God's sake.

JACOPO: Hear me out, please.

GIANNICCO: Listen to him, dear Master.

MARESCALCO: The pole horse has a bad foot, and I have to go. Don't be a pain in the ass, for heaven's sake.

JACOPO: Go ahead, play the fool as usual.

MARESCALCO: I too am a courtier.[29]

JACOPO: Don't say later on that I didn't warn you.

MARESCALCO: Come along, Giannicco.

GIANNICCO: I'm coming. [*To* JACOPO] He'll definitely take her, sir. [*He and the* MARESCALCO *leave*]

JACOPO: He will if he wants to keep breathing. My, my, what an old lady! I

---

28. A scudo was a coin used widely in sixteenth-century Italy, of varying value depending on who coined it and the amount of gold or silver it contained. While its value fluctuated, a scudo was always a major coin, and four thousand scudi would have been a large fortune, at the high end of what an upper-class man could hope for in a dowry.

29. The Marescalco is claiming his right to be treated with respect because he is a courtier. People of lower rank such as a mere stablemaster could be (and were) treated by their superiors in a much more high-handed way.

have the feeling that this business is going to get him in trouble. [AMBROGIO *enters*] But Ambrogio, where are you going?

ᴥ SCENE III ᴥ

AMBROGIO and MESSER JACOPO

AMBROGIO: Actually, it's quite remarkable how you're always talking to yourself—always mumbling that your servant's a thief or a drunk, or that he gets up at vespers, or that he licks the plates or gambles or fools around with women, or that he's always telling lies or can't carry a message, or that you send a birdbrain when you send him on an errand, or that he's so lazy he even sleeps when riding a horse. So now what are you complaining about?

JACOPO: I was very upset and muttering to myself about how the Marescalco doesn't want the very beautiful and rich wife the Duke has decided to give him.

AMBROGIO: Is that possible?

JACOPO: I'm afraid so. And if it weren't for me he'd have crucified his boy just a moment ago.

AMBROGIO: What for?

JACOPO: Simply for telling him that people are saying that he'll get a wife this evening.

AMBROGIO: [*Laughing*] That's really rich!

JACOPO: Another man with such luck would be thanking God, and he's damning Him.

AMBROGIO: Lords are always doing favors for those who don't deserve them or don't appreciate them.

JACOPO: Lords do other things that are more cruel, as well.

AMBROGIO: We should go and see how he looks when he has to face getting married.

JACOPO: Are you suggesting that he won't submit to the wedding like a good philosopher?

AMBROGIO: [*Laughing*] You got it! Where will the wedding be held?

JACOPO: At the Count's house.

AMBROGIO: Great. If you want to go, let's meet later at that market of philosophy, the barbershop.[30]

---

30. The barbershop was a male hangout where news and gossip were exchanged; see act III, scene ix.

JACOPO: Well said. Goodbye.

AMBROGIO: Goodbye.

❧ SCENE IV ❧

The BALIA[31] and GIANNICCO

BALIA: Where, where are you going, so lost in thought? What's up?

GIANNICCO: [*Mumbling irately*] God da— . . . by the whor—. . .

BALIA: I can't make out what you're saying. How's my nursling?[32]

GIANNICCO: Ask the fires of hell.

BALIA: That's a fine way to talk!

GIANNICCO: I don't want to stay with him anymore, and if I leave . . . if I leave . . .[33]

BALIA: He treats you better than you deserve, you little rascal.

GIANNICCO: I'm not kidding—he wanted to cut me up into little pieces.

BALIA: My God, in little pieces! But why?

GIANNICCO: Because I told him that all of Mantua is full of the news that the Lord is going to give him a wife.

BALIA: [*Excitedly*] What's this?

GIANNICCO: I swear on the Gospels. And he was swearing like a traitor that he doesn't want her. But he'll take her even if it kills him.

BALIA: [*Fervently to herself, as if in prayer*] O blessed Saint Nafissa,[34] put your

---

31. A *balia* was the woman who breast-fed and brought up a child—a wetnurse. Wetnurses are regular characters in Renaissance comedies, often playing the affectionate, protective role that in other cultures is usually associated with a child's mother (indeed, in the next scene the Balia refers to the Marescalco as "my little son"). That mothers seldom appeared in such a role in Renaissance comedies is suggestive. Compare the Balia in Aretino's comedy with the mother in Machiavelli's *La mandragola*, for example. In *La calandra*, Bibbiena used the more formal term *nutrice*, which we translated there as "wetnurse." Here we have used the Italian term, in part because this character lacks any other name in the comedy, but also because it seems to have a more affectionate connotation than "wetnurse."

32. I.e., the Marescalco.

33. Throughout this scene Giannicco is threatening to leave the Marescalco and, it is implied, perhaps turn him in to the authorities as a sodomite as well. Given that the younger passive partners in such relationships were seldom punished severely and often not punished at all if they turned in their older partners, this threat was a dangerous one for the Marescalco.

34. Jokingly known in the Renaissance as the patron saint of prostitutes and sexual intercourse. In his *Dialogues* Aretino describes a convent with a sexually explicit mural depicting the "miracles" of this saint, who gave her services to much of the male population of Rome.

hands before you, *et in mulieribus . . . nomen tuum . . . vita dulcedo . . . panem nostrum . . . beneditta tu . . .* if he takes a wife . . . *ad te suspiramus . . .* I will become a holy woman . . . *et homo fattus est.*[35] [*To* GIANNICCO] Tell me, Giannicco, child, are you pulling my leg?

GIANNICCO: Shit![36] If I don't tell—

BALIA: [*Interrupting*] Don't swear like that. I believe you. [*To herself again, fervently*] *Sub Pontio Pilato, vivos et mortuos*[37] . . . my prayers, my fasts will be answered. I'll make a vow to the Madonna of the Friars to not use oil or salt on cabbage the Fridays of March and to fast on bread and water the four yearly periods of fasting . . . *lagrimarum valle . . . a malo.*[38] Amen. Yes, yes, if he takes a wife, she'll be the meal ticket of my old age.

GIANNICCO: Do you want anything else? [*Preparing to leave*]

BALIA: Where are you going? Wait here and leave everything to me.

GIANNICCO: I don't want to stay with him anymore.

BALIA: Wait for me here, I said.

GIANNICCO: I'll wait, but if he— . . . enough, enough. I know what's up, so get going. [*The* BALIA *leaves*]

SCENE V

The BALIA, alone

BALIA: Get going yourself and go ahead and make fun of dreams. But in the end, dreams are not what people think—they're not to be laughed at. Well, I don't need to go to my confessor now, instead I want to find my little son. I'll surely find him in the stalls because there's always some horse that's sick. [*The* MARESCALCO *enters*] But here he is now. As my dear departed husband used to say, "Who needs brains when they have a bit of God-given luck?"

---

35. On the face of it these Latin phrases ("and in wifedom . . . your name . . . sweet life . . . our bread . . . blessed art thou . . . we ask of you . . . and he made man") suggest that the Balia is running through her prayers. But there may be a deeper joke here, for the phrases also echo the prayers used in love magic; thus we have not jumped to the conclusion that they are parts of specific Christian prayers. As magical prayers were often a pastiche of common prayers, many elements would be similar. The crucial difference was that magical prayers forced the saints, the Virgin Mary, and God to help with problems, whereas regular prayers asked for their aid and grace.

36. He actually says *potta* (cunt), but the English connotations of that term are too strong for the context.

37. "Under Pontius Pilate, the living and the dead."

38. "Tearful valley . . . from evil."

☜ SCENE VI ☞

The MARESCALCO and the BALIA

MARESCALCO: Where are you going at this hour?

BALIA: I was going to my confessor for something important.

MARESCALCO: Can you tell me what was so important?

BALIA: I might tell you, and I might not.

MARESCALCO: Stop beating around the bush and tell me.

BALIA: I was going to have him explain a dream to me, but since I've figured it out just now, I've come to you without going to him.

MARESCALCO: So let's hear this dream.

BALIA: It seemed to me that last night near dawn I was in the garden sitting at the foot of the fig tree, and while I was listening to a little bird that was improvising a song, along came a bestial man who found the singing of the little bird annoying. He threw stones at it. But the little bird kept singing, and he kept throwing stones. And while that bird sang and he threw, I argued with the man and he argued with me. But in the end the little bird was allowed to stay on the fig. Have you understood my dream?

MARESCALCO: Sure. But the real issue is to understand how you've understood it.

BALIA: The little bird that was singing is your boy, Giannicco, who was sweetly describing your wife to you. The bestial man is you. You were threatening him because he spoke about her. And I am myself; seated beneath the fig I would do and say anything to see you take this wife, who will be so good for you.

MARESCALCO: It's plain to see that the world is enjoying my suffering. Listen to how my own Balia laughs at my expense! Oh well, as long as my lord enjoys having this joke at my expense, I'll be patient. For I hold him dear, and after all, when a master jokes with his man, it's a sign of affection.

BALIA: [*Angrily*] Come, come now, wake up and throw off your blasphemy and sinful ways.

MARESCALCO: What do you mean, blasphemy and sinful ways?

BALIA: You know what I'm talking about.

MARESCALCO: What, have I crucified Christ?

BALIA: No, but ...

MARESCALCO: What do you mean, "No, but"?

BALIA: I mean ...

MARESCALCO: Well, what?

BALIA: Well, that you've done worse than that.

MARESCALCO: What?

BALIA: You know very well what. Now it's time to follow my advice: take a wife, my son, and establish some honor for yourself. Stop running after youthful pleasures[39] and begin your family and household, because now you're on your own, as you know. The Lord will give you a noble title, and you'll be called Sir So and So from Such and Such.

MARESCALCO: Dear God, dear God, what torments I suffer!

BALIA: Poor little one, poor bad one, poor sweet one, do you know what it means to take a wife?

MARESCALCO: Not only do I not know, I don't want to know!

BALIA: It's paradise, simply heaven, to take a wife.

MARESCALCO: Sure, if hell were heaven.

BALIA: Please, listen to me, and with your whole body and soul.

MARESCALCO: All right, you've got my attention; tell me.

BALIA: Listen, then. Having a wife is like being in heaven. You return home, and your good wife comes to greet you at the top of the stairs. Laughing and with a loving heart, she gives you a welcome that touches your very soul. She helps you off with your jacket and then, full of joy, she turns to you, and noting that you're all sweaty and tired, she dries you off with some towels so white and so delicate that they soak up your cares. Then she puts the wine to cool and sets the table and fans you for a bit. And then she has you pee.

MARESCALCO: Ha, ha!

BALIA: What are you laughing about, silly boy? Once you've peed, she sits you down to dinner, and she excites your appetite with certain little sauces and little dishes that would rouse the dead. And while you eat, she never stops bringing you, with her sweetest little ways, now this plate and now that one, and she offers you every tasty mouthful, saying, "Taste this, taste that, try a bit of this, for my love, or if you love me taste this." With such words, all honeyed and sugarcoated, she'll send you not just to paradise, but several thousand miles at least above it.

MARESCALCO: What does this wife do after dinner?

BALIA: After the husband has shoveled down his food, she calls him to bed.

39. Literally, "give up your youthful ways" *(lascia andare le gioventudini)*, which in the context refers to the Marescalco's sexual relations with young men, as does her reference to "blasphemy and sinful ways." As the Balia notes, the time for such youthful pleasures is past, he needs to take on the correct sexual and gender roles of an adult male, by getting married and starting a family.

But before she puts him in, she washes his feet carefully with water boiled with laurel, sage, and rosemary, and after she has cut his toenails and scrubbed his feet well, she dries them carefully and helps him into bed. Once she has cleaned up the table and the bedroom and said her prayers, she climbs in next to him, all content. Then embracing her sweet mate and kissing him all over, she says to him, "My heart, my soul, dear hope, dear life blood, sweet son, handsome father, am I your little girl? Your joy, your daughter?" When a man is treated like that, isn't he in paradise?

MARESCALCO: It doesn't seem so to me. But what's the point of all those kisses?

BALIA: They serve to sweetly plant the seed of little babies in a holy way. Then when morning comes the thoughtful wife brings you fresh eggs and your white shirt, and while she helps you dress, mixing some kisses with sweet little words, she makes so many sweet little sounds that you find in her the peace that the angels find in paradise.

MARESCALCO: Have you finished yet?

BALIA: Finished? Why, I've hardly begun. Imagine it's wintertime, and the husband returns home dog tired and all limp, covered with snow and frozen. The valiant wife changes your clothes and revives you in an instant before a warm fire. And as soon as you are warmed, the dinner is ready, and with fresh dainty soups and unusual tasty dishes you are totally reinvigorated. And if you should have some worries, as often happens, she asks humbly, "What's wrong? What are you thinking? Don't let it bother you. God will help you. God will provide." And she'll say all this in such a way that all your worries will turn to happiness. Then there come the little babies, little pets, little playthings. Oh, God, what content, what sweetness a father feels when his little boy touches his face and his breast with those tender little hands, saying, "Papa, my Papa, oh, Papa." And I've seen harder men than you wilt at the sound of that "Papa." Oh, when will I see you in that state?

MARESCALCO: On the feast day of Saint Con-man, which falls three days after the Last Judgment.

BALIA: Well, have you understood me, at least?

MARESCALCO: Let's say I've overunderstood you. But you should talk with one of those poor dogs who must suffer with a real wife who seems to be possessed by every demon that exists, suffering her at the table, in bed, in the morning, in the evening, outside and inside. Such a man is truly tortured by her high-handed ways, her hardheadedness, her lack of understanding. Why, I've heard it said that the French disease,[40] with all its little delights—awful swellings, horrible boils, and terrible pains like those of its dear sister, the gout—is nothing compared with the pain of having a wife.

BALIA: May God punish the man who filled you up with such trash!

MARESCALCO: Well, the man who has a wife is a martyr.

BALIA: [*Ignoring the* MARESCALCO] May he be killed!

MARESCALCO: Look, a male servant is good enough to do all those things that you have taken so long to describe. And whenever you get tired of him, you can send him off to the whorehouse—something you can't do with a wife.

BALIA: Clearly you don't deserve anything better than those filthy tablecloths and sheets washed in cold water with no soap that they use in your dirty courts, you delinquents. [GIANNICCO *enters*] But here's your boy now. He'll support me.

☙ SCENE VII ❧

GIANNICCO, the MARESCALCO, and the BALIA

GIANNICCO: Go on, throw me out! I never would've thought you'd want to kill me just because I told you about this wife thing.

MARESCALCO: Still howling? Still howling?

GIANNICCO: Well, is it so awful to say that you're going to take a wife? Must I be in the doghouse for that?

MARESCALCO: I don't like hearing you say it.

GIANNICCO: But if you are to have a wife, why can't I say it like everyone else?

BALIA: He's right.

MARESCALCO: He's full of shit!

GIANNICCO: For just a few words asking about a wife.

MARESCALCO: By the blood of Chr—

GIANNICCO: [*Interrupting*] There's no need to take God's name in vain over a wife.

MARESCALCO: By God, I'm going to let you have it!

BALIA: Calm down, you big dolt.

GIANNICCO: I don't deserve a beating for just mentioning your wife.

MARESCALCO: In the name of the Whore!

BALIA: Calm down.

---

40. *Mal francioso:* syphilis, a disease that had recently burst upon the European scene. It seems to have made its first appearance in Italy in 1494, when the French invaded; hence the popular name.

GIANNICCO: If the Lord wants to give you a wife, what fault is it of mine?

MARESCALCO: I'm going to do something I'll regret!

GIANNICCO: The Duke is responsible for you getting a wife, not Giannicco.

MARESCALCO: I'm going to lose it in a moment!

BALIA: Punish him when he deserves it.

GIANNICCO: The Lord is the reason that you're getting a wife, not me.

BALIA: That's clear as day.

GIANNICCO: His Excellency, and not your boy, is giving you a wife.

MARESCALCO: I'll give you something!

GIANNICCO: Go ahead, what are you going to give me?

BALIA: You deserve every punishment there is. Don't be so sure of yourself. Now get in the house right now!

GIANNICCO: Nyah, nyah!

BALIA: Get in the house, you beastly boy!

MARESCALCO: Go on, now. Get in the house.

GIANNICCO: I'm going, dear Master, saintly Master, good Master.

MARESCALCO: You too, Balia.

BALIA: [*On the verge of tears*] As you wish. Oh, oh, oh!

❧ SCENE VIII ❧

The MARESCALCO, alone

MARESCALCO: How much better off I'd have been if I'd worked on my own. But I was led astray by the sweet smell of the court. On my own I could have had a good time with what I would have made. But instead I decided to give that up and live miserably. And people did warn me that in these damn courts there was only envy and backstabbing, and the devil take the hindmost. Now, by God, I'm in a real fix. I must admit that His Excellency spoke to me about this a month ago, but I thought he was just kidding me. Now he's all too serious. What cruelty!

❦ SCENE IX ❧

The PEDANT and the MARESCALCO

PEDANT: *Bona dies. Quid agitis, magister mi?*[41]

MARESCALCO: Ah, pardon me, Professor. I'm very upset and didn't see you.

PEDANT: *Sis letus.*[42]

MARESCALCO: Speak Italian; I have things on my mind other than your astrological jargon.

PEDANT: *Bene vivere et laetari:*[43] I bring you good news, really good, really very good.

MARESCALCO: What news for me could possibly be good?

PEDANT: His Excellency, His Most Illustrious Lordship, loves you and thusly this very evening, gathering you to the matrimonial yoke, he will join you to such a well set-up *puella*[44] that *totum orbem*[45] will envy you.

MARESCALCO: Are you serious, or are you just trying to make me lose my temper?

PEDANT: *Per Deum verum.*[46] Our Lord will certainly give her to you.

MARESCALCO: There's no way I'll ever go that route.

PEDANT: Ah, my friend, harken unto the words of the Holy Gospels.

MARESCALCO: [*Angrily*] What do you want me to do with them?

PEDANT: Don't get all worked up.

MARESCALCO: Are the Gospels against taking wives?

PEDANT: Against? *Imo*[47] the opposite, and you should listen to their words. The verses of the Evangelist proclaim *idest:*[48] The Maker of *coeli et terrae*[49] in the Gospels says that the tree that does not bear fruit should be cut down and burned. Based on this wisdom, so that you like the tree should make fruit and so that the human race should grow and multiply, our most magnificent Duke has chosen you to glory in a most uprighteous consort. And His Excellency has conferred *nobiscum*[50] and ordered that *ego agam oratiunculam*[51]—that is, that I prepare the sermon for the marriage, to put it vulgarly.[52]

---

41. "Good day. How are you, my good sir?"
42. "Be happy."
43. "Live well and enjoy life."
44. "Young girl."
45. "The whole world."
46. "In God's name, it is true."
47. "Quite."
48. "As follows."
49. "Heaven and earth."
50. "With us."
51. "I give a little sermon."

52. *Idiotamente*—clearly intended to have a double meaning of both "commonly" and "in the vernacular." Some have read *idiotamente* as "appropriately." See the edition of G. B. de Sanctis, 49, n. 23.

MARESCALCO: Oh! Fine. This seems perfectly diabolical. Certainly I've often worried that I would die poor and despised at court, like most courtiers. But to be punished for my many faults with the cruel penance of a wife—well, the idea never crossed my mind.

PEDANT: My dear and unique Marescalco, *animadverte*[53] the Old Testament and, *oculata fide*,[54] you will see how all those men were expelled from the Temple and forbidden *ignem et aquam*[55] who were without children and who thusly had given the universal order a kick in the ass.[56] These men were marked and damned by the Prime Mover, the Giver of Life, and, going *de malo in peius*,[57] were mocked in the end even by the vulgar herd, just as *ars deluditur arte*,[58] as our Cato said. And on the contrary, as Dione the historian—translated by us grammarians from Greek into Latin and from Latin into our native language—wrote, argued, expressed, and said that the Great Octavian, ever Augustus, with prolix oratory exalted *usque ad sidera*[59] those who had many children, and, *per antifrasim*,[60] with great insults rejected the sterile and useless. The heretofore cited Dione also explicates the evils that befell those close to Augustus who did not produce most sweet offspring.

🏵 SCENE X 🏵

GIANNICCO, the MARESCALCO, and the PEDANT

GIANNICCO: [*Rushing in*] Master, the horses are fighting, they're killing each other. Listen, listen to the uproar!

MARESCALCO: The devil take it! Get going, I'm coming. [*He rushes off*]

53. "Turn your soul to."
54. "Guided by faith."
55. "Fire and water"—in other words, the basic necessities of civil life in society.
56. *Conculcavano* (here translated "gave a kick in the ass to") is a rare term probably used by Aretino because it suggests anal intercourse (*con cul cavano*) while referring to going against the presumed universal order of things, which is to use sexual intercourse for reproduction.
57. "From bad to worse."   58. "Art is mocked by artfulness."
59. "To the stars."   60. "In contrast."

ᗡ SCENE XI ᘒ

GIANNICCO and the PEDANT

GIANNICCO: What were you talking about with my master? Tell me, if it's something you can discuss.

PEDANT: We were speaking about matrimonial *copule*.[61]

GIANNICCO: What, my lord, about scrofula?

PEDANT: I mean *copule.*

GIANNICCO: What are these cups?[62]

PEDANT: They are connubial couplings.

GIANNICCO: Is that something you eat on Saturdays, my lord?

PEDANT: What's this about Saturdays? Or Fridays, for that matter? I was speaking with him about copulation with the female, because carnal copulation is the first article of divine law as well as human, while sins of the flesh[63] adulterate both human and divine law. Thus his lord, that is, the Most Excellent Excellence of His Excellent Lordship, has promised this very evening the incarnation of the matrimony of your master.

GIANNICCO: Right. Now I've got it. I've got your drift, all right. You two were going at it hammer and tongs about *in mulieribus,*[64] right?

PEDANT: You said it, *tu dixisti.*[65]

GIANNICCO: Well, is he going to take her or not?

PEDANT: I hope to God that I will bind him up with such efficacious reasoning that we will win him over, for *verba ligant homines, taurorum cornua*—

GIANNICCO: [*Interrupting*] Just like you.

PEDANT: —*funes, idest vincula.*[66]

---

61. "Sexual intercourse." The following exchange hinges on that common form of wordplay in Renaissance comedies, the mishearing of like-sounding words: *scrofule* (scrofula), *copule* (sexual intercourse), *pocule* (cups).

62. *Pocule* (cups) could be verbalized *po in cul* and taken as a reference to sodomy.

63. I.e., copulation outside of matrimony.

64. "Taking a wife" (with the double sense of "in matrimony" and "sexually").

65. "You said it."

66. "Men are bound by words, and bulls by their horns . . . are roped, that is, yoked": a misrendering in Latin of the popular saying, "Words bind men while cords bind the horns of bulls." By having Giannicco interrupt the Pedant in midstride and thus leave hanging "are roped," Aretino suggests that the fate of men bound in marriage is to wear horns—a commonplace in Renaissance antimarriage literature and a recurring theme in this comedy. "Yoked" as in the yoke of matrimony was a common way of referring to marriage.

GIANNICCO: Oh well, the yoke is on you.[67]

PEDANT: I don't think you can fully penetrate my subtlety.

GIANNICCO: Why not?

PEDANT: Quite clearly not.

GIANNICCO: Aren't you saying that men tie up the hay and yoke the mad?

PEDANT: Ha, ha!

GIANNICCO: Here comes my master. Meet me later in the square, I need to speak with you.

PEDANT: Very well.

ᵜᕲ SCENE XII ᕲᵜ

GIANNICCO, the MARESCALCO, and the PEDANT

GIANNICCO: Oh, you've ruined our gallant and perfumed discussion.

MARESCALCO: Oh, what a wild beast that Arabian stallion is!

PEDANT: Horses and mules are always kicking each other.

GIANNICCO: Listen, the Balia is calling. Here we are! We're coming!

MARESCALCO: Goodbye, Professor.

PEDANT: *Me vobis commendo.*[68]

GIANNICCO: Quick, let's get going, for I'm afraid the cat may eat the partridge that you stole this morning from the Lord's plate.[69]

Act II

ᵜᕲ SCENE I ᕲᵜ

GIANNICCO and the KNIGHT'S PAGE

GIANNICCO: While my master is arguing with his Balia about his wife, I want to find the Pedant, Mr. Latin,[70] and have a few words with him. But here comes the Knight's page.

---

67. Another case of mishearing: *vincula*, the word the Pedant uses for "yoke," heard as *v'incùla*, "up your ass."

68. "I commend myself to you."

69. The meaning of this apparently witty quip is unclear. The critical editions pass over it in silence. If it is directed at the Pedant, as it appears, it may be simply a cutting remark about how he lives by freeloading at the Lord's expense. Birds, however, often have phallic implications in Renaissance literature, and *gatta* (cat) regularly had the same double meaning as "pussy" today.

70. *I cujus*, implying one who always uses Latin declensions, hence "Mr. Latin."

PAGE: What's up, Giannicco?

GIANNICCO: Not much, little brother.

PAGE: I'd like to . . .

GIANNICCO: What?

PAGE: I'd like to find some old fart and tie these firecrackers to his ass!

GIANNICCO: Let's go for it. See that old goat strolling over there?

PAGE: I see him, and he looks like he's practicing walking with his nose in the air.

GIANNICCO: He's the one who teaches the little boys their Our Fathers.

PAGE: What now?

GIANNICCO: I'll get his attention. You circle around behind, hang the firecrackers on him, and then light them.

PAGE: [*Laughing*] There's no one I'd rather give it to than this soup slurper, this bean eater, this lasagna pit!

GIANNICCO: Follow along behind me slowly, now.

PAGE: I'm with you.

ᵔᴥ SCENE II ᵔᴥ

GIANNICCO, the PEDANT, and the KNIGHT'S PAGE

GIANNICCO: Good day to the Magnificent Paternity that is Your Lordship.

PEDANT: Good day to you, and good year as well.

GIANNICCO: I told my master's Balia that you'd make him take a wife, whatever it takes. And above and beyond the good it will do for your soul, she said that she wants to give you four handkerchiefs of Rhenish cloth and a pair of handsome shirts. But the question remains, will he take this wife or not?

PEDANT: Of course he will take her.

GIANNICCO: She will be forever in your debt.

PEDANT: Who?

GIANNICCO: The Balia. And I told her that Your Lordship—

PEDANT: [*Interrupting*] Gran mercé for giving me that "Lordship." [*The* PAGE *creeps up behind him and begins attaching the firecrackers*]

GIANNICCO: —is a valiant man with his weapon in hand.[71]

---

71. *Arme* can mean both "weapons" and "phalluses," and the double meaning is innocently echoed by the Pedant in the next line with *arma virum* (manly weapons).

PEDANT: Both with *arma virum* and with books, I do not give quarter to any man. And I share with you my condolences for the injustice done to you by those who did not allow you to study, for you are ideally suited to be penetrated by reason.[72]

GIANNICCO: Yeah, well, I had a weasel, but it died three days ago. It was worth a fortune, because it caught every single little pigeon.

PEDANT: I said reason, not weasel. [*The firecrackers go off, and the* PEDANT *begins running around the stage*] Oh, my God, Jesus, and Maria!

GIANNICCO: You're running out on me, eh? By the body of that I won't name . . . I'll find you later anyway. Run along.

PEDANT: [*To the* PAGE] How could you! In this manner! Is this any way to treat us, the *preclari*[73] disciplinarians of the philosophical schools?

GIANNICCO: Leave his disciplining to me, by the blood, by the body of—

PEDANT: [*Interrupting*] A boy whore, a presumptuous little jailbird, dares to outrage us, the most dignified educators of the grammatical discipline!

GIANNICCO: Professor, these are just ordinary boyish pranks. They mean nothing.

PEDANT: Mean nothing? Such things are very serious indeed for one of my station, and the Lord will not take them lightly. Oh, oh, oh, I promise you that!

GIANNICCO: Don't get all upset.

PEDANT: Our immediate responses *non sunt in potestate nostra*[74] because *ira impedit animum*.[75] Now go with God's grace, young man, because I want to bring charges before His Excellency. Then, I swear to you by the majesty of these professor's robes, by the reputation of my station in life, and by the seriousness of my learning, that I am going to give that page such a beating, I am going to give him so many—

GIANNICCO: [*Interrupting*] Please, no.

PEDANT: No?

GIANNICCO: Calm down.

PEDANT: I am not going to be able to finish reading the *Buccolics* to my students if I do not leave now. *Dominus providebit*.[76]

GIANNICCO: You're leaving at the right time for that, but without much of

---

72. In the following exchange, Giannicco mishears the Pedant's *indole* (reason) as *dondola* (weasel), which also means a swing or male genitals. And *pipione*, the little pigeons that the weasel always caught, has the double meaning of testicles and soft pigeonlike breasts.

73. "Distinguished."

74. "Are not under our control."

75. "Rage blinds the soul."

76. "The Lord will provide."

His grace. Well, who's this hurrying along? He seems to be a footman of the court. I'll just go into the house.

❧ SCENE III ☙

The DUKE'S FOOTMAN and the MARESCALCO

FOOTMAN: Here's his house. I'll knock. Knock, knock, knock!

MARESCALCO: [*Opening the door*] What's up?

FOOTMAN: The Lord wants to see you.

MARESCALCO: What does His Excellency want with me?

FOOTMAN: I'm not sure, but I think I know.

MARESCALCO: Please tell me, brother.

FOOTMAN: It's about your wife.

MARESCALCO: So this is the reward for my service! It's certainly cruel that against my every wish I am forced to take a wife!

FOOTMAN: Are you saying that the Lord is mistreating you by making you rich?

MARESCALCO: Enough!

FOOTMAN: You really don't believe that the Lord is going to make you rich, then?

MARESCALCO: I believe in God and that these lords have strange whims and great power. If I wanted a wife and were willing to dower her myself, asking for his favor in every way possible and with a hundred thousand petitions, I'd never get it. But because I don't want her, he wants to stick me with her by force. I suppose that lords are like women: they chase after those who flee them and flee those who follow, and they have no greater pleasure in life than to make those who serve them suffer. Let's go.

❧ SCENE IV ☙

The BALIA and GIANNICCO

BALIA: Do you think that the Lord wants to be obeyed?

GIANNICCO: Even the eyes of those hanged, being eaten by crows, can see that.

BALIA: Oh, kind Lord, good, sweet, saintly, and loving Lord! What greater blessing can he give than to make the Marescalco take this wife? In this way he will provide an example to those lewd men, those pigs who run after falsehood and sin who should be burned by the hundreds every day.[77]

GIANNICCO: Don't get carried away, Balia.

BALIA: You're the cause of all this sin, you little jailbait.

GIANNICCO: And you're going to be tossed in a blanket.[78]

BALIA: Who would do such a thing?

GIANNICCO: All the men of the court.

BALIA: Why?

GIANNICCO: Because courtiers are the enemies of women.

BALIA: As far as I'm concerned, the whole court should be drowned in the lake, the shameless rogues.

GIANNICCO: Look, here comes that holy fool Ser Polo,[79] better dressed than a wise man. He just turned the corner.

BALIA: Let's go back inside. If my son should return I don't want everything to be ruined because he can't find us.

GIANNICCO: Let's go, I think I see him coming.

＊ SCENE V ＊

The MARESCALCO and AMBROGIO

MARESCALCO: What a life; even madmen are taking pleasure in my troubles, even Ser Polo is kidding me now!

AMBROGIO: I swear to God that the Lord has done you a great favor. He spoke with you as a friend. Now take her and satisfy him; it'll be to your advantage.

MARESCALCO: So you think it's a good thing to take a wife, eh?

AMBROGIO: Very good indeed.

MARESCALCO: Have you ever had a wife?

---

77. The Balia's use of the term *ribaldone* (lewd men) and her aggressive, abusive language imply that she is attacking sodomites again. So does her call for the burning of these men—one of the traditional penalties for sodomy in the Renaissance.

78. A typical form of Renaissance charivari, a punishment carried out (usually by a group of young men) to discipline behavior deemed incorrect according to the customary rules of a community. Tossing people in a blanket was a dishonoring but relatively mild form of correction. As lower-class women often did not wear underwear, the shaming could have a strongly sexual element.

79. Zuan Polo, a Venetian poet and buffoon very popular at the courts of Mantua and Ferrara at the time of this comedy.

AMBROGIO: I have had one and still do.

MARESCALCO: If she were to leave you, would you go running after her to get her back?

AMBROGIO: Maybe, maybe not. But since it's the wish of the Lord, you'd better not make a mistake. He's a devil of a lord. One must pray to God that he doesn't get some strange whim, for if he does—well, you would be better off forgetting about worldly honors. But let's not talk about lords, for it's more dangerous to take their names in vain than that of Our Lord God. Now about your wife—

MARESCALCO: [*Interrupting*] Let's avoid that "your," if you want me to listen.

AMBROGIO: All right, the woman people are saying will be yours.

MARESCALCO: That's better.

AMBROGIO: People are talking about her exceptional qualities.[80] And it's clear that if women had only a fraction of the thousands of graces they were proclaimed to have before marriage, husbands would all be blessed.

MARESCALCO: But how many live up to such promises?

AMBROGIO: Not a one, and to be honest with you I must admit that they told me that my wife was the sibyl and the all-seeing Morgana.[81] But now that I have taken her I find that her real skill[82] is to make children for me without me having to do anything at all. Why, I'd say my children, or at least those that people call mine, are about as much mine as Christ is the son of Joseph.

MARESCALCO: And you haven't killed her?

AMBROGIO: Why should I?

MARESCALCO: To wipe out your shame!

AMBROGIO: [*Laughing*] Why should I be any smarter than all those great teachers who, rather than punishing their wives for giving them horns, turn their lovers into brothers and friends?

MARESCALCO: I won't have a wife giving me horns!

AMBROGIO: But to continue, your—

MARESCALCO: [*Interrupting*] What did I tell you?

AMBROGIO: I forget.

MARESCALCO: Don't say "your."

AMBROGIO: Oh, right. I'll say "this one" or "that one," then. But I must say that the one that the Lord wants to be yours is praised to the skies.

80. *Virtù.*

81. In the ancient world a sibyl was a woman with the power to tell the future. In Greece the most famous was at Delphi. Morgana was a fairy associated with the popular Arthurian romance cycle.

82. *Virtù.*

MARESCALCO: Tell me your honest opinion.

AMBROGIO: That's what I'm here for.

MARESCALCO: Should I marry her or not? Tell me what you really think.

AMBROGIO: Well, when . . .

MARESCALCO: You're having trouble spitting it out.

AMBROGIO: Do you want to hear my real opinion, or do you want me to say something that will make you happy?

MARESCALCO: The truth.

AMBROGIO: Don't take her. Don't get involved. Good God, if you do, you'll rue the day.

MARESCALCO: Now I really believe you and know that you love me. I'm your man from here on out!

AMBROGIO: Listen to just a small part of their perfidy.

MARESCALCO: I'm listening.

AMBROGIO: You return home in the evening, tired, upset, and full of those cares that a working man has, and there's your wife greeting you with "What kind of time is this to get home? You've come from either the tavern or some sluts, I can tell. Is this any way to treat your poor wife? Like this? You treat me like this?" And you, having been looking forward to a relaxing dinner, find yourself all agitated instead. After suffering a bit in silence, if you should now answer angrily, she'll yell in your face, "You don't deserve a woman like me, you're not worthy of me" and other similar insults that wives use. So, having lost your appetite, you climb into bed, and after a thousand recriminations she climbs in by your side with a "May the man be hanged and quartered who gave me to you, I could have been married to a count or a knight." And then, putting on many airs, she'll begin to give you a full account of her genealogy, telling you about how she was descended from the Gonzaga family.

MARESCALCO: And yet the Lord wants me to take her? Oh no, never!

AMBROGIO: Sooner or later you'll have to bawl her out for one of the thousands of things they do that require reproach. As soon as you open your mouth, she'll turn on you with "I did no such thing. You're crazy, get yourself some glasses, you're mad, cool off, I say you're a fool, you go too far, pull yourself together, you're dreaming, you're delirious, you're a dolt, a monkeybrain, a bum! What a joy you are! What a great catch! How many fools like you has God created and left hanging out to dry? Did you hear me? I'm not afraid to tell you off! Do you think I'm afraid of you?" And if the good husband doesn't close his ears to all that noise—constantly becoming louder, the more she thinks she's being heard—he'll go both deaf and mad at the same time.

MARESCALCO: Oh, oh, oh, God help me!

AMBROGIO: And then one must really suffer when they insist that fine cloth is worthless or dark bread is white cake. There's simply nothing you can say to shut them up. They just go on and on.

MARESCALCO: They have no respect.

AMBROGIO: And how hard it is to be quiet when they begin to gossip and run on continuously without ever, ever giving any rest to their tongues! They run on with the most bogus and stupid scuttlebutt that you ever heard, and heaven forbid you should interrupt them or stop listening. As far as envy is concerned, I don't need to tell you that if they so much as see a new veil on another woman, they puff up, they explode! And they want you to listen to everything calmly, without saying a word.

MARESCALCO: May the devil take them all!

AMBROGIO: And disrespectful—they're as disrespectful as the devil's horns, always running off at the mouth, just to irritate you.

MARESCALCO: May they all become sterile!

AMBROGIO: And contrary—I can't tell you how contrary they are, always grumbling, always complaining.

MARESCALCO: May they be drawn and quartered!

AMBROGIO: And malicious—I can't tell you how they always have something bad to say about everyone: "She has black teeth. She has a mouth that's too big. So and So has a complexion that's too pale. That one's too small. This one doesn't speak well. That other one carries herself badly. She hangs around church too much. She's always preening on the balcony. Who's doing this, who's doing that?" They insult everyone else as if they themselves had all the virtues, manners, and beauty there is.

MARESCALCO: I'm overwhelmed.

AMBROGIO: And disobedient—in disobedience they go to the limit. A husband is just like the Podestà of Sinigalia:[83] he gives orders only to find that he must do everything himself.

MARESCALCO: Tell me, after all this, if a man takes a wife, should he continue on with her or just give up and die?

AMBROGIO: There's a remedy for everything.

MARESCALCO: What remedy do you have, man, now that you're married?

AMBROGIO: I give her a little knuckle blessing upside the head, as is custom-

---

83. A proverbial ruler who gave orders that no one followed.

ary.[84] But getting back to the subject: I should tell you that when she's from a more noble family than you, she'll always hold her family up to you.

MARESCALCO: It seems like I can already feel her giving me a hammer[85] on the head at every word.

AMBROGIO: If she's richer than you, you'll hear about it every time she's unhappy about something: "If it wasn't for me, you'd be in rags. I picked you up out of the mud. Do I deserve this? I could have had any husband. I've been wasted marrying you, cut off from my wealth. You're consuming me, eating me up, gulping me down, devouring me completely."

MARESCALCO: This will come up every day because of her dowry.

AMBROGIO: If you dress her richly, everyone will have something to say about it: "Who does he think he is? Who does she think she is?" If you let her go out dressed modestly, they'll say, "That cheapskate! He ought to be ashamed. He could afford to dress her better, what with the dowry she brought him. She's being suffocated. She was crazy not to have become a nun rather than marry him." If you scold her for being too forward, you're labeled a jackass. If you give her free rein, you're viewed as not upholding your honor. If you allow her to roam about, the neighbors will begin to talk. If you keep her locked up, everyone will call you jealous and cruel.

MARESCALCO: What the hell is one to do with these wives?

AMBROGIO: If anyone knows, I hope he'll tell you.

MARESCALCO: Oh, oh, oh! But what is this you're telling me?

AMBROGIO: You haven't heard the half of what husbands suffer every day—tales that can't be told!

MARESCALCO: Well, at least tell me something about the caresses that they give their husbands.

AMBROGIO: The best you can expect is that they will pick a hair or two off your clothes, scratch a scab or two with just one finger, help you off with your shirt, straighten your cap, cut one fingernail, or give you a clean handkerchief. But these and other little things are the tricks they use to blind you to their betrayals. [*He laughs*]

MARESCALCO: Why are you laughing?

---

84. That is, he hits her on the head from time to time. The term used, *abronuncio*, comes from the ecclesiastical Latin *abrenunitare*, which was used in baptism and exorcism rituals as a blessing that drove out demons.

85. The word *marescalco* denotes both the Master of the Horse and the hammer used to drive the nails to shoe horses. Thus he imagines his wife both calling him and hitting him over the head.

AMBROGIO: I laugh, but I should be throwing up!

MARESCALCO: Why?

AMBROGIO: When I think of their faces in the morning when they get up— it's enough to say that even chickens, who'll eat anything, would be disgusted by them. Apothecaries surely don't have more jars of medicines and unguents than they do. And they never stop plastering, powdering, smearing their faces with this stuff. I won't say anything about how they construct their faces, tightening the skin with astringents so that where they were once firm and soft, they become wrinkly and flabby before their time, with black teeth.

MARESCALCO: Ha, ha, ha!

AMBROGIO: But what can we say about those who paint their faces with a ton of makeup? Certainly it would be better if they spread out the color evenly over their cheeks rather than smearing it all in one spot like clowns.

MARESCALCO: Little fools, big gossips, birdbrains!

AMBROGIO: And the construction work that goes into building their hair-styles is more than what gets done in a whole year at the Venetian Arsenal.[86] But I'm going to make you laugh by telling you what happened to a certain flashy sweet young thing.

MARESCALCO: What happened?

AMBROGIO: A little cat jumped up on the lap of this nymphet, and as she leaned forward to kiss it, the cat put its dirty paws on both her cheeks, leaving perfect prints there for all to see!

MARESCALCO: [*Laughing*] I'd rather be in hell, but if that woman were married to me I'd give her one hell of a beating if she painted her face like that.

AMBROGIO: It's not as easy to beat them as you might think.

MARESCALCO: Why not?

AMBROGIO: Because they bewitch you, they blind you, and they befuddle you.

MARESCALCO: There must be something that could be done.

AMBROGIO: Well, all I can say is that the sack of Rome or of Florence was nothing compared with the way they wreck, slash, and destroy those poor sap husbands who have faith in them. And in order to have their wives seen in public richly tailored and covered with gold, these husbands themselves go around all down-at-heel, looking even seedier than today's courtiers. Actually because these

---

86. One of the most famous shipyards of the Renaissance, reputedly able to build an entire fleet in a year and a warship in a day. By referring to the Arsenal's famed productivity, Aretino—who was living in Venice by the time he finished this play—slips in a compliment to his Venetian hosts.

wives are out going from churches to parties and on to banquets done up like duchesses and empresses, their husbands must stay home for months, even years, living in poverty. I know a certain man who sold everything he owned so that his wife could buy furs and gilded caps dripping with jewels, strings of pearls, royal necklaces, and papal rings. In the end, with husbands selling and wives buying both the temporal and the spiritual world, they all fall into the hands of our *hebreos fratres.*[87]

MARESCALCO: Ah, that's what distinguishes men from beasts!

AMBROGIO: What would you say of those men who, in order to be able to hitch up fine horses to their wives' carriages, themselves ride decrepit mules, trying to hide their disgrace by throwing a fine blanket over the poor beast? Even common people would sneer at them in the streets.

MARESCALCO: What wretches!

AMBROGIO: I won't go on about all the time wives waste discussing how they're going to do up their hair, pluck their eyebrows, brighten their teeth, and generally do themselves up. They're constantly inviting over first a hairdresser, then a Jewish hawker of hats, fans, and perfumed gloves, and next some woman who gathers herbs—unfortunately, those herbs are no use for maintaining what little beauty they might have but good only for making them old, grizzled, and rancid.

MARESCALCO: Heaven help us!

AMBROGIO: But every one of their vices (and you should call every deed of theirs a vice) would matter nothing at all if only their dishonored, destroyed, and broken husbands could be sure of their . . . I can't say it.

MARESCALCO: Go ahead, man, spit it out!

AMBROGIO: It's the horns.

MARESCALCO: You've hit the mark again! Oh, oh, that's the way to tell the truth, man to man!

AMBROGIO: Well, now you've heard some of the hundred thousand things I could tell you about wives. You should know, however, that the gentlemen of Venice deserve eternal praise for everything they've accomplished, but especially for the sumptuary laws (worthy of divine praise!) with which they limit the disorderly appetites of their women.[88] For their unequaled riches, matched only

87. "Jewish brothers." Antisemitism was a common theme in Renaissance comedy. Jews were associated with pawnbroking (a trade formally forbidden to Christians as a form of usury) and with having sold Christ to the Romans (a topos of medieval and Renaissance anti-Jewish rhetoric). This passage appears to refers to both associations.

88. Here begins a stretch of praise for Venice and its noble rulers—a type of advertising for

by their unequaled prudence and power, wouldn't last a day of adorning their wives if they hadn't imposed the necessary provisions, laws, and limits on such activity.

MARESCALCO: How would they dress each day?

AMBROGIO: As if they were on a triumphal arch, as Ciola[89] says. The women of Venice are as beautiful as they are noble, and as noble as they are splendid. Therefore, there would be so much wearing of the fashionable curls on curls, the wide sleeves, the elegant slashes, the fine embroideries, the jewels, and the stylish clothes that the wealth earned by all the worthy efforts[90] of the Venetians would melt away like snow under a hot sun.

MARESCALCO: You ought to have used a better comparison, saying, "The treasure would be eaten up as the Marescalco is eaten up by despair when he thinks of marrying." But from what I've heard, Venetian wives have less need of fancy dress than angels, because they're so incredibly beautiful.

AMBROGIO: You're right. Now, is there anything else that I can do for you?

MARESCALCO: More? I don't know what more you could tell me. Your outstanding, saintly, and divine counsels have so confirmed my commitment not to take a wife that I won't be budged by all the dukes of the world, never mind this Duke of Mantua.

AMBROGIO: Goodbye, then. But wait a second, here come some people for you, just as I'm leaving. [*He leaves*]

❧ SCENE VI ❧

The BALIA, GIANNICCO, and the MARESCALCO

BALIA: Here he comes, all crestfallen. The Lord must have twisted his arm.

GIANNICCO: No danger of that.

BALIA: Why?

GIANNICCO: Because the Lord is too good for that, and besides, he ought to hang him, God forgive me for saying it.

BALIA: What?!

GIANNICCO: [*Seeing the* MARESCALCO *coming up to them in a rage*] Yes, sir?

---

which Aretino might have expected to be rewarded. He often referred in his works to favors he had received from the great and famous, and heaped abuse on those who had treated him shabbily.

89. There was more than one Ciola in Renaissance literature. The likeliest candidate for this reference is Ser Ciolo in Francesco Sacchetti's *Il trecentonovelle*, LII.

90. *Virtù.*

MARESCALCO: Who's talking to you?

GIANNICCO: Me? I thought I heard something.

MARESCALCO: Don't give me a hard time, you—

BALIA: [*Interrupting*] Why are you so upset?

MARESCALCO: Screw the poor bastard that fathered me!

BALIA: How would you act if you were being asked to take some medicine?[91]

GIANNICCO: But medicine is so bitter, and a wife so sweet.

MARESCALCO: Yeah, well, medicine eliminates the sickness from the body, while a wife eliminates the good from both the body and the soul.

GIANNICCO: [*To the* BALIA] Would you believe it? Now he's worrying about his soul.

BALIA: What would you say if you were given a wife of sixty when you were only twenty-five? Or if you were an old man, what would you say if you had to take a wife of sixteen like old— . . . but I won't speak of him. What would you think then, eh?

MARESCALCO: I imagine that if I were that old man, I'd be fulfilling the fantasies of every other man in town—with my own wife.

GIANNICCO: Oh, well said!

MARESCALCO: My boy, my boy!

GIANNICCO: My master, my master!

MARESCALCO: You are a tempting little devil. Now, Balia, if you don't teach me some magic charm to change the Lord's whim to give me a wife, I'll throw myself out of a window or cut my throat or give myself body and soul to the Great Devil.

BALIA: Don't say that, my son, don't say it.

MARESCALCO: I want to live as I wish, sleep with whom I like, eat what pleases me, without the scolding of a wife.

BALIA: Since you're willing to risk your neck on this out of stubbornness, I've come up with a plan that will keep the Lord from ever mentioning the matter again.

MARESCALCO: Really?

BALIA: Really.

MARESCALCO: My sweet, dear mother, how?

BALIA: Spells.[92]

---

91. Her implication is, "What a baby you are!"

92. The following exchange plays on the similar sounds of *incanti* (spells), *canti* (songs), and *cacai* (I have crapped).

MARESCALCO: That won't work.

BALIA: Why not?

MARESCALCO: Because I don't have any friends who can sing.

BALIA: Have you lost your hearing? I said spells.

MARESCALCO: You said songs.

BALIA: I've crapped.

MARESCALCO: All right, all right, how are we going to do these spells, by witchcraft or by necromancy?

BALIA: Forget necromancy and witchcraft! Come in the house and leave this to me. By the holy cross, you'll miss me when I'm gone!

MARESCALCO: Oh, what a life. . . . But if these spells work and save me from this plague, this martyrdom, this living death of taking a wife, I'll take a holy vow—

BALIA: [*Interrupting*] Get going!

MARESCALCO: I'm coming! [*Continuing*] —to visit the Holy Sepulcher, Santiago de Compostela in Galicia, *et in finibus terra.*[93]

⤳ SCENE VII ⤶

The COUNT and the KNIGHT

COUNT: By my faith, sir Knight, it's wonderful that the Duke is giving a wife to this man who's never looked with interest at a woman.

KNIGHT: In this case His Excellency only desires that he not look at her until he marries her.

COUNT: [*Laughing*] I've never seen a man as upset by a disaster as this one is because he has to marry. Why, I bet he'd rather be tortured by ten drops on the cord than have her.[94]

KNIGHT: Actually, a thousand! Over the years I've seen at least twenty people reply more warmly to the executioner when he asks their pardon for what he's about to do to them than the Marescalco replies to those who mention this joke.

COUNT: [*Laughing*] Here comes his boy; let's find out what his master is up to.

93. "And the ends of the earth."

94. The *tratto di corda* was the most widely used form of judicial torture during the Renaissance. It involved tying the victim's hands behind his back, hoisting him into the air by the hands, and them letting him drop, stopping him abruptly just before he touched the ground and leaving him hanging. People were usually assigned a specific number of drops or a specific period of time, to control the amount of physical damage done.

ᵗᵒ SCENE VIII ᵒᵗ

GIANNICCO, the COUNT, and the KNIGHT

GIANNICCO: [*Singing*]

> Oh, open up, Marcolina,
> And be on your way on tiptoe,
> Oh, open up, Marcolina . . .

COUNT: Giannicco, what news of your master?

GIANNICCO: [*Singing*]

> Dear Mama, marry me, for I cannot hold out any longer.
> Dear Papa, marry me, as I feel the stirrings . . .

COUNT: What's your master up to, Giannicco?

GIANNICCO: Oh, he's fine, fine. He's just despairing, hanging himself, killing himself, like a criminal who doesn't want the infestation of a wife. And at the moment he's after his Balia to give him some evil arm to use against the Lord's whim to make him take one.

KNIGHT: [*Laughing*] You mean an evil charm.

GIANNICCO: That's it, sir. One of those.

COUNT: Ha, ha, ha!

GIANNICCO: Do you want to hear the advice I gave him, my lords?

COUNT: Go ahead, my fine young man.

GIANNICCO: I told him that if she was beautiful and rich, he should take her the Half Way, and that way we would all luck out.

COUNT: What are you talking about?

GIANNICCO: It's like this, sir: he'll have to put out for a few days after the marriage, but soon the usual handsome young guys will begin flocking around like roosters; then he can have his fill of the cocks and I'll have my fill of the hen.[95] Well, what do you think?

COUNT: Solomon himself couldn't have given better advice.

KNIGHT: [*Laughing*] What did he think of the idea?

---

95. The wordplay of Giannicco's proposal turns on the double meanings of *uccello* (which means both "bird" and "phallus") and *civetta* (literally, "owl," but in common parlance denoting both a woman who attracts men with her beauty and the female genitals).

GIANNICCO: He wanted to have me boiled and roasted. But let me run this errand for him at the palace, for I see him coming out of the house. [*He leaves, singing*]

> The young widow, when she sleeps alone,
> Has no reason to complain of me.
> She has no reason,
> She has no reason.[96]

✣ SCENE IX ✣

The KNIGHT, the COUNT, and the MARESCALCO

KNIGHT: [*To the* COUNT] Let's start on our way, pretending that we're in a hurry. [*To the* MARESCALCO] Good day, Marescalco. I'm pleased by all your good fortune. *Ad maiora.*[97]

COUNT: Sir, I'm pleased by the favor that the Lord has shown you in giving you this beautiful and rich mate.

MARESCALCO: May my enemies enjoy such favors and fortune! But there are enough problems to go around. Good day to you.

KNIGHT: [*Walking off with the* COUNT] As far as problems go, he's got a point.

✣ SCENE X ✣

The MARESCALCO and the BALIA

MARESCALCO: Come on out, everybody's gone.

BALIA: I'm coming.

MARESCALCO: You're sure, now, that if I say these words in his ear, he won't say any more about giving me a wife?

BALIA: Absolutely. You need to take this powder as well and do as I told you.

---

96. The Balia's earlier dream seems to be coming true: Giannicco is singing, and in her dream he was the singing bird—perhaps in more than the literal sense. As noted earlier, the Italian word for "bird" also means "phallus," and the bird in the dream is sitting on a fig, the Italian word for which also means "vagina"; it seems as if Giannicco's bird is anxious to move on from his master's love and find figs of his own. In such details a Renaissance audience may have heard a comment on male/male sexual relationships: Giannicco is growing up and leaving behind his youthful relationship with the Marescalco, but the Marescalco has not done the same, just as the Balia complained early on.

97. "May it ever increase."

But tell me, how are you going to make the sign of the cross on the ground several times without anyone noticing?

MARESCALCO: I'll drop my beret, and when I stoop to pick it up I'll make the sign of the cross like this and this, and then I'll say in his ear the words you taught me while throwing the powder behind me.

BALIA: All right, let's give it a try, and remember, you mustn't forget the words. Pretend I'm the Duke.

MARESCALCO:

> I conjure you for Tubia
> So that you take with you on your way
> The Lord's whim
> So that a wife he will not give me
> On the Holy Epiphany.[98]

BALIA: Too loud and too quick.

MARESCALCO:

> I conjure you, Epiphany,
> For the wife of Tubia—

BALIA: You've got it backwards, and you're making a mess of it! Now I remember how slow you were learning to say grace at the table. Why, you were eighteen before you could learn the Hail Mary! Now try it again from the start.

MARESCALCO:

> I conjure you, evil wife,
> That you don't get the whim—

Oh, God damn you and the whore who shat me forth into this world! These songs or spells—to hell with this magic and necromancy. I'm simply not made to take a wife, and before they make me marry, day will become night and night, day.[99] Go on into the house now, I want to say a few words to the Professor, whom I see coming.

98. Although Aretino is clearly joking, the spell is similar in form to actual spells used in the popular magic of the period.

99. This speech appears to express a strong Renaissance sense of sexual identity that is not heterosexual, and the Balia's troubled response seems to confirm that reading.

BALIA: You've made it perfectly clear where you stand. Oh, oh, the devil has you by the hair, and he rides you as he pleases!

✺ SCENE XI ✽

The PEDANT and the MARESCALCO

PEDANT: These cheeky adolescents, these effeminate Ganymedes, they bring shame upon *istam urbem clarissimam!*[100] Here the guardians of the treasures of Virgilian letters are at the mercy of *capestri sine rubore* and *cineduli subiaceno*[101]— gallows-bait!

MARESCALCO: What are you all worked up about?

PEDANT: *Me tedet*[102]—I am overcome—by the fact that this *alma et inclita*[103] city of Mantua that *genuit*[104] me, and also that selfsame Vergilius Maro, is full of hermaphrodites. *Honorem meum nemini dabo,*[105] but a most presumptuous little crook still wet behind the ears attached to my hindquarters some firecrackers, and lighting them he has *combusto*[106] my hair and my backside, that is to say my toga, *cum sulphure!*[107]

MARESCALCO: Oh, what a stink! [*Laughing*] You smell like the master who makes the gunpowder in Ferrara. I'm laughing, though I should be crying. Who did this to you?

PEDANT: The Knight's girlfriend, his little traitoress of a page, his secretary.[108] I am going to take this matter to His Excellency, and if perchance he does not act on it, the memory of ink on paper shall proclaim it *a posteritate!*[109]

MARESCALCO: I'm sure that when the Lord hears about this he'll see to it that the lad gets a hundred thousand lashes.

PEDANT: Were we not the one who illuminated the obscure darknesses and subtle discourses surrounding the Priapae[110] with our daily and nightly studies?

---

100. "This very great city."

101. "Shameless and thoroughly corrupt sodomite boys."

102. "I am upset."   103. "Proud and glorious."

104. "Gave birth to."   105. "I give my honor up to no man."

106. "Burned."   107. "With sulfur."

108. The Pedant uses words with feminine endings to describe the Page, implying that he is the passive partner in a sexual relationship with his master the Knight.

109. "In posterity."

110. A collection of erotic Latin poems focusing on the phallus. The phallus was widely worshipped in antiquity as the symbol of the masculine lifegiving forces in nature. Greek homes

And did not we dedicate to the Knight our sententious macaronic discourses, for whose penetrating style I beseeched the laurel wreath?[111] It is a difficult thing to continue living at a heroic level of eloquence in this *ferrea e plumbea etate.*[112] I want to explain to you *ad unguem*[113] about your wife, but the extreme explosiveness of my anger impedes me from discoursing on the matter. Another time I will expound for you what the *armiclarissimo prencipe*[114] has confided to me. Now I will go to the palace, where I will *ambulabo usque ad vesperam*[115] in the cloister and then protest *vocem magnam.*[116] That noose-bait! I'll never forgive him, not even if he gets down on his knees before me and begs, that ass of a gallows-bird!

MARESCALCO: Don't get all up in arms with a boy. Leave your anger to me, for I'm up to my neck in this mess, and my heart is in my throat trying to deal with it. I'm going in now. Goodbye.

PEDANT: *Et ego quoque discedam. Vale!*[117]

Act III

✺ SCENE I ✺

The JEW and GIANNICCO

JEW: Who wants to buy, who wants to buy my little trinkets, my pretty things, my rare things? Who wants to buy, who wants to buy?

GIANNICCO: This person singing so out of tune, seeking buyers for his fakes, seems, from his red eyes and yellow face, to be the Jew. It's him, all right. What a good stoning I'd give him if it weren't for the laws that protect them![118]

---

and gardens were regularly protected by erect stone phalluses, and even during the Roman period the cult of Priapus was quite popular.

111. Great poets in ancient Rome were awarded laurel wreaths, a practice revived in the Renaissance. See n. 11.

112. "Squalid and backward age."   113. "Fully."

114. "Prince most excellent in arms."   115. "Pace back and forth until vespers."

116. "At the top of my lungs."   117. "I too must be off. Goodbye."

118. This scene explains in part why anti-Jewish sentiments could run so high in the cities of the Renaissance. The laws that Giannicco complains about were in place largely to allow Jews to make small loans to lower-class people, usually as pawnbrokers. Because lending money at interest was forbidden by the church to Christians as usury, the practice of allowing Jews to perform this needed service to get the poor through hard times was encouraged by urban governments. Needless to say, when it came time to pay off those debts, those who had needed the loans were in a less friendly mood, and as a result Jews became scapegoats for lower-class poverty. Local

JEW: Who wants to buy my nice things, my pretty little things?

GIANNICCO: [*Tipping his cap*] A very good day to you, most reverend Abraham.

JEW: You are quite correct, Giannicco, to tip your hat to me.

GIANNICCO: [*Aside*] It's hard enough to do. [*To the* JEW] But look, I want to make you rich.

JEW: That would be good, Giannicco, my gallant lad.

GIANNICCO: What kind of baubles do you have for brides?

JEW: Actually, I don't have anything except fans, skullcaps, makeup, perfumed waters, bracelets, necklaces, earrings, tooth powders, pins, belts, and other similar things to ruin a husband.

GIANNICCO: If that's the case, you must have something to ruin my master, for with a broken heart, with a broken liver, and out of breath, he'll marry this evening.

JEW: [*Laughing*] A wife, eh?

GIANNICCO: Yep, a wife, you treacherous dog! Oops—forgive me, Your Lordship, for that little verbal slip.

JEW: God will forgive you if you're telling me the truth.

GIANNICCO: On the Gospels. But if you don't believe me, what can I do? In the Count's house this evening, the Lord will marry him to a pretty little dish much against his wishes. And if you bring him your little traveling market, he'll buy everything. You can trust me on this, and if you don't, you can bugger off.

JEW: There's little to be lost in going twenty more paces. I'll go to him, and if he doesn't want my wares, I'll sell them to someone else, that's all.

GIANNICCO: Don't let him know that it was my idea.

JEW: Why not?

GIANNICCO: Because all this is being kept secret—just about like a public announcement.

JEW: I'll do as you wish, my pretty boy. Who wants to buy my pretty trinkets, my lovely things? [*He leaves*]

GIANNICCO: I'll make the Marescalco damn heaven itself, just as he often makes me. Now the Jew is knocking at his door. I'll hide myself here to hear with what good will he responds to the Jew's offer!

---

governments would from time to time drive out resident Jews, often violently, thus canceling the accumulated debts and winning the support of the populace. But credit for the poor remained necessary, and usually Jews were invited back to repeat the cycle.

ꙮ SCENE II ꙮ

The JEW, the MARESCALCO, and GIANNICCO

JEW: Knock, knock, knock!

MARESCALCO: [*Opening the door*] Either I'm here or I'm not here. If I'm here, I don't want to be here, and if I'm not here, why do you want to break down my door, you shifty scoundrel?

JEW: Speak with some respect, please.

GIANNICCO: [*Aside*] By the devil, take him to court!

MARESCALCO: I'm in the right. Why don't you knock more quietly?

JEW: I've come to furnish you with a thousand fine little things, and you get all worked up!

MARESCALCO: What need do I have of fine little things?

GIANNICCO: [*Aside*] To stick them where the sun doesn't shine.

JEW: What need? Why, for your wife, whom in the name of God you're going to marry this evening. Oh, look at this fine fan and how nicely perfumed it is. Here, smell. [*Thrusting the fan at him*]

MARESCALCO: First madmen and now the synagogue crowd are making fun of my problems! I've been set up, and I'm in danger of becoming a laughingstock. I'll be lucky if I survive this without exploding.

GIANNICCO: [*Aside*] If you explode, that would no doubt be a great loss!

JEW: I can assure you that for this cap I'll give you a good price—half what I'd charge someone else.

MARESCALCO: Leave me alone.

JEW: Don't be rash. Don't miss out on this necklace—made in France, and what gold! Only the finest, I promise you.

MARESCALCO: I'm afraid I may do something crazy.

GIANNICCO: [*Aside*] Someone tie him down!

JEW: Come, now. I'll sell you these bracelets for ten scudi and four sesini,[119] and I'm not charging you for the workmanship. Such a deal—you'll never find another like it. I'll make good my loss dealing with some poor dupe.

MARESCALCO: You're trying to get me banished from this realm.[120]

GIANNICCO: [*Aside*] Oh boy!

MARESCALCO: I don't give a damn any longer.

---

119. Sesini were small copper coins of little value, like pennies. For scudi, see n. 28.
120. I.e., banished for having murdered him.

GIANNICCO: [*Aside*] Hell, keep pushing him, Jew. Maybe, just maybe . . .

JEW: This pendant is antique and worth a fortune. Name your price.

MARESCALCO: Be quiet, Jew, I'm begging you.

JEW: If you'll let me have a few words with a certain merchant, I can give you six months to pay.

GIANNICCO: [*Aside*] What fun!

JEW: You're not answering. How about if we make it a year?

MARESCALCO: Look at what my cruel luck has brought me to: one of those who crucified Christ is mocking a person of my rank, and it's illegal for me to punish him! And just yesterday that pig, Mainoldo,[121] who weighs a ton, tripped me up in the middle of the court, but one must take all such insults without a murmur.

GIANNICCO: [*Aside*] What a crybaby!

JEW: I'm asking one hundred scudi for the lot, and the pendant alone is worth that. And look at the beautiful color of this diamond—like the clearest water.

MARESCALCO: If it weren't for the fact that my enemies would be pleased . . . but enough. Master Abraham, go with God.

JEW: [*Losing his patience*] I'm not going to force my kindness on anyone. If you offered me two hundred and in cash, I wouldn't sell them to you now. And to think that it was all because of your boy that I degraded my goods offering them to the likes of you!

MARESCALCO: My boy, eh? I have to take that on top of all the rest!

❧ SCENE III ☙

GIANNICCO and the MARESCALCO

GIANNICCO: [*To himself*] I don't know who told me that it's not true that the Lord is going to give him a wife.

MARESCALCO: Is that you?

GIANNICCO: Yes, I think I'm me.

MARESCALCO: Do you know who I am?

GIANNICCO: Oh, you're the one who says cruel things.

MARESCALCO: Cruel things, eh?

---

121. A jeweler and antiques dealer in Mantua whom Aretino made fun of more than once in his writings and who in real life suffered as the butt of a number of his cruel jokes.

GIANNICCO: Yes, sir.

MARESCALCO: Yes, sir, eh?

GIANNICCO: What are you driving at?

MARESCALCO: What are you doing gossiping with the Jew about my affairs?

GIANNICCO: Me? With the Jew?

MARESCALCO: You, with the Jew, exactly.

GIANNICCO: May God be my witness. Oh, these Jews, what assassins, cuckolds, thieves—may they all be killed and burned like the one who was executed when the emperor was here![122] Whatever Jew told you this was lying through his teeth, the traitor. It's more than a year since I've been alone with a Jew.

MARESCALCO: I haven't lost my hearing yet.

GIANNICCO: It's true that among other things a certain person covered with strings of needlework and several thousand whorish trinkets hung all over him and with I don't know what kind of gold around his neck who's asking people to doff their caps to him said to me, "If your master who has taken a wife wants to buy a beautiful and new gilded carriage, I'll sell him one" and swore that it would be ideal for your horses. I told him that your horses weren't suited to carriages. And if it weren't for the fact that I don't want to spend time in jail, I'd have given him more than mere words.

MARESCALCO: Don't get involved in any violence. But tell me, what are people saying about my predicament?

GIANNICCO: Some are saying one thing, some another.

MARESCALCO: Oh, really?

GIANNICCO: Really, they're saying that you're a brute, Master, for not taking her. And I've heard it also said, although I don't remember by whom, that there will be no wife.

MARESCALCO: Oh, God, if only that were true!

GIANNICCO: Master, watch out that your stubborn fancy doesn't destroy you. Go on, take a wife. Do it. [*Aside*] If he's this crazy before he's been given her, imagine what he'll be like after he's lived with her for a year or two. But here comes one of the servants of the Lord.

---

122. The emperor Charles V visited the city in 1530 and 1532. No record has been found of such an execution in those years, but Aretino seems to be referring to a recent historical event.

ᔥ SCENE IV ᔤ

The DUKE'S FOOTMAN, the MARESCALCO, and GIANNICCO

FOOTMAN: Have you seen the jeweler?

MARESCALCO: He was in the neighborhood a little while ago.

FOOTMAN: The Lord is asking for him.

MARESCALCO: Why?

FOOTMAN: How should I know? Let me go look for him, in God's name.

GIANNICCO: Maybe he wants him so that gambling with him he can win some precious stones and coins.

ᔥ SCENE V ᔤ

The MARESCALCO and GIANNICCO

MARESCALCO: I'm afraid, I'm worried, I'm trembling all over.

GIANNICCO: Why?

MARESCALCO: That guy! It's as clear as the nose on your face that he's looking for the jeweler on my account.

GIANNICCO: What do you mean, on your account?

MARESCALCO: For the marriage rings; for my doom!

GIANNICCO: Of course, that's it. But go ahead and take her. How bad can it be? Saint Julian did worse killing his daddy and mommy.[123]

MARESCALCO: He should have killed his wife. Those who slit their throats go directly to heaven in flesh and blood.

GIANNICCO: You could cut your wife's throat, if you go to heaven for it. And it seems to be customary these days.

MARESCALCO: How do you know it's customary?

GIANNICCO: From experience—perhaps you can't learn these things from study.

MARESCALCO: Let's change the subject. Go to the palace and see why the Lord has called the jeweler. When you find out, come back home. I'll be waiting for you here.

---

123. I.e., did a worse thing and still became a saint. Saint Julian was a legendary saint, protector of travelers, who supposedly killed his parents. He was a popular figure in Renaissance literature and is referred to in the famous traveling-salesman story in Boccaccio's *Decameron*, II, 2.

GIANNICCO: I'll do just that, Master. I'll fly. . . . But these two coming along talking to each other appear to be the jeweler and the footman. I'd better hurry up and beat them to the court.

♁ SCENE VI ♁

The DUKE'S FOOTMAN and the JEWELER

FOOTMAN: How should I know why the Lord wants you?

JEWELER: If His Excellency wants to gamble with me today, I'm ready to win big.

FOOTMAN: Be careful.

JEWELER: Oh, I'll win, there's no doubt. But what are they saying at court?

FOOTMAN: That the pope[124] will go to Avignon and not Nice—actually, I mean to Marseilles. And that the duke of Orleans[125] has taken the pope's niece[126] as his wife, and everyone is amazed by that.

JEWELER: This pope is a fearsome man, and I'm afraid that he's going to turn the world upside down, but that's none of my business. Our Duke is loved by all and never gives anyone anything to complain about, may God keep him well for a hundred years.

FOOTMAN: Oh, I forgot, His Lordship will be giving a wife to his Marescalco this evening at the Count's house.

JEWELER: Ah, then he wants me for the rings. Oh, I'll serve His Excellency excellently! Let me show you this little box of matchless and glorious stones.

FOOTMAN: Be careful not to go about with that box after dark.

JEWELER: Why?

FOOTMAN: Because you'll be relieved of it as well as of your life, which is worth more.

JEWELER: This little box is worth more.

FOOTMAN: The devil you say! Are you serious?

JEWELER: Yes sirree, I wouldn't give up these jewels for a thousand lives.

FOOTMAN: Yeah, right—lives of your grape vines, maybe.[127]

---

124. Pope Clement VII (1523–34).

125. Future king of France, Henry II (1519–59).

126. Catherine de'Medici (1519–89). They were married in 1533. Their marriage produced three kings of France: Frances II (1559–60), Charles IX (1560–63), and Henry III (1574–89). For most of this time Catherine de'Medici was a major figure in the political and cultural life of France.

127. A play on *vite*, which can mean either "lives" or "grape vines."

JEWELER: No, I mean the lives of a thousand men.

FOOTMAN: You might be right if you were speaking of a certain kind of man.

JEWELER: No, I mean men that are my equals, even if it's true that there are hardly a dozen men who would fit that bill.

FOOTMAN: Ha, ha, ha!

JEWELER: Let's get back to jewels. Look at this unset cameo.

FOOTMAN: I see it.

JEWELER: I've been offered one hundred scudi for it!

FOOTMAN: A loose camel[128] is too expensive for me, but how much would it cost tied up?

JEWELER: I really couldn't say.

FOOTMAN: And then that camel that was running around loose at Pietole, he wasn't worth all that much.[129]

JEWELER: Actually, I said cameo.

FOOTMAN: Oh, yeah, yeah, I get you now.

JEWELER: Look at this lapis lazuli. Oh, what a lovely aquamarine blue it is for only fifty scudi an ounce!

FOOTMAN: Who would have the nerve to want it along with leprosy, as if the disease of Saint Lazarus wasn't enough!

JEWELER: But no, no! I said lapis, not leprosy, and I said lazuli, not lazars.

FOOTMAN: When you talk slow I catch your drift, but when you get running along my ears can't keep up.

JEWELER: This is a carbuncle, the very twin of the one in the Treasury of Saint Mark.[130] It's like pure fire, and it's perfect, and it's so brilliant that it's virtually blinding.

FOOTMAN: Keep your carbuncle to yourself! Take my advice and don't even admit that you have one.

JEWELER: Why?

FOOTMAN: In order to avoid being quarantined in your house. And as for me, I'm going to tell the Lord that I didn't find you.

JEWELER: Why all the fuss?

FOOTMAN: Do you want me to admit that I spoke with someone who has a carbuncle?

---

128. *Camello scioto*, a mishearing of *cameo sciolto* (unset cameo).

129. A reference to some as yet unidentified contemporary event.

130. Another compliment to Venice. The Treasury of Saint Mark was (and still is) in Saint Mark's Cathedral in Venice. It contained a rich horde of precious stones and jewelry from all over the world.

JEWELER: Oh, you're thinking of carbuncles, plague sores, and I'm speaking about carbuncles, stones, valued by us jewelers more than emeralds and diamonds.[131]

FOOTMAN: Really, huh?

JEWELER: But of course!

FOOTMAN: Well, that seems all right, then.

JEWELER: Look at this finely worked gold chain.

FOOTMAN: Let me put it on.

JEWELER: All right, but don't touch it, or it'll lose its shine.

FOOTMAN: With this gold chain around my neck, I could be one of our mincing fops who dance around their mistresses. Without such chains, however, those dandies wouldn't be much, as either suitors or lovers. They wear them long so that everyone will notice them. And to make it all as impressive as possible, they have their chain made so fine that as soon as it's touched, it breaks. Gold chains should be instead like the one that the king of France sent all the way to Venice to give to Pietro Aretino.[132] It weighs eight pounds!

JEWELER: Who told you that?

FOOTMAN: Some scoundrels dying of envy.

JEWELER: That king deserves to rule the world!

FOOTMAN: Do you have chalcedonies?

JEWELER: Yes, I have one to be set. But look at this rosary of the finest agate.

FOOTMAN: What's agate?

JEWELER: It's a stone like these onyxes, these cornelians, and these turquoises. They all have great inner gifts[133] of magical power.[134]

FOOTMAN: Well, then, give one to me as a present. By God, I'd like to see its powers.

JEWELER: I can't.

131. He actually says carbuncles of Saint Rocco. Saint Rocco was revered for his ability to intervene with God to secure relief from the plague; hence plague sores were called carbuncles of Saint Rocco. To keep the plague from spreading, people who had been exposed to it were commonly locked up for forty days (the word "quarantine" is derived from *quaranta*, the Italian for "forty"). This confinement could cause extreme hardship, and many people tried to avoid it, as the Footman is prepared to do here.

132. Aretino was extremely proud of this chain, given to him by Frances I (1515–47). It figures prominently in many of the portraits of him, and he seldom missed an opportunity to refer to it in his writings, as if to establish it as the benchmark against which to measure all other gifts given him by the rich and powerful.

133. *Donate*. Here and in the Footman's reply, the word's double meaning is at play: like the English "gift," it can mean either a present or an inner quality.

134. *Virtù* (and again in the Footman's reply).

FOOTMAN: Why not?

JEWELER: It's already promised. But look at this mother of pearl. What do you think? Isn't it worthy of a queen?

FOOTMAN: It looks to me more like the great-great-grandmother of pearl than just the mother. Why, as an earring it would rip off the ear of a cow, never mind a woman!

ᓬ SCENE VII ᖇ

AMBROGIO, the DUKE'S FOOTMAN, and the JEWELER

AMBROGIO: [*To the* FOOTMAN] You certainly are quick! Four—no, actually almost six hours ago the Lord sent you on an errand, and you're still fooling around. [*To the* JEWELER] And you must serve His Excellency gallantly, as he calls for you even if you don't deserve the honor.

FOOTMAN: This great display of jewels on sale that he was showing me is huge enough to fill in the Mincio.[135]

JEWELER: I'm ready to serve our Lord.

AMBROGIO: Let's get going. Heavens, you two are slower than molasses in springtime.

JEWELER: Let's go, let's go.

FOOTMAN: Yes, let's go.

ᓬ SCENE VIII ᖇ

AMBROGIO, alone

AMBROGIO: The person who doesn't rush to court is either a miracle worker[136] or a real philosopher. Why bother studying at the University of Bologna? If you want to have a doctorate in three days, you should instead send your sons to court. The court is truly a learned school—how many different types of men, with different customs, with strange humors and beastly spirits, live there! It's common knowledge that even scholars, who are so subtle and so clever that they can trick and mock anybody, when they have to deal with

---

135. The river and the lake that it formed surrounding Mantua.

136. *Legno di India*, a miraculous "cure" for syphilis. It came from the Guaiacum tree found in the New World, where syphilis was thought by many to have come from. It was also called "holy wood."

courtiers immediately turn into ungainly dolts. And in the end, the man who is really the most intelligent at court is the one who is capable of flights of fancy to match his lord's desires—flights of fancy that go far beyond the capabilities of those courtiers lost in blind obsequiousness. Such a man is capable of going along with things that even Ser Polo, the court fool, would reject out of hand. If anyone doubts this, just look at the Marescalco and his wife problems. [*Laughing*] That poor fellow is at his wits' end! But then again, lucky are the men who go to court already crazy—they, at least, have already taken care of the problem.

ᴙᴁ SCENE IX ᴃᴙ

MESSER JACOPO and AMBROGIO

JACOPO: [*Entering and hearing the last of* AMBROGIO*'s soliloquy*] What's all this about wise men and madmen?

AMBROGIO: Oh, I didn't see you—I was just talking to myself about the prank[137] being played on our Marescalco, which has him looking for his confessor.

JACOPO: His confessor! Why?

AMBROGIO: Because he believes that having to take a wife is a death sentence—he doesn't see that it's all just nonsense.

JACOPO: It's not nonsense at all; he's actually going to have a beautiful and rich wife.

AMBROGIO: What do you think of our Lord?

JACOPO: I'd say that God couldn't have given us a better one.

AMBROGIO: You speak wisely. And he wouldn't be a Gonzaga if he weren't good, kind, and openhanded. But where did you hear that His Excellency was going to give him a wife?

JACOPO: From a first-rate source.

AMBROGIO: Where?

JACOPO: A perfect place for information, I'd say.

AMBROGIO: Could you name the man?

JACOPO: One who knows what's up.

AMBROGIO: Who is it that knows so much?

JACOPO: My barber.

AMBROGIO: [*Laughing*] Certainly a place worthy of credit, the barbershop,

---

137. *Burla.* See the discussion of the *burla* in the introductory essay.

where all the travelers of the whole world come bearing news. Let's go to the palace now so that we can find a good seat for the marriage oration.

JACOPO: Let's go. After all, we're paid not to give a damn and be mindless. Speaking of which, here comes the communal Pedant, babbling on about his usual muttonheaded blather.

AMBROGIO: Let's move along, for if he should hook up with us he'll deafen us with those annoying discourses of his.

✤ SCENE X ✤

The PEDANT, alone

PEDANT: [*Singing*]

Scribere clericulis paro doctrinale novellis
Rectis as es a, a, tibi dat declinatio prima.[138]

I was penetrated right to my intestines, right to my bowels, right to my uterus by the kind reception given me by His Most Excellent Lordship. So much so that I did not tell him about the audacious and insolent ribaldry that uncouth little piece of ass[139] subjected me to. But *ad rem nostram:*[140] given that His Most Illustrious Kindness has selected me to deliver the prologue, the sermon, the oration for the marriage of our companion, *nolo mirari,*[141] I want to enter into a discussion with Cicero's letters, and I hope to win such glory with my audience, speaking before the prefects and governors of this *aurea*[142] city, that *omnia gratis et cito obtineam.*[143] But here comes that professoricide.

138. "I proclaim a new method to teach young clerics to write, / The rule as, es, a, a, gives you the endings of the first declension." These are the first lines of a medieval Latin grammar by Alexandre Villadieu regarded as outdated in Aretino's day; thus once again the Pedant reveals the hollowness of his supposed learning.

139. *Ghiotticulo* (literally, "glutton-ass") seems to mean someone with a gluttonous ass, in other words someone eager to be sodomized. The term *ghiotto* (glutton) figures in various forms in the sexual insults of this comedy. It serves regularly as a metaphor for someone who has an overactive sexual appetite or is promiscuous, and it seems to be particularly associated with younger males engaged in sodomy as passive partners.

140. "Concerning our own affairs."

141. "Which is in no way surprising to me."

142. "Golden."

143. "I will obtain all that I ask, freely and immediately."

⸾꙳ SCENE XI ꙳⸾

The KNIGHT'S PAGE and the PEDANT

PAGE: Your Majesty, Your Magnificence, Your Lordship, have you seen the lord Knight, my master?

PEDANT: Hah! You little ass of gallows-bait![144] Hah! You little whore-ass![145] You dare to fool with the teacher of Mantua's *condiscipuli*[146] in the street, do you?

PAGE: What are you ass-scissoring and lusting corruptly after now?[147] Please tell me if you have seen him.

PEDANT: I swear to you by the Holy Gospels that I will have you given such a beating that you will be an example to all the little boy-whores.[148]

PAGE: Professor, can you say this in Latin? "The wall's pissing on me."[149]

PEDANT: *Mingere possa tu le interiora*,[150] you little glutton-killer.[151]

PAGE: How does the cross of the holy cross relate to the ABCs, Professor?

PEDANT: What a great disgrace it is that a shameless faggot[152] like you should provoke a great intellectual like me! Oh, oh, oh!

PAGE: Is it true, Professor, that they keep the K in the alphabet because it's an erect soldier?[153]

---

144. *Forchicula.* The first in a series of insults alluding to sodomy with the addition of the syllable *cul*, suggesting *culo* (ass).

145. *Meretriculo.*

146. "Students."

147. *Forbiculate e mandragolata.* These insults turn on references to sodomy. The Pedant's insistent use throughout this scene of words containing *cul* is echoed and then allusively extended with the Page's *mandragolata*, which may well have drawn on the popularity of Machiavelli's *La mandragola* and seems to be used by Aretino as a term implying sexual trickery or corruption.

148. *Cinediculi.*

149. In the Renaissance, when men regularly urinated against walls, the reversal of the normal order of things with a wall urinating on a young man would have seemed quite funny and clever. Much Renaissance humor was built upon such unexpected and often revealing reversals.

150. "You can piss out your innards" (i.e., as far as I'm concerned).

151. Critics have found this insult difficult to interpret. *Ghiotticidio* (glutton-killer) seems out of place in this exchange. However, the ending *-icidio* echoes the (feminine) term used earlier by the Pedant, *precettoricida*, translated as "professoricide," and may thus be another reference to the Pedant's claim that the Page had tried to kill him. If this repeating of forms is deliberate, it would suggest that in his rage the Pedant was revealing that he was a glutton—indeed, perhaps even a glutton for sodomy, the two concepts having been linked in the previous scene with the term *ghiotticulo* (glutton-ass) (see n. 139).

152. *Sfacciaticulo.*

153. An allusion both to the phallic shape of the letter and to the fact that *cazzo* (phallus) begins

PEDANT: *Verum est*[154] that I will give you this! [*Making a threatening gesture*]

PAGE: We're coming to fisticuffs, eh?

PEDANT: I cannot contain my urbane anger—take this! [*Swinging at the* PAGE]

PAGE: By the body of Chri— [*Picking up a stone*]

PEDANT: Put down that stone!

PAGE: I am going to tell what you did to me, you . . .

PEDANT: *Mentiris per gutter!*[155]

PAGE: It was you that wanted it, you wicked Pedant!

PEDANT: Begone, *maledictus homo!*[156]

PAGE: I have you by the ass. Take this! [*Making an obscene gesture*]

PEDANT: You give me the fig, do you?[157] [*The* PAGE *runs off, and the* PEDANT *turns to go in the opposite direction*] Here is my *domiculo e tuguriale albergulo.*[158] My cerebral cavity is spinning.[159] I must go inside *per requiescere aliquantulum.*[160]

Act IV

❧ SCENE I ☙

The MARESCALCO, alone

MARESCALCO: Giannicco ought to be back by now. O God, who would have ever thought that such a cruel fate awaited me? How many unlucky men have I comforted in my day who had their honor and fortunes destroyed on account of their wives? How many sad stories have I heard from first one fellow and then another about this wife and that one? And how many men have I seen pointed out by someone saying, "Last night I did it with his wife" and adding, "He's a dupe, a cuckold, a jerk"? And I know many men who—aware of the evil reputation that their wives have given them—are so ashamed that they begin to fear

---

with a *K* sound, and a reference to a serious scholarly debate going on at the time about whether the letter *K* should be kept in the alphabet.

154. "It's true."

155. "You're lying through your teeth."

156. "O evil man."

157. An obscene gesture made by inserting one's thumb between the first two fingers of the same hand and flashing it at the person to be insulted. Given the double meaning of "fig" (see n. 96) and the look of the fingers being penetrated by the thumb, the meaning of the gesture should be self-evident.

158. "Domicile and humble abode." The Pedant's *culs* are multiplying.

159. *Giricula.*

160. "To repose a bit."

that everyone is talking about them, and they no longer go to church or to public squares or frequent the court. [*Seeing* GIANNICCO *enter*] I see my little bad boy returning, and he's laughing. Perhaps he wasn't summoned by the Lord for the wedding rings.

🍂 SCENE II 🍂

The MARESCALCO and GIANNICCO

MARESCALCO: Well?

GIANNICCO: I don't want to give you any more bad news, but the wife is still yours.

MARESCALCO: What do you mean, "still"?

GIANNICCO: What do I know? But the jeweler was called for you.

MARESCALCO: Are you absolutely sure that it wasn't for someone else?

GIANNICCO: I saw the rings.

MARESCALCO: That doesn't mean anything. He's always showing his jewels to people.

GIANNICCO: Do you think I'm blind?

MARESCALCO: No, but sometimes you can mistake one thing for another.

GIANNICCO: By the body of Saint— . . . you make me want to swear.

MARESCALCO: Maybe he was aware that you were there, and he just pretended to buy them.

GIANNICCO: He said he was buying them for you.

MARESCALCO: Aren't there other "you's" besides me in the world?

GIANNICCO: He even said "Master."

MARESCALCO: And surely there are other "Masters."

GIANNICCO: You can interpret things as you like. I'm telling you that you should get your hair washed, and have a shave and a good bath as well, because tonight you're going to meet your wife, marry her, and sleep with her. Is that crystal clear?

MARESCALCO: Oh, by all that's holy, by that whore Fortune! Me, really? Take a wife? A wife for me? And what have I done to deserve this?

GIANNICCO: Oh, the rings are splendid—one is red like a cooked shrimp, and the other is green like green sauce.

MARESCALCO: What do I care about the colors? Oh, damned fate, shitty fate!

GIANNICCO: One stone is called something like "carubino" or "serafino"—at least I know it ends in "ino." The name of the green one I don't remember, but it's something like "hot" or "emerald."[161] Whatever. . . . But what really matters is that I've warned you about the wife thing; now it's up to you.

MARESCALCO: What do I care about the names of the stones?

GIANNICCO: Evidently nothing, but it's quite important to realize that they cost four large ducats.[162]

MARESCALCO: Four ducats, eh?

GIANNICCO: Four or three and a half, more or less.

MARESCALCO: Ah well, that serves me right, or terribly. I would have been better off shoeing geese—yes, geese!—instead of horses and leaving the womanizers, drinkers, backbiters, and flatterers to preen and prance at court. All the favors and ease are theirs anyway and certainly not for the likes of me. [*Noticing the* COUNT *and the* KNIGHT *entering looking for him*] But now it looks like it's my turn.

❧ SCENE III ☙

The COUNT, the KNIGHT, the MARESCALCO, and GIANNICCO

COUNT: We're pleased to serve you, my good man, and our great friend. The Lord has commanded us that we are to bring you at eight to the Count's house, where everything has been set up for the wedding.

KNIGHT: The bride and the wedding will be fitting for a great lord, not for someone without rank, so you will be eternally grateful and obligated to His Excellency.

MARESCALCO: If one feels an obligation to someone who ties a stone around one's neck when one is drowning, you're right. But I'm more obligated to my patron, the Duke, more than liberality and virtuous deeds[163] are to Cardinal Ippolito de'Medici, as the statue of Pasquino said in Rome.[164] But what have I

---

161. *Caldo* (hot), *smeraldo* (emerald).

162. A significant price to have paid. *Ducati largi* were Venetian coins originally minted in gold and highly valued during the Renaissance, although their precise value varied with the amount of precious metal they contained and the monetary policy of Venice.

163. *Virtù.*

164. Aretino is again shamelessly flattering the Medici favorite mentioned in the Prologue (see n. 4). The statue of Pasquino in Rome was a monument where people posted political comments, predictions, and diverse slanders and compliments, especially during carnival. What the statue had to say via these writings was widely reported and often had considerable weight. These sayings of Pasquino were known as *Pasquinate*, and Aretino, was reputed to be the author of some of the most vicious.

done against the Duke? Heaven knows I'd never do His Majesty any harm, like Fra Benedetto.[165] Still, I would rather be thrown into a latrine than take a wife.

GIANNICCO: What language! But to you a latrine would seem like perfume.

MARESCALCO: Shut up, unless you want me to take it out on you.

GIANNICCO: I'm silent.

COUNT: Good Master, I'm your friend, and friends always give good advice to friends. And I'm warning you that if the Lord hears your silly bitching, he'll throw you out, and that's all there is to it.

KNIGHT: And that's not just talk.

COUNT: Don't say I didn't warn you. You should certainly realize that there's not another lord like our Duke of Mantua in the world, as everyone agrees. He's the only prince who gives gifts, caresses, and fortune to his courtiers. Even the best men of the pope and the emperor aren't as well dressed as you, as you could have seen for yourself when they were in Bologna.[166] Why, a few loving words of His Lordship's are worth more than the deeds of other rulers. It's only because his humanity makes us all his companions that you have the nerve to defy his orders.

KNIGHT: The Count is speaking to you as a true friend. Remember, after the fact there's no use in repenting. Fortune is offering you her graces up front; be sensible and take her.

GIANNICCO: And if she offered up her behind?

COUNT: Shut up, kid.

GIANNICCO: What do you mean, "Shut up kid"? Can't I speak on my master's wedding day?

KNIGHT: He's right. But listen to the Count, who's your friend. Look, there are plenty of Marescalcos, but there is only one Duke of Mantua.

COUNT: By God, that's exactly it, and if you aren't careful, you'll be sorry later. You should take this wife and not waste any more time. But no, someone like you has to be forced to accept favors, because you're a blockhead. Take her and be quick about it. I shouldn't have to say it again.

KNIGHT: Don't put yourself in the position of having to say afterwards, "I made a mistake."

COUNT: Do you know what's the worst thing in the world?

GIANNICCO: My master.

165. Possibly Benedetto Poncetti, a favorite of Federico Gonzaga, whom Aretino had attacked in print in 1528.

166. In 1530, when Charles V was crowned emperor in Bologna by Pope Clement VII.

MARESCALCO: Yes, I know.

COUNT: What?

MARESCALCO: Taking a wife.

COUNT: Rubbish. The worst thing in the world is to lose the favor of those in power—lords. And it's much easier to lose than to regain. Now don't do something that will make ours turn against you, for even though he's very forgiving, when he gets his dander up, things can get really serious. He may allow one mistake or two or three, even nine or ten, but then he'll punish you for all of them just when you think he's forgotten. Still, I'll leave it up to you. You're the master.

KNIGHT: That's just like what the country bumpkin said to the barber who was accidentally cutting his throat as he shaved him: "I'll leave it up to you because you're the master."

MARESCALCO: You two are enough to make me curse heaven itself. What do you think I could do with a wife? How am I going to live with her? When I have to leave, whose house am I going to put her in, who can I ask to look after her, who will I leave her to? With you, maybe, because you're so careful about looking after the interests of your friends and relatives? No, I won't get married. You can tell the Lord that he can cut me to pieces, burn me alive, tear me apart with pincers, but I'm not going to take her, not even for you! In the end I want to be a man, not some deer with horns.

GIANNICCO: Does being a deer mean being a cuckold, Master?

MARESCALCO: And you, shut up!

GIANNICCO: Thanks be to God!

COUNT: Be quiet, boy. [*Turning to the* MARESCALCO] We'll report your mule-headedness to the Lord, and if he asks us to knock some sense into you, we'll do our duty.

KNIGHT: You were always a horse's ass, and if it were up to me I would treat you like one.

COUNT: Enough! The wretch will eat the bread of repentance.

MARESCALCO: I'm as honorable a man at my social level as you are at yours, and you're out of line speaking to me like this.

KNIGHT: Our mistake has been in dealing with you with words and not with deeds.

COUNT: You might as well stop worrying about it: if the Lord orders it, you'll either gain a wife or lose your skin. [*Turning to the* KNIGHT] Let us return to court, sir Knight.

KNIGHT: Let us go, sir Count. [*They leave*]

MARESCALCO: O cruel fate, what do you think of my situation now? Should I take her? By God, no. You say yes, and I say no. But who's this coming up to me so slowly? Ah, it's the Pedant.

᙭ SCENE IV ᙭

The MARESCALCO and the PEDANT

MARESCALCO: I didn't recognize you. Where are you headed?

PEDANT: *Cogitabam—idest,*[167] I was thinking—about the innate goodness of our Dominator, Protector, and Monarch whose beneficence has placed on my shoulders the responsibility for the nuptial discourse during the decorous celebration of your wedding.

MARESCALCO: In other words, I am to take her?

᙭ SCENE V ᙭

MESSER JACOPO, the PEDANT, GIANNICCO, and the MARESCALCO

JACOPO: [*Entering and overhearing the* MARESCALCO] Even a blind man can see that you'll take her. But after all, who wouldn't?

PEDANT: Listen to me, companion: *per Deum,*[168] in God's name, she is one of the most nicely formed *puelle*[169] of Mantua.

JACOPO: It's more important that she's good, for beauty without goodness is like a house without a door, a ship without wind, a fountain without water.

PEDANT: That would be Seneca in chapter 17 of *De agilibus mundi.*[170]

GIANNICCO: What? Is the Pedant blaspheming?

JACOPO: [*To* GIANNICCO] Be quiet. [*To the* MARESCALCO] You idiot, you idiot, you idiot! I'm going to call you that three times so that you'll get the message. Don't you realize, you animal, and I'll call you that as well, that if your father hadn't taken a wife, you wouldn't exist? And I've heard a preacher from Padua say that it's better to be born and end up in hell than never to have been born.

PEDANT: That would be Augustine in *De civitate Dei.*[171]

---

167. "I was thinking, that is."
168. "In God's name."
169. "Girls."
170. *On the Movements of the World.* There is no such work by Seneca.
171. *The City of God.* Actually it appears that Augustine did not say this there.

JACOPO: How can a man go so stubbornly astray? Don't you want there to be another you in this city after you're gone? Why, without you the horses would be much less well cared for. I say this because of the miraculous cures that you have accomplished for leg sores, worms, fevers, problems with hooves and shoeing, and so forth. Still, when your time comes, when you become old or worn out by disease, when you are gone, your sons will take up your place, and our land will not feel any loss.

PEDANT: Oh, what an egregious disquisition on progeny and childlessness!

GIANNICCO: What did you say, Pedant?

JACOPO: Now come here and hear me out, as one should a friend. I want to tell you a little bit about the happiness I find in the prudence, the ability, and the chastity of my wife.

MARESCALCO: Tell me about these miracles, but mind you, no lying.

PEDANT: Our Messer Jacopo is neither mendacious nor loquacious, so listen to him; hear what he has to say.

JACOPO: I took my wife—may her memory be blessed—in the year that the old duke,[172] remembered for his generous and glorious nature, was put in charge of the papal armies. But no, I'm confused, it was the year that His Excellency was made Captain of the Church,[173] and I must have been at the time twenty or twenty-one years old, still penniless and unwashed, as most courtiers are,[174] when I got this good wife. I can't help but cry when I remember it.

GIANNICCO: Don't cry, sir.

PEDANT: The call of the flesh continues to seduce.

MARESCALCO: What humbug!

JACOPO: So my good wife came into my life, and she took me to live with her in her noble house. In that place, well furnished with soft beds and fine furnishings, she brought me back to life. As a result, day by day appreciating ever more the finer things of life, I became another man. She, in turn, sagely understood my nature, and everything she said, everything she arranged, and everything she did turned out just as I would have wished, and there was nothing else I could have asked for. When I fell ill with something—I don't recall what—oh, God, what care, what compassion, what love she lavished on me! She didn't eat, sleep, or rest during my illness. What's more, at every little sigh of mine, at every little

172. Gianfrancesco Gonzaga II (1466–1519).

173. 1521.

174. I.e., as most of them are at that age.

stirring, she was there asking, "What's wrong? What would you like? What's bothering you?" Then, when she gave me pesto[175] or bread in broth to make me feel better, she used such sweet words that she made those dishes that seemed bitter to me taste like sweet honey. Anyone who saw her with the doctor asking anxiously about my health would have understood what it is to have a wife. And who could describe how her sweet care for me redoubled when I recovered my health?

PEDANT: Aristotle gives a similar account in *The Ethics*.[176]

MARESCALCO: Hurry it up, if you have more to say.

JACOPO: Take it easy. I can say that there is no luscious fruit, no healthy food, that my most sweet wife did not bring me. I was cured thanks to God's mercy and hers. Then my first son was born, and I derived such happiness from this that I forgot the court, my service there, and my concerns about being rewarded for my merits. In sum, I was transformed from a courtier into a lover of peace and quiet. I hardly ever left home, and if I did, every moment away seemed an eternity. As the boy grew, watching him play at the table, in the room, and in the bed, I felt an extraordinary pleasure.

PEDANT: Listen to what Virgil says on this: "*Mihi parvulus aula luderet Aeneas.*"[177] The queen of Carthage, Dido, never would have plunged the cruel steel into the side of her milky, ivory-white breast if Aeneas had given her a *puerulo da poter seco ludere in domo*.[178]

GIANNICCO: You know it all by heart, Professor—the Bible, the New Testament, everything.

PEDANT: These are not texts for nasty adolescents.[179] Ask me no more questions, for I will not reply.

MARESCALCO: Little children and madmen wreck a home.

GIANNICCO: And what about chickens?

JACOPO: I've lost the thread of my argument.

GIANNICCO: The Pedant here made you lose your track. Pedant, don't interrupt him.

MARESCALCO: [*Laughing*] What comic lines for a comedy!

175. A kind of pounded meat, not the Genoese pasta sauce popular today.

176. No such passage exists in Aristotle's *Ethics.*

177. "The little Aeneas played with me in my hall." For a change, this citation is accurate; see Virgil, *Aeneid*, IV, 328–30.

178. "A little child that she could have played with at home."

179. *Adulescentuli.*

JACOPO: I'll finish my argument another day. For now it's enough that I reassure you that this is a good thing to do. A man without a wife is like a fly without a head.

PEDANT: Plutarch in his *De insonio Scipionis* said the same thing.[180]

JACOPO: I wanted to tell you about the time I was in danger of being banished for the affair that you know about already. Thanks to the industriousness of my wife, not only was I not banished, but the matter was settled peacefully with my opponents in eight days. Nor should you think ill of her because with our little boy in her arms she went before the Lord and with great humility brought tears to the eyes of everyone with her sweet words on my behalf.

MARESCALCO: Sure, sure, and I'd like to believe that there's much more you could say. But the question is, does one rose make a springtime? If there were here a hundred married men, what do you think they would say about their wives, if they were willing to speak truthfully?

JACOPO: I won't deny that there are some bad wives. Why, even among the Apostles there was Judas.

PEDANT: *Omnis regula patitur exceptionem, latine loquendo.*[181]

JACOPO: But this bride—one can say "your" bride—is well known as a woman without equal, an angel, a real angel.

GIANNICCO: If she's an angel, take her, Master.

MARESCALCO: [*To* GIANNICCO] If you say one more word, I'll break your bones with my fists, I'll brain you with my knuckles, I'll gouge out your eyes with my fingers!

PEDANT: *Irascimini, et nolite peccare,* as is said in the Apocalypse.[182]

MARESCALCO: Messer Jacopo, I don't want to waste your time, so let's not talk about it any more, if you want to be my friend. Is that clear?

JACOPO: [*Becoming angry*] What do I care about your friendship? I'm advising you as a brother to change your ways. Get on the right path, or one day you'll be scratching your ass and crying over your stupidity. Without the kindness of the Lord, you would be ruined and go around with nothing, like Don Franzino.[183] And you would fall apart if you weren't able to put on your leather apron and spend all day kissing the feet of horses.

---

180. *On the Insomnia of Scipio.* Once again the Pedant has erred in his citation. There was a famous work *The Dream of Scipio.*

181. "Every rule has its exception, speaking in Latin."

182. "Be angry, but sin not," actually said in Ephesians 4:26.

183. Possibly a character in popular lore.

MARESCALCO: I am an honorable man.

JACOPO: You can be whatever you like, but I'll never be happy with you,[184] even if you want to be my friend. Let's go, Professor, to San Sebastiano—actually I meant to say the Palazzo del Te. Perhaps Giulio Romano has discovered some divine history.[185]

PEDANT: *Eamus.*[186] What a beautiful building that palace is, created from Romano's little model.[187] He has successfully imitated *Vittruvio prospettivo prisco.*[188]

JACOPO: Let's go. [*He and the* PEDANT *leave*]

SCENE VI

The MARESCALCO and GIANNICCO

MARESCALCO: I'd like to run after that stupid old man and give him a good knifing! That would teach him to try to talk me into taking a wife, something he'd happily refuse himself. But it's always that way: someone who's broken his neck because of a mistake wants everyone else to break theirs. But in the end, one man knows as much as another.

GIANNICCO: Give it to the old fool. Oh, that evil old man, that wicked man! But Master, here comes the jeweler for you.

SCENE VII

The JEWELER, the MARESCALCO, GIANNICCO, and the BALIA

JEWELER: [*Showing him two jewels*] Take a look. Go ahead, touch. Good luck, *proficiat.*[189] Knowing that they were being bought for you, I got you two jewels that would be fit to remake the Turkish helmet made in Venice by the famous

---

184. I.e., if you continue like this.

185. San Sebastiano was the name of a church in Mantua as well as one of the city's Gonzaga palaces. The magnificent Palazzo del Te is another of the Gonzaga palaces, designed and decorated by Giulio Romano (1492–1546), an architect, artist, and friend of Aretino. Once again Aretino seems to be flattering his friends and supporters.

186. "Let's go."

187. *Modelliculo.*

188. "The ancient perspective of Vitruvius." Vitruvius was an author of the first century B.C. whose *De architectura* is the only ancient work on architecture to survive. It had a great influence on Renaissance architecture and architectural theory.

189. "May you flourish."

jeweler Luigi Cavorlino.[190] Oh, what a lively spirit, oh, what a gentleman, oh, what a perfect friend he is!

MARESCALCO: Run along, run along, and mind your own business.

JEWELER: My business is that of my friends. But you must be under the influence of the moon, for today it's foolish. But I'm off to see the medals, statues, and vases that the abbot found in the remains of an ancient outhouse. I've heard there is a head of Saint Joseph done by Polyclitus and a foot of the old In-the-Beginning Himself done by Phidias.[191] After that, I need to get organized to go to Venice to trade ten thousand green quartzes for garnets and pearls, which I want to use to adorn my gold-brocaded robe. And whoever says my robe was made from the saddlecloth of Bartolomeo Colleoni[192] is lying: I'm a Knight of the Church and a papal jeweler. Do you understand, Marescalco?

MARESCALCO: Sure, run along, now. [*To* GIANNICCO] What an ass he is! [*Seeing the* BALIA *hurrying towards him*] And now what does my Balia want?

GIANNICCO: I know what she wants.

MARESCALCO: Beastly boy, beastly boy!

Giannicco. I really do know.

MARESCALCO: All right, what?

GIANNICCO: For you to take her to the wedding.

MARESCALCO: [*Hitting him*] Take this for weddings! And this for wives! And this for husbands!

GIANNICCO: Is this the way you treat those who give you pleasure?

MARESCALCO: [*Hitting him again*] Take this for the pleasures you give! And this for your services! And this for your merits!

BALIA: [*To the* MARESCALCO] Don't disgrace yourself so in public. Enough, I say! Get going, go inside! Enough is enough!

MARESCALCO: [*To* GIANNICCO] Traitor!

GIANNICCO: Everyone is going to know about this in the end. Just you wait. Beating me, eh?

BALIA: [*To the* MARESCALCO] Stop it, I say. Aren't you ashamed to be running after him in the streets?

---

190. One of Aretino's Venetian friends and a noted goldsmith. One of his famed works was a Turkish helmet of gold covered with gems.

191. A poke at the lively Renaissance trade in fake ancient artifacts. Polyclitus and Phidias were famous sculptors of ancient Greece, much too early in time to have created anything to do with Saint Joseph, and rather late to have done the foot of the old In-the-Beginning Himself, i.e., God.

192. Perhaps a reference to the famous equestrian statue of the noted condottiere Bartolomeo Colleoni in Venice, with an implicit joke about testicles (see n. 23).

MARESCALCO: [*To* GIANNICCO] Rascal, glutton![193]

GIANNICCO: I'll tell all over!

MARESCALCO: [*To* GIANNICCO][194] Why, you little whore!

BALIA: [*To the* MARESCALCO] Come now, calm down.

GIANNICCO: Enough, enough. [*He runs off*]

MARESCALCO: [*Held back by the* BALIA] Let me go, you old witch. By the body of— . . . you're making me lose my temper!

BALIA: [*Losing her temper*] It's a waste of time to help this guy. What haven't we suffered for this madman who wants to destroy us all today? As far as I'm concerned, you can drop dead. I'm going home, and get this through your head, I'm no longer your Balia. [*She leaves*]

MARESCALCO: [*Yelling after her*] You ugly old bearded witch, go to the devil! I've gotten rid of the whole lot of them: Count, Knight, Giannicco, Balia, and that big shit Messer Jacopo. Now I want to see if they're going to force a wife on me. Let the Lord order me to give up my life for him, which in the end would mean less to me than if he ordered me or even begged me to take a wife. By my faith, I will not take a wife! By God, he will not give the Marescalco a wife! Ah, no, no, let him think of something else, and if his goal is to kill me, why, he can at least have me executed quickly rather than nailing me to that cross.

﹛ SCENE VIII ﹜

The DUKE'S FOOTMAN and the MARESCALCO

FOOTMAN: Greetings.

MARESCALCO: Good day.

FOOTMAN: What a cold reply! But I really am your friend.

MARESCALCO: For God's sake, don't make problems for me.

FOOTMAN: What do you mean, problems? You ought to be dancing in the streets, and instead you're crying.

MARESCALCO: Why should I dance?

FOOTMAN: Because of your wife, your favor with the Lord, and the dowry.

---

193. For the sexual connotations of *ghiotto* (glutton), see n. 139.

194. Because the word used here, *puttana* (whore), is feminine, some have assumed that the Marescalco has suddenly begun to attack the Balia, but the context makes clear that he is continuing to trade insults with Giannicco. This is consistent with Aretino's tendency to use feminine endings for words relating to Giannicco and the Page, alluding to their passive sexual roles.

MARESCALCO: Don't torment me any more, please.

FOOTMAN: Even the hose that you're wearing could be mine,[195] do you understand?

MARESCALCO: If you weren't the Lord's footman, you would have to shut up or else something unpleasant would come your way. And if you don't quit it, I'll put aside the respect I owe and maybe, just maybe . . .

FOOTMAN: What "respect" are you talking about, and what "maybe"? You're not worth the trouble, and if it weren't for the fact that I'd lose face for getting involved with a craftsman who's hardly bright enough to hold two nails and a hammer, never mind a sword, I'd show you that you're out of your league. Yes, you are going to take a wife! You are going to have her and accept her, whether you want to or not! Yes, *your* wife, *your* wife, yes! Have you got my gist?

MARESCALCO: Even when a man wants to, he can't just mind his own business. His day is ruined a thousand times over, thanks to these pains in the neck.

FOOTMAN: What are you saying?

MARESCALCO: I'm in your debt. Go with God.

FOOTMAN: I can see that you two are going to make a happy couple. I don't know who has more to be miserable about, she about you or you about her. But anyway, take her and don't go on about it.

MARESCALCO: Dear God, dear Christ, dear Jesus, what torture! I beg you, brother, to speak about something else or go on your way.

FOOTMAN: We are speaking about something that means your happiness. Take her!

MARESCALCO: My life is finished.

FOOTMAN: She's very pretty.

MARESCALCO: The world is totally destroyed!

FOOTMAN: More than four thousand scudi . . .

MARESCALCO: I'll have to disappear.

FOOTMAN: . . . part in goods, part in money.

MARESCALCO: That's it!

FOOTMAN: A noblewoman.

MARESCALCO: Patience!

FOOTMAN: Very young.

MARESCALCO: Please! I'm going into my house to get away from you. [*He goes in*]

FOOTMAN: [*Calling after him*] And don't forget about those hose! [*Laughing*]

195. I.e., could be mine if you didn't have the Lord's favor.

Well, I've done what the Lord wished: he ordered me to harass him. He really is suffering. But I must get back to court.

Act V

⌇ SCENE I ⌇

MESSER JACOPO, MESSER JACOPO'S SON, and the MARESCALCO

JACOPO: Given my long friendship with the Marescalco, I really can't stay angry with him very long, even though I might want to, for he really is a good man and deserves to be loved. I'll wait here outside his house until he comes out, and with the example and the testimony of my oldest son I'll regain his friendship and press him to take a wife willingly so that he won't have to take her unwillingly without gaining either rank or favor. But here he comes.

MARESCALCO: Perhaps I should flee this city to escape my torments. But here's trouble.

JACOPO: Master, the arguments that arise between friends are like the winds: they quickly die down. So let's let our grievances go up in smoke and speak calmly together.

MARESCALCO: Sure, I've put it behind me, and I'm your friend again—as long as you don't start blabbing about that subject, which would cut me to the quick.

JACOPO: Here's one of the first fruits that I harvested from the wifely tree. Here's the seat of my life, here's the staff of my old age, here are the eyeglasses of my latter years. This is my son, this is my companion, this is my brother. He sustains me, he serves me, he guides me. And in my old age, God willing, he'll no longer be my son but will serve as a father himself, and as I now sustain our little household, he'll then sustain it.

MARESCALCO: May God protect him. I'm not such a lucky man, that I could hope to have a son like him.

JACOPO: Listen to me all the same: he sings, he plays an instrument, he rides, he fences, he writes well, spells well, dances well, eats even better, and would be capable of serving the sultan himself. And if you had such a son yourself, wouldn't you cherish him as much as the gifted artists and writers cherish the kindness of our Lord?

MARESCALCO: Be quiet; here come the Count and the Knight. What could they want?

JACOPO: [*To his son*] Go on, now, my son, it's getting to be time to give the young horses a run.

SON: Father, that tailor is a nasty man.

JACOPO: Why?

SON: Because I hoped to have my new outfit this morning, but the cloth isn't even cut yet.

MARESCALCO: Hmmm.

᷽ SCENE II ᷞ

The COUNT, the KNIGHT, MESSER JACOPO, and the MARESCALCO

COUNT: Are you still angry with us?

KNIGHT: Here we are, your friends more than ever.

JACOPO: He's more flexible than a reed.

COUNT: Please forgive us for our harsh words earlier.

KNIGHT: Our love for you made us lose our tempers.

JACOPO: Like I lost mine with you.

MARESCALCO: Your Lordships are my patrons, and it's wrong for clients to get angry with their patrons. As long as you aren't here to talk to me about a wife, I'm ready to serve you in everything.

COUNT: Brother, we thank you. We have returned to you at the behest of the Lord, who has asked us to plead with you, not order you, on his behalf that you be willing to consent to his wish that this evening you marry the sweet young thing.

MARESCALCO: I feel like I'm dying!

KNIGHT: Ah, back to your old childishness.

MARESCALCO: What suffering!

COUNT: Listen, you would be wiser to bless our words and our very steps.

MARESCALCO: All right, let's hear it, I'm listening.

COUNT: His Excellency, above and beyond the other favors he has done you, after you have given her the ring, wants to make you a knight, an honor worthy of a king.

JACOPO: What more could you ask for—lasagna?

KNIGHT: Certainly the highest honor you can give to anyone, even a prince, is to call him Knight.

MARESCALCO: This seems even worse than taking a wife.

COUNT: Are you out of your mind?

KNIGHT: Poor fellow!

JACOPO: Silly fool!

MARESCALCO: A knight, the golden spur? I'm thinking of the Jeweler, who even though he may be widely recognized as crazy at least has remained sensible enough to not want to be called a knight. Such titles tend to place you at the right hand of the Lord, and that can sometimes lead to unpleasant consequences.

COUNT: What a character!

MARESCALCO: I've heard that when a lord wants to flatter someone a bit, he makes him a knight. It seems like a title suitable for someone who needs prestige rather than real things.

KNIGHT: It's a title that anyone would welcome, and it was created not just for the prestige of the nobility but to ennoble the deserving.

MARESCALCO: My lords, a knight without riches is like a wall without a crucifix: in plain language, everyone pisses on it.

JACOPO: He's talking nonsense.

KNIGHT: He's not sane enough to even write a will.

COUNT: Let's forget it and return to the bride. You should know that she is learned.

KNIGHT: That's true. That new madrigal that's being sung to the tune of Marchetto[196] was composed by her.

JACOPO: I don't sing anything else these days.

MARESCALCO: So she's learned?

COUNT: Most learned.

MARESCALCO: A poetess?

KNIGHT: She is, exactly as we have told you.

MARESCALCO: Oh, I understand, all right. I feel them already, I can see them sprouting. She composes, eh? When women begin to write songs, their husbands begin to grow horns. Let me explain. The other day two young women, reading the *Furioso* by Ariosto, in the part where Ruggiero is under the control of the fairy Alcina—[197]

COUNT: [*Interrupting*] By the way, this young woman doesn't read anything but the lives of the saints, and one day I'm sure we'll be lighting candles at her feet, like with Lena da lo Olio.[198]

---

196. Marchetto Cara, a famous singer as well as composer and lutist. He lived his later years at the court of the Gonzaga, where he died in 1527.

197. For these events in *Orlando furioso* by Ludovico Ariosto (1474–1533), see VII, 9–32.

198. Apparently the Bolognese noblewoman Elena Duglioli dall'Olio (d. 1519), renowned for her sanctity and made a saint in 1534. The reference, however, may be tinged with irony, as Aretino attacked her in 1534, labeling her a whore.

MARESCALCO: Let me finish.

KNIGHT: Listen, listen! Just make up your mind to do it. It'll be better for you if you do.

MARESCALCO: Okay, you go ahead and talk, and I'll be quiet.

COUNT: Now is the time to focus a bit on the truth.

MARESCALCO: Just let me say a few words, and then you can talk all you want.

COUNT: Go ahead.

MARESCALCO: It's not so much that those young girls were reading Ariosto as . . . well, I don't know how to say it, but looking at another book . . .

KNIGHT: What book?

MARESCALCO: That book where there are pictured those birds that have their nests in codpieces of velvet.[199]

KNIGHT: And then what?

MARESCALCO: Just looking at those pictures, they got all hot and bothered.

KNIGHT: [*Laughing*] Oh my, my, my, my, my!

COUNT: You're taking things much too seriously. If you're so blind, I must tell you that you're overlooking the good fortune that comes with taking a woman of such reputation.

MARESCALCO: And I must tell you that I'm not so blind as to overlook the dishonor that comes with taking a woman of bad reputation.

COUNT: This woman is held by everyone to have a good reputation.

KNIGHT: If she didn't have a good reputation, the Lord wouldn't give her to you.

MARESCALCO: Oh, these lords, these lords, these lords—they're an evil lot. Let's leave it at that.

COUNT: How many husbands do I know who if it weren't for their wives would go begging?

MARESCALCO: How many husbands do I know who if it weren't for their wives would go about celebrating?

JACOPO: There's nothing worse than . . . but I don't want to say it.

MARESCALCO: Go ahead.

JACOPO: Than to insist on having the night without the day.[200]

MARESCALCO: You're confusing my small error with your great one.

199. As noted earlier, *uccello* has the double meaning of "bird" and "phallus."

200. The Italian proverb is "refusing to put water with wine," but the sense is "refusing to put the male with the female"—in other words, not to engage in heterosexual intercourse. The thing "nothing worse than" that Jacopo was referring to was refusing heterosexual relations with a wife in favor of sodomy.

COUNT: Let's not lose track of our main concern. Have you talked with Messer Jacopo about the happiness of having a wife?

MARESCALCO: Yes.

COUNT: And what did you learn from him?

MARESCALCO: That he hates me so much that he wants to see me dead.

JACOPO: What are you talking about? Dead?

MARESCALCO: That's right, dead. You advised me to do what Ambrogio, a good and honest man, warned me against, contradicting everything you said.

KNIGHT: Ambrogio, eh?

JACOPO: And you believe Ambrogio?

COUNT: Do you trust Ambrogio?

MARESCALCO: I believe Ambrogio and trust him like the *verbum*[201] of God. But wait, I just thought of something.

COUNT: What?

MARESCALCO: A thing that I saw a young woman of the court do.

COUNT: What did she do?

MARESCALCO: When she broke one of her nails, her cries of pain created a furor all over the palace. But when she had her ears pierced to hang some junk on them, she laughed as heartily as I would laugh if the Duke were to change his mind about my wife.

COUNT: What's that got to do with anything?

MARESCALCO: This: wives are all investments on which you can lose everything.

COUNT: Your wife isn't the type to pierce her ears. She's not like that.

MARESCALCO: If she pisses like the others, she must be like the others.

KNIGHT: What a character!

MARESCALCO: What a character, eh? Do you believe that even if this woman couldn't afford to have brocades like a queen, she would be willing to be second to any other woman in other vanities? Woman are creatures of the devil, may cancer eat them all!

COUNT: Let's get this over once and for all. Get it through your head that it's better to do what must be done. Tonight it's your destiny that you must take a wife.

201. "Word."

❧ SCENE III ❧

The PEDANT, the MARESCALCO, the COUNT,
the KNIGHT, and MESSER JACOPO

PEDANT: [*Entering quickly*] *Sapiens dominatur astris.*

MARESCALCO: Here's the man who'll defend me. What did you just say,
Professor?

PEDANT: I said that the wise man rules over destiny, that is, the stars. It is
true, however, that you must take a wife. Read Ptolemy, Albumasar, and the
other astronomers about how *fatis agimur.*[202] It's the old *sic fata volet,*[203] the old *sic
erat in fatis.*[204]

COUNT: What do you say to that?

MARESCALCO: I say I'd shove it up the rears of Albumasar and Ptolemy and
all the astrologers that have been and will be.

KNIGHT: Oh, oh, oh!

JACOPO: Professor, listen, persuade him with your philosophy to take her.
Say more.

PEDANT: Most willingly. *Volentieri, libenter, quis habet aures audiendi audiat.*[205] Hear
me out my friend, *quia amici fidelis nulla est comparatio.*[206] Everything that is, is the
will of God, and especially marriages, where He always has a hand in the action.
Et iterum,[207] again I say that this your marriage is a product of His working this
morning above in heaven, and this evening down here below it will happen, for
as I said, God has taken it into His hands.

MARESCALCO: It would have been much better for me, and for the honor of
Messer Lord God, if He had put His hands to a letter of credit for one
thousand ducats that I could draw from a bank.

---

202. "We are guided by fate." Ptolemy (ca. A.D. 90–168) was regarded in the Renaissance as the
most famous and influential of ancient astronomers. Albumasar (805–885) was an Arab astron-
omer and astrologer whose work was often seen as continuing and expanding on the work of
Ptolemy. Astrology and astronomy are spoken of here as essentially interchangeable—something
that was widely accepted in the premodern world, with astrology often being seen as the practical
side of astronomy.

203. "What fate has decreed."

204. "It was in the fates."

205. "Willingly, let him who has ears capable of hearing, hear me."

206. "Because there is nothing like a faithful friend."

207. "And moreover."

COUNT: Given the fact that He has given you four thousand ducats as a dowry, don't you see that He has, in fact, taken the matter into His hands?

PEDANT: Let me finish. Marescalco, I tell you that there could well be born a son of *seminis eius*,[208] which from the mother's side will have that *pulcherrima gratia*[209] that Alfonso d'Avalos[210] has, who with his martial and Apollonian presence makes the rest of us seem mere apes with tails. And the *acerrimus virtutum ac vitiorum demonstrator*[211] said it well when he said that while his innate generosity left him stripped bare, as a result he displayed and shined forth more splendor than even the Roman Fabrizio[212] did in his *paupertate*.[213] Even if *veritas odium parit*.[214]

KNIGHT: Take note.

COUNT: Listen up.

JACOPO: Pay attention.

MARESCALCO: I took note, I listened up, I paid attention.

PEDANT: And who knows if your boy would learn that *strenua eloquenzia*[215] with which the most invincible duke of Urbino[216] addressed Charles V, emperor of the Italians, as he told him of the Italian campaigns of the soldiery of Italy, Gaul, Spain, and Germany, which amazed His Majesty, just as Quintus Maximus Fabii once did to the Roman Senate when explaining to them the tactics he used to hold at bay Hannibal the Carthaginian.

KNIGHT: And he's just getting warmed up!

PEDANT: Of course.

COUNT: The words of the learned are certainly enjoyable.

MARESCALCO: [*With irony*] These are the *little* pleasures, all right.

PEDANT: Your son might equal the qualities of Alessandro de'Medici, another Alexander the Great; or the much feared Signor Giovanni de'Medici, *terrore*

208. "His seed."

209. "Most beautiful grace."

210. Alfonso d'Avalos (1502–46) was another of Aretino's patrons. Most noted as a commander in the emperor's army, he was also a patron to writers and artists and served as governor of the Duchy of Milan.

211. "Hard judge of virtue and vice."

212. Caius Fabritius was a consul in ancient Rome and a general during the Republic. The Pedant is referring to the story that when Fabritius was envoy to Pyrrhus, he refused the rich gifts that were offered to him.

213. "Poverty."

214. "Truth generates hatred."

215. "Bold eloquence."

216. Francesco Maria I della Rovere (1490–1538).

hominumque deumque;[217] or Paolo Luzzasco, his teacher and disciple; or, in his goodness and generosity, Massimiliano Stampa. Now, as for *pictoribus atque poetis*,[218] he might equal Fortunio of Viterbo, for instance, famed in Hebrew, Greek, Latin, and Italian.[219]

KNIGHT: You know lots of names.

PEDANT: *Ego habeo in catalogo*[220] all the *nomi virorum et mulierum illustrium*,[221] and I have learned them by heart. Now, if he were a poet, he might be another Pietro Bembo, *pater Pieridum*,[222] or a Molza di Modena, who with his melodious flute stopped rivers, or a learned Giovanni Guidiccioni di Lucca, or a sweet-voiced Alamanno of Florence, or an elegant clear Bernardo Capello di Adria, not to mention a young Venier or even, consider it, a witty Tasso.[223]

MARESCALCO: What do all these names have to do with me?

PEDANT: Think of them as the precious gems adorning an embroidered robe—the pearls, opals, sapphires, amethysts, and rubies. What do you think? And then your son might be like the miraculous Giulio Camillo, who shines forth the light of wisdom no less then the heavens, or the most famous Agostino Bevazzano from the Veneto, or the Unico Aretino, or a Giovanni Pollio from Arezzo. But wait, consider: he could be another witty Firenzuola or Vittorio Fausto, who has enough learning to sink his quinquireme.[224] Or he could be another Antonio Mezzabarba, whose legal studies have kept him too long from the Muses, or a Ludovico Dolce, whose fame flourishes.[225]

217. "The terror of both men and gods."

218. "Painters and poets."

219. Alessandro de'Medici (1510–37): first duke of Florence. Giovanni de'Medici dalle Bande Nere (1498–1526): famous condottiere much admired by Machiavelli. Paolo Luzzasco: another contemporary condottiere. Massimiliano Stampa (d. 1552): governor of Milan, who exchanged letters with Aretino. Fortunio Spira: a contemporary poet. This section on the famous men to whom the future son of the Marescalco might be equal is a thin excuse for Aretino to curry favor with a long list of patrons, friends, and potential friends. Interestingly, this scene seems to mock his own obsequious courting of power and patronage.

220. "I have a list of."

221. "Names of famous men and women."

222. "Father of the Muses."

223. Pietro Bembo (1470–1547): literary arbiter and love poet who became a cardinal in 1539. Francesco Maria Molza (1489–1544): noted humanist from Modena. Giovanni Guidiccioni (1500–1541): poet and papal official. Luigi Alamanni (1495–1556): Florentine poet and humanist who also served the French king, Frances I. Bernardo Cappello (1498–1565): noble Venetian poet and humanist. Domenico Venier (1517–82): another noble Venetian poet who early in his career was a follower of Aretino and Bembo. Bernardo Tasso (1493–1569): poet and father of Torquato Tasso.

224. A warship with five banks of oars.

225. Giulio Camillo (ca. 1485–1544): Venetian humanist noted for his command of languages.

COUNT: You sound like a parish priest reading the calendar of saints to the peasants.

KNIGHT: Ha, ha, ha!

JACOPO: Ha, ha, ha!

PEDANT: And what do you think about that comedy recited in Bologna before many princes written by Agostino Ricchi when he was still a young adolescent, imitating the best of the Greeks and Latins?[226]

MARESCALCO: O dear devil, save us!

PEDANT: Have you seen the Roman Academy in San Petronio? Doesn't Paolo Giovio seem to you another Livy, another Sallust? I myself saw there Claudio Tolomei, a most erudite mine of learning, and there I met Cesano, more liberal than liberty itself, and also our Gian Giacomo Calandra, whom everyone knows, our modern Statius, and Don Onorato Fascitello, the *luminare maius*[227] of the order of the great Saint Benedict.[228]

KNIGHT: This could go on until nightfall.

COUNT: He's really got it going!

JACOPO: Ha, ha, ha!

PEDANT: Quiet, *silentium! Si pictoribus—*[229]

MARESCALCO: [*Interrupting*] Oh, God, what a way to die!

COUNT: Ha, ha, ha!

PEDANT: *Si pictoribus,* your son might equal Titian, *emulus naturae immo magis-*

Agostino Bevazzano (d. ca. 1571): poet and humanist from Treviso. The "Unico Aretino" was the poet Bernardo Accolti (1458–1535), not Pietro Aretino. Giovanni Pollio Lappoli: contemporary humanist and priest. Agnolo Firenzuola (1493–1543): humanist and sometime cleric known for his erotic short stories. Vittore Fausto (ca. 1490–1540): Venetian humanist interested in reviving ancient Greek naval technology (the text mentions a quinquireme; Fausto helped build such a ship based on ancient designs). Antonio Isidoro Mezzabarba: contemporary Venetian lawyer and humanist. Ludovico Dolce (1508–1568): prolific Venetian writer on a wide variety of topics.

226. Agostino Ricchi (1512–64) was actually eighteen when he wrote the comedy referred to here, *I tre tiranni.*

227. "Major light."

228. Paolo Giovio (1483–1552): historian, diplomat, and humanist. Livy (59 B.C.–A.D. 17) and Sallust (86–35 B.C.): Roman historians. Claudio Tolomei (1492–ca. 1555): humanist and linguist who aggressively defended Tuscan as the ideal literary form of Italian. Gabriele Maria Cesano (1490–1568): longtime friend of Aretino, a bishop and humanist particularly interested in language. Gian Giacomo Calandra (1488–1543): diplomat and court official at Mantua often responsible for distribution of patronage. Statius (A.D.45–96): Roman poet. Onorato Fascitello (1502–67): Benedictine poet and humanist. Saint Benedict (ca. 480–547): founder of the Benedictine Order, whose rule became the model for Western monasticism.

229. "Silence! As for painters."

ter,[230] or certainly the most divine Venetian Friar Sebastiano Luciani, or perhaps Giulio Romano *Romanae curiae,*[231] or Raphael from Urbino, *alumno.*[232] And as for *marmorarea facultate*[233] (even if the preeminence of sculpture has not yet been decided),[234] one must mention first that your son might be a mini-Michelangelo or a Jacopo Sansovino, *speculum Florentiae.*[235]

MARESCALCO: My lords, with your permission I will sit down for the rest of this. Go on with the comedy.

COUNT: Ha, ha!

KNIGHT: Ha, ha, ha!

JACOPO: Ha, ha, ha, ha!

PEDANT: Go ahead, sit down, my friend, sit down, my brother. Without doubt, among the practitioners of Vitruvian architecture, your son will be another Baldassare da Siena *vetus,*[236] or a Serlio da Bologna *docet,*[237] or a Luigi Anichini from Ferrara, inventor of the technique of carving on Eastern crystal. In music he will be another Adrian, a wonder of nature, or a Pre Lauro, or a Roberto, and in *cimbalis bene sonantibus*[238] another Giulio da Modena or a Marcantonio. Don't you hear him already playing like Francesco from Milan or Alberto from Mantua? And in surgery I see him already as an Asclepius, like Paolo of Vicenza, and being made a Roman citizen by the Senate in the Capitolio.[239]

230. "A rival of Nature, or verily her master."

231. "Of the Roman Curia."

232. "His student."

233. "Working in marble."

234. A reference to the ongoing debate about which was the nobler art, painting or sculpture.

235. "The mirror of Florence." Titian (ca. 1487–1576): Venetian painter and close friend of Aretino. Sebastiano Luciani, known as Del Piombo (1485–1547): painter who worked first in Venice, then in Rome. Romano: see n. 185. Raphael (1483–1520): painter who worked primarily in Rome. Michelangelo (1475–1546): sculptor, painter, architect, and poet. Jacopo Sansovino (1486–1570): architect and sculptor who worked in Florence, Rome, and Venice, where he was part of the close circle of Aretino's friends.

236. "The elder."

237. "Learned."

238. "On the sweet-sounding cymbals."

239. Baldassare Peruzzi (1481–1536): painter, set designer, and architect. Sebastiano Serlio (1475–1554): architect, writer on architecture, and friend of Peruzzi. Luigi Anichini (ca. 1500–?): Venetian engraver. Andrian Wallaert (1480–1562): Flemish composer who worked for a time in Venice. It is not clear who Pre Lauro or Roberto were. Giulio Segni (or de Mutina) (1498–1561): composer, singer, organist, and harpsichord player. Marcantonio Cavazzoni (ca. 1490–ca. 1570): composer, organist, and singer. Francesco Canova (or da Milano) (1497–ca. 1543) and Alberto Ripa (or da Mantova) (1480–1551): lutists and composers. Asclepius: Greek and Roman god of medicine. Paolo Vicentino: a surgeon at the time of Pope Clement VII.

MARESCALCO: Play the pipes; the first act is finished.

KNIGHT: Ha, ha, ha, ha!

COUNT: Ha, ha, ha!

JACOPO: Ha, ha!

PEDANT: Clearly, clearly, he would have that same integrity, that same faith, that same ability, as Messer Carlo of Bologna, whose prudence calms the heart of the most excellent Duke Massimo. *Al tandem,*[240] he might rise to the level of the most reliable Aurelio or the splendid knight Vincenzo Firmano, and share in the courtly manners of not only Ottaviano Ceresara but of all the gentlemen of the court of His Excellency.[241] And if God were to decide that he should be a woman—

MARESCALCO: [*Interrupting*] I'm getting out of here.

PEDANT: —if God decides that he will be a woman, she will have many of the qualities of the most famous Marchesa of Pescara.[242]

KNIGHT: Now we need to tie you down.[243]

PEDANT: Why?

KNIGHT: Because even God would have trouble making another woman with a thousandth of her glories—even if Madonna Bianca, wife of Count Manfredi, were to be reborn, she who is now the wonder of heaven as she was once the wonder of this world.[244]

COUNT: Exactly. He couldn't have been husband to a better wife, nor she wife to a better husband.

JACOPO: That's true.

MARESCALCO: Now you can see, *cuius figurae,*[245] that your blabbing on doesn't accomplish anything.

PEDANT: *Certum est*[246] that she was nursed by the ten Muses.

KNIGHT: Sir, there are only nine, unless you want to include among them your housekeeper.

PEDANT: What do you mean, nine? I count Clio, one; Euterpe, two; Urania,

---

240. "Finally."

241. Carlo da Bologna (d. 1540): treasurer of Mantua. It is not clear who Aurelio was. Vincenzo Guerrieri of Firmo (d. 1563) and Ottaviano dei Ceresara: courtiers at the court of Mantua.

242. Vittoria Colonna (1490–1547).

243. I.e., like a raving madman.

244. Manfredi di Collalto was a papal official. About his wife we know little beyond the fact that Aretino wrote a sonnet in her honor in 1540, well after her death.

245. "From your own examples."

246. "It's certain."

three; Calliope, *quattuor;* Erato, *quinque;* Thalia, *sex;* Venus, seven; Pallas, eight; Minerva, *novem, verum est.*[247]

MARESCALCO: Play the pipes again for the second act.

KNIGHT: Ha, ha, ha!

COUNT: Ha, ha, ha, ha!

JACOPO: Ha, ha, ha, ha, ha!

MARESCALCO: I don't have anything to laugh at at this party.

PEDANT: Given that my speech was *ex abrupto,*[248] I do not want to forget to tell you that your baby girl would have that prudence, that presence, that magnificence that the gentlewomen of Venice use to amaze the amazing city of Venice.

MARESCALCO: If I believed that I could have a daughter who would even begin to resemble one of their old shoes, I'd gladly get down on my knees and give my wife the ring.

KNIGHT: Glory to Mohammed! Finally, something to your liking.

PEDANT: Now, may Christ protect you from evil, honorable Marescalco.

MARESCALCO: My friends, to the Professor I don't need to say anything else except that these children of mine will be, if male, gamblers, pimps, robbers, traitors, and lazy scoundrels and, if females, at best, whores. Goodbye.

COUNT: Wait a minute. You're the type of man and she's the type of woman who should expect nothing from sons and daughters except good manners and great accomplishments.[249]

PEDANT: You speak wisely, *quia*—because—*arbor bona bonos fructus facit.*[250]

MARESCALCO: Some good fathers and mothers have terrible children, and I know well that many foolish fathers had no part in making their children.

COUNT: Let's go inside your house, and once we've talked this through completely, you'll admit for yourself that it would be for the best to satisfy and obey the Lord.

PEDANT: Good, good!

KNIGHT: Let's go.

MARESCALCO: As Your Lordships wish.

KNIGHT: After you, Your Lordship Count.

COUNT: No, after you, Your Lordship Knight.

---

247. "Four . . . five . . . six . . . nine, that is correct." As usual, the Pedant has botched his list, adding the goddesses Venus, Pallas, and Minerva and leaving out the Muses Melpomene, Polyhymnia, and Terpsichore.

248. "Off the cuff."

249. *Virtù.*

250. "A good tree produces good fruit."

KNIGHT: You first, Count.

COUNT: You first, Knight.

KNIGHT: Really, Your Lordship—

COUNT: Actually, Your—

PEDANT: [*Moving to enter first*] *Cedant arma togae.*[251]

JACOPO: [*Following the* PEDANT] I'm with you, Professor. Who cares anymore about these Spanish, Lombard courtier games from Naples?

᠀᠐ SCENE IV ᠂

OLD WOMAN, CARLO (dressed as a bride), a MATRON, and a GENTLEWOMAN

OLD WOMAN: This is going to be the best party ever! The Lord has told the whole court that this evening he'll give a wife to his Marescalco. With everyone believing that, he had us dress Carlo da Fano instead as the promised bride. [*Laughing*] Here he is, come on out!

CARLO: [*Entering, dressed as a bride*] I am a miracle! [*Laughing as he looks at himself*] Once a man, I've become a woman, and the Marescalco will marry me.

MATRON: By my faith, anyone would believe that you're a young girl. [*Laughing*] You have the airs, the speech, the manner, and the walk.

GENTLEWOMAN: By the holy cross, you're right. I know that his cheeks had no need of rouge.

MATRON: Have you learned how you must hold your eyes?

CARLO: Lowered, like this?

MATRON: Perfect.

CARLO: With my head held humbly and bowed a little, this way, right?

MATRON: Exactly. Look prudent, modest, and respectful, and as your bridegroom approaches fix your eyes on the ground and don't look anyone in the eye. And when the vows are said, hesitate until the third time you are asked before saying yes, understand?

CARLO: Yes, madam.

MATRON: Try it a bit.

CARLO: With my eyes just so, looking down, with my mouth like this, and curtsying like this and this, and the third time I'll reply, "Y-y-yes, s-s-sir."

GENTLEWOMAN: [*Laughing*] I could just die! I've never seen a bride do it so well!

251. "Arms give place to scholarly robes."

MATRON: Don't mess it up by laughing.

CARLO: Don't worry.

GENTLEWOMAN: And when you kiss him, don't forget to put your tongue in his mouth, as the Lord asked.

CARLO: I won't forget.

GENTLEWOMAN: Here we are at the Count's house. Go on in, Matron.

MATRON: You first, gentle lady.

GENTLEWOMAN: After you, Matron.

MATRON: Really, it should be you first.

GENTLEWOMAN: Actually, it should be you.

OLD WOMAN: I should go in first, I'm the oldest.

CARLO: No, I'm first—after all, I am the bride!

MATRON: And so he is. Go on in, bride, and the rest of us will follow as a group.

❧ SCENE V ☙

The COUNT, the KNIGHT, JACOPO, the MARESCALCO, and the PEDANT

COUNT: We have been instructed to bring you to your wedding either by love or by force.

KNIGHT: You should forgive us. We have to obey the Lord—that's all there is to it.

JACOPO: If you come to any harm resisting, don't complain later.

MARESCALCO: Fine. Follow orders. Kill me right now and save me all the suffering.

COUNT: Now take these rings, an emerald and a ruby. They are gifts from the Lord.

MARESCALCO: This gift would be great for—

KNIGHT: [*Interrupting*] Let's just go on, one step at a time, until everything is in order.

MARESCALCO: That's easy for you to say. You're going to a wedding, and I'm going to my execution.

JACOPO: You're still stuck on that!

KNIGHT: Here we are at the Count's house; let's go in. And soon, right here in front of this door, in this beautiful square, I want you to marry her. And a thousand years from now people will still be saying, "Here the Lord Duke married the fondly remembered Marescalco to that gentlewoman."

MARESCALCO: Actually they will say, "Here the Marescalco was executed by the Lord Duke as a reward for his faithful service."

COUNT: Enough. Go on in first, bridegroom.

MARESCALCO: The honor of going first means nothing to me.

PEDANT: One must observe the decorum of the events of the occasion, as I will *etiam*[252] observe that decorum in the oration that His Excellency has ordered me to give before your wedding. Enter, *igitur, adunque, tamen,*[253] nonetheless, enter, bridegroom.

MARESCALCO: Mock me, scorn me, insult me—I'll submit to it all, since I have no other option.

COUNT: Come in, everyone.

⟶ SCENE VI ⟵

AMBROGIO and MESSER PHEBUS

AMBROGIO: I'd give up a year of masses, a year of sermons, a year of vespers rather than miss the fun!

PHEBUS: Me too. But do you know what worries me?

AMBROGIO: No.

PHEBUS: That the Lord may get mad at all this disobedience and send him to the gallows.

AMBROGIO: Isn't he already sending him to the gallows by giving him a wife?

PHEBUS: As far as I'm concerned, he's sending him to heaven giving him a bride so rich and pretty. I wish to God I were in his place.

AMBROGIO: Come on, think about the living!

PHEBUS: What do you mean, the living?

AMBROGIO: Just what I said, the living.[254] If you knew what wives are like, you too would try to avoid one, just like him.

PHEBUS: How bad can a wife be?

AMBROGIO: Have you ever had the amorous affliction?

PHEBUS: What's that?

AMBROGIO: The French disease.[255]

PHEBUS: Why do you call it the amorous affliction?

---

252. "Also."
254. I.e., not what happens in heaven.

253. "Therefore, then, nevertheless."
255. Syphilis. See n. 40.

AMBROGIO: Because it's born between the thighs when *omnia vincit Amor.*[256]

PHEBUS: Well, what does it matter if one has a disease that almost the whole world has? If I had it, would I become some kind of criminal?

AMBROGIO: No, that's not the point.

PHEBUS: Then why bring it up?

AMBROGIO: To make a comparison that hits home about what it means to take a wife.

PHEBUS: Go ahead, tell me, then.

AMBROGIO: A wife in the home is just like the French disease in the body: just as one's body then always has some pain, now in a knee, now in an arm, and now in a hand, so in the house where there is a wife there's always some disturbance. Moreover, he who has a wife is like a man with that disease in that he must suffer either her rages, or her stubbornness, or her ostentatious display, or her filthiness. There never was and there never will be a man with a wife without ifs, ands, or buts, just as there never was and never will be a man with that worldwide disease who can relax for a moment without some sharp little pain here or there in his body. But is that the boy and the Marescalco's Balia that I see coming?

✸ SCENE VII ✸

AMBROGIO, GIANNICCO, the BALIA, and MESSER PHEBUS

AMBROGIO: What's up, my pretty boy? Are we going to have peace and a wedding?

GIANNICCO: The peace has been concluded, and the wedding will be concluded. Peace, because I could never bring myself to leave him to live with someone else. So even though he treated me badly, I'm not going to leave him.

AMBROGIO: There's wisdom in your words.

BALIA: I feel the same way. All those evil things he said to me don't matter an iota, because after all, I brought him up, and his marriage will bring peace to us all.

PHEBUS: That's right.

BALIA: Once he gets over his little rages, he means more than bread to me.[257]

AMBROGIO: Well, let's get going so that we don't miss this long-awaited holy event.

---

256. "Love conquers all."

257. Bread remained the main food people ate during the Renaissance. Thus, as having one's daily bread was crucial, the Balia is claiming that the Marescalco was someone she could not live without.

PHEBUS: Let's cut down through this little street here. That way we can enter the Count's house from the back.

ᴏ SCENE VIII ᴏ

The DUKE'S FOOTMAN, alone

FOOTMAN: Will this marriage business with this Marescalco never end? All day long I've been running here and there, and just as I was settling down to play a little game of cards the Lord ordered me to tell the Count that it's time to go ahead with the wedding. This is his door, I'll knock hard. Knock, knock, knock!

ᴏ SCENE IX ᴏ

The COUNT'S MAIDSERVANT and the DUKE'S FOOTMAN

MAIDSERVANT: Who's that down there knocking?

FOOTMAN: Come to the window.

MAIDSERVANT: Who's knocking?

FOOTMAN: A servant of the Lord.

MAIDSERVANT: What do you want?

FOOTMAN: Is that you, my sweetheart?

MAIDSERVANT: Yes, my hope.

FOOTMAN: Tell the Count that it's time to have the ring ceremony, by the order of the Duke.

MAIDSERVANT: I'll tell him. Ah, me!

FOOTMAN: Why that sigh?

MAIDSERVANT: It's a sigh of wishing that you had a ring to give to your Giorgina.

FOOTMAN: I'll do all that I've promised you, but you do remember you-know-what, right?

MAIDSERVANT: At three by the door of the stalls, right?

FOOTMAN: Yes, my lady.

MAIDSERVANT: At three, right?

FOOTMAN: I've got it, my queen of queens.

MAIDSERVANT: Spit three times.

FOOTMAN: I'll do exactly as you say, my empress of empresses.

MAIDSERVANT: Don't lose track of the time.

FOOTMAN: How could I lose track, heart of my heart?

MAIDSERVANT: Do something to be sure you don't fall asleep.

FOOTMAN: I will, my sugar of sugar-coated almonds and my sweet nut paste in marzipan.

MAIDSERVANT: Three, now; don't forget.

FOOTMAN: I won't forget, my milk of milk candy and my little box of jewel boxes. Catch this kiss that I'm blowing you. [*Aside, as he leaves*] I've certainly made a fool of that slut, and the bells will ring three and four as well, but I've no intention of going there. But what flock of people is this coming along? I'll head off this way.

᪥ SCENE X ᪥

The COUNT, the KNIGHT, MESSER JACOPO, the PEDANT, MESSER PHEBUS, AMBROGIO, the MARESCALCO, GIANNICCO, the BALIA, the MATRON, CARLO (dressed as a bride), the GENTLEWOMAN, and the OLD WOMAN

COUNT: You might as well buck up and make the best of it.

KNIGHT: That's what I've been saying all along.

MARESCALCO: If I had to die only once without a wife it would be a kindness, but having to die a thousand times with one is a cruel torture that would knock the crap out of anything the emperor Nero dreamed up.

COUNT: Look, the bride is coming out with a pretty company. What a wench! She really is beautiful.

KNIGHT: My God, some people have all the luck!

MARESCALCO: Oh my, I'm dying, I'm about to explode . . . I . . . I . . . *commen . . . spirtum me.*[258] [*Slipping to the ground in a faint*]

COUNT: Vinegar, vinegar, he's passing out. Marescalco, oh, Marescalco!

KNIGHT: This is the strangest case in the world. When other men see a beautiful girl they come to life, but this one is dying.

COUNT: He doesn't seem to be breathing.

GIANNICCO: Master, pray to the Madonna in the Church of San Piero.[259]

BALIA: If he revives, I vow to say every morning the prayer of Saint Alexis[260] at the foot of my staircase.

258. "Commend . . . my soul."
259. The Cathedral of Mantua.
260. A popular saint prayed to when someone was seriously ill. According to legend, Alexis fled on the eve of his wedding to live the life of an ascetic.

PEDANT: *Altaria fumant*,[261] but *sine Cercere e Bacco, friget Venus.*[262] Don't lose it, old boy.

COUNT: Wet his wrists well.

MARESCALCO: Oh my, my heart!

KNIGHT: Buck up, everything will be all right.

PEDANT: It's all fumes that come from the *cerebro*.[263]

BALIA: How quickly his color has returned!

GIANNICCO: Oh, I tell you, he's naturally hard.

MARESCALCO: Are you here, Balia, and you, my Giannicco?

BALIA: I forgive you your nastiness.

GIANNICCO: You won't find any others like your sweet little Giannicchi.

MARESCALCO: I didn't notice you, Messer Jacopo.

JACOPO: I couldn't let you down, so I'm here.

COUNT: Enough is enough. Let's get on with it.

KNIGHT: On with this great event!

COUNT: Professor, you will give the sermon. Please bring over the bride so that the will of the Lord may be done. [*Threateningly*] And you, Marescalco, you are ready to obey, right?

MARESCALCO: No, my lord.

COUNT: Either you can say yes, or [*showing him a knife*] I'll slit your throat with this.

KNIGHT: He would be really upset if they didn't play a funeral dirge at his wedding.

MARESCALCO: Don't hurt me, and I'll tell you why I can't marry her.

COUNT: Why?

MARESCALCO: I have an open hernia.

KNIGHT: [*Laughing*] Bind yourself up in matrimony, then!

MARESCALCO: Ask my Balia. [*Aside*] I won't say, "Ask my boy, who knows better."

BALIA: I don't want such a lie on my conscience. It's not true.

GIANNICCO: Well done, Balia. Honesty is the best policy.

COUNT: Enough of this show. On with *the* show.

MARESCALCO: All right, call her over. Come over here. For my sins . . . my sins . . .[264]

261. "The altars are all steamed up and ready to go."
262. "Without Ceres [food] and Bacchus [wine], Venus [love] freezes."
263. "Brain."
264. I.e., this is my punishment for my sins.

KNIGHT: Come along, ladies, and bring the young bride.

MATRON: Here we are, my lord.

COUNT: It's up to you, Professor, to dust off the old lines of the marriage ceremony.

MARESCALCO: I'm sweating and freezing.

PEDANT: The parsimony of the *sobrio prandio*[265] does not incline me to spew forth my discourse. Nonetheless, let us begin *latine*,[266] because Cicero in his *Paradoxes* says that we should not speak of holy matrimony in the vulgar tongue.

COUNT: Speak to us as much as you can in everyday language, because all this "ibus, ibas" business is too constipated to be understood.

AMBROGIO: His Lordship the Count is right.

PEDANT: Do you want me to lose the gravity of my oration? One must first pace a bit, glancing now up, now down, in the manner of the followers of Demosthenes. *Silentium!*[267]

In principio creavit Deus caelum et terram. Praeterea,[268] He made *pisces per aequora, et inter aves turdos, et inter quadrupedes gloria prima lepus.*[269] I have been saying that God the Father, after He created heaven and earth, created fish for the sea and birds for the air and for the woods deer and bucks. *Ulterius, ad similitudinem suam,*[270] He mixed up from clay the masculine and the feminine, *postea*[271] he bound them, *idest,* He coupled them together so that they would grow and multiply *sine* adultery *usquequo* they filled up the seats that the overweeningly proud and ungodly followers of Lucifer had emptied. And the Lord made man *principaliter*[272] to trample *leonem et draconem,*[273] and He made him a rational animal with his sight, his touch, and his other faculties *solum*[274] so that his desires would be different from those of the beasts, *et ideo*[275] so that he would copulate with women,[276] as is shown in Genesis, where Adam and Eve are discussed. For this

265. "Frugal meal."

266. "In Latin."

267. "Silence!"

268. "In the beginning God created heaven and earth. Shortly thereafter."

269. "Fishes for the water, and to the thrushes, among birds, and to rabbits, among four-legged creatures, went the first glory." During the Renaissance, rabbits, suggestively, were associated with males attracted to males.

270. "Later, in his own image."

271. "After which." And, in the rest of the sentence, "that is," "without," "until."

272. "Above all."

273. "Lions and dragons."

274. "Solely."

275. "And that is."

276. Aretino playfully alludes to the fact that men are distinguished from beasts by the fact that

reason, our illustrious Lord's Most Excellent Lordship couples his *celeberrimo*[277] Marescalco here with the beautiful lady to whom I now turn and say, "Are you willing, most beautiful Madonna, to take as your legitimate spouse the one and only Marescalco of His Most Excellent Excellency?"

MARESCALCO: O God, make her lose her voice!

PEDANT: Are you willing, most courteous lady, to take for your perpetual husband the personal Marescalco of the Most Excellent and Illustrious Lord Duke Federico, First Duke of Mantua?

MARESCALCO: It would be a miracle if she lost her voice.

PEDANT: Are you willing, most delicious lady, to take for your singular consort the Marescalco *de nobilibus*?[278]

CARLO: Y-y-yes, s-s-sir.

MARESCALCO: Gouge out my other eye!

PEDANT: *Spectabili viro domino Marescalco, placet vobis,*[279] are you willing, to take for your bride, your wife, your woman, your consort, your lad—

MARESCALCO: [*Interrupting*] Didn't I tell you I couldn't because I have this open hernia?

GIANNICCO: Rubbish. He's totally closed up!

COUNT: [*Threatening the* MARESCALCO *with the knife*] Either you decide to say yes or you decide to have me finish you off right here.

GIANNICCO: Say yes, Master.

BALIA: Oh no, Lord Count!

MARESCALCO: [*In a low voice*] Yes, sir. I want her. I'm willing. Mercy!

COUNT: Speak up, man.

MARESCALCO: I like her. I want her. Mercy! Yes, sir!

KNIGHT: *Te Deum laudamus.*[280]

COUNT: Kiss each other as you put on the ring.

CARLO: [*Pretending to resist*] Ooh, oooh!

MATRON: I've never seen a more modest bride.[281]

God made them with sexual tastes different from beasts' (i.e., they preferred to copulate with women). This may explain the frequent references to the Marescalco as a beast: he clearly does not prefer to copulate with women.

277. "Most illustrious."

278. "Of noble status."

279. "Most notable Lord Marescalco, is it pleasing to you."

280. "Let us give thanks to God."

281. We follow the reading of De Sanctis, who assigns this speech to the Matron. Petrocchi assigns it to the Marescalco.

KNIGHT: Let's see what she's like in the morning.

COUNT: Go ahead, kiss her. [*They kiss.*]

GIANNICCO: He's finished now.

MARESCALCO: [*Angrily*] Your tongue, eh? Already the fun begins. God might be able to make her a martyr, but neither God nor her mother can make this one a virgin. O horns, I haven't been able to avoid your sad tune! Give me patience!

GENTLEWOMAN: Ungrateful lout!

MARESCALCO: This is what one gets for putting one's faith in lords. Oh, oh, oh, oh!

CARLO: He must be a beastly man.

MARESCALCO: Well, at least I want to see the goods that I've bought with my ruin.

PEDANT: "Ruination" is the word Petrarch used.

MARESCALCO: [*Touching* CARLO] Hold still, don't wiggle so. Move a little this way. Come a little closer . . . closer yet. Oh my! This is really wonderful!

CARLO: Ha, ha, ha!

MARESCALCO: Oh, what an ass, what an ox, what a buffalo! Oh, what a fool I am! [*Laughing*] This is Carlo, the page!

COUNT: What the devil—it's Carlo!

KNIGHT: Let me see. [*Laughing*] My God, it's Carlo!

COUNT: I guess we've been had.

KNIGHT: [*Still laughing*] Had is right!

AMBROGIO: It's really him. [*Joining the laughter*] I guess we can be called Mantuan nincompoops!

PHEBUS: It's better than in Boccaccio's *Decameron.*

PEDANT: It's a boy? In fine, *nemo sine crimine vivit.*[282]

BALIA: He's in seventh heaven, the big rogue, isn't he?

MARESCALCO: Well, doesn't it seem better to you, for me to see you laughing at a lie than for you to see me crying at the truth?

BALIA: You can never pull the frog from his mud.

PEDANT: As Aesop said in the *Fables.*

JACOPO: [*Laughing*] You're not complaining now, Marescalco!

---

282. "Well, in the end no one lives without crime."

◆ SCENE XI ◆

The COUNT'S SERVANT, the COUNT, the MARESCALCO,
the PEDANT, and GIANNICCO

SERVANT: Please, all, come in. The dinner is ready, and after dinner you can finish laughing at the joke.[283]

COUNT: First the bride, then the ladies, and then you, old woman.

KNIGHT: Everyone enter behind the bride.

MARESCALCO: I'll enter, given that I am the *quondam*[284] spouse. Come in, friends!

PEDANT: Every lout wants to be called *quondam*, as if a common laborer deserved to be called *quondam*. This *quondam* has great significance, just great.

COUNT: What are you babbling about, Professor? Give a heroic farewell to the audience, then come on in and have a meal and a drink on the house.[285] Let's go, sir Knight.

PEDANT: Why, neither I nor any of my relatives was ever a barber, and I am used to having my hair combed rather than combing the hair of others.

GIANNICCO: Ha, ha, ha!

PEDANT: What are you laughing at, you little ass?[286]

GIANNICCO: I'm laughing because it's clear you're not familiar with the language of mercenaries. "On the house" among mercenaries means to eat at the expense of others.

PEDANT: Really?

GIANNICCO: Absolutely!

PEDANT: Homer, the father of our Greek studies, died trying to figure out such an enigma.[287] I thank you for having explained to me such a strange riddle, which not even Averroes[288] would have been able to solve.

---

283. *Burla.*

284. In this case *quondam* means survivor or heir of the deceased. It was a term frequently used in noble titles to trace descent, which explains the Pedant's next comment.

285. *Pettinare* (literally, to have a free meal). The Pedant mishears it as *pettinarsi* (to comb one's hair). Hence his remark about being descended from barbers.

286. *Asinellulo,* suggestive of the sound of the Pedant's favorite insult.

287. There was an ancient story that Homer died of disappointment at being unable to solve a fisherman's riddle.

288. Arab philosopher (1126–98) especially famous for his commentaries on Aristotle. The University at Padua, which had a strong influence on the intellectual life of nearby Venice, was famed as a center for the study of Averroes.

GIANNICCO: Aren't I a scholar?

PEDANT: You have a speculative dimension. Now go in, and I'll be along shortly.

GIANNICCO: Don't waste too much time, if you don't want to eat with gloves on.[289]

PEDANT: How can I eat with gloves on if I don't have any?

GIANNICCO: You'll have to pay me if you want me to teach you this one.

PEDANT: We shall reconsider the matter later.

GIANNICCO: Take care of these people here and say a few unkind words about wives so that they'll all adore you.

PEDANT: Really?

GIANNICCO: Yes, sir.

SCENE XII

The PEDANT, alone

PEDANT: The servant boy has advised me how to win the grace of you, the audience, and I am pleased to do so, because in order to observe the correct order of things in saying good night to you all, as earlier in my nuptial oration I spoke in favor of marriage, now I should speak against it. And having *cogito*[290] about how I should do this, I think I have decided what I should say, and here it is. Spectators, we are destined, with God's grace, when school lets out, to compose another comedy concerning the triumph of the Marescalco divided into four parts. In the first we will consider the happiness of those men who have remained without a wife. In the second we will consider the unhappiness of men whose wives refuse to die. In the third we will speak of the ruin that falls on the shoulders and on the backs of those who are forced to take a wife. In the fourth and last we will conclude by considering the beatitude of those who do not have a wife, do not want a wife, and have never had a wife. *Isto interim*[291] . . . what was it I wanted to say? Could you remind me? I wanted to say, um, . . . ah yes, I've got it. *Isto interim*, please be well and applaud.

---

289. *Mangiarete con i guanti.* Giannicco's remark may be a play on *mangiarsi i guanti*, meaning to destroy oneself in love, or it may be sexual slang with homoerotic overtones.

290. "Thought."

291. "At this point."

꧁ ꧂

Gl'ingannati

(The Deceived) [1]

By the Academy of the Intronati of Siena [2]

CHARACTERS:

GHERARDO: an old man

VIRGINIO: an old man

CLEMENZIA: a *balia* [3]

LELIA: a young girl

SPELA: GHERARDO's servant

SCATIZZA: VIRGINIO's servant

FLAMMINIO: a lover

PASQUELLA: GHERARDO's maid

ISABELLA: a young girl

GIGLIO: a Spaniard

CRIVELLO: FLAMMINIO's servant

The PEDANT

FABRIZIO: a young man, [4] son of VIRGINIO

---

1. First performed on 12 February 1532 during carnival season.

2. Like most Renaissance academies, the Intronati (Dazed) of Siena were an aristocratic group of literati, humanists, and intellectuals. Theoretically modeled on ancient academies of learning, the group played a significant role in the upper-class intellectual and festive life of the time, often sponsoring and performing comedies. Although there have been various attempts to identify a single author for this comedy within the academy, the declaration in the Prologue that it was a joint effort remains the best attribution we have. See the discussion of the name in the introductory essay.

3. I.e., wetnurse.

4. *Giovinetto.*

STRAGUALCIA: FABRIZIO's servant
AGIATO: an innkeeper
FRULLA: an innkeeper
CITTINA: the daughter of the *balia* CLEMENZIA

Prologue

I can tell even from here, most noble ladies, that you are amazed to see me
here before you in these clothes and amid this scenery, as if we were about to
present some comedy to you. You must not have expected a comedy, for up until
last year, as you may be aware, the Intronati were concerned with other things.
Then the other day you found out how they felt about you and learned that they
no longer wanted to run after you or have anything to do with you, like those
who no longer want to be bitten, chewed, and cut to the quick by you. So, as you
saw, they burned those things that were capable of arousing their fantasies and
increasing their desire for you as well as for your beauties.[5]

Now I want to make you forget all those strange things. These Intronati, to
tell you the truth (and you can believe me, because I heard them say it), are very
sorry to have become involved in such madness and are scared stiff that you
(being quite capable of it) will have taken their hard points so deeply to heart
that in the future you will withhold your tongues from them and turn your
backs on them every time you see them. That's why they've shoved me out here as
their ambassador, orator, legate, lawyer, or poet, hoping that you'll stick the
matter, in whatever way it enters best, into the very backside of your memory.

I find that I come before you [*looking at his crotch*] with a large mandate, in good
shape. So have faith in me, or I'll be forced to show it to you, as long as I've
brought it along. I tell you that I'm here specifically to make this peace with you
and to get you back together with them, if you are willing; for to tell you the
truth, their affairs have gone cold and flaccid without you and have almost faded
away, and if you don't make it up with them, they will dwindle away to nothing.
Hey, do it! Do it, ladies, it will give only pleasure. After all, you know how they
are: if you look at them even once with a little pity, they'll let you control them,
they'll be putty in your hands (but only for you, because with others they
wouldn't be so capable), and they'll let you sweetly torture them, touch their,

5. The Intronati had earlier made fun of the coldness of the women of Siena in a ceremony that
included a sacrificial bonfire of gifts from their mistresses and the reciting of misogynist poetry.
We have tried to capture the convoluted style of the original, which calls attention to the
Prologue's erotic allusions and double entendres.

um, hearts with your words, always be on top and always come first. Well, what do you think? Are you content? Will you do it? You're not responding. But then you aren't refusing either, which is a good sign. Look, they were so eager to make this peace that they've put this comedy together in barely three days, and today they want you to see and hear it, if you are willing.

Now you understand what this scene is doing here, who I am, and what I'm here to do for you. This comedy, from what I've heard, they call *The Deceived*, not because they were ever deceived by you. Oh, no! You have never tricked them—they know you all too well for that; rather, you have always compelled them, for they simply couldn't ever resist you. So they call the comedy this because almost all of the characters involved are deceived. Still, dear ladies, for all the ill will in which I hold you, there are some deceptions here that, God willing, I would be glad to play on you if you were the victims and I was the trickster, and to tell the truth I wouldn't even care if you turned the tables and got on top of me. The story is new and not taken from any source outside of their fevered brains—the same place where on the night of the Befana they decided your fate[6] in such a way as to make you think that the Intronati were wronging you with what they said and that they have evil tongues. If you were to taste their tongues, perhaps you wouldn't feel that way but would defend them instead and take their parts as good companions wherever necessary.

I am well aware that there are plenty of people who will say that this comedy is just a grab bag. To them I make no reply, because however things turn out, it's enough if you enjoy it, for the Intronati have always addressed themselves to giving pleasure above all else. And they think it will be easy for them to do this for you ladies, especially those of you who are pregnant, who normally prefer ground-up coal, thread tea, brick dust, and the like to comedies.[7] As far as the men in the audience are concerned, we really don't care whether they like it or not, because the Intronati have ordered that none of them may see or hear this unless they're already blind. Still, if there's some stuck-up scumbag of a man, drawn by an uncontrolled urge to criticize us, who is here and who really wishes

6. I.e., with the antiwoman ceremony mentioned earlier. Celebrated on 6 January, the night of the Befana was an ancient festival, still practiced in various ways in Italy today. Given that a full month separates that festival from the first performance of this comedy, some have argued that this passage does not refer to the Intronati's ceremony, which earlier was said to have taken place "the other day." Still, the sense of this passage suggests that this was when it occurred, or at least was planned. That supposition is also supported by the nature of the festival itself, which focused on driving out or burning an evil old woman, the Befana.

7. The implication is that pregnant women with their strange tastes are likely to enjoy this strange comedy.

to see and hear it, he'll have to cut out his eyes if he wants to understand it. I imagine you think it's strange that only blind men should watch this comedy. But it's true, and if you just have a little patience you'll understand, for I'll show you why.

Whatever beauty there is in the world today is without doubt here in Siena, and whatever beauty there is in Siena is present in this hall. This cannot be denied, because I can't believe that those who aren't here could be as beautiful as you or even close, since they stay away rather than be compared with you. How do you imagine men could come here to marvel at scenes or comedies, or to listen to or watch what we do or say, with you beautiful women here before them? What more beautiful game, what more beautiful spectacle, what more pleasing or beautiful thing could a man see than you ladies? Nothing, certainly. So now I have shown you why men may not see or hear this comedy unless they are blind, and you see I'm not quite as full of it as you thought. But you ladies will see and hear it just fine, because we know you well enough indeed to know that you're too well mannered ever to get carried away or lose self-control from looking at our beauty. Nor should those males who try so hard to be pretty—all dressed up, all shaved, who think they're so sophisticated because they have a well-kept beard, wear good boots, and know how to bow with their hat in hand and sigh loud enough to be heard all the way to the Becci fountain[8]—think that you will ignore our comedy in order to pay attention to them. If they think that, they will be the deceived and thus will steal the name of our comedy. Now, it's possible that you'll see a Spaniard in our comedy whose strange talk will ruin your pleasure a bit and make it hard to follow our plot. But let me give you a good tip: don't pay any attention to him, for you don't speak his language and you won't be able to follow what he says; instead, give your attention to what the Italians say, and everything will be fine.

But you know, I see some men over there watching you so intently that they haven't heard a thing I've said, so I might as well speak to you frankly and intimately for a second. Is it possible, then, seeing how ungrateful you are, that these Intronati will always need to complain about you and return to this subject over and over again and in every place? And all the suffering they have endured for you and all the work they have put into praising you—has this still not been able to move you to grant them a bit of pleasure? Oh, in God's name, ease up a bit and call them to you one at a time and try to listen to what they have to say and what they want from you. I'm absolutely sure that what they

---

8. A fountain outside the walls of the city, thus used to describe any place that was distant.

want is only a trifle, and you're so rich in it that it would cost you nothing to give it to them, and in fact to give it to the whole city as well. Tell me, honestly, what do you think they really want? They aren't looking for anything from you beyond your graces, and when you come to know their penetrating wit— whether it be large or small—you can say "I like this" or "I don't like this" so that those who don't appeal to you can turn their wit elsewhere and work on penetrating other subjects. But it's a serious matter that you insist on keeping them in this constant dither and won't ever resolve matters by using that blessed word "yes." Do you understand what I'm trying to say? Watch out that you don't make them genuinely give up in despair, and remember my words, because I know just what I'm talking about. Eventually you'll lose them for good, and then there will be no way to get them back, and you'll be sorry when it's too late. And you can be sure of this: that there are other options. Enough.

Now that I think about it, don't expect any explanation of the plot, because the person who was supposed to do it isn't up to it. For now you can do without an explanation. It's enough that you know that this city behind me is Modena this year,[9] and that the people who appear in this story are for the most part from that city. But if they make some mistakes with the dialect of Modena, just overlook it, because they haven't learned it very well yet. As far as the rest is concerned, I'm sure you're intelligent enough to pick it up without any trouble. You will learn, above all else, two things: how important good fortune and the right moment are in love, and how important patience accompanied by good advice is. Two young girls will demonstrate this with their wisdom, and by following their wisdom you will benefit as well, so you ladies should be grateful to us. These men, meanwhile, even if they don't enjoy our play, should still have plenty to thank us for, since for four hours, more or less, we'll be giving them the opportunity to contemplate your divine beauty. But I see two old men coming out on stage, so I will leave, unhappy to leave your beauty, even if I plan to return to see you again. Goodbye, all.

9. In other words, during this carnival season the stage setting is being used to represent Modena, and presumably in performances of other comedies in other years, it was used to represent other cities.

Act I

⟡ SCENE I ⟡

GHERARDO and VIRGINIO

GHERARDO: Virginio, if you want to make me happy, as you've promised, let's arrange this holy matrimony quickly and get me out of this hopeless mess that has somehow overwhelmed me. And if something is holding you back, like not having enough money for clothes or furnishings for the house or if you're unable to pay for the wedding right now, don't worry—I know all too well that you lost everything in the terrible sack of Rome.[10] Just tell me, and I'll take care of everything. It wouldn't be any problem for me to spend another ten scudi, especially if we could move this up a month to satisfy my eagerness. Thank God I have the money. And you know as well as I do that neither of us are spring chickens any longer, we're pushing our prime a bit, and maybe . . . well, anyway, the older one gets the less time one has to lose.

Don't be surprised Virginio, if I press you, because I swear that since I've begun to dream of this, I haven't had half a night's sleep. Look at how early I was up this morning! Why, in order not to disturb you I heard the first mass at the cathedral before I came here. But if you have had a change of heart and have decided that your daughter's too young for me, since I'm already well into my middle years and perhaps a bit beyond, tell me straight out. I'll take care of it by turning my thoughts elsewhere. We'd both then avoid the problem, for, as you know, there's no lack of others who would like to have me for a relative.

VIRGINIO: None of these things are holding me back, Gherardo. If it was in my power to give you my daughter today, I would. But I lost virtually everything in the sack of Rome—including Fabrizio, my beloved son. Still, thank God, I have enough left that I hope I can pay to dress and marry my daughter without having to ask for help. Don't worry that I want to break my promise, either. As long as the girl agrees, she's yours, for as you know, a merchant needs to keep his promises.

GHERARDO: Unfortunately, these days the promises of merchants are more upheld in words than in deeds. But you aren't like the others, I'm sure. Still, seeing myself put off day after day makes me worry that something is wrong. And knowing how forceful you are, I know that when you want to, you can make your daughter do what you want.

---

10. Carried out in 1527 by the troops of the German emperor Charles V.

VIRGINIO: Let me explain. You know that I had to go to Bologna to close a deal that I had with Messer Buonaparte Ghisilieri and the Cavalier da Casio. I was living alone in my country home and didn't want to leave my daughter in the hands of the female servants there, so I sent her to the convent of San Crescenzio to stay with Sister Camilla, her aunt. She's still there, because I only returned last night, as you know. Just now I sent a servant to have them send her home.

GHERARDO: Are you sure she's in the convent and not somewhere else?

VIRGINIO: Why shouldn't she be there? Where else do you think she would be? What are you suggesting?

GHERARDO: Well, I've been there several times on business of my own, and I've asked to see her but without success. And certain sisters have told me that she's not there.

VIRGINIO: That's because those good sisters want her to become a nun in order to get what little remains of my wealth after I die. But their plan won't work, for I'm not so old that I can't still father a couple of sons when I take a wife.

GHERARDO: Us, old? Why, I can tell you that I feel as strong and hard as I *bone* did when I was twenty-five, especially in the morning before I pee. Even if I have this white beard, between my legs I'm still as green as Boccaccio![11] And I defy any of these pansy-boys who prance around Modena trying to act tough with their hat feathers standing up stiff in the Guelph style, with their swords at their thigh, with their daggers hanging behind their ass, with their silk tassels—I defy them to outdo me at anything, except perhaps running.

VIRGINIO: You've a great heart, even if I don't know how you'll hold up.

GHERARDO: You just ask Lelia how it held up after her first night with me!

VIRGINIO: In God's name, take it easy with her! She's still young, and it's not good to be too forceful in the beginning.

GHERARDO: How old is she?

VIRGINIO: When we were prisoners of those swine, the Germans, during the sack of Rome, she was thirteen.[12]

GHERARDO: That's perfect for me. I don't want a wife who's too young or too

---

11. Giovanni Boccaccio, best known in the Renaissance for his racy collection of short stories, *The Decameron*. Gherardo may be referring to the Introduction to the Fourth Day of the stories in which Boccaccio remarks that like a leek he may have a white head, but he still has something that is green.

12. Meaning that in 1532, when the action of the comedy took place, Lelia would be eighteen— not particularly young by Renaissance standards for upper-class brides.

old. I have the most beautiful clothes, the most beautiful jewels, the most beautiful necklaces, and the most beautiful accouterments for a woman of any man in Modena.

VIRGINIO: Excellent! I'm satisfied for her well-being and yours.

GHERARDO: Press ahead, then!

VIRGINIO: As far as the dowry's concerned, we'll stick to our agreement.

GHERARDO: Do you think I would change my mind? Goodbye.

VIRGINIO: Good day to you. [GHERARDO *leaves;* CLEMENZIA *enters*] Ah, here's her *balia* now. I'll send her to bring Lelia home. That will save me the trouble.

✌ SCENE II ☙

CLEMENZIA and VIRGINIO

CLEMENZIA: [*To herself*] I wonder what to make of the fact that all my hens were so excited this morning. They made so much noise that it was as if they wanted to throw the house into confusion, or else make me rich with their eggs. Something strange is going to happen to me today; they never make such a commotion unless there's bad news or something goes wrong.

VIRGINIO: [*Aside*] This woman must be talking with angels or with the blessed preacher of the Church of Saint Francis.[13]

CLEMENZIA: [*To herself*] And another strange thing happened to me that I don't know how to interpret, even if my confessor told me that I shouldn't believe in such signs.

VIRGINIO: What are you doing, talking to yourself? The day of the Befana has already passed.[14]

CLEMENZIA: Oh! Good day, Virginio. In God's name, I came by to visit you for a little, but you'd already gone out. I'm very glad to see you back!

VIRGINIO: What were you mumbling to yourself just now? Were you plan-

---

13. There are several allusions in the comedy to the preacher of the Church of Saint Francis in Modena. Referred to variously as Fra Cipolla, Cipollone, and Cipollini, he was apparently merely a well-known literary type: a corrupt friar known for seducing the women of the town. The name also recalls Boccaccio's con-man friar.

14. In the Renaissance, Epiphany, 6 January, was a day when gifts were given. Virginio may be referring to Clemenzia's habit of angling for gifts and saying that if she is preparing to ask him for one, she is wasting her time. "Befana," however, also denoted an old hag or witch, and thus he may be saying that she was muttering under her breath like an old hag and that her day has past (see n. 6).

ning to talk me out of some bushels of grain or bottles of oil or some lard, as usual?

CLEMENZIA: Sure! [*Aside*] How easy it is to talk a magnanimous tightwad like him out of something! Is he perhaps putting away money for his children?

VIRGINIO: What were you saying, anyway?

CLEMENZIA: I was saying that I didn't know what to make of the fact that a pretty kitty that disappeared fifteen days ago turned up this morning. And then she caught a mouse in my dark room, and while playing with it, she upset a flask of Trebbiano wine that the preacher of the Church of Saint Francis had given me for doing his wash.

VIRGINIO: This is a sign that there'll be a wedding. But you wanted me to give you another flask of wine, right?

CLEMENZIA: Of course.

VIRGINIO: See, I do know how to read signs! But where's Lelia, your nursling?[15]

CLEMENZIA: Oh, the poor child, it would've been better if she'd never been born!

VIRGINIO: Why?

CLEMENZIA: You ask why? Isn't that Gherardo Foiani going around saying that she's his wife and that everything's arranged?

VIRGINIO: He's telling the truth. Why not? Don't you think it's good that she'll be set up in an honorable house with a rich man, well furnished with all the goods one could ask for and without anyone else in the house, so she won't have to fight with a mother-in-law, a daughter-in-law, or a sister-in-law (usually they're at each other like cats and dogs)? And he'll treat her like a daughter.

CLEMENZIA: That's the problem: young girls want to be treated like wives, not daughters. They want men who sweep them off their feet, bite them, lay into them first from one side and then the other, not someone who treats them like a daughter.

VIRGINIO: You think all women are like you, and you know that I know you well enough! But she's not like that—even if Gherardo is more than ready to treat her as a wife.

CLEMENZIA: How? Why, he's already well over fifty!

VIRGINIO: What does that matter? I'm almost that old, and you know I'm still capable of giving you a good ride, right?

---

15. *Allieva*, literally "the child you nursed." Like the Balia in *Il marescalco*, Clemenzia plays a highly maternal role in this comedy.

CLEMENZIA: Oh my, there are few men your equal! But if I thought that you would really give her to him, I'd drown her first.

VIRGINIO: Clemenzia, I lost everything. Now I have to make do as best I can. If one day Fabrizio were to be found and I'd given everything away for her dowry, he'd die of hunger. And that I don't want. This way I can marry her to Gherardo with the proviso that if Fabrizio doesn't turn up within four years, she'll have a dowry of one thousand florins. If he does, she'll get only two hundred from me, and Gherardo will make up the rest.[16]

CLEMENZIA: Poor child! [*Aside*] I know that if she did as I wish she would . . .

VIRGINIO: What's she up to? How long has it been since you saw her?

CLEMENZIA: More than fifteen days. I wanted to visit her today.

VIRGINIO: I think those sisters want to make her a nun, and I'm afraid that as usual they've tried to put a bug in her ear. Go to the convent and tell them I want her to return home.

CLEMENZIA: You know, I need you to lend me two carlini[17] to buy some wood. I don't have a stick.

VIRGINIO: Devil, you never give up! Get going now, and I'll buy you some myself.

CLEMENZIA: I want to go to mass first.

◄∂ SCENE III ◊►

LELIA (dressed as a boy) and CLEMENZIA

LELIA: [*Aside*] Leaving the house alone at this hour requires real courage when one considers the evil ways of the rowdy young men of Modena! Oh, it would serve me right if one of those young rogues forced me into one of these houses to see for himself whether I was a boy or a girl! That would teach me to be out so early! But I'm here because I love that fickle and cruel Flamminio. Oh, how unlucky I am! I love someone who hates me, who is always cursing me. I serve someone who doesn't even recognize me. And to make matters worse, I help him

16. Gherardo would not just be fictitiously crediting Lelia with a thousand-florin dowry that would remain in his hands; she would automatically regain her dowry if he should die before she did. As a result, her financial security after his death would not be contingent on his willingness to share his family's wealth with her via his will. Such dowry agreements were often used to provide financial security for women when they married, especially when there was great age discrepancy between partners. Some Renaissance city-states, however, were less assertive than others in protecting the dowry rights of widows.

17. A small coin used in Modena for everyday expenses.

in his pursuit of another woman—who would believe it!—without any other hope than to satisfy my desire to see him one day at a time. And actually up to this point everything has gone pretty well.

But what am I to do now? What strategy can I use? My father has returned, Flamminio has come to live in the city, and I can't stay here without being recognized. But if that should happen, I'd be dishonored forever and become a scandal in the whole city. So I'm out at this hour to ask the advice of my *balia*, whom I saw come this way from the window. Together we can decide on the best strategy. But first I want to see if she recognizes me in this get-up!

CLEMENZIA: [*Aside*] My goodness, Flamminio must have returned to Modena, for I see his door is open. Oh, if Lelia knew, she would be eager to return home! But who is this young showoff cutting back and forth in front of me in the street this morning? [*To* LELIA] What are you up to, you little pansy, tripping me up? Get lost! What are you doing? What do you want from me? If you only knew how much I'm attracted to your type!

LELIA: God give you a good day, Lady Sponger.

CLEMENZIA: Save your "good days" for someone you ought to have said good night to.

LELIA: Even if I did say good night to someone else, I want to say good day to you, if you'll let me.

CLEMENZIA: Don't give me a hard time, or I'll tell you what you'll make me do to you this morning!

LELIA: Are you waiting for the preacher of the Church of Saint Francis, perhaps, or are you going to Fra Cipollone?[18]

CLEMENZIA: Shoo! Go to hell! What's it to you where I'm going or who I'm going to see? Keep your nose out of my business! What preacher? What Fra Cipollone?

LELIA: Oh, don't get all upset, Lady-Full-of-Threats-but-without-Deeds!

CLEMENZIA: [*Aside*] I'm certain I know this kid, but I don't know from where, even though it seems like I've seen his face a thousand times. [*To* LELIA] Tell me, boy, where do you know me from, and why are you so nosey about my affairs? Lower that cape a bit so I can see your face better.

LELIA: Come on! Are you pretending you don't recognize me?

CLEMENZIA: If you keep hiding behind that cape, neither I nor anyone else will recognize you.

LELIA: Come this way a little.

18. See n. 13.

CLEMENZIA: Where?

LELIA: Over here. [*Pulling back her cape*] Now do you recognize me?

CLEMENZIA: Is that you, Lelia? Oh, my life is ruined! What a disaster! Yes, it's you! Good heavens! What does this mean, my dear child?

LELIA: Be quiet. You're acting like a madwoman. If you keep shouting, I'll leave.

CLEMENZIA: [*Aside*] Is she the least bit ashamed? [*To* LELIA] Have you become a woman of the world, a whore?

LELIA: Yes, I'm of the world. How many women have you seen from outside the world? As far as I'm concerned, I don't remember ever being outside the world.

CLEMENZIA: But have you lost, then, the name of virgin?

LELIA: The name, no—not as far as I know, especially here in Modena. For the rest, you'll have to ask the Spaniards who held me prisoner in Rome.

CLEMENZIA: Is this the honor you owe to your father, your house, yourself, and to me who nursed you? Why, I could cut your throat with my own hands! Come along, now, I don't want you to be seen out here in these clothes.

LELIA: Oh, please calm down!

CLEMENZIA: Aren't you ashamed to be seen like this?

LELIA: Am I perhaps the first woman who ever dressed like this? I've seen hundreds in Rome. And in Modena there are plenty of women who go about their business every night dressed like this.

CLEMENZIA: They're wicked women!

LELIA: Oh well, among so many wicked women isn't there room for one good one?

CLEMENZIA: I want to know why you're running around like this and why you left the convent. Oh, if your father knew, he'd have your head, poor child!

LELIA: That would solve my problems. Do you think I value my life all that much?

CLEMENZIA: Why are you running around like this? Tell me.

LELIA: I'll explain, if you'll listen. And then you'll understand my misfortune and why I left the convent dressed like this and what I need you to do for me. But come this way a bit so that if anyone passes by they won't recognize me talking with you.

CLEMENZIA: You're driving me crazy. Tell me quickly, or I'm going to die of desperation! Oh my!

LELIA: You know that after the horrible sack of Rome, my father, having lost everything, including my brother Fabrizio, in order not to live alone took me away from the Lady Marchesana in whose service he had left me earlier. Our poverty forced us to return to our home here in Modena to escape our evil fortune and live as well as we could with what little we had. And you know that my father, because he had been a close friend of Count Guido Rangone,[19] was not well received here by some.

CLEMENZIA: Why are you telling me what I already know better than you do? And I know that this was the reason that you both went to stay on your farm at Fontanile and I went with you.

LELIA: Exactly. You remember also how difficult and hard my life was then. My thoughts were not only far from love but far from virtually everything human. For I was afraid that having been in the hands of Spanish soldiers, everyone would be pointing at me. I was certain that no matter how honorably I lived, people would never stop talking. Remember how many times you scolded me and urged me to be happier?

CLEMENZIA: If, as you say, I know this already, why are you telling me again? But go on.

LELIA: Well, if I hadn't repeated it, you wouldn't be able to understand the rest. It so happened that at that time, because Flamminio Carandini was one of our faction, he became a close friend of my father. Day after day he came to our house and sometimes very secretly he would look at me, sigh, and lower his eyes. You were the one who pointed it out to me. I began to enjoy his manners and conversation and his way of carrying himself much more than I did at first. But I wasn't thinking of love. Still, visiting our house, he made me aware of how much he was taken with me, first with one thing and then with many signs of love, sighs, longing gazes, and glances, so that although I'd never been in love before, feeling that he was worthy of love I began to turn my thoughts towards him, and eventually I fell for him so completely that to see him was my only desire.

CLEMENZIA: I knew all this already, also.

LELIA: And you will remember that when all the soldiers finally left Rome, my father wanted to go back partly to see if any of our possessions were still there, but mainly to see if he could learn anything about my brother. And because he didn't want to leave me alone, he sent me to Mirandola to live with my aunt Giovanna until he came back. How unhappy I was to be separated from my Flamminio, you know well, for many times you dried my tears! I remained at Mirandola for a year. Then when my father came back, as you know, we returned

19. Guido Rangone (1485–1539) was a condottiere who served at one time or another with both imperial and papal forces.

to Modena, and I was more than ever in love with Flamminio. Since he was my first love, I was very happy, assuming that he would love me as he did before.

CLEMENZIA: Silly little girl! How many men of Modena do you know who'd be able to love a woman a whole year rather than deceiving first one for a while and then another?

LELIA: When I found him, in fact, I might just as well have never existed as far as he was concerned. And what was worse, he was committed heart and soul to winning the love of Isabella, the daughter of Gherardo Foiani, who not only is very beautiful but also is his only heir, if that old madman doesn't decide to marry and have other children.

CLEMENZIA: Gherardo believes that his marriage with you is all arranged, and he's going around saying that your father has given his word. But all this still doesn't explain why you're running around dressed like a man or why you've left the convent.

LELIA: Let me finish, and you'll understand. But as far as Gherardo is concerned, I can tell you that he'll never have me. After my father returned from Rome, he had to go to Bologna on business. And because I didn't want to return to Mirandola, he put me in the convent of San Crescenzio with our relative, Sister Amabile, while he was away, which was supposed to be for a short time only.

CLEMENZIA: I knew all this.

LELIA: Living there, I found that the reverend mothers didn't talk about anything except love. So it seemed to me that I could reveal my love as well to Sister Amabile de'Cortesi.[20] Taking pity on me, she worked day and night to get Flamminio to come to the convent to talk with her and the other nuns so that hidden behind a curtain, I could comfort my eyes and ears looking at him and hearing his voice—which was my greatest desire. One day, listening to him, I heard him lamenting the death of a young boy in his service and singing his praises. And he said that if he could find another boy like that, he would trust him with everything he owned and be the happiest person in the world.

CLEMENZIA: [*Aside*] Woe is me! I'm afraid that this "boy" business is going to make my life very unhappy.

LELIA: I immediately decided that I wanted to see if I could become that lucky boy. So as soon as he left, I broached the subject with Sister Amabile. Since Flamminio was not living in Modena, I wanted to see if I could become his servant and get away with it.

20. "Sweetness of Courtesy."

CLEMENZIA: [*Aside*] Didn't I say that this "boy"— . . . I'm ruined!

LELIA: She agreed with me and showed me how I should act, giving me some clothes that she had recently made for herself so that she could leave the convent every now and then on her own business dressed as a man like the other sisters. So one morning early, I left the convent in these clothes, and being outside of Modena, I was quite confident and things went very smoothly. I went to the villa where Flamminio was living, which as you know is not far from the convent, and I waited there until he came out. In this I must thank Fortune, for the minute Flamminio saw me he asked me very courteously where I was from and if I had anything to ask him.

CLEMENZIA: Didn't you die of shame on the spot?

LELIA: Actually, with the help of Love, I answered him earnestly that I was a Roman seeking my fortune because of my poverty. He looked me up and down from head to toe several times so closely that I was afraid he would recognize me. Then he said that if I was agreeable he would gladly take me on and that he would treat me well and as a gentleman. And although I felt a bit embarrassed, I accepted.

CLEMENZIA: Listening to you, I wish I'd never been born! What good did you see in such craziness?

LELIA: What good? Does it seem to you a small thing for a woman in love to be able to see her lord all the time, to speak with him, touch him, hear his secrets, meet his friends and discuss things with him, and be sure that if she's not enjoying him, at least no one else is?

CLEMENZIA: These are the ways of a foolish child. They don't accomplish anything beyond adding wood to the fire, unless you think they make the man you love happier. But how do you serve him?

LELIA: At the table, in the bedroom. And I know that he's been so pleased with me in these fifteen days that if I'd been wearing my regular dress, I would feel truly blessed!

CLEMENZIA: Wait just a minute—where do you sleep?

LELIA: In a small room off his bedroom, alone.

CLEMENZIA: What would happen if one night, moved by an evil lust, he should call you to sleep with him?

LELIA: There's no sense worrying about problems before they occur. If it happens, I'll think it over and decide.

CLEMENZIA: What will people say when they learn about this, you naughty little girl?

LELIA: Who's going to say anything, if you don't tell? Now, this is what I want you to do, because I've learned that my father returned last night, and I imagine he'll send for me: see to it that for four or five days he doesn't. Or tell him that I've gone with Sister Amabile to Roverino and that I'll return in four or five days.

CLEMENZIA: Why?

LELIA: I'll tell you. Flamminio, as I told you earlier, is in love with Isabella Foiani, and often, very often, he sends me to her with letters and messages. She, however, has fallen madly in love with me thinking that I'm a man and gives me the sweetest caresses ever. Meanwhile, I'm pretending that I don't want to be her lover unless she makes Flamminio forget about her. I've already brought matters to a head, and I'm hoping that in the next three or four days everything will come together and he'll leave her.

CLEMENZIA: I'm afraid that your father has already asked me to get you. So I want you to come to my house now so that I can send for your clothes. You shouldn't be seen like this. And if you don't do as I say, I'll tell your father everything.

LELIA: If you do, you'll be responsible for me going where neither of you will ever see me again. Do as I ask, please! [*Seeing* GHERARDO *coming out of his house*] But I can't tell you the whole story now. I hear Flamminio calling me. [*Calling as if to* FLAMMINIO] My lord! [*To* CLEMENZIA] Wait for me an hour from now at your house; I'll meet you there. And you should know that if you want to find me, you should ask for Fabio degli Alberini, which is the name I've taken. Don't forget. [*Calling as if to* FLAMMINIO] I'm coming, sir! [*To* CLEMENZIA] Goodbye.

CLEMENZIA: My goodness, she saw Gherardo, who's headed this way, and she's disappeared. What am I to do now? I can't tell her father, and I can't let her stay here like this. I'll keep quiet until we speak again.

⁂ SCENE IV ☙

GHERARDO, SPELA, and CLEMENZIA

GHERARDO: If Virginio keeps his promise, I'm going to be giving myself the best time of any man in Modena. What do you think, Spela? Wouldn't that be something?

SPELA: I think it would be much better if you gave something to your nephews, who need it, or to me, since I've served you so long that I've worn the soles off my shoes. I'm afraid that this wife will send you over the edge or give you a set of— . . . actually, I'm sure of it.

GHERARDO: You'll see that she'll be well paid by me.

SPELA: I believe you. While other men would satisfy her with good hard coin, you'll pay her with tiny little halfpennies![21]

GHERARDO: [*As* CLEMENZIA *approaches*] Here's her *balia*. Be quiet, while I cleverly ask her how Lelia is.

CLEMENZIA: [*Aside*] What a handsome lily fresh from the garden that Gherardo is to want a wife so young! Who would ever think it was a good idea to hand that poor child over to this wheezing old geezer? By the holy cross, I'd suffocate her before I'd let her be given to that run-down, moldy, drooling, rancid snotnose. I want to work him over a bit. I'll go over to him. [*To* GHERARDO] God give you a good day and a good morning, Gherardo. You look like a little cherub this morning.

GHERARDO: And may God give you a hundred thousand and more ducats.

SPELA: [*Aside*] Those would be better given to me.

GHERARDO: Oh, Spela, how happy I'd be if I were Clemenzia!

SPELA: Because you would've gotten to try a bunch of husbands rather than just the one wife you've had? Or are you trying to say something else?

CLEMENZIA: And according to you, just how many husbands have I tried, Spela? May God have the flies skin you alive! Are you jealous that you weren't one of them?

SPELA: Sure, by God! But I don't know if I could have handled all the pleasure!

GHERARDO: Shut up, you idiot. I wasn't saying that at all.

SPELA: What were you saying, then?

GHERARDO: I meant that if I were she, I would so often have hugged, kissed, and held to my breast my sweet Lelia, made of sugar, of gold, of milk, of roses, and so much else that I'm at a loss for words.

SPELA: Oh, oh, my master, let's go indoors! Get going! Hurry up!

GHERARDO: What?

SPELA: You have a fever, and staying out here in the air will make it worse.

GHERARDO: I have only the pain in the butt that I hope God will give you. What fever? I feel perfectly fine.

SPELA: I'm sure that you have a fever, and I'm certain that it's a big one.

GHERARDO: I know that I feel fine.

SPELA: Does your head hurt?

---

21. Coins poured into a purse were seen as a metaphor for sexual intercourse, the intercourse being all the more satisfying if the coins were large and of good metal.

GHERARDO: No!

SPELA: Let me take your pulse. Does your stomach hurt, or do you feel some sort of vapor rising to your brain?

GHERARDO: You've lost your mind! Do you want to make me into a Calandrino,[22] perhaps? I tell you, I don't have any problem other than missing my Lelia, so delicate, so sweet.

SPELA: I'm certain that you have a fever and that you're very sick.

GHERARDO: How can you tell?

SPELA: How? Can't you see that you're out of your mind, raving, frenzied, and that you don't know what you're saying?

GHERARDO: It's love that makes me act like that, right, Clemenzia? *Omnia vincit amor!*[23]

SPELA: [*Aside*] Right! What a beautiful Neapolitan[24] saying! *Facetis manum,*[25] everybody: it's never been said before.

GHERARDO: That sweet cruel one, your little daughter, sweet traitor . . .

SPELA: [*Aside*] This isn't a fever, this is terminal idiocy. Oh my! Woe is me! What can I do?

GHERARDO: Oh, Clemenzia, I want to hug and kiss you a thousand times!

SPELA: [*Aside*] I'm afraid we need ropes to tie the madman down.

CLEMENZIA: Watch out! I've no desire to be kissed by an old man.

GHERARDO: Do I seem to you that old?

SPELA: [*Aside*] What do you think? At least my master's eyes haven't fallen out of his mouth yet—oops, I mean his teeth.

CLEMENZIA: Well, now that I take a better look at you, I can say that you aren't as old as you seem.

GHERARDO: Tell Lelia that. And listen, if you put in a good word for me with her, I'll give you a veil.

SPELA: [*Aside*] Wow, the big spender! And what will you give me?

CLEMENZIA: If you were as much in the graces of the duke of Ferrara as you are in the graces of Lelia, how lucky you would be! Yes, of course! But who are you kidding? If you really loved her, you wouldn't be doing this to her or trying to ruin her life.

22. The famous fool in Boccaccio's *Decameron* who was the victim of the constant pranks of his friends. By the sixteenth century he had become the proverbial fool in common parlance.
23. Latin: "Love conquers all."
24. Neapolitans were often stereotyped as fast talkers who tried to take advantage of others in love.
25. "Please clap."

GHERARDO: What do you mean, ruin her life? I'm trying to give her a good life, not ruin it.

CLEMENZIA: Why have you kept her waiting a whole year with your negotiations over whether or not you would marry her?

GHERARDO: What? Does Lelia think that was my fault, then? Why, if you should find that I didn't ask her father every day, that this hasn't been my greatest desire, that I didn't wish to marry her immediately, may you see me laid out in my coffin sooner rather than later.

CLEMENZIA: With God's grace, let's hope that's the case! I'll tell her everything. But do you realize that she'd prefer to see you dressed differently? Now you look like an old goat.

GHERARDO: What do you mean, old goat? What have I done?

CLEMENZIA: Nothing, but you're always out all wrapped up in animal skins of one kind or another.

SPELA: [*Aside*] To win her love, then, he'd be better off if he had himself skinned alive or at least went naked through the streets. Can you believe it?

GHERARDO: I have the finest clothes of any man in Modena. Still, I'm grateful for your advice, and she'll soon find that I have a different look. But where will I be able to see her when she returns from the convent?

CLEMENZIA: At the Bazzovara gate. I'm going to get her right now.

GHERARDO: Why don't you let me come with you? We could talk as we walk.

CLEMENZIA: No, no. What would people say?

GHERARDO: I'm dying. Oh, love!

SPELA: [*Aside*] I'm bursting with laughter. Oh, heaven above!

GHERARDO: Oh, how blessed you are!

SPELA: [*Aside*] Oh, you're crazier by far!

GHERARDO: Oh, Clemenzia, so lucky!

SPELA: [*Aside*] Oh, blockhead, so ducky!

GHERARDO: Oh, milk of kindliness!

SPELA: [*Aside*] Oh, brains of emptiness!

GHERARDO: Oh, Clemenzia, so joyful and dear!

SPELA: [*Aside*] Oh, you, so full in the rear!

GHERARDO: Go on now, Clemenzia! Goodbye. [CLEMENZIA *leaves*] Come along now, Spela, I want to refashion myself. I've decided to dress myself more stylishly to please my wife.

SPELA: This is going to end badly.

GHERARDO: Why?

SPELA: Because you're already beginning to do things her way. She's going to wear the pants in the family.

GHERARDO: Go to the shop of Marco, the perfume maker, and buy me a jar of musk. I'm ready to lead the life of a lover.

SPELA: Where's the money?

GHERARDO: Here, take this bolognino.[26] And be quick about it. I'm going home.

⌖ SCENE V ❧

SPELA and SCATIZZA

SPELA: [*Alone*] If anyone wished to wrap up all the foolishness in the world in one package, they could wrap up my master and the job would be done. And now that he has embarked on this mad passion of love, it's even more true. He shaves, he combs his hair, he paces back and forth before her house, he goes out at night to parties armed with a dagger, he goes about all day caterwauling with that raspy, coarse voice of his and a lute even more out of tune than his singing. And he has even given himself to writing efistulas[27] (may he come down with one)—snotnets, rhyndes, stramboats, mad-gals, and a thousand other things that belong in comedies. It's enough to make the asses of this world die laughing, never mind the dogs! Now he wants to start putting on musk. In God's name, it's enough to make even one's balls go crazy. But here's Scatizza, who ought to be coming back from the convent.

SCATIZZA: [*Muttering to himself*] Why, these fathers who have their daughters made nuns must be just like the great men of the time of Bartolomeo Coglioni.[28] Can they really believe that their daughters spend all their time on their knees before a crucifix praying to God that he reward them for putting them in the convent? It's true that they pray to God, and the devil as well, but asking rather that they break the necks of those who've had them locked up in there.

26. A small coin.

27. The wordplay is based on Spela's confused recollection of words having to do with writing and literature: *epistole* (letters) becomes *fistole* (fistulas, or boils); *sonetti* (sonnets) becomes *sognetti* (little dreams), which we have rendered as snotnets, and so on.

28. "Great men" is ironic. Bartolomeo Colleoni (1400–1476) was a famous condottiere frequently referred to in jest because his name sounded like *coglioni* (testicles). There still stands in Venice an equestrian statue of him that has served for centuries as a source of local jokes and proverbs.

SPELA: [*Aside*] I want to hear this story.

SCATIZZA: [*Still muttering to himself*] As soon as I knocked at the supposedly locked door into the inner cloisters, the room filled with nuns, all young and as beautiful as angels. I started to ask for Lelia. On one side some laughed, on the other side some giggled, and then they all began to play around with me as if I were a sweet hard candy.

SPELA: God bless you, Scatizza! Where are you coming from? Sure, you have the sweetest candy. Let me try some.

SCATIZZA: A pox on you and that madman, your master!

SPELA: Leave me alone, and keep the pox for yourself. But where are you coming from?

SCATIZZA: From the nuns of San Crescenzio.

SPELA: All right, but what about Lelia? Has she returned home?

SCATIZZA: May the gallows return for you! Can God allow that imbecile, your master, to think that he's going to have her?

SPELA: Why not? Doesn't she want him?

SCATIZZA: I really doubt it. Does she strike you as being meat for his teeth?

SPELA: She's right not to want him. But what did she say?

SCATIZZA: She didn't say a thing. What could she say, considering that I didn't get to see her? When I got there and asked for her, those hungry nuns wanted to make a snack of me.

SPELA: They wanted more than a snack! More like the meat course. You clearly don't know them.

SCATIZZA: I know them better than you, may the pox take them! You should have been there. The first one wanted to know if I was lovesick, then another if I would marry her. Yet another said that Lelia was all wet in the bath and drying herself off, and one said that she was all tied up at the moment in the sleeping quarters. One asked me, "Did your father have any male children?" Oh! I was about to say to her, "I have a large co— . . . cock-a-doodle-do," but finally I realized that they were just kidding around and that they didn't want me to talk with Lelia.

SPELA: You really weren't very clever. You should've marched right in and told them you wanted to look around for her yourself.

SCATIZZA: Are you crazy? Go right in there by myself? Come on, man, come on. Do you want to see me ruined? Oh, there isn't a stallion in the Maremma[29]

---

29. A rural region of Tuscany noted for its fine horses and rustic backwardness.

who could stand up to them alone! Nuns? A pox on them! But I can't hang around here any longer, I have to get back to my master.

SPELA: And I have to buy some musk, for my own crazy one.

Act II

SCENE I

LELIA (dressed as a boy) and FLAMMINIO

FLAMMINIO: It's very disheartening that after all this time you still haven't been able to win a kind word for me from that cruel and ungrateful Isabella. Still, to see you always welcomed so warmly and listened to so willingly makes me think that she doesn't hate me. And as far as I know, I've never done anything to displease her. You'd know from what she said if she was upset with me about anything. But please tell me again, Fabio, what she said to you last night when you took her my letter.

LELIA: I've already told you twenty times.

FLAMMINIO: Well, tell me again. What's it to you?

LELIA: What's it to me? It makes me sad to see you so downcast; it makes me suffer as much as you. Since I'm your servant, I don't want to give you anything but pleasure, and I worry that her replies will make you unhappy with me.

FLAMMINIO: Don't worry, my dear Fabio. I love you like a brother, and I know that you love me, so you can be sure I'll never let you down, as you'll see with time. Say your prayers and don't worry about anything else. But what did she say?

LELIA: As I told you already: that the greatest pleasure you could give her in the whole world would be to leave her alone and stop thinking about her because she's fallen in love with someone else; and that she can't stand the sight of you anymore and you're wasting your time courting her, because when all is said and done, you're going to find yourself empty-handed.

FLAMMINIO: Did it seem to you that she really meant it, or is she upset with me about something? There was a time when every now and then she seemed to like me, and I really can't believe that she dislikes me that much, for she accepts my letters and messages. I'm prepared to court her until the day I die. At least I want to see what the future has to offer. What do you think, Fabio? Don't you agree?

LELIA: I don't, sir.

FLAMMINIO: Why not?

LELIA: Because if I were in your shoes, I'd want her to be happy with my courtship. What woman would pass up a man like you, noble, accomplished, gentle-mannered, and handsome? Take my advice, Master: drop her and find someone else who loves you. You'll have no trouble finding another and, yes, perhaps one just as beautiful. Tell me, haven't you ever loved another who appreciated your attentions here in Modena?

FLAMMINIO: Of course. There was one among the others called Lelia—in fact, many times I have been tempted to say that you remind me of her. She's reputed to be the most beautiful, wise, and well-mannered young woman in these parts—I should point her out to you someday. She would be very pleased if I showed her a bit of favor. She's rich and has been at court. And she was my love for about a year, showing me much favor, until she went off to Mirandola. Then my evil fortune made me fall in love with this woman who's been as cruel to me as the other was gentle.

LELIA: Master, turn about is fair play. You have ignored someone who loves you; it's only fair that now you are being ignored.

FLAMMINIO: What are you trying to say?

LELIA: If that poor young woman was your first love and she continues to love you more than ever, why have you abandoned her to run after another? I'm not sure that God can ever forgive such a sin. Heavens, my lord Flamminio! You're clearly very much in the wrong.

FLAMMINIO: You're still a boy, Fabio, and you don't understand the power of love. Look, I'm forced to love and adore this new woman, and I can't think about anyone else. I don't know how to, and I'm not capable of it. So go talk to her again and see if you can wheedle out of her why she's so upset with me that she doesn't want to see me.

LELIA: You're wasting your time.

FLAMMINIO: I'm willing to waste this time.

LELIA: You're not going to accomplish anything.

FLAMMINIO: That's life!

LELIA: Give up on her, I say.

FLAMMINIO: I can't. Go on, do as I ask.

LELIA: I'm going, but . . .

FLAMMINIO: Come back immediately with her reply. I'll walk on to the cathedral.

LELIA: As soon as the moment is right, I'll give it my best shot.

FLAMMINIO: Fabio, if you can do it, I'll be very pleased with you! [*Walks off towards the cathedral*]

LELIA: [*Aside*] We split up just in time, because here comes Pasquella looking for me.

↝ SCENE II ↜

PASQUELLA and LELIA (dressed as a boy)

PASQUELLA: [*Alone*] I don't believe there's a greater pain or hassle in the whole world for someone like me than to serve a young girl in love. And that's even more true when that girl doesn't have to fear her mother, sister, or other person, like my mistress. Recently she's fallen so madly in love and become so lathered up that she can't find any peace, day or night.[30] She's always scratching between her legs, stroking her thighs, or running up onto the porch or over to the window or running down the stairs or up the stairs. She just can't seem to stop; it's as if she had quicksilver in her feet. For God's sake, oh, yes, I too was young once and in love as well, and I did some little things that I shouldn't have done, but I also calmed down from time to time.

It would be better, however, if only she'd decided to fall in love with someone of worth, someone mature, a man who would know how to take care of his business and scratch her itch. But she's all caught up with a fancy boy who looks like he would have trouble buttoning up his pants without help if they were unbuttoned. And all day long she sends me to find this lover-boy, as if I didn't have any work to do around the house. Can his master really think that he's acting on his behalf? [*Noting* LELIA] But this is certainly him coming along now. What luck! [*To* LELIA] Fabio, God give you a good day. My dear boy, I was looking for you.

LELIA: And may God give you a thousand scudi,[31] my dear Pasquella. What's your pretty mistress up to? What does she want from me?

PASQUELLA: What do you think she's doing? She's crying, she's all upset, she's a mess because you haven't visited her yet this morning.

LELIA: My goodness, what does she want? Does she want me to get there before the sun comes up?

PASQUELLA: I imagine she'd like to have you stay the whole night, I'm afraid.

LELIA: Well, I have other things to do. I have to serve my master. Do you understand, Pasquella?

---

30. This description of a young woman madly in love uses the language of contemporary love spells, which called for the victims to find no peace day or night until they gave in to their passion. The behavior reported for Isabella is exactly the behavior such spells were supposed to induce.

31. See n. 65.

PASQUELLA: Well, I'm sure your master would feel that you were serving him in coming here, right? But wait, are you perhaps sleeping with him?

LELIA: I wish to God he liked me that much! If that were the case I wouldn't be in the mess I'm in.

PASQUELLA: Oh my! But wouldn't you rather sleep with Isabella?

LELIA: Not me.

PASQUELLA: What? You're not serious!

LELIA: I wish I weren't!

PASQUELLA: Hmmm. Well, let's change the subject. My mistress told me to ask you to come visit her right away because her father isn't at home and she needs to speak with you about something important.

LELIA: Tell her that she's just wasting her time if she doesn't get rid of Flamminio first. She knows that I'd be ruined otherwise.

PASQUELLA: Come tell her yourself.

LELIA: I said I had other things to do. Didn't you hear me?

PASQUELLA: What do you have to do that's so important? Run over to see her, and you can hurry right back.

LELIA: Oh, you're a pain in the neck. Get lost.

PASQUELLA: Won't you come?

LELIA: I said no. Can't you understand?

PASQUELLA: In good faith and in all honesty I'll tell you, Fabio, you're too arrogant. Remember that you're just a young dandy, and you don't really understand how lucky you are. But this fascination with you isn't going to last forever, you know. You're going to grow a beard, your cheeks aren't going to remain so fresh, your lips so red. You won't always be so sought after by everyone—no, sir.[32] Then you'll realize what a fool you've been, and you'll regret what you missed when it's too late. Tell me, how many men do you think there are in this city who'd be delighted if Isabella even smiled at them? And you think you can just laugh at such a sweet dish![33]

LELIA: Well, why doesn't she smile at one of them, then, and leave me alone? I'm not interested.

32. As a good-looking young boy without a beard, Lelia/Fabio would have been attractive to both men and women in the sexual world of the Renaissance. The description of Fabio matches the Renaissance stereotype of the younger partner in male/male relationships and also reflects the fascination with androgyny—often associated with young males—during the period. This fascination seems to have been seen as a refined taste, and lower-class characters in these comedies often express their preference for "real" men or more manly youths.

33. *Pane unto*, literally bread soaked in grease or oil, a common metaphor for something desirable, often used to imply a sexually attractive woman.

PASQUELLA: My God! It's obvious that these youngsters today don't have enough good sense to get by.

LELIA: Come on, Pasquella! Don't keep preaching at me, you'll only make it worse.

PASQUELLA: Stuck up, stuck up, you're going to miss being so stuck up when you grow up! Come on, my dear, sweet Fabio, my soul! Come, for goodness sake, quickly. If you don't, she'll just send me out again to find you because she won't believe I've talked with you.

LELIA: Fine. Relax! I'll come, Pasquella. I was just kidding.

PASQUELLA: When, my sweet?

LELIA: Soon.

PASQUELLA: How soon?

LELIA: Soon enough. Now get lost.

PASQUELLA: I'll be waiting for you at the door, all right?

LELIA: Yeah, yeah.

PASQUELLA: And, uh, you know that if you don't show up, I'll be mad.

❧ SCENE III ☙

GIGLIO and PASQUELLA

GIGLIO:[34] [*Aside*] For the life of me, if this isn't the lucky old bag who serves the most beautiful young thing in this city! What I wouldn't give to have two words alone with her! By the vow of virginity of all the clerics of Rome, I swear I'd make her howl like a cat in heat! But for now, let me see if I can sweet-talk this old bag into helping me with her mistress. [*To* PASQUELLA] Good day, kind and gentle Madonna Pasquella. Where are you coming from this morning?

PASQUELLA: Oh! Good day, Giglio. I'm coming from mass. Where are you going?

GIGLIO: Seeking my fortune. I'm looking for a woman who would give me some kindness.

PASQUELLA: Oh, sure! That's exactly what you Spaniards need! Why, there's not a one of you who doesn't have a dozen women hanging around.

GIGLIO: It's true that I have two myself, but I can't visit them anymore without danger.

---

34. Throughout the comedy, Giglio speaks with a heavy Spanish accent, mixing Spanish with Italian.

PASQUELLA: What? Are they gentlewomen of the Easylay family, perhaps?

GIGLIO: Yes, by my word, exactly. But now I want a mother who'll wash my shirts sometimes and mend by socks and jacket and keep me like a son. And I'll help her with good service.

PASQUELLA: Keep looking, keep on looking; no doubt you'll find plenty. A man like you who already has his gentlewomen will have no trouble finding servants.

GIGLIO: I've already found someone, with your permission.

PASQUELLA: Who?

GIGLIO: You yourself.

PASQUELLA: Really! But I'm too old for you.

GIGLIO: Old? I swear by the Virgin Mary of Monserrat that you seem to me a sweet thing of fifteen or twenty. Old? Don't ever say such a thing again, because I can't bear to hear it. If you decide to be kind to me, you'll see soon enough whether I treat you like a young woman or an old one!

PASQUELLA: No, no, Spanish Rooster, get lost! I don't want to get involved with Spaniards. You're like horse flies, either you bite or you harass, and you're like coal, either you burn or you blacken. We've had plenty of experience with you by now, unfortunately for us! We know you well, thank God. And there's clearly nothing to be gained from becoming involved with you.[35]

GIGLIO: Gain? I swear to God that you will gain more from me than from the most important gentleman of this city! And although I may appear to you now to be down on my luck, I can tell you that I come from one of the most noble families in all of Spain.

PASQUELLA: It's a miracle that you didn't claim to be a lord or a knight! All the Spaniards who come here make themselves lords. And then take a look at how they behave!

GIGLIO: Pasquella, accept my friendship. It will bring you great benefit!

PASQUELLA: What will you do for me? Make me a lady, maybe?

GIGLIO: I'm not asking you to be anything except my mother. And I want to be your son and sometimes also your husband, if that would please you.

PASQUELLA: [*Laughing*] Oh, leave me alone!

GIGLIO: [*Aside*] Ah, she's laughing. Let's see if this puts her in the carnival spirit.

---

35. Given that Spanish armies had ravaged much of Italy in the early sixteenth century and that many independent city-states had fallen under the control of the emperor, whose rule was often maintained by Spanish troops and bureaucrats, such anti-Spanish sentiments were widespread.

PASQUELLA: What did you say?

GIGLIO: That I want to give you a rosary to say during carnival.[36]

PASQUELLA: And where is it?

GIGLIO: Here it is.

PASQUELLA: Oh, it's beautiful! Why don't you give it to me?

GIGLIO: If you'll be my mother, I'll give it to you.

PASQUELLA: I'll be whatever you want, if you give it to me.

GIGLIO: When can we talk alone together for an hour?

PASQUELLA: Whenever you wish.

GIGLIO: Where?

PASQUELLA: Oh, I don't know where.

GIGLIO: Isn't there someplace in the house where you can keep me tonight?

PASQUELLA: Yes, there is. But what if my master should find out?

GIGLIO: What? Don't worry, he won't find out anything!

PASQUELLA: Look, I'll see if it's possible tonight. Come by the house, and I'll tell you if you can come in or not. Now give me that rosary. Oh, it is beautiful!

GIGLIO: Good. I'll be here to find out at nightfall.

PASQUELLA: Right, yes! But give me the rosary.

GIGLIO: I'll bring it with me when I return. I want to have it perfumed a little for you first.

PASQUELLA: There's no need for that. Give it to me as it is; I don't want it more perfumed.

GIGLIO: Look, this piece is broken. I'll have it replaced with a bit of gold, then I'll give it to you this evening. There's no rush, it will be yours.

PASQUELLA: [*Aside*] It will be mine when I have it. One can't rely very much on the word of you Spaniards, I'm afraid. I'm not the only one who says that you're like the tax collector: whatever happens, you never give, only take.

GIGLIO: What are you saying, my mother?

PASQUELLA: I have to go inside, my mistress is waiting for me.

GIGLIO: Wait just a little longer. What's the rush? What do you have to do for your mistress?

PASQUELLA: Oh, you wouldn't believe it. May the devil take me if these

---

36. Both passages use the term *festa*, meaning party, feast day, or festival, but we have translated it as carnival because the term captures the sexual innuendos of this exchange and because Renaissance comedies were normally performed during this season. See act II, scene vi, in which Crivello and Scatizza mention that these events are taking place during carnival.

young girls nowadays don't fall in love before they're dry behind the ears and if they aren't ready to use the pestle and mortar before the needle and thread.[37]

GIGLIO: What are you trying to say?

PASQUELLA: Dying to say?[38] Why, I'm just trying to say that she really would like to start grinding away!

GIGLIO: But it's not possible, she's still too young. Please tell me who she's in love with.

PASQUELLA: I wish it weren't true, or at least that she was in love with someone worthy of her.

GIGLIO: Tell me, on your life, who is he?

PASQUELLA: I don't want to say. Look, you must keep this a secret. Do you know that boy who serves Flamminio de'Carandini?

GIGLIO: Who? That kid that goes around all dressed in white?

PASQUELLA: Yes, him.

GIGLIO: Good God! Is it possible? How could she want to be served by him? He's more fit for being screwed than for screwing.

PASQUELLA: You got that right.

GIGLIO: And that boy, does he love the girl?

PASQUELLA: Well, more or less.

GIGLIO: Doesn't her father know about this?

PASQUELLA: I don't think so. Actually, he has twice discovered him in the house and given him a thousand little caresses, taking his hand and chucking him under the chin as if he were his son. And he says that he thinks he resembles a daughter of Virginio Bellenzini.

GIGLIO: Ah, damn that boy! Ah, that old pig, that lecher! Yes, yes, I know what he's after.

PASQUELLA: Ugh! You've kept me too long. I must go.

GIGLIO: Remember that I'll come tonight. Don't forget your promise!

PASQUELLA: And you, don't forget that rosary!

37. I.e., the girls are more interested in sex (using the pestle and mortar) than in domestic responsibilities (using the needle and thread).

38. Pasquella has misheard what Giglio said in his mixture of Spanish and Italian.

◌ SCENE IV ◌

FLAMMINIO, CRIVELLO, and SCATIZZA

FLAMMINIO: You haven't gone to look for Fabio, and he hasn't returned. I don't know what to make of his delay.

CRIVELLO: I was going, and then you called me back. Is that my fault?

FLAMMINIO: Well, go now, and if he's at Isabella's, wait for him outside and when he comes out send him here immediately.

CRIVELLO: Well, how can I tell if he's there or not? Do you want me to ask her if he's there?

FLAMMINIO: What an ass! Do you think that would be a good idea? It's clear that I don't have anyone to serve me who's worth a fig besides Fabio. God help me reward him as he deserves! And you, what are you muttering about? Do you have something to say, you knave? Isn't it true?

CRIVELLO: What do you want me to say? I say yes, of course. Fabio is good. Fabio is handsome. Fabio serves well. Fabio with you, Fabio with your girl. Fabio is everything, Fabio does everything. But . . .

FLAMMINIO: But what?

CRIVELLO: He may not be entirely the right stuff.

FLAMMINIO: What are you suggesting with this "stuff" thing?

CRIVELLO: That you can't always trust him. Look, he's a foreigner, and one day he could carry off your stuff.

FLAMMINIO: I wish I had as much faith in you others as I have in him! [SCATIZZA *enters*] Here's Scatizza, ask him if he's seen Fabio. I'll be at the Porrini bank. [*He leaves*]

CRIVELLO: Hello, Scatizza. Have you seen Fabio?

SCATIZZA: Who? Your boy with the right stuff? That little bastard! You can have him.

CRIVELLO: Where are you headed?

SCATIZZA: To find my old boss.

CRIVELLO: He left just a moment ago.

SCATIZZA: Where did he go?

CRIVELLO: That way. Come on, and we'll catch up with him. Hurry up! I have a funny story to tell you about what happened to me with my Caterina— the best story ever!

ᴥ SCENE V ᴦ

SPELA, alone

SPELA: Could there be a worse thing in the world than to serve a master who's crazy? Gherardo sent me to buy musk. When I told the apothecary that I had only one bolognino, he insisted that I had forgotten what Gherardo wanted and suggested that maybe he had asked for a jar of unguent for mange instead, since that's what he really needs. Then he insisted that Gherardo wouldn't know what to do with musk. So I began to explain Gherardo's mad love so that he would believe me, and he, along with several other young fellows who were there, almost died laughing. He even wanted me to take him a jar of asafetida,[39] so I left with their laughter ringing in my ears. Now if my master wants that musk, he'll have to give me more money.

ᴥ SCENE VI ᴦ

CRIVELLO, SCATIZZA, LELIA (dressed as a boy), and ISABELLA

CRIVELLO: So that's it. And if you want to come, I'll do everything to find a girl for you too.

SCATIZZA: See what you can do, and I promise you that if you find me a cute serving girl, we'll have a great time together. I have the keys to the granary, to the wine cellar, to the pantry, to the wood, and if you get me an easy lay, I'll make sure we live the life of lords. In the end you can be sure our masters won't make us rich in any other way.

CRIVELLO: Good, I'll ask Bita to find you some easy piece so that all four of us can have a good time together this carnival.

SCATIZZA: Yeah! But it's already the last day of carnival.[40]

CRIVELLO: We'll have us a good time during Lent, then, while our masters are praying and only dreaming of women. But wait a second, Gherardo's door is opening. Let's hide over here for a bit.

SCATIZZA: Why?

39. A foul-smelling substance used as a medicine.

40. This places the events of the comedy at the same time as its performance: the last day of carnival, 12 February 1532.

CRIVELLO: Oh, let's say out of good manners. [*They move off as* LELIA *and* ISABELLA *appear in the doorway*]

LELIA: All right, Isabella! But don't forget what you promised.

ISABELLA: And don't forget to come see me. Listen to me a second.

CRIVELLO: [*To* SCATIZZA, *unheard and unseen by* LELIA *and* ISABELLA] If I were in the place of that pansy, I know my master wouldn't be able to forgive me.

SCATIZZA: You'd have the chick for yourself, eh?

CRIVELLO: What do you think?

LELIA: Now what else do you want?

ISABELLA: Listen a little.

LELIA: I'm listening.

ISABELLA: Do you see anyone out in the street?

LELIA: Not a living soul.

CRIVELLO: What the devil is she up to?

SCATIZZA: No good; they're too close.

CRIVELLO: Let's wait and see.

ISABELLA: Listen, just a word.

CRIVELLO: They're very close together.

SCATIZZA: That's it! That's it!

ISABELLA: You know, I would like . . .

LELIA: What would you like?

ISABELLA: I would like . . . come a little closer.

SCATIZZA: Get closer yet, you animal!

ISABELLA: See if there's anyone out there.

LELIA: Didn't I tell you there's no one?

ISABELLA: Oh, I'd like you to come back after dinner when my father will be away.

LELIA: All right. But when my master passes by, be sure to shut the window in his face and run off.

ISABELLA: If I don't, you needn't love me anymore. [*She touches* LELIA]

SCATIZZA: Where the devil does she have her hands?

CRIVELLO: Oh, my poor master! But that's it, of course, I've got it now!

LELIA: Goodbye.

ISABELLA: Wait a second. Do you really want to leave?

SCATIZZA: Go ahead, kiss her. May you get the pox!

CRIVELLO: She's afraid to be seen.

LELIA: Go on, now. Go back in the house.

ISABELLA: I want one favor from you.

LELIA: What?

ISABELLA: Come this way a little more into the doorway. [*She tries to kiss* LELIA]

SCATIZZA: The deed is all but done!

ISABELLA: [*As* LELIA *pulls away*] Oh, you're so difficult!

LELIA: We'll be seen. [ISABELLA *grabs* LELIA *and kisses her*]

CRIVELLO: Oh my! Oh my! Oh damn! Why not me?

SCATIZZA: Didn't I tell you he'd kiss her?

CRIVELLO: I'll tell you right out, I would rather have seen that kiss than earn a hundred scudi.

SCATIZZA: I saw it, but I would rather have had it!

CRIVELLO: My God! What will my master do when he hears about this?

SCATIZZA: In the devil's name, who would want to tell him?

ISABELLA: Forgive me. You're so good looking and my love for you is so strong that I couldn't resist doing what you may well consider immodest for a young girl. But God knows, I couldn't stop myself.

LELIA: You don't need to ask me for forgiveness, madam, for I know only too well my own feelings and the things that I've done because I loved too much.

ISABELLA: What things?

LELIA: Oh, what things? . . . Deceiving my master, that's hardly good.

ISABELLA: Oh, to hell with him!

CRIVELLO: That's what faith in such trash will get you! It serves him right. No wonder the little fraud has been encouraging my master to forget this love!

SCATIZZA: Everyone looks after good old number one. And in the end, all women are the same.

LELIA: It's late, and I must find my master. Goodbye.

ISABELLA: Wait a second. [*She kisses* LELIA *again*]

CRIVELLO: Wow! And now it's two! May he dry up and go limp!

SCATIZZA: My God, I've got a leg so hard it seems ready to explode!

LELIA: Close the door, now. Goodbye.

ISABELLA: I'm totally yours.

LELIA: And I'm yours. [ISABELLA *goes in, closing the door, and* LELIA *walks slowly away soliloquizing, unheard by* CRIVELLO *and* SCATIZZA] On the one hand I'm having the best time ever playing with this woman who believes I'm a man. On the other, I want to get out of this muddle and am not sure how. It's clear that she's already at the kissing stage, and who knows what will happen the next time we're together? And if she discovers my disguise, I'll lose everything. I need to find Clemenzia and see what she suggests. [*Looking offstage*] But here comes Flamminio.

CRIVELLO: Scatizza, my master told me that he would meet me at the Porrini bank. I want to give him the good news. But if he doesn't believe me, you must support me.

SCATIZZA: You can count on me. Still, if it were up to me, I'd keep quiet and hold this knife to Fabio's throat so he'd be forced to do whatever you wish.

CRIVELLO: No, I want to get him. He has ruined me.

SCATIZZA: It's up to you. [*He and* CRIVELLO *leave in the opposite direction from where* FLAMMINIO *enters; inside the house,* ISABELLA *slams the shutters closed as* FLAMMINIO *passes by the window*]

᭕ SCENE VII ᭕

FLAMMINIO and LELIA (dressed as a boy)

FLAMMINIO: [*Aside*] Can I be so madly in love and think so little of myself that I want to love and serve a woman who despises me, who tortures me, who doesn't give a damn about me, who doesn't even want to give me the pleasure of a glance? Am I so worthless, so vile that I don't know how to end this shame and torture? But here's Fabio. [*To* LELIA] Well, what have you accomplished?

LELIA: Nothing.

FLAMMINIO: Why did it take you so long to return? Are you becoming gallows-bait?

LELIA: It took longer because I wanted to talk with Isabella.

FLAMMINIO: Why didn't you talk with her?

LELIA: She didn't even want to listen to me. If you want my advice, I'd suggest you find another game and take care of yourself, because from everything I've seen to this point, you're wasting your time. She seems absolutely determined never to do anything that would please you.

FLAMMINIO: Well, even if God said it, He would be wrong. Yet do you know that just now, when I was walking by her house, the minute she saw me she ran from the window with such distaste and anger—almost as if she had seen something horrible or frightening?

LELIA: Forget her, I say. Is it possible that in this entire city there isn't some other woman who merits your love as much as she does? Haven't you ever been attracted to another woman?

FLAMMINIO: I wish it weren't true! But I'm afraid that that might be the root of all my problems, because I loved with all my heart that Lelia, daughter of Virginio Bellenzini, whom I told you about. And I'm afraid that Isabella may think I'm still in love with her, and that's why she doesn't want to see me. But I'll convince her that I don't love Lelia anymore—in fact, that I hate her and can't stand even to hear her name. And I'll promise her absolutely never to go near Lelia again. I want you to tell her this clearly.

LELIA: Oh dear!

FLAMMINIO: What's wrong? You seem about to faint. How do you feel?

LELIA: Oh dear!

FLAMMINIO: Where does it hurt?

LELIA: Oh dear! My heart.

FLAMMINIO: How long have you had this? Lean on me a moment. Does your body ache?

LELIA: No, sir.

FLAMMINIO: Is your stomach upset?

LELIA: It's my heart that hurts.

FLAMMINIO: Mine too, and perhaps even more than yours. But you've lost your color. Go on home and put some hot towels on your chest and have your back rubbed; maybe that will do the trick. I'll be back soon, and if you need it, I'll send for the doctor to take your pulse and see what's wrong with you. Give me your arm for a moment. You're freezing! . . . That's better. Go on, now, slowly. [*Aside*] Life is so strange! I wouldn't trade this Fabio for all my wealth, for I don't believe there's anyone more able or willing to serve me in all the world or better mannered than this young man. Moreover, he shows me so much love that if he were a woman, I would think that he's ill because he loves me. [*To* LELIA] Fabio, go on home now and warm your feet. I'll be there shortly. Tell the others to set the table. [*He leaves*]

LELIA: [*Walking off*] O poor wretch! Now you have heard with your own ears from the mouth of this ungrateful Flamminio just how much he loves you! Poor, sad Lelia! Why waste any more time serving this cruel man? Your patience, your prayers, your favors have done no good. Now even your deceptions have failed. Poor me! Rejected! Cast aside! Fled! Hated! What am I doing serving the man who rejects me? Why am I staying with the man who cast me aside? Why do I follow the man who flees me? Why do I love the man who hates me? Ah, Flamminio! You have eyes only for Isabella. He wants no one but Isabella! He can have her. Take her! For I'll either leave him or die. I've decided no longer to serve him in these clothes and never to cross his path again so that he won't ever have to see the woman he finds so hateful. I'll go find Clemenzia. She's waiting for me at home. Together we'll plan what to do with my life. [*She runs off*]

᠂᠊ᔓ SCENE VIII ᕪᶜᠸ

CRIVELLO and FLAMMINIO

CRIVELLO: And if it isn't true, you can have me hung by the neck if cutting my tongue out isn't enough. That's what happened.

FLAMMINIO: When did it happen?

CRIVELLO: When you sent me to look for him.

FLAMMINIO: How? Tell me again, because he told me he didn't get to talk with her today.

CRIVELLO: It would be better if he confessed. But I'll tell you that while I was waiting to see if he would show up at her house, I saw him come out. And as he was about to leave, Isabella called him back inside the doorway and then, after looking around to see if there was anyone to see them, not seeing anyone, they kissed each other.

FLAMMINIO: How come they didn't see you, then?

CRIVELLO: Because I was hidden in that portico across the way, and they couldn't see me.

FLAMMINIO: How did you see them, then?

CRIVELLO: With my eyes. Do you think that I saw them with my elbows?

FLAMMINIO: And he kissed her?

CRIVELLO: I don't know if she kissed him or he her, but I believe they kissed each other.

FLAMMINIO: Did they each put their faces so close together that they could kiss?

CRIVELLO: Their faces no, but their lips yes.

FLAMMINIO: Aha! Can two people bring their lips close without doing the same with their faces?

CRIVELLO: All right, I suppose if people had their mouths in their ears or in the back of their necks it would be possible, maybe, but given where they are now, you're right.

FLAMMINIO: Look, you'd better have seen things clearly, because later you can't say, "Well, it seemed to me." This is a very serious thing that you're saying.

CRIVELLO: As great as the giant Mangia, who rings the clock on the tower of Siena.[41]

---

41. Mangia was the name of the giant automaton that struck the hours on this mechanical clock, and thus was used to describe anything really big.

FLAMMINIO: How did you see it?

CRIVELLO: Looking, with my eyes wide open, and as I was there to look, I really didn't have anything else to do but see.

FLAMMINIO: If this is true, you've killed me!

CRIVELLO: It's true. She called him. They came together. She embraced him. She kissed him. So now if you want to die, go ahead.

FLAMMINIO: I'm not surprised that the traitor denied being there! Now I understand why the rogue encouraged me to leave her—so that he could have her for himself! I won't deserve to be called a man if I don't launch a vendetta against him that will stand for all time as an example to servants who betray their masters. But in the end, if I don't have better proof, I don't want to believe you. I know that you're not trustworthy and that you must hate his guts, so you're saying this to get me to get rid of him. But in the name of God whom I hold dear, I'll make you tell the truth or kill you! Tell me! Did you really see it?

CRIVELLO: Yes, sir.

FLAMMINIO: He kissed her?

CRIVELLO: They kissed.

FLAMMINIO: How many times?

CRIVELLO: Two times.

FLAMMINIO: Where?

CRIVELLO: In the entrance hall.

FLAMMINIO: You're a rotten liar! A little while ago you said they were in the doorway.

CRIVELLO: I meant to say near the doorway.

FLAMMINIO: Tell the truth! [*Beating him*]

CRIVELLO: Ouch, ouch! I'm beginning to be sorry I told you.

FLAMMINIO: Did it really happen?

CRIVELLO: Yes, sir. But I forgot: I have a witness.

FLAMMINIO: Who is it?

CRIVELLO: Scatizza, Virginio's servant.

FLAMMINIO: He saw them too?

CRIVELLO: Just like me.

FLAMMINIO: And if he doesn't confirm what you said?

CRIVELLO: Kill me.

FLAMMINIO: I will.

CRIVELLO: And if he confirms it?

FLAMMINIO: I'll have to kill two people.

CRIVELLO: Oh, my God, why?

FLAMMINIO: Not you two; Isabella and Fabio.

CRIVELLO: And then you should burn down that house with Pasquella and everyone in it.

FLAMMINIO: Let's find Scatizza. If I don't pay them as they deserve . . . if I don't make people talk . . . if the whole city doesn't see . . . I'll have such a great revenge! . . . That traitor! That's what trust gets you.

Act III

✎ SCENE I ✑

The PEDANT, FABRIZIO, and STRAGUALCIA

PEDANT: This city seems completely changed since I was last here. Actually I was here only briefly with the delegation from Ancona, and we stayed at the Guicciardino. Still, we were here about six days. [*To* FABRIZIO] Do you recognize anything?

FABRIZIO: It's like I've never seen it before.

PEDANT: That makes sense. After all, you left when you were so young that it's no wonder. Wait, I recognize this street. That's the palace of the Rangoni, over there's the Grand Canal, and that church you see there at the head of the street is the cathedral. Have you ever heard the saying "Were you ever the pussy of Modena" or "You think you're the pussy of Modena"?[42]

FABRIZIO: A thousand times. Show it to me, please.

PEDANT: See that statue above the door of the cathedral?

FABRIZIO: That one?

PEDANT: That's it.

FABRIZIO: Wow! That's a scream!

PEDANT: Now you understand.

FABRIZIO: I've also heard the saying "You're trying to lead the bear of Modena."[43] What does that mean, and where's this bear?

PEDANT: There are sayings of the *antiqui de quibus nescitur origo.*[44]

---

42. A proverbial way of saying "You're full of yourself" or "You're putting on airs," based on a statue of a naked woman with her legs spread over the door of the cathedral displaying her genitals in a manner that Renaissance viewers took to be prideful. It was reportedly an ancient fertility symbol.

43. I.e., taking on something impossible or disreputable.

44. "Ancients whose origins are not known." This pedant, like that of *Il marescalco*, regularly spouts Latin.

FABRIZIO: I really have the feeling, Professor, that this place is going to bring me good things.

STRAGUALCIA: And it's going to bring me even better things, because I smell the sweet perfume that comes from a roast, and it's making me die of hunger.

PEDANT: Oh! Don't you know what Cantalicius said? *"Dulcis amor patriae."*[45] And Cato: *"Pugna pro patria."*[46] *Hoc, in summa,*[47] there is not a sweeter thing than one's fatherland.

STRAGUALCIA: I believe that Trebbiano wine is much sweeter, Tutor. Boy, could I use a cup of that now! My back's broken from carrying this baggage.

PEDANT: These streets seem newly paved. When I was here before they were all dirty and muddy.

STRAGUALCIA: Are we going to stand around and count the cobblestones? Let's get going! Let's hurry up and find a place where we can eat, that's what I want.

PEDANT: *Iandundum animus est in patinis.*[48]

FABRIZIO: Whose coat of arms is that over there with the auger on it?

PEDANT: That's the coat of arms of this community, and it's called the Trivella. And just as in Florence they cry "Marzocco, Marzocco!" and in Venice "San Marco, San Marco!" and in Siena "Lupa, Lupa!" here they cry "Trivella, Trivella!"

STRAGUALCIA: I would rather we yell "Frying pan, frying pan!"

FABRIZIO: That one I recognize: it's the arms of the duke.

STRAGUALCIA: Tutor, why don't you carry this baggage yourself for a bit? My lips are so parched with thirst that I can barely talk.

PEDANT: Buck up. You can quench your thirst later!

STRAGUALCIA: When I'm dead, *then* you'll make me a heavenly broth to drink.

FABRIZIO: I'm glad that I really like this place, even at first sight. What about you, Stragualcia?

STRAGUALCIA: It seems like heaven to me: here too one doesn't eat or drink. Let's get going and not waste any more time looking at the place. We can look at it at our leisure after we eat.

PEDANT: There you see the most egregious bell tower that exists in the whole structure of the universe.

---

45. "Sweet is the love of one's fatherland." Giovanni Battista Cantalicio (ca. 1450–1515) was a minor humanist and grammarian.

46. "Fight for one's fatherland."

47. "Thus, in sum."

48. "For some time his soul has been among the dishes."

STRAGUALCIA: Is that the one the people of Modena wanted to put a sheath over and whose shadow they claim makes a man go crazy?[49]

PEDANT: Yes, that's it.

STRAGUALCIA: I know that as far as I'm concerned I'm not going to leave the kitchen. Whoever wants to wander around can do so. Now let's find a place to stay.

PEDANT: You're in a great rush.

STRAGUALCIA: A pox on you! Here I am dying of hunger, and I haven't had a thing to eat this morning besides that half a hen that you left me on the boat.

FABRIZIO: Whom can we find to show us to my father's house?

PEDANT: Actually, it seems to me that first we should find a place to stay at an inn and rest a bit there. Then we can look for him at our leisure.

FABRIZIO: I like that idea. These seem to be inns.

⁀꙳ SCENE II ꙳⁀

AGIATO, FRULLA, the PEDANT, FABRIZIO, and STRAGUALCIA

AGIATO: Oh, kind sirs! This is the inn for you, if you want lodging. Come to the Mirror, to the Mirror!

FRULLA: Oh, you're most welcome here! I've been your host other times. Don't you remember your Frulla? Come in here, where all the people of your quality put up.

AGIATO: Come stay with me. You'll have good rooms, a good fire, excellent beds, freshly washed sheets, and you'll not lack for anything that's yours.

STRAGUALCIA: I should certainly hope so!

AGIATO: I meant to say you won't lack for anything that's your desire.

FRULLA: I'll give you the best wine in Lombardy, big fat birds, sausages like this, pigeons, large chickens, and whatever you ask for. And you'll really enjoy everything.

STRAGUALCIA: This is what I want most of all.

PEDANT: And you, what do you say?

AGIATO: I'll give you sweetbreads, mortadella, wine from the mountains, and above all you'll enjoy fine, delicate things.

FRULLA: I'll give you lots of food, and you can forget delicate things. If you

---

49. A reference to the series of contemporary jokes about the supposedly bizarre behavior of the people of Modena.

stay with me I'll treat you like lords, and you can pay me as you wish. At the Mirror, however, you'll pay for everything, even the candles. You decide.

STRAGUALCIA: Master, let's stay here, it's clearly better.

AGIATO: If you want to lodge well, it would be better for you to stay with me. Do you want people saying that you're staying at the Joker?[50]

FRULLA: My Joker is a hundred times better than your Mirror.

PEDANT: *Speculum prudentia significat iuxta illud Catonis, "Nosce teipsum."*[51] Do you understand, Fabrizio?

FABRIZIO: I understand.

FRULLA: See for yourself who has more guests, [*tauntingly to* AGIATO] you or me.

AGIATO: See for yourself where the important people stay.

FRULLA: See where they are better treated.

AGIATO: See who has more fine things.

STRAGUALCIA: Enough of these fine things, fine things, fine things. I want just one thing, to fill my whole body, and you can keep your fine things, as far as I'm concerned. Too many fine things are fine for the Florentines.[52]

AGIATO: They all stay with me.

FRULLA: They used to stay with you, but over the last three years they've all come over to my sign.[53]

AGIATO: Young man, put that baggage down here, for I see that it's tiring you out.

STRAGUALCIA: Don't worry about that, I've no desire to lighten the load on my shoulders until I'm sure I'm going to load up my belly.

FRULLA: Would a couple of fat capons do the trick? Bring the bag over here, and these are all yours.

50. The name of Frulla's inn was the *Matto*, often translated literally as the Fool, although the name seems to refer to the playing card known as the *Matto*, or Joker. As the Joker was the wild card in many card games and cards were often played at inns, the name would have indicated a congenial if not overly fine inn. The Italian term conveys all three meanings—wild card, joker (trickster), and fool—and the ambiguity is regularly played for a laugh.

51. "The mirror signifies prudence, according to the proverb of our Cato: 'Know thyself.'"

52. Florentines were the traditional enemies of the people of Siena. This discussion alludes to the growing upper-class emphasis on manners, fine things, and delicacy as opposed to the older ideals, which were being left to the lower classes, that focused on having plenty: plenty to eat and plenty of pleasure, no matter how earthy and unrefined.

53. Since this comedy was set in 1532, Frulla's comment suggests that Florentines have been staying under the sign of the Fool (or the Joker/Trickster) since 1529, when Florence fell again under the control of the Medici family. The anti-Florentine sentiment would not have been lost on a Sienese audience.

STRAGUALCIA: Well, why not! But they'll only be an appetizer!

AGIATO: Look at this prosciutto! Doesn't it look like crimson silk?

PEDANT: That's not bad.

FRULLA: Who knows about wine?

STRAGUALCIA: Me, me! Why, I know more than the French.

FRULLA: See if you like this, then. If not, I can give you at least ten others.

STRAGUALCIA: Frulla, for my money you are a much better innkeeper than he is. He's got it backwards: he shows you something that will make you want to drink[54] before he lets you see whether the wine is any good. [*Tasting the wine*] Oh, Master, this is good. Go ahead, take the bag.

PEDANT: Wait a moment. You, what do you have to say?

AGIATO: I say that gentlemen don't worry about stuffing their stomachs with a lot of food but rather eat small helpings of food that is fine and delicate.

STRAGUALCIA: He must be running a hospital or an inn for the ill.

PEDANT: [*To* AGIATO] You're making sense. What will you give us?

AGIATO: Ask for what you wish.

FRULLA: I'm amazed at you gentlemen. When there is plenty of food, a man may eat as much or as little as he likes, which is not the case when there is little. Moreover, when a man begins to eat, his appetite grows and he needs to fill up with bread.

STRAGUALCIA: "You are wiser than the law," as they say. I've never met a man who understands my needs better than you. Let's go, because I think I love you.

FRULLA: Go on into the kitchen, brother, and take a look around.

PEDANT: *Omnis repletio mala, panis autem pessima.*[55]

STRAGUALCIA: Learned fool! One of these days I'll rearrange your teeth, if I live long enough. [*He enters the* JOKER]

AGIATO: Come with me, gentlemen, for it's not a prudent thing to stand around outside in the cold.

FABRIZIO: Oh, come now, we're not that fine and delicate!

FRULLA: Listen, my lords, that inn, the Mirror, used to be the best inn in Lombardy. But ever since I opened the Joker, he's lucky if ten people stay there in a year. And my inn is better known than any other in the whole world. Lots of Frenchmen come here, and all the Germans who come through town.

AGIATO: You're lying. The Germans go to the Pig.[56]

---

54. I.e., the salty prosciutto.

55. "Every excess in food is bad, but too much bread is the worst thing."

56. Germans were often portrayed as porcine. German stereotypes were generally negative, given

FRULLA: Visitors from Milan, Parma, and Piacenza stay with me.

AGIATO: The Venetians, Genoese, and Florentines stay with me.

PEDANT: Where do the Neapolitans stay?

FRULLA: With me.

AGIATO: Are you kidding? Most of them stay at the Love.[57]

FRULLA: And how many of them stay with me?

FABRIZIO: The duke of Malfi,[58] where does he stay?

AGIATO: Sometimes with me, sometimes with him, sometimes at the Sword, sometimes at the Love, depending on what he wants.

PEDANT: Where do the Romans stay? Because we have come from Rome.

AGIATO: With me.

FRULLA: That's a lie. You won't find one who has stayed there all year. It's true that some old cardinals out of habit have stayed there, but all the new ones belong at the Joker.

STRAGUALCIA: [*Coming out of the* JOKER] I won't leave this place unless I'm dragged out. The others can go where they like. Master, there are so many big pots around the fire, so many soups, so many savories, so many sauces, such great spits of roasted pigeon, partridge, thrush, and goat, capons, boiled meats, roasts, and wonderful macaroni, lasagna, pies—if he were getting ready for carnival or the entire court of Rome, he would still have enough to satisfy everyone.

FRULLA: Did you try the wine?

STRAGUALCIA: And what wine!

PEDANT: *Variorum ciborum commistio pessima generat digestionem.*[59]

STRAGUALCIA: *Bus asinorum, buorum castronorum, tatte, battate, pecoronibus!*[60] What the devil are you up to? May you catch the pox, you and all the other pedants in the world! You're a scoundrel, as far as I'm concerned. Let's stay here, Master.

FABRIZIO: Where do the Spanish stay?

---

the German role in the sack of Rome and in the numerous armies that devastated Italy from 1494 to midcentury.

57. Another popular stereotype: Neapolitans were reputed to be great lovers (or at least to think of themselves as such).

58. Alfonso Piccolomini, a general of Emperor Charles V and at the time of this comedy the Capitano del Popolo of Siena and a supporter and member of the Intronati. There are several gently humorous references to him in the play.

59. "Mixing various foods is terrible for the digestion."

60. Stragualcia is making fun of the Pedant's Latin with some pseudo-Latin of his own. It does not translate neatly, but a Renaissance audience would have caught the drift: "Asshole of asses, castrated oxen, beating, beaten, in the name of the muttonhead!"

FRULLA: I avoid having any dealings with them. They stay at the Bandit.[61] But what else could you want? There isn't anyone who comes through here who doesn't stay with me, except for the Sienese, who are so friendly with the Modenese that when they visit they have a hundred friends who put them up in their homes. Lords and great professors, poor and rich, soldiers and good men, they all run to the Joker.

AGIATO: All the doctors, judges, friars, and learned men come to my inn.

FRULLA: And I'll tell you that there hardly passes a day that someone doesn't leave the Mirror to come and stay with me.

FABRIZIO: Tutor, what should we do?

PEDANT: *Etiam atque etiam cogitandum.*[62]

STRAGUALCIA: Body of mine, it's time to fatten up. For once I'm going to eat my fill and really pig out.

PEDANT: I am thinking, Fabrizio, that we are rather low on funds.

STRAGUALCIA: Tutor, inside there I saw the innkeeper's young son, handsome as an angel.

PEDANT: Come on, then! Let's stay at the Joker. In any case, your father, if we find him, will pay the innkeeper.

STRAGUALCIA: [*Aside*] I thought that bit about the boy would be just the bait to catch that old bird! I've already had three glasses of wine, although I'm claiming only one. And I'm not going to leave the kitchen until I've tasted everything. Then I'll have a nap by that good fire. And to hell with anyone who wants to hold back!

AGIATO: Watch out, Frulla. You've cheated me once too often, and one of these days we're going to have it out once and for all.

FRULLA: Whenever you like. I'm ready and waiting.

‍ SCENE III ‍

VIRGINIO and CLEMENZIA

VIRGINIO: Is this the way you've taught her to behave? Is this the honor she pays me? Oh, how unlucky I am! I've worked so hard to overcome my evil fortune, and for this? To see my patrimony without heirs; to see my house ruined; to see my daughter a whore; to become the subject of common gossip; to

---

61. Another national slur: the Spanish were often portrayed as grasping and thievish.
62. "This is a matter for much thought."

be unable to show my face in public; to be pointed out by children in the streets; to be held up as a warning by the old; to be put in a comedy by the Intronati; to be made an example of in tales; and to be made the subject of the gossip of every woman in this city? Maybe these women aren't gossips, eh? Maybe they don't like to malign others, eh? But I imagine it doesn't really matter, because everyone knows everything already. Actually, I'm certain, for if even one woman knows it, in three hours the whole town knows it. I'm a disgraced father, a miserable and sad old man who has lived too long! What can I do? What should I think?[63]

CLEMENZIA: You'd be better off making less noise so you can concentrate on making sure she returns home before the whole town finds out. But I think Sister Blabbermouth is as full of hot air as is the idea that Lelia is really running around town dressed as a man! Be sure that the nuns aren't just saying this because they hope you'll make her a nun and leave everything to the convent.

VIRGINIO: How could she be lying? She even told me that Lelia is a servant of a Modenese gentleman and that he hasn't realized she's a woman.

CLEMENZIA: Anything is possible, but me, I can't believe it.

VIRGINIO: And I certainly can't believe he hasn't figured out that she's a woman.

CLEMENZIA: I didn't mean that.

VIRGINIO: I have to say it, because my honor's on the line. Actually, I created the problem myself by giving the girl to you to bring up even though I knew what you were.

CLEMENZIA: Virginio, enough of such talk. If I've been a sinner, it's because you made me one. You know very well that before you, there was no one but my husband. And young girls need to be treated differently than you have treated Lelia. Aren't you ashamed to be trying to marry her off to a croaking old fool who could be her grandfather?

VIRGINIO: What do you have against old men, you slut? They're a thousand times better than young ones.

CLEMENZIA: You've lost your senses, and that's why everyone is deceiving you and telling you such foolish gossip.

VIRGINIO: If I find her, I'll drag her home by the hair.

---

63. Although played for laughs, these lines reflect the significant disciplining power of honor. The entire community monitored honorable behavior. When honor was lost—in this case because Lelia dressed as a man had broken free from the restraints placed on women—everyone knew it immediately, as Virginio laments. And, crucially, not just Lelia's reputation and standing in the community would be destroyed by her breaking free but also that of her family, and especially Virginio, the male head of the family ultimately responsible for her honorable behavior.

CLEMENZIA: That way you'll be like those men who flaunt the horns on their own heads instead of sensibly hiding them.

VIRGINIO: I don't care. People will find out anyway. The best that I can do is chop them off.

CLEMENZIA: Do what you think best, just be sure you don't chop off your head along with the horns.

VIRGINIO: I've been told how she's dressed, so I'm going to find her, and when I do there'll be hell to pay.

CLEMENZIA: Do as you please. For myself, I'm off; no sense preaching to the deaf. These men!

SCENE IV

FABRIZIO and FRULLA

FABRIZIO: While my two servants are sleeping, I'm going to visit the town. When they wake up, tell them to head towards the main square.

FRULLA: You know, my lord, if I hadn't seen you dressed in those clothes, I'd swear that you were the young servant of a local gentleman who dresses like you, in white, and is the spitting image of you.

FABRIZIO: Might he be some brother of mine?

FRULLA: He could.

FABRIZIO: Tell the Professor to find the person we've come to see.

FRULLA: I'll take care of it.

SCENE V

PASQUELLA and FABRIZIO

PASQUELLA: My goodness, here he is.[64] I was afraid I was going to have to search the whole city for him. Fabio, how good to see you! I was looking for you, so you've saved me the time and effort of finding you. My dear, my mistress wants you to come to see her right now about something of importance to you and her—I don't know what.

FABRIZIO: Who is your mistress?

---

64. Pasquella has mistaken Fabrizio for Lelia dressed as Fabio.

PASQUELLA: You know very well who she is, you. My goodness, you two make a fine couple!

FABRIZIO: Actually, we're not a couple! But if she wants to couple, I'm ready.

PASQUELLA: I mean that you two aren't very quick. I'd like to be still young like you and able to enjoy such a feast! And I know that if I were you, I'd have already put aside my suspicions and scruples. But you'll get down to it soon enough, right?

FABRIZIO: Please, madam! You don't know me. You've mistaken me for someone else, so leave me alone.

PASQUELLA: Oh, don't get me wrong, dear Fabio, I'm saying this to help you out.

FABRIZIO: I haven't gotten anything wrong. But my name isn't Fabio, and I'm not who you think.

PASQUELLA: Well, you two will have to work things out to your own satisfaction. But you know, there are very few young women her equal in wealth or beauty in this city. And I'd rather see you get down to it instead of running back and forth all the time, giving others reason to talk without gaining anything for yourself and with little honor for her.

FABRIZIO: [*Aside*] What's all this about? I don't understand. Either she's mad or she has mistaken me for someone else. But I want to see where she's leading me. [*To* PASQUELLA] Let's go.

PASQUELLA: Oh! I think I hear people in the house. Wait here a bit until I see if Isabella is alone. I'll call you if no one's there. [*She enters the house*]

FABRIZIO: I want to see how this story ends. Maybe this woman is the servant of some courtesan and she thinks she'll get some money out of me. If that's the case, she's mistaken. I'm virtually a student of the Spanish, and in the end I'll be more likely to have a scudo of hers before she has a carlin of mine.[65] One of us will be deceived, and it won't be me. I'm going to move away a bit from this house so that I can see the type of people who go in and out and judge what type of person this woman is.

---

65. Another dig at Spaniards as being tight and grasping. A scudo was a large coin of significant worth, a carlin a small coin of little value.

ᙏ᙮ SCENE VI ᙮ᙎ

GHERARDO, VIRGINIO, and PASQUELLA

GHERARDO: Please forgive me, but if that's what's happened, I'm going to turn her down. I'm afraid that your daughter did this because she didn't want me, and worse yet I'm convinced that she did it because she has had other lovers.

VIRGINIO: Don't think that, Gherardo. Do you think I would have told you any of this if that were the case? Please don't ruin our arrangements.

GHERARDO: Please don't talk to me about it anymore.

VIRGINIO: Oh! Are you going to betray your word?

GHERARDO: Yes, if someone's deeds betray me, I see no reason to keep my word. In the end you don't even know if you can get her back. You're trying to sell me the proverbial bird in the bush. Look, I heard everything you said to Clemenzia.

VIRGINIO: As long as I don't have her, I won't try to give her to you, but if I get her back, wouldn't you be willing to marry her immediately?

GHERARDO: Virginio, I had the most honorable wife who ever lived in this city, and I have a young daughter who's a pure dove. How can you ask me to take into my home a woman who has fled from her father and goes from house to house like a whore dressed as a man? Don't you understand that if I do that I won't be able to marry my daughter off?[66]

VIRGINIO: After a few days no one will be talking about it anymore. What does it really matter? And no one else besides us knows about it.

GHERARDO: Soon everyone in town will be talking.

VIRGINIO: That's not true.

GHERARDO: How long has she been gone?

VIRGINIO: Since yesterday or this morning.

GHERARDO: I wish to God it were true. But are you sure she's in Modena?

VIRGINIO: Absolutely.

GHERARDO: All right. Find her, and then we can speak again.

VIRGINIO: Promise that you'll take her?

GHERARDO: I'll think about it.

VIRGINIO: Go ahead, say yes.

GHERARDO: I can't say that, but . . .

VIRGINIO: Go ahead, speak up. [PASQUELLA *enters*]

---

66. Another indication of the significance of honor and its disciplining potential.

GHERARDO: [*Aside to* VIRGINIO] Quiet! [*To* PASQUELLA] What are you doing here, Pasquella? What is Isabella doing?

PASQUELLA: What do you think? She's busy praying before her little altar.

GHERARDO: May she be blessed! I have a daughter who's always praying. Who could ask for more?

PASQUELLA: Oh, you've described her perfectly. She goes without meat every day that God requires it, and she says her prayers like a little saint.

GHERARDO: She's just like her blessed mother.

PASQUELLA: Exactly. Oh, the good that wretched woman did! She punished herself more and wore more hair-shirts than anyone else in recent history, and she made charity her life; and if it weren't for her love of you there wouldn't have been a friar, priest, or poor man who came to her door who wouldn't have received everything she had to offer.

VIRGINIO: Now those were good deeds!

PASQUELLA: Why, many times she'd get up an hour or two before dawn to go to the first mass of the Friars of Saint Francis, for she didn't want to be seen or thought to be a paud like certain saint sniffers I know.

GHERARDO: What? "Bawd"? What do you mean?

PASQUELLA: That's right, "bawd." How do you say it?

VIRGINIO: That's an insult!

PASQUELLA: I know I've heard her say it.

GHERARDO: You meant to say "fraud."

PASQUELLA: Maybe. But what I really wanted to say is that her daughter is even more like that than she was.

GHERARDO: God willing.

VIRGINIO: [*Seeing* FABRIZIO][67] Oh, Gherardo, Gherardo! Here's the person we were talking about! Oh, unhappy father that I am. She may hide or run, now that she's seen me. Grab her!

GHERARDO: Be sure you're not making a mistake. Maybe it's not her.

VIRGINIO: Who wouldn't know her? Don't I see all the signs that Sister Blabbermouth told me to look for?

PASQUELLA: [*Aside*] Things are looking bad. I'm afraid I'm in trouble.

---

67. Virginio too mistakes Fabrizio for Lelia dressed as Fabio.

❧ SCENE VII ☙

VIRGINIO, GHERARDO, and FABRIZIO

VIRGINIO: [*To* FABRIZIO] Good day, young lady. Is this any way for a young lady to dress? Is this the way you honor your family? Is this the happiness you give to this poor old man? If only I'd been dead when I fathered you! It seems that the only reason you were born was to dishonor me and bury me alive! Oh, Gherardo! What do you think of your bride? Do you think she is bringing honor to us?

GHERARDO: I wouldn't say so. My bride, hardly!

VIRGINIO: Tramp! Disgrace! It would serve you right if this man didn't want you as his wife any longer and no one else would take you! But he won't hold your foolishness against you; he wants to have you.

GHERARDO: Not so fast!

VIRGINIO: [*Pointing to* GHERARDO's *house*] Get in that house over there, you disgrace! It's clear that the milk your mother gave you the day that I sired you was damned.

FABRIZIO: Old man, don't you have sons, relatives, or friends in this city who can take care of you?

VIRGINIO: What a reply! What are you talking about?

FABRIZIO: Well, in view of your need of a doctor, I'm amazed that they've let you out of the house. In any other city they'd keep someone like you tied down.

VIRGINIO: I ought to have kept you tied up! Why, I'd like to cut your throat! Bring me a knife.

FABRIZIO: Old man, you don't know me very well. And perhaps you're insulting me like this because you think I'm a foreigner. But I'm as much from Modena as you and the son of as good a father and family as you yourself.

GHERARDO: [*Aside*] She really is pretty. If there's no other problem than what one can see, I'll take her.

VIRGINIO: Well, then, why did you run off from your father and the place where I sent you?

FABRIZIO: You never sent me anywhere that I know, but I was forced to leave.

VIRGINIO: Forced, eh? Who forced you?[68]

FABRIZIO: The Spaniards.

---

68. "Forced" here has a sexual implication as well, which the following clarifications by Fabrizio only seem to confirm.

VIRGINIO: And now where have you come from?

FABRIZIO: From the military camp.

VIRGINIO: From the military camp?

FABRIZIO: Yes, from the military camp.

GHERARDO: [*Aside*] If that's how it is, the marriage is off!

VIRGINIO: You're ruined!

FABRIZIO: And you too, old man!

VIRGINIO: Gherardo, please put her in your house so that she won't be seen in this state.

GHERARDO: I will not. Send her to your own house!

VIRGINIO: In the name of our friendship, let her in!

GHERARDO: I said no.

VIRGINIO: Listen a second. [*He and* GHERARDO *move off to talk privately*] This way you'll be sure she won't run off.

FABRIZIO: [*Alone*] I've known many crazies from Modena, whom I'll not name, but I've never seen any like this old man who weren't tied down or locked up. What a strange humor he's in! He's out of his mind, at least from what I can tell, because he seems to think that young men are young women. Oh, this is even more intriguingly strange than the story Molza[69] told about a Sienese woman who thought she had become a Cretan vase, especially since women are usually held to be more foolish than old men, who for a host of reasons ought to be very wise.[70] And not for a hundred scudi would I want to miss the chance to tell the tale of this madness during carnival![71] But they're coming back. Let's see what they have to say.

GHERARDO: I'll tell you the truth, on the one hand I think I will, on the other I think I won't. Perhaps you could question her a little more closely.

VIRGINIO: [*To* FABRIZIO] Come here.

FABRIZIO: What do you want, old man?

VIRGINIO: You are a real sad case, you.

FABRIZIO: Don't insult me. I won't accept such treatment.

VIRGINIO: You disgrace!

69. F. M. Molza (1489–1544), a poet and playwright from Modena who also lived in Siena and Rome. Andrea Barbieri has suggested that Molza was actually the author of this comedy. See Andrea Barbieri, " 'Gl'Ingannati' di Molza, uomo di teatro," *Giornale storico della letteratura italiana* 176 (1999): 388–95.

70. We have not followed the Cerreta edition's emendation that would make Molza the subject of this last phrase: "Molza for a host of reasons ought to have been very wise."

71. Of course, with a nice irony, that is exactly what Fabrizio is doing, as the comedy was being performed during carnival.

FABRIZIO: Oh, oh, oh, oh, oh, oh!

GHERARDO: Let him speak. Can't you see that he's all worked up? Do as he says.

FABRIZIO: What does he want from me? What do I have to do with you or him?

VIRGINIO: You still have the nerve to speak? Tell me, who is your father, eh?

FABRIZIO: I'll tell you: Virginio Bellenzini.

VIRGINIO: I wish to God it weren't true! You're going to make me die before my time.

FABRIZIO: An old man of sixty dying before his time? Everyone should live so long! Why, you can go ahead and die anytime you like; you seem to have lived too long already.

VIRGINIO: It's all your fault, you tramp.

GHERARDO: [*To* FABRIZIO] Enough of such talk, my little daughter, my dear sister. You shouldn't talk that way to your father.

FABRIZIO: That's it—the madmen are joining ranks. Both of them seem to be suffering from the same delusion. [*Laughing*] What a strange case!

VIRGINIO: How can you still laugh?

GHERARDO: It's a bad sign that you make fun of your own father.

FABRIZIO: What father, what mother? I've never had another father than Virginio or another mother than Giovanna. You seem to be off your rocker. What do you think, that I have no father?

GHERARDO: [*Going off again to talk privately with* VIRGINIO] Virginio, you know what? I'm afraid that melancholy has caused this poor young woman to lose her mind.

VIRGINIO: Alas! I suspected it right away when she began treating me so aggressively.

GHERARDO: Actually, that could be for another reason.

VIRGINIO: What?

GHERARDO: When a woman has lost her honor, she thinks the whole world is hers and becomes aggressive.

VIRGINIO: She seems merely crazy to me.

GHERARDO: Still, it's strange that she remembers her father and mother yet doesn't seem to recognize you.

VIRGINIO: Let's make her go into your house; it's right here. We can't get her to mine without alerting the whole city.

FABRIZIO: [*Aside*] What are these two senile brothers of ancient Melchizedek plotting now?

VIRGINIO: Let's try to lure her into the house with kindness and then lock her up with your daughter in her room.

GHERARDO: All right, let's try.

VIRGINIO: [*Coming back with* GHERARDO *to speak with* FABRIZIO] Look here, my daughter, I don't want to stay angry with you. I'll forgive everything if you'll try to be good.

FABRIZIO: Thank you, sir.

GHERARDO: Now that's the way good daughters behave.

FABRIZIO: [*Aside*] Now the other one's cooked.

GHERARDO: Look here, it's not honorable to be seen talking out here dressed up like that. Come into the house. Pasquella, open the door!

VIRGINIO: Go in, my daughter.

FABRIZIO: I'm certainly not going to do that.

GHERARDO: Why not?

FABRIZIO: Because I don't like entering the houses of strangers.

GHERARDO: I'm blessed! She'll be a perfect wife, like Penelope![72]

VIRGINIO: Didn't I tell you that my daughter was beautiful and good?

GHERARDO: Her manners show through.[73]

VIRGINIO: [*To* FABRIZIO] I only want to have a word with you.

FABRIZIO: You can have it out here.

GHERARDO: No, out here is not the place! This house is yours because you're going to be my wife.

FABRIZIO: What wife? Why, you old bugg— . . . you humbugger!

GHERARDO: Your father has betrothed you to me.

FABRIZIO: What are you thinking? Do you think I'm one of those pansy boys that you can . . . eh?

VIRGINIO: [*To* GHERARDO] Come on! Don't get her all upset. [*To* FABRIZIO] Listen, my child. I don't want to do anything that you don't want.

FABRIZIO: Look, old man, you're mistaken about me.

VIRGINIO: Just a few words inside.

72. In the *Odyssey*, Penelope, the wife of Odysseus, waited twenty years for him to return from his wanderings, all the while resisting a host of suitors—the proverbial good wife.

73. Reading *abito* as "manners" makes this a positive comment, but reading it as "dress" has the opposite effect: Gherardo believes that Fabrizio is Lelia dressed as a man, and so her dress shows that she is bad (though perhaps sexually exciting in a man's clothing).

FABRIZIO: [*Going in the house*] As many as you like. Do you think I'm afraid of you?

VIRGINIO: Gherardo, now that you have her inside let's have her locked up with your daughter in her room until we can send for her clothes.

GHERARDO: As you wish, Virginio. Pasquella, bring the key to Isabella's room and call Isabella.

Act IV

✥ SCENE I ❧

The PEDANT and STRAGUALCIA

PEDANT: It would serve you right if he gave you a good beating to teach you that when he goes out, you should go with him instead of getting drunk and then sleeping it off.

STRAGUALCIA: And he ought to load you up with kindling, sulfur, pitch, and gunpowder and then set you alight[74] to teach you not to be what you are.

PEDANT: Drunkard! Drunkard!

STRAGUALCIA: Pedant! Pedant!

PEDANT: Wait till I find our master!

STRAGUALCIA: Wait till I find his father!

PEDANT: Oh! What do you want to tell his father about me?

STRAGUALCIA: And you, what can you say about me?

PEDANT: That you're a fool, a crook, a fraud, a thug, a madman, a drunkard!

STRAGUALCIA: And I can say that you're a thief, a gambler, a gossip, a cheat, a swindler, an impostor, a braggart, a fathead, a disgrace, an ignoramus, a traitor, a sodomite, and an evil person!

PEDANT: It seems we've met.

STRAGUALCIA: Right.

PEDANT: Enough. I don't want to get mixed up with your sort; there's no honor in it for me.

STRAGUALCIA: Yes, by God! One finds in you all the nobility of the Ma-

---

74. A reference to the ways in which sodomites were executed during the Renaissance. In saying that being set alight would teach the Pedant "not to be what you are" (*a non esser quel che voi séte*), Stragualcia is accusing him of being a sodomite: having a sexual identity, not just of engaging in a sexual practice. This seems to contradict Foucault's contention that the concept of sexual identity did not exist until modern times.

remma.[75] Will you ever be anything but the son of a mule driver? Aren't I from a better family than you? Is it right that this fool should lord it over everybody just because he knows how to say *cuius masculini?*[76]

PEDANT: Alas! "Poor and nude, philosophy journeys through this world." Latin has come on hard times when it comes from the mouth of an ass.

STRAGUALCIA: The ass will be you, and I'll give you a good beating[77] if you don't change your tune.

PEDANT: You should remember the proverb *"Furor sit laesa saepius sapientia."*[78] You're about to make me lose my temper, Stragualcia. Back off, you big ugly manure shoveler, you villain, you archvillain!

STRAGUALCIA: Hey! Pedant, archpedant, pedant, greatest pedant! Is there any insult worse than "pedant"? Is there a worse type? Is there a greater fraud? Is there a worse profession? Maybe it wouldn't be so bad if they didn't go around all puffed up because others call them "Messer So and So" or "Professor Such and Such," or if they deigned to respond to someone who doffs his hat to them before they're a mile past. "Good day to you, Sir Crap, Sir Turd, Professor Diarrhea, Sir Shit!"

PEDANT: *Tratant fabrilia fabri.*[79] You're talking about exactly what you are.

STRAGUALCIA: I'm talking about what you like.

PEDANT: Could you get your ass out of my way?

STRAGUALCIA: I would never let my ass be in your way, although I imagine you would like to have had it in your way.

PEDANT: By the body of— . . .

STRAGUALCIA: By the body of— . . . You'd better watch out if you're going to start swearing at me! [*Aside, but said so that the* PEDANT *can overhear*] He ought to realize that I know about all his evil deeds and that if I wanted to, I could have him burned. Yet he still insists on busting my ass.[80]

---

75. A region of Tuscany noted for its poverty and rusticity. Some have suggested that Maremma here is a contraction for *mare e mondo* (sea and land) and should be read as ironically referring to the whole world.

76. "This sweet male-icity." Most editors have focused on the incorrectness of Stragualcia's invented Latin, but the invented term *masculini* appears to be a Latinized version of the Italian *mascolino*, used in the Renaissance to refer to passive sodomites. See Leone Ebreo, *Dialoghi d'amore*, ed. S. Caramella (Bari: G. Laterza, 1929), 129.

77. Possibly another reference to the punishment the Pedant would receive as a sodomite: the passage could be read as "I'll load you down with firewood."

78. "Wisdom too often offended becomes anger."

79. "Those who work in the area speak of it."

80. Stragualcia continues to allude to the Pedant's being a sodomite.

PEDANT: You're lying! I'm not that kind of man.

STRAGUALCIA: [*Aside*] He would be one of the first pedants who wasn't.

PEDANT: I've decided, Stragualcia, that this house is not big enough for both of us.

STRAGUALCIA: How original! Is this the first time I've heard you say this? Look, you aren't about to leave unless someone chases you out the door with a broom. Answer me this: who are you going to find to feed you, to study with you, to give you a place to sleep, if not this young man who's as good as they come?

PEDANT: For God's sake, as if I couldn't find another post if I wanted to. Why, there's even someone who made me an excellent offer.

STRAGUALCIA: Come on, come on, do you expect me to believe that crap?

PEDANT: Enough, and you would be wise to keep quiet. Now go back to the inn and look after our master's things. We can settle this later.

STRAGUALCIA: I'll return to the inn willingly, and I'll take care of things on my own, but you'll pay in the end. [*Aside as he leaves*] If I didn't threaten this bugger every now and then, I couldn't live with him. He's lower than a rabbit. When I threaten him, he keeps quiet, but if I let him get on top of me he'd do his worst, given his tastes! It's a good thing I know his character.

PEDANT: [*Alone*] Frulla told me that Fabrizio will be someplace around the central square. I'd better get going.

SCENE II

GHERARDO, VIRGINIO, and the PEDANT

GHERARDO: As far as the dowry is concerned, what we agreed to is agreed to. I'll give her the dowry you asked for, and you'll add a thousand florins if you don't find your son.

VIRGINIO: That's fine.

PEDANT: [*Aside as he approaches* GHERARDO *and* VIRGINIO] If I'm not mistaken, I've seen this gentleman before. But I don't remember where.

VIRGINIO: [*To the* PEDANT] What are you staring at, my good man?

PEDANT: [*Aside*] Clearly this is my master.

GHERARDO: Let him stare at whatever he wishes. He seems to be a stranger here, and as you know, in other places they don't even think twice about staring at anyone they want to.

PEDANT: If I stare, it's not *sine causa*.[81] Tell me, do you know a Messer Virginio Bellenzini who lives in this city?

VIRGINIO: Yes, I know him. Actually, I have no closer friend. But what do you want with him? If you're thinking of staying with him, I should tell you that he's busy with other things and he can't put you up. You'd be wise to find other lodgings.

PEDANT: You are clearly he. *Salvete, patronorum optime!*[82]

VIRGINIO: Could you possibly be Messer Pietro de'Pagliaricci, my son's tutor?

PEDANT: Yes, it is I.

VIRGINIO: [*Beginning to weep*] Oh, my son! Alas! What news do you have of him? Where did you leave him? Where did he die? Why did you wait so long to contact me? Did those traitors, those Jews, those dogs kill him? My poor son! He was the only good I had in the world. O my dear Professor, tell me immediately, please!

PEDANT: Don't cry, sir, please.

VIRGINIO: O Gherardo, my son-in-law, here's the man who taught my poor son while he was alive. O Professor! O my son! Where are you buried? Don't you know? Why don't you tell me? I'm dying to know, and I'm dying of fear that I'll learn what I don't want to.

PEDANT: Oh, don't cry, Master. Why are you crying?

VIRGINIO: Shouldn't I cry for such a sweet son? So wise, so learned, so well brought up! And those traitors, they've taken him away from me, killed him.

PEDANT: May God keep you both well, you and him. Your son is alive and well.

GHERARDO: [*Aside*] I'm the loser, if this is true. I'm out a thousand florins.

VIRGINIO: Alive and well? If that were true, he would be with you now.

GHERARDO: Virginio, do you know this fellow well? Could this be some kind of trick?

PEDANT: *Parcius ista viris, tamen obiicienda memento.*[83]

VIRGINIO: Explain, Professor.

PEDANT: Your son was taken prisoner by a certain Captain Orteca during the sack of Rome.

81. "Without good reason."
82. "Greetings, O finest of masters!"
83. "Go easy with the personal insults, remember that they will be repaid in time" (from Virgil's *Eclogues*, III, 7).

GHERARDO: [*Aside*] Oh boy, now the story begins.

PEDANT: And because the captain captured him along with two others, he decided to trick them by secretly sending your son and me to Siena. But a few days later he began to worry that those gentlemen of Siena—who are great lovers of law and fair play and friends of our city and above all else good men—would free your son. So he moved him from Siena to a castle of the lord of Piombino. In the meantime he made us write *per usque millies*[84] asking for the ransom he had set of one thousand ducats.

VIRGINIO: My poor son! Did they torture him as well?

PEDANT: No, in fact they treated him like a gentleman.

GHERARDO: [*Aside*] I'm afraid I can see what's coming.

PEDANT: We never had any reply to the letters we sent.

GHERARDO: [*Aside to* VIRGINIO] You understand that this is the way he intends to get his hands on your money.

VIRGINIO: [*To the* PEDANT] Go on.

PEDANT: Then the Spaniard took us with him on campaign in Correggio, where he was killed. After that the court took control of his property, and we were freed.

VIRGINIO: Where is my son, then?

PEDANT: Closer than you think.

VIRGINIO: In Modena?

PEDANT: If you promise me some refreshment, *quia omnis labor optat praemium,*[85] I'll tell you.

GHERARDO: This is what he's after, the fraud!

PEDANT: [*To* GHERARDO] You're mistaken. I, a fraud? *Absit!*[86]

VIRGINIO: I'll promise you anything you want. Where is he?

PEDANT: At the inn of the Joker.

GHERARDO: [*Aside*] It's done: the thousand ducats are played and lost. But what does it matter to me? As long as I have Lelia, I'm fine. I'm rich enough as it is.

VIRGINIO: Let's go, Professor. I can't wait to see him and embrace him and kiss him and hold him in my arms!

PEDANT: Master, oh, *quanto mutatus ab illo!*[87] He's no longer a child to hold in your arms. You wouldn't recognize him. He's grown up, and I'm sure he won't

---

84. "An infinite number of times."
85. "As every labor deserves its reward."
86. "Away with you."
87. "How the times have changed him."

recognize you either, what with how much you've changed. *Praeterea*,[88] you have that beard now which you didn't have before, and if I hadn't heard your voice I wouldn't have recognized you. And Lelia, how is she?

VIRGINIO: Well. She's all grown up and rounded out.[89]

GHERARDO: Rounded out? You mean she's pregnant? If that's the case, you can keep her! I don't want her.

VIRGINIO: Oh no! Oh no! I mean she's become a grown, shapely woman. Oh, Tutor, I haven't embraced you yet. [*He takes the* PEDANT *in his arms and kisses him on both cheeks*]

PEDANT: Master, not that I want to brag, but the things I have done for your son—I could tell you! And in turn there was never a thing I asked of him that he didn't do immediately.

VIRGINIO: How did his studies go?

PEDANT: He didn't lose any time, *ut licuit per varios casus, per tot discrimina rerum.*[90]

VIRGINIO: Call him out here, but don't tell him anything. I want to see if he recognizes me.

PEDANT: He left the inn a little while ago. Let's see if he has returned.

᪥ SCENE III ᪥

The PEDANT, STRAGUALCIA, VIRGINIO, and GHERARDO

PEDANT: Stragualcia! Oh, Stragualcia! Has Fabrizio returned?

STRAGUALCIA: Not yet.

PEDANT: Come here. Say something to my old master. This is Messer Virginio.

STRAGUALCIA: [*To the* PEDANT] Are you still angry?

PEDANT: Don't you know that I never stay angry with you?

STRAGUALCIA: Good.

PEDANT: Now give your hand to Fabrizio's father.

STRAGUALCIA: [*To the* PEDANT] You should give me your hand.[91]

88. "Moreover."

89. *Grossa*, which, as Gherardo's reply indicates, can mean "pregnant" as well as "filled out" or "large."

90. "Accomplishing everything he could, given the travails and dangers."

91. The confusion here arises from the richness of the gesture of giving someone your hand, which during the Renaissance could be construed in various ways: as a sign of submission to a superior, a sign of friendship, a sign that an agreement had been reached, and even—although clearly not in this case—a sign of intent to marry.

PEDANT: Not to me, to this gentleman.

STRAGUALCIA: Is this our master's father?

PEDANT: Yes.

STRAGUALCIA: [*Giving* VIRGINIO *his hand*] O magnificent Master, you are just in time to pay the innkeeper. Welcome!

PEDANT: This man was a good servant to your son.

STRAGUALCIA: Are you suggesting that I won't be in the future?

PEDANT: No.

VIRGINIO: You are most welcome, my son! I think I ought to reward all those who have given my son such support.

STRAGUALCIA: You can reward me with a very little thing.

VIRGINIO: Tell me what.

STRAGUALCIA: Get me a job as a servant with this innkeeper, who's the greatest guy in the world and the best supplied and the wisest and the one who best understands a traveler's needs of any innkeeper I've ever met. As far as I'm concerned, this is paradise.

GHERARDO: He has an excellent reputation as a host.

VIRGINIO: Have you eaten?

STRAGUALCIA: A little.

VIRGINIO: What have you had?

STRAGUALCIA: A couple of partridges, six thrushes, a capon, a bit of veal, and only two tankards of wine.

VIRGINIO: Frulla, give him what he wants and leave the bill to me.

PEDANT: Now are you happy?

STRAGUALCIA: [*With a Spanish accent*] Let me kiss your hands. This is the way masters should be! Tutor, you're too cheap and want everything for yourself. How many people have told you that? Frulla, bring these gentlemen something to drink.

PEDANT: That's not necessary.

STRAGUALCIA: I know you'll drink. I'll pay. It's no big deal. Some sweetbreads, a slice of salami . . . won't you have some? Tutor, come on, have something to drink.

PEDANT: All right, to make peace with you.

STRAGUALCIA: Oh, he's good, Master. You should love the Tutor, for he loves your son more than his own eyes.

VIRGINIO: May God reward him!

STRAGUALCIA: First it's your turn, then God's. [*To* GHERARDO] And you, sir, have some wine.

GHERARDO: I really shouldn't. [*Accepts a glass of wine and takes a sip*]

STRAGUALCIA: Please, come on in until Fabrizio returns, and then, since dinner is all ready, let's eat here this evening.

PEDANT: That's not a bad idea.

GHERARDO: I'll leave you, as I have a little matter to take care of at home.

VIRGINIO: Be careful that she doesn't get away.

GHERARDO: That's exactly why I'm going home.

VIRGINIO: She's all yours, now. Take care of things as you see fit. As far as I'm concerned, you can do as you please. [*He and the others go into the inn as* GHERARDO *heads towards his house*]

GHERARDO: [*Alone*] In the end one can't have everything. Patience! [*Looking offstage*] But if I'm seeing clearly, that's Lelia, who has somehow escaped! That silly servant girl has let her get away!

ᷤ SCENE IV ᷤ

LELIA (dressed as a boy), CLEMENZIA, and GHERARDO

LELIA: [*As* GHERARDO *approaches, unseen*] Don't you think, Clemenzia, that Fortune enjoys toying with me?

CLEMENZIA: Relax and leave it to me. I'll find some way to make it all work out for you. But go and change those clothes before you're seen like that.

GHERARDO: [*Aside*] I want both to greet her and to find out how she escaped. [*To* CLEMENZIA *and* LELIA] May God make you happy, Clemenzia, and you too, Lelia, my sweet bride. Who let you out? The maid, was it? I'm glad you went to your *balia*'s house, but to be seen in these clothes isn't very honorable for me or for you.

LELIA: [*Aside*] Oh no, he has recognized me! [*To* GHERARDO] Who are you speaking to? What Lelia? I'm not Lelia.

GHERARDO: Oh! Didn't your father and I lock you up with my daughter Isabella a few minutes ago, and didn't you admit that you were Lelia? And do you think I wouldn't recognize my own wife? Go and change those clothes.

LELIA: [*As she enters* CLEMENZIA*'s house*] You're crazy if you think I'd want a husband!

CLEMENZIA: You go home too, my dear Gherardo. All women are a bit strange, some in one way, some in another. And you should know that there are very few, in fact probably none, who don't do something a little offbeat now and then. Such things, however, are best kept secret.

GHERARDO: As far as I'm concerned, it will remain a secret. But how did she get out of my house? I had locked her up with Isabella.

CLEMENZIA: Who? Her?

GHERARDO: Her.

CLEMENZIA: You're deceiving yourself! She's been with me the whole day. And in a playful moment she decided to put on these clothes and asked me if they suited her, as young girls sometimes do.

GHERARDO: Are you trying to kid me? I'm telling you, we put her in my house with Isabella!

CLEMENZIA: Where are you coming from now, then?

GHERARDO: From the inn of the Joker, where I went with Virginio.

CLEMENZIA: Did you drink anything?

GHERARDO: Just a sip.

CLEMENZIA: Well, go and sleep it off. You clearly need to.

GHERARDO: Let me speak with Lelia a bit before I leave. I have some good news for her.

CLEMENZIA: What?

GHERARDO: Her brother has returned safe and sound, and her father is waiting for him at the inn.

CLEMENZIA: Who, Fabrizio?

GHERARDO: Fabrizio.

CLEMENZIA: If it's true, I'll give you a kiss.

GHERARDO: How beautiful happiness is! But as far as the kiss is concerned, I would prefer to give it to Lelia.

CLEMENZIA: I'm going to run and tell her.

GHERARDO: And I'm going to give hell to that imbecile who let her escape!

ᘖ SCENE V ᘊ

PASQUELLA, alone

PASQUELLA: Oh dear! I had such a scare that I've run out of the house. [*To the audience*] Ladies, you won't believe what's happened if I don't tell you. So I will tell you, but not those dirty-minded men, who would just laugh. Those two old muttonheaded dolts were absolutely convinced that that young man was a woman, and they locked him up with my mistress, Isabella, in her bedroom and gave me the key. After a while I decided to go in to see what was up, and I found them hugging and kissing! So I decided to find out whether it was a man or a woman. My mistress had the person down on the bed, and she called me to help her while she held his hands. And he was letting her win, so I opened the front of his clothes, and all of a sudden I felt something slap my hand, and I wasn't sure whether it was a large pestle or a big stick or that other thing. But whatever it was, it was in great shape. And when I saw how big it was, I took off, sisters, and locked the door behind me! And I can tell you that as far as I'm concerned, I have no intention of going back in there alone. And if one of you ladies doesn't believe me and wants to see for herself, I'll lend her the key. But here comes Giglio. I want to see if I can get that rosary and make a fool of him; these Spaniards think so much of themselves that they don't believe there's anyone else in the world as clever as they are.

SCENE VI

GIGLIO and PASQUELLA

GIGLIO: [*Aside*] There's Pasquella. I bet she's been getting herself pretty worked up, waiting so long for me. She already knows, the slut, how good we Spaniards are with women. Oh, these Italian whores really get off on us!

PASQUELLA: [*Aside*] I've already figured out how to deceive this guy. Leave it to me.

GIGLIO: [*Aside*] This low-life washerwoman, she thinks I'll give her the rosary. The emperor be damned if I don't get her to love me so much that she buys me dozens of socks and shirts and jackets. I'll use her as I please, and afterwards I'll take off with my rosary without a word. Maybe she's already forgotten it.

PASQUELLA: [*Aside*] If he lets me get my hands on that rosary just once, he'll never see it again or you can cut out my eyes. And if he complains, I'll have my Spela give him a beating like he's never had before.

GIGLIO: [*To* PASQUELLA] Oh, blessed is the mother who gave birth to such a beautiful woman, so well formed, so true! I think that you have been longing for me.

PASQUELLA: [*Aside*] What beautiful bull they dish out! [*To* GIGLIO] I've been waiting here in the doorway for more than half an hour to see if you'd come by, because my master was out and we could have had some time alone together.

GIGLIO: My God, I am devastated that I was held up by other business. But let's go in now.

PASQUELLA: I'm afraid my master will return; he's been gone for a while. But you've forgotten the rosary, eh?

GIGLIO: No, madam, I have it here with me.

PASQUELLA: Show me. Oh! You were going to fix it. Why haven't you?

GIGLIO: I'll get it fixed later. To tell you the truth, it slipped my mind.

PASQUELLA: Well! I see how much I mean to you, womanizer that you are! I'd like to—

GIGLIO: [*Interrupting*] Don't get angry, madam, with your son. You know I don't have any women friends other than you.

PASQUELLA: It hasn't taken me long to catch you in a lie. A little while ago you said you had two gentlewomen for friends.

GIGLIO: I gave them up for you. I don't want anyone else besides you. Don't you understand me?

PASQUELLA: All right. But is that string of beads really a rosary? It seems pretty long to me.

GIGLIO: I don't know how many beads there are.

PASQUELLA: That's a sign that you don't say it very often. I'm beginning to wonder if you even know your Our Father. Oh well, give it to me for a second, and I'll count the beads.

GIGLIO: Take it. [*He hands it to her*] But let's go into the house.

PASQUELLA: Should we? Take a look around to see if anyone would see you come in.

GIGLIO: [*Looking around*] There's no one around.

PASQUELLA: Let's go in. [*Opening the door a crack*] Oops, oh dear, my hens are all here at the door! Wait a second, Giglio. Move over there. If they get away it'll take all day to round them up.

GIGLIO: Hurry up.

PASQUELLA: Back, back, my pretty ones, my pretty ones, shoo, shoo! May you break your necks! Some of them are getting away. Watch out, watch out, Giglio!

GIGLIO: Where are these hens? From here I don't see any hens, or cocks for that matter.

PASQUELLA: You don't? They're over here. Move back a little and let me close the door for a bit so that I can put them back where they belong. [*She enters the house, closing and locking the door*]

GIGLIO: Hey, you're locking the door! Why are you doing that?

PASQUELLA: Because I don't want any cocks opening it.

GIGLIO: Hurry up before someone comes along and disturbs us.

PASQUELLA: It doesn't matter who comes along, as no one is opening anything.

GIGLIO: [*Aside*] Damn her, the old hag. [*To* PASQUELLA] Tell me why you aren't opening up.

PASQUELLA: My dear Giglio, don't you realize that first I must say this whole rosary? You can forget about this evening. And I forgot, I also have a prayer to say that I mustn't overlook.

GIGLIO: What foolishness is this? What rosary, what prayer?

PASQUELLA: What prayer? Do you want me to teach it to you? It's a good one: "Ghost, ghost, that wanders day and night, if you have come all hard to me, all hard you'll have to leave. Evil with evil, you've come to me at the wrong time thinking to have me, and you will remain deceived. Amen."[92]

GIGLIO: I don't understand your prayer. If you don't want to open the door, give me back my rosary and I'll go my way. [*Aside*] In the name of all the holy martyrs, if this ugly old babbling untrustworthy bat has tricked me . . . [*To* PASQUELLA] Lady Pasquella, open up at once, if you value your life!

PASQUELLA: [*Singing*] "What is my lover doing that he doesn't come? The love of another girl keeps him away from me."[93] Alas!

GIGLIO: What? Don't say that, my lady Pasquella! He's right here, waiting for you to let him in.

PASQUELLA: [*Singing*] "I cannot serve you, my dear lord." Oh dear!

GIGLIO: [*Aside*] More songs, that damn woman. She doesn't realize that I'm out here. I'll knock on the door, I swear to God. [*Knocking*]

PASQUELLA: Who's there?

GIGLIO: Your little boy.

PASQUELLA: What do you want? My master's not at home. Do you want to leave a message?

GIGLIO: A word.

PASQUELLA: Wait a bit, he should be here shortly.

GIGLIO: Open up so that I can wait inside. Come on. [*Aside*] May the whole world be damned if I don't burn down this house if she doesn't give me my rosary! [*Pounding on the door*]

PASQUELLA: Hello! Who's there? Could you be a little more discreet? Forgive me, but who are you? Oh my! Are you trying to break down the door?

---

92. From Boccaccio's *Decameron*, VII, 1, where the wife of Gianni Lotteringhi used these words to warn her lover that their tryst must be canceled because her husband had unexpectedly returned home.

93. These lines and the next sung by Pasquella were from popular songs of the day. See V. Santoli, "Cinque canti popolar delle Raccolta Barbi," *Annali della Scuola Normale di Pisa*, 2d series, vol. 7 (1938): 138.

GIGLIO: I swear by God and even Saint Litany that I'll burn down this door if you don't give me back my rosary!

PASQUELLA: Maybe you should look elsewhere. We usually don't grow roses in our garden.

GIGLIO: You misunderstand, I'm saying my rosary beads, my Our Fathers.

PASQUELLA: What business is it of mine if you say your Our Fathers? Are you suggesting that I should become a false convert[94] like you Spanish Jews, and that I'd need to learn them over again like you?

GIGLIO: Damn you, you whore, you old hag! Now you're calling me a false convert?

PASQUELLA: You know what? If you don't get away from that door, I'm going to throw water on you.

GIGLIO: Go ahead, throw your water. I'm going to burn down your door. [PASQUELLA *dumps a bucket of water on him*] Damn you! She has drowned me, this woman, hag, old whore, tramp! To hell with all that's holy!

PASQUELLA: Did you get all wet? I didn't notice you. [GHERARDO *enters*] But here comes my master. If you want something, ask him and don't bother me anymore.

GIGLIO: If that old man finds me here, I'll be in big trouble. I'd better get out of here.

⁀ᴗ SCENE VII ᵔᴗ

GHERARDO and PASQUELLA

GHERARDO: What were you up to with that Spaniard here by the door? What do you have to do with him?

PASQUELLA: He was asking about some rose garden. But I didn't pay any attention to him.

GHERARDO: Well, you sure did exactly as I told you! I'd like to break your neck.

PASQUELLA: Why?

GHERARDO: Why did you let Lelia escape? Didn't I tell you not to let her out?

---

94. *Marrano*, a pejorative term used for a Jew who had falsely converted to Christianity to escape the persecutions set in motion in Spain by the forced conversions that began there in 1492. Many Jews who were forced to convert fled to Italy to avoid further persecution. The term was a particularly stinging insult for a Spaniard in Italy, as Giglio's outraged reaction suggests.

PASQUELLA: What do you mean, escape? Isn't she in the room?

GHERARDO: God damn you!

PASQUELLA: I know she's there, I'm sure of it!

GHERARDO: And I know she isn't there, because I just left her in the house of her *balia*, Clemenzia.

PASQUELLA: Why, I just left her in the bedroom on her knees running through her Our Fathers with Isabella.

GHERARDO: Maybe she got back before me.

PASQUELLA: I tell you, she never left. The room has been locked the whole time.

GHERARDO: Where's the key?

PASQUELLA: Right here.

GHERARDO: Give it to me. And if she's not there, I'll break your neck!

PASQUELLA: And if she is there, will you give me a blouse?

GHERARDO: All right.

PASQUELLA: Let me open the door.

GHERARDO: [*Leaving with the key*] No, I want to open it myself. You'd find some excuse.

PASQUELLA: Oh my! I hope he doesn't find them still going at it. But it's been a while since I left them.

❧ SCENE VIII ☙

FLAMMINIO, PASQUELLA, and GHERARDO

FLAMMINIO: [*Entering*] Pasquella, how long ago did my Fabio leave?

PASQUELLA: Why?

FLAMMINIO: Because he's a traitor, and I'm going to punish him. And because Isabella has left me for him, she'll get what she deserves, too. Oh, what a fine thing—for a noblewoman to fall in love with a mere serving boy!

PASQUELLA: Oh, don't get all worked up! The caresses she gave him, she gave as a sign of her love for you.

FLAMMINIO: You can tell her that one day she'll be sorry. And you can tell him that when I find him (I have this knife in my hand for this), I plan to cut off his lips and ears and cut out one of his eyes and give them all to her on a plate. That way she can kiss them as much as she likes!

PASQUELLA: [*Aside*] That's how it goes! "While the dog barks, the wolf eats his fill."

FLAMMINIO: You just wait and see. [*He leaves in a rage*]

GHERARDO: [*Entering in a rage*] Oh, my God! Is this what things have come to? This is it, then? I'm ruined! That traitor Virginio! That dirty traitor! He's made an ass of me. Oh, God! What can I do?

PASQUELLA: What's wrong, Master?

GHERARDO: What's wrong? Who is that man with my daughter?

PASQUELLA: Oh, don't you know? Isn't it Virginio's baby girl?

GHERARDO: Baby girl, eh? A baby girl that will make my daughter have babies of her own! Oh, how I'm suffering!

PASQUELLA: My, don't say such things! What's wrong? Isn't it Lelia?

GHERARDO: I'm telling you, that's a man in there.

PASQUELLA: What? That can't be true. You can't be right!

GHERARDO: I saw him with my own eyes.

PASQUELLA: How?

GHERARDO: On top of my daughter, alas!

PASQUELLA: Oh, these kids today are great pranksters.

GHERARDO: I wish it were a prank!

PASQUELLA: Are you sure it was a man?

GHERARDO: Yes. I tell you, I opened the door suddenly and there he was with only his doublet on, and he didn't have time to cover himself.

PASQUELLA: You're sure you saw everything? Look, maybe it was a woman!

GHERARDO: I tell you, it was a man, and he was well enough endowed to make two men.

PASQUELLA: What did Isabella say?

GHERARDO: What do you think she said? That I should be ashamed, maybe?

PASQUELLA: Why don't you let that young man go? What do you want to do with him?

GHERARDO: What can I do? Haul him before the courts and have him punished.

PASQUELLA: But maybe he'll escape.

GHERARDO: Impossible. I locked him back in. But there's Virginio. Just the man I'm looking for. [*He leaves*]

🎗 SCENE IX 🗝

PEDANT, VIRGINIO, and GHERARDO

PEDANT: I'm really surprised that he still hasn't returned to the inn. I don't know what to say.

VIRGINIO: Was he armed?

PEDANT: I think so.

VIRGINIO: Then I'm afraid he may have been arrested for carrying arms. We have a Podestà[95] who's as tough as nails.

PEDANT: I don't think they would treat a foreigner so badly.

GHERARDO: [*Entering*] Good day to you, Virginio. Is this the way a gentleman acts? Is this the way to treat a friend? Is this the way you wanted to become my relative? Who did you think you were fooling with? Did you think I would accept this? I'd like to—

VIRGINIO: [*Interrupting*] Why are you upset with me, Gherardo? What have I done to you? I wasn't the one who wanted to become your relative; you've been nagging me about this for a year. Well, if you've changed your mind now, we can forget about it.

GHERARDO: Why, you have some nerve acting as if I was the one in the wrong! Dirty traitor, fraud, crook, swindler! But the courts will learn everything.

VIRGINIO: Gherardo, such language is not fitting for one of your station and even less so to use with me.

GHERARDO: He doesn't even want me to complain, this swine! You've become all haughty because your son has returned, eh?

VIRGINIO: You're the swine.

GHERARDO: Oh, God! If I were young again, I'd cut you to pieces.

VIRGINIO: Would it be possible to find out what you're talking about?

GHERARDO: You housewrecker!

VIRGINIO: I'm too patient with this man.

GHERARDO: Thief!

VIRGINIO: Forger!

GHERARDO: You're lying. Just wait . . .

VIRGINIO: I'm waiting.

---

95. An official in many Renaissance cities who oversaw the justice system. He was normally hired for a term of six months from outside the city and brought with him a group of patrollers and notaries who ran the policing and judicial apparatus. The idea was that the city would thus have impartial justice.

PEDANT: [*Restraining* GHERARDO, *who takes off his vest and approaches* VIRGINIO *threateningly*] Ah, my good man, why this madness?

GHERARDO: Let me go!

PEDANT: Sir, put your vest back on.

VIRGINIO: Who do you think you're dealing with? Give me back my daughter.

GHERARDO: I'll cut both your throats! [*He runs into his house*]

PEDANT: Why is this gentleman so upset with you?

VIRGINIO: I've no idea. Perhaps it has something to do with the fact that a little while ago we put my daughter Lelia in his house because he wanted to take her as his wife. Now you see how he is. I'm afraid he might harm her.

PEDANT: [*Seeing* GHERARDO *coming out of his house with a pike*] Ah, ah, good sir! Let's not get started with weapons! No weapons!

GHERARDO: Get out of my way!

PEDANT: What is the problem?

GHERARDO: This traitor has ruined me.

PEDANT: How?

GHERARDO: If I don't cut him to pieces, if I don't slice him into quarters with this pike . . . [VIRGINIO *flees*]

PEDANT: In God's name, please tell me what's wrong.

GHERARDO: Let's go into my house and I'll explain, since that traitor has fled. Aren't you his son's tutor? Weren't you at the inn with us?

PEDANT: Yes.

GHERARDO: Come in.

PEDANT: With faith in your word.

GHERARDO: Oh, you can count on that!

Act V

SCENE I

VIRGINIO (with a large shield and a mail shirt), STRAGUALCIA, SCATIZZA
(with a small round shield), several of VIRGINIO's servants
(with various makeshift weapons), GHERARDO, the PEDANT, and FABRIZIO

VIRGINIO: All of you, come with me. Stragualcia, you too.

STRAGUALCIA: With weapons or without? I don't have any weapons.

VIRGINIO: Get some from the inn. [STRAGUALCIA *goes into the inn*]

SCATIZZA: You know, Master, with a large shield like that you should have a lance.

VIRGINIO: I don't need a lance. This is enough for me.

SCATIZZA: This small round shield would be more noble, since you're wearing a mail shirt.

VIRGINIO: No, this covers me better. Oh! This muttonhead seems to think he's caught me trying to swindle him somehow. And I'm afraid he may have killed my poor daughter.

STRAGUALCIA: [*Coming out of the inn with a roast on a spit and a bottle of wine*] This is a fine weapon, Master. I'm going to run this spit through him like a woodcock!

SCATIZZA: Oh! But what are you going to do with the roast?

STRAGUALCIA: I have military experience, and I know that the first thing you need to do is be sure you have field rations.

SCATIZZA: And the wine, what's that for?

STRAGUALCIA: To refresh the troops, if the first attack is rebuffed.

SCATIZZA: Sounds good to me, and it's likely.

STRAGUALCIA: Do you want me to run them all through—the old man, the daughter, the servants, the whole household and all of them, like chicken livers to be roasted? Why, I'll run this spit through the old man's ass and up and out through his eyes. The others I'll run through side by side like thrushes.

VIRGINIO: The door is open. They may have set some kind of ambush.

STRAGUALCIA: Bushes? That's bad. I'm more afraid of being beaten with switches than swords. But the Tutor is coming out.

PEDANT: [*Coming out of the house and speaking to* GHERARDO, *who remains inside*] Leave this to me, and I'll make peace for you, Messer Gherardo.

STRAGUALCIA: Look at that, Master. It's the Tutor, and it seems that he has mutinied and gone over to the enemy. You can't count on his type to stay loyal! Do you want me to start with him, running him through so that I can say "one down"?

PEDANT: Messer Virginio, my master, why are you armed?

STRAGUALCIA: Aha! Didn't I tell you?

VIRGINIO: What has happened to my daughter? Hand her over. I want to take her home. And have you found Fabrizio?

PEDANT: Yes.

VIRGINIO: Where is he?

PEDANT: He's here inside. And he has taken a very beautiful bride, with your permission.

VIRGINIO: A wife, eh? And who would that be?

STRAGUALCIA: [*Aside*] That was quick. This is rich, rich!

PEDANT: The beautiful and well-mannered daughter of Gherardo.

VIRGINIO: Oh! The same Gherardo who just now wanted to kill me?

PEDANT: *Rem omnem a principio audies.*[96] Come on into the house, and you'll hear the whole story. Come on out, Messer Gherardo.

GHERARDO: [*Coming out of the house*] Oh, Virginio, this is the strangest case ever! Come in.

STRAGUALCIA: [*Aside*] Should I run him through? But his meat is hardly worth roasting.

GHERARDO: Have your men put down their weapons. This is a matter for laughter.

VIRGINIO: Can I trust you?

PEDANT: Yes, certainly, on my word.

VIRGINIO: All right, go on home everyone! And put down your weapons and bring me my vest.

PEDANT: Fabrizio, come out and meet your father. [FABRIZIO *comes out*]

VIRGINIO: Oh! Isn't this Lelia?

PEDANT: No, this is Fabrizio.

VIRGINIO: O my dear son!

FABRIZIO: O my father, I've searched so long for you!

VIRGINIO: O my dear son, I've cried so long for you!

GHERARDO: Come in, come in, and you'll hear the whole story. And I should tell you also that your daughter is safe in the house of Clemenzia, her *balia*.

VIRGINIO: O dear God, how grateful I am to You!

SCENE II

CRIVELLO, FLAMMINIO, and CLEMENZIA

CRIVELLO: I saw him with these eyes and I heard him with these ears in the house of Clemenzia.

FLAMMINIO: Are you sure it was Fabio?

CRIVELLO: Do you think that I don't know him?

FLAMMINIO: Let's go. If I find him . . .

CRIVELLO: You'll ruin everything. Be patient, and wait until he comes out.

FLAMMINIO: Not even God could give me enough patience.

CRIVELLO: You're going to ruin the cake.

96. "You will hear the whole story from the beginning."

FLAMMINIO: I *am* going to ruin myself! [*Knocks fiercely at the door*]

CLEMENZIA: Who's there?

FLAMMINIO: A friend of yours. Come down to the door.

CLEMENZIA: Oh! What do you want, Messer Flamminio?

FLAMMINIO: Open the door and I'll tell you.

CLEMENZIA: Wait a second until I come down.

FLAMMINIO: [*To* CRIVELLO] As soon as she opens the door, go in and see if he's there, then call me.

CRIVELLO: Leave it to me.

CLEMENZIA: [*Opening the door*] What do you want, Signor Flamminio?

FLAMMINIO: What's my boy doing in your house?

CLEMENZIA: What boy? [*Blocking* CRIVELLO *as he tries to push past her into the house*] And you, Crivello, where are you going, you rascal? Do you think you can enter my house by force?

FLAMMINIO: Clemenzia, by the holy, inviolate, sacred body, if you don't hand over that . . .

CLEMENZIA: What do you want me to hand over?

FLAMMINIO: My boy, who's hiding in your house.

CLEMENZIA: There's no serving-boy of yours in my house, even if there is a serving-girl.

FLAMMINIO: Clemenzia, this is not the time to fool around. You've always been a friend of mine. You've helped me out, and I've helped you. But this is too important.

CLEMENZIA: This must be some madness induced by love. Calm down, Flamminio, cool down a bit.

FLAMMINIO: I said, hand over Fabio.

CLEMENZIA: I'll hand him over.

FLAMMINIO: Enough! Make him come down here *now.*

CLEMENZIA: Oh, calm down, for God's sake! You know, if I were young and you liked me, I wouldn't give you the time of day. By the way, how's Isabella?

FLAMMINIO: I wish she were cut into pieces!

CLEMENZIA: Hah! I don't believe you.

FLAMMINIO: You don't believe me? I can tell you that she's cleared things up for me just fine.

CLEMENZIA: Really! Well, you young colts deserve every setback, because you are the most ungrateful people in the whole world.

FLAMMINIO: You can't say that about me. Every other accusation might fit, but to be called ungrateful, no. There's not a man alive who dislikes such behavior more.

CLEMENZIA: I'm not talking about you. But there was once here in this city a young girl who, realizing that she was admired by a knight—one of your peers here in Modena—fell so in love with him that she lost sight of everything else.

FLAMMINIO: Lucky man! Happy man! I certainly couldn't say as much for myself.

CLEMENZIA: It so happened that her father sent this poor girl, so in love, away from Modena. Fearing that her lover would forget her, she cried so much that it was a wonder to see. And in fact he immediately found another girl, as if she had never existed.

FLAMMINIO: I'd say that such a man should be called a traitor, not a knight.

CLEMENZIA: Listen, it gets worse. When the young girl returned after several months, she found that her lover loved another who didn't love him. Abandoning her house and her father and putting her honor at risk, she decided to serve him. So she dressed herself as a young manservant and took a job with her lover as his servant.

FLAMMINIO: This happened in Modena?

CLEMENZIA: And you know them both.

FLAMMINIO: I would rather be this lucky lover than the lord of Milan.

CLEMENZIA: Do you want to hear the rest? This lover of hers, not recognizing her, used her as his go-between with his new love. And to make him happy, this poor girl did everything he asked.

FLAMMINIO: Oh, what a virtuous woman! What constant love! This love could serve as a lesson for future centuries. Why can't I be so lucky?

CLEMENZIA: Well, you wouldn't give up Isabella for such a love anyway.

FLAMMINIO: Why, I'd almost be willing to say I'd give up Christ for someone like that. Please, Clemenzia, tell me who this woman is.

CLEMENZIA: I'd be glad to. But first I want you to tell me, on your oath as a gentleman, what you would do with such a poor girl if such a thing happened to you. Would you kick her out when you learned what she'd done? Would you kill her, or would you judge her worthy of some reward?

FLAMMINIO: I swear in the name of the power[97] of the sun that you see in the sky, and with the proviso that I be banned forever from the company of my peers, gentlemen and knights, that I would take her as my wife—even if she were

97. *Virtù.*

ugly; even if she were poor; even if she were of low birth; even over the daughter of the duke of Ferrara.

CLEMENZIA: That's a big oath. Are you ready to stand by it?

FLAMMINIO: Yes, I'm saying it, and yes, I would do it.

CLEMENZIA: [*Turning to* CRIVELLO] You're a witness.

CRIVELLO: I heard him, and I know he would do it.

CLEMENZIA: Now I want to introduce you to this woman and to this knight. Fabio, oh, Fabio! Come down here. Your master is looking for you.

FLAMMINIO: What do you make of this, Crivello? Do you think I should kill this traitor? He's at least a good servant.

CRIVELLO: Oh well! I'm hardly surprised! I thought something strange like this would happen. Go ahead, pardon him. What else is there to do? That tart Isabella never really loved you anyway.

FLAMMINIO: You're right.

❧ SCENE III ❧

PASQUELLA, CLEMENZIA, FLAMMINIO,
LELIA (dressed as a woman), and CRIVELLO

PASQUELLA: [*Coming out of* GHERARDO*'s house and speaking with someone inside*] I'll take care of it. I'll tell him what you told me and what I've learned. [LELIA *comes to the door of* CLEMENZIA*'s house where the others are standing*]

CLEMENZIA: This, Messer Flamminio, is your Fabio. Take a good look. Do you recognize him? Are you surprised? And this same girl is that young woman I told you about, so loyal and so true to her love. Take a good look, and see if you recognize her. Have you lost your voice, Flamminio? Well, what do you have to say now? And you, you are that young man who thought so little of the love of his mistress. Don't think that you're one of the deceived here! You can see for yourself that I'm telling the truth. Now keep your word, or I'll take you before the courts as someone who has broken his pledge.

FLAMMINIO: I don't believe there's ever been a more perfect deception than this one. How could I have been so blind that I never recognized her?

CRIVELLO: I was more blind than anyone. I looked at her closely a thousand times and never realized. I'll be damned! Oh, what a fool I've been!

PASQUELLA: [*Interrupting*] Clemenzia, Virginio told me to tell you to come to our house right now because he has married off Fabrizio, his son who returned today. And he needs you to put the house in order, because, as you know, he has no other woman.

CLEMENZIA: What wife? Whom did he marry him to?

PASQUELLA: Isabella, the daughter of Gherardo, my master.

FLAMMINIO: Who? Isabella, the daughter of Gherardo Foiani, your master, or another Isabella?

PASQUELLA: Another? No, it's her. Flamminio, it's like they say: "Some people have all the luck."

FLAMMINIO: You're sure it's true?

PASQUELLA: Absolutely. I was there for the whole thing. I saw him give her the ring, and then they embraced, they kissed, and they rejoiced. And even before he gave her the ring she gave him . . . well, let's just say, I'm sure.

FLAMMINIO: How long ago did this happen?

PASQUELLA: Now, just now. Then they sent me running here to tell Clemenzia and to bring her back.

CLEMENZIA: Tell them I'll be there shortly. Go on, now.

LELIA: [*Aside*] O God, You've made things come together so well! I'm dying of happiness.

PASQUELLA: Don't take too long, I've so much to do that I'm all in a dither! I need to go now to buy some makeup. Oh! I forgot to ask if Lelia's here, because Gherardo has agreed to marry her.

CLEMENZIA: You know very well that she's here. Do you really want to see her married to that poor old excuse for a man, your master? He ought to be ashamed of himself!

PASQUELLA: You don't really know my master. Why, if you knew how manly he can be, you wouldn't talk about him like that.

CLEMENZIA: Sure, sure, I believe you. I bet you've tested his manliness.

PASQUELLA: Just like you with your master. Anyway, I'm off.

FLAMMINIO: She's to be married to Gherardo?

CLEMENZIA: Yes, woe is me! Isn't this poor girl unlucky?

FLAMMINIO: But he has already lived his life.[98] Look, Clemenzia, I believe that it's clearly the will of God that she not be wasted like this, for He has taken pity on her virtue and on my poor soul. And so, lady Lelia, if you're willing, I

---

98. A succinct statement of the generational conflict that runs through this and many other Renaissance comedies. Old men have wealth and power, and young men are waiting to take their places as husbands, lovers, and heads of households. With upper-class males being labeled youths until they married and not marrying until their late twenties or early thirties, and then having to compete with older, richer men, such conflict was ubiquitous in life and literature.

don't want any other wife but you, and I swear to you as a knight that if you won't marry me, I'll never marry another.

LELIA: Flamminio, you are my lord. You know exactly what I did and why, and so you know that I've never had any other desire but this.

FLAMMINIO: You've proven it perfectly. Please forgive me if I've made you unhappy, not recognizing you. I'm very, very sorry, and I recognize my error.

LELIA: You could never do anything, Signor Flamminio, that would make me unhappy.

FLAMMINIO: Clemenzia, I don't want to wait any longer and take the chance that something unforeseen might ruin this good fortune. I want to marry her now if she's willing.

LELIA: I'm most willing.

CRIVELLO: Oh, thank God! And you, my master, Lord Flamminio, are you willing? By the way, you should know that I'm a notary. And if you don't believe me, here's my diploma.[99]

FLAMMINIO: I'm very willing and as happy as I've ever been in my life.

CRIVELLO: Give each other your hands in marriage, and then you can go to bed. Oh! But I forgot to tell you that you should kiss her! [*They kiss*]

CLEMENZIA: Here's what I think we should do now. You two stay here in my house while I go tell Virginio everything and break the bad news to Gherardo.

FLAMMINIO: Fine, and you can tell Isabella as well.

SCENE IV

PASQUELLA and GIGLIO

GIGLIO: [*Aside*] By the king's life, it's that old bag Pasquella who's trying to trick me out of my goods. How glad I am to have run into her.

PASQUELLA: [*Aside*] Damn this pain in the ass! Just my luck to have him underfoot! He can break his neck along with all the others who have come from Spain, as far as I'm concerned! What excuse can I find now?

---

99. It is unlikely that a servant would be a notary (a quite lucrative and prestigious profession), and equally unlikely that he would be carrying his diploma with him. But before the Council of Trent defined more tightly the legal requirements for a marriage, all that was required to form a legally binding marriage was an exchange of consent. Thus, even if Crivello wasn't a notary, by formerly securing the consent of both Flamminio and Lelia he was in fact marrying them. Crivello's timely claim may also be a sendup of the unlikely coincidences that tie up the loose ends in most Renaissance comedies.

GIGLIO: Lady Pasquella!

PASQUELLA: [*Aside*] Things are going well, I've already become a lady.

GIGLIO: You've tricked me and taken my rosary, and you haven't done what you promised.

PASQUELLA: Shush, shush, shush! Be quiet, be quiet!

GIGLIO: Why? Is there someone around to hear us?

PASQUELLA: Shush, shush, shush!

GIGLIO: I don't see anyone here. You're not going to deceive me again! What are you up to?

PASQUELLA: You're trying to ruin me.

GIGLIO: You're trying to trick me.

PASQUELLA: Go away. Leave me alone now, and I'll talk with you later.

GIGLIO: Give me back my rosary, and we can talk whenever you like. I don't want you to be able to say that you've deceived me.

PASQUELLA: I'll give it to you. But do you think I have it here? Do you think it's that important to me? Why, I can have all the rosaries I want!

GIGLIO: Why did you lock me out and then start singing and say such strange things like "Ghost, ghost" and I don't know what prayers and other stuff?

PASQUELLA: Be quiet. You're going to ruin me. I'll explain everything.

GIGLIO: What? Why don't you tell me?

PASQUELLA: Move a little over this way, in this corner, so that my mistress won't see you.

GIGLIO: Are you trying to trick me again?

PASQUELLA: You're so sure that I'm tricking you! Am I really the type to deceive someone? Is that what you think, eh?

GIGLIO: All right, but tell me right now what's going on.

PASQUELLA: Listen. When we were talking before, Isabella, my mistress, came down very quietly and was hidden near me and heard everything. When I was rounding up my chickens, she went into the room there and from a hole in the wall watched everything we did. I, realizing this, pretended that I hadn't seen her. And I pretended that I wanted to deceive you. In the end, when I showed her the rosary, she, believing that I had tricked you, took it away and, laughing, wrapped it around her arm. But I'll get it back tonight and give it to you if you don't want me to have it.

GIGLIO: Is all this true? You'd better not be trying to deceive me!

PASQUELLA: Dear Giglio, may I never see you again if it isn't true. Do you think I don't cherish your friendship? But you Spaniards don't believe in Christ or anything else!

GIGLIO: Well, why don't we do now what we agreed to earlier?

PASQUELLA: I can't stay here with you because my mistress has just gotten married, and tonight we'll have the celebration. I have so many things to do. Wait a little longer. [*Aside*] Oh, what a nuisance these Spaniards are!

GIGLIO: Tomorrow! Tomorrow morning, all right?

PASQUELLA: Leave it to me. I'll remember you when the time is right. Don't worry. [*Aside as she hurries off*] Ugh, ugh, ugh! How disgusting!

GIGLIO: I swear to God, I'll slash your face if you're deceiving me again!

SCENE V

CITTINA

CITTINA: [*Coming out of* CLEMENZIA's *house*] I wonder what that strange noise is in the downstairs room. I hear the bed making a thumping, a drumming sound, as if it were possessed by some spirit. Oh my! I'm really scared. Oh! I hear someone complaining and moaning softly, "Oooh, not so hard!" And oh! I hear someone saying, "My life, my happiness, my hope, my sweet dear wife!" Oh! I can't make out the rest. I'm tempted to knock. And oh! Now one of them says, "Wait for me." They must be getting ready to leave. And the other one is saying, "Come quickly too." It sounds like they're going to break that bed. Oh, oh, oh! That bed is bouncing so fast, so fast! By all that's ho . . . hole . . . holey,[100] I'd better go tell Mama.

SCENE VI

ISABELLA, FABRIZIO, and CLEMENZIA

ISABELLA: I was certain that you were the servant of a local knight. You look so much like him that you must be his brother.

FABRIZIO: Others today have mistaken me for someone else. Even the inn-keeper seemed confused.

ISABELLA: Here comes Clemenzia, your *balia*. She'll want to speak with you.

---

100. In her agitation, Cittina has misspoken. Meaning to say *in buona fede* (in good faith, or in the name of my good faith), she has instead said *in buona fica* (in good pussy, or in the name of a good pussy). We have very few descriptions of actual sexual relations from the Renaissance, and it is interesting that this scene suggests an ideal of sexual satisfaction for both partners and a fairly open communication of desires between them.

CLEMENZIA: [*Aside*] This must be him, for he looks exactly like Lelia. [*To* FABRIZIO] O Fabrizio, my dear child, welcome home! How are you?

FABRIZIO: Excellent, my dear balia. How's Lelia?

CLEMENZIA: Good, good. But let's go into the house, there's a lot I need to explain to you.

❧ SCENE VII ❧

VIRGINIO, CLEMENZIA, and STRAGUALCIA

VIRGINIO: I'm so happy to have found my son that I'm satisfied with everything.

CLEMENZIA: It was all the will of God. It certainly has turned out better than if you had married your daughter off to that broken-down Gherardo. But let me go into the house to see how things are going. I left the newlyweds all alone and very, very close. [*She goes in and after a moment calls*] Come in, come in. Everything's fine. [VIRGINIO *follows her;* STRAGUALCIA *stops in the doorway*]

STRAGUALCIA: Spectators, don't wait for them to come back out of the house, because that will make a long story even longer. If you want to come to dinner with us, I'll be waiting for you at the Joker. And bring along some money, because no one's treating. But if you don't want to come—and it looks to me like that's the case—be happy and enjoy yourselves. And you members of the Intronati, how about some applause? [*He enters the* JOKER]

❧ ❧

La veniexiana

(The Venetian Comedy) [1]

Anonymous

CHARACTERS:

ANGELA: a young widow
BERNARDO: a porter
GIULIO: a young foreign dandy, still beardless
NENA: ANGELA's servant
ORIA: VALIERA's servant
VALIERA: a young noble wife, newly married

1. According to its most noted modern editor, Giorgio Padoan, this comedy was probably written and performed during the carnival season of 1535. There is, however, no contemporary record of its performance, and Padoan's dating is based upon a series of apparent archival matches that allow him to claim that he has found the actual individuals on which the story is based. The comedy was lost and apparently unknown until it was rediscovered in 1928 by Emilio Lovarini in a manuscript collection in the Marciana library in Venice. Padoan also doubts, primarily on stylistic grounds, that the author of the work was the Venetian nobleman Giovan Francesco Valier (d. 1542), to whom it has often been attributed. Padoan has even created a debate about the title itself, and we have followed his reading, *La veniexiana*, over *La venexiana*. Finally, there is uncertainty over what the title means. The best interpretation seems to be "The Venetian Comedy," since the other suggested title, "The Venetian Woman," runs into problems with the fact that there are two dominant female characters.

Prologue

The ancients innocently imagined Cupid, the son of Venus, as a blind, winged child, armed with a quiver of arrows, thus expressing the nature of love: blindly irrational, flying here and there, and imprudent, able to penetrate to the core of every man and so completely confounding his intellect that he becomes a child once again and returns to his pristine state of foolishness. This is in fact due to the senses, which, overwhelmed by an attraction to something, represent it as being different from what it actually is, making it seem either better or worse. As a result, with judgment blinded, desire forces every sense to fall into line. While this is a universal condition, it has a greater effect on the female sex, since their sensual nature far outruns their limited intellect.

Today you will come to understand this clearly, O spectators, when you hear of the boundless love that a fellow noblewoman of yours felt for a foreign youth. And you will hear of her boldness and her determination to have him, and then the happy play and pleasure that she enjoyed with him. At the same time, you will learn of the love of another woman for the same youth, which was all the more intense because of the first one's love. Thus, seeing the happiness of the one and the suffering of the other, you will be able to see how strong Love is in women, and how we are conquered by his power.

Give us your attention, everyone, and in some stretches of what follows, don't be disturbed if certain things that are usually passed over in silence are portrayed here without shame: for in order to show clearly the nature of Love, we have to show clearly all his effects. And take care that, having learned about Love, you deal with him with the aid of your reason and not your senses, otherwise wisdom may quickly turn to sadness. And don't imagine that women are any different from you except when they are dressed up as women. When they take off their feminine dress, they are not objects of love but lovers just like you.[2]

---

2. This concept—that dress / culture is what separates women from men—sounds similar to the modern notion of gender, although such a reading would be anachronistic. A more appropriate interpretation would be that in matters of love, when culture is stripped away men and women become equivalent: active participants rather than mere objects—a startling break with the Renaissance stereotype of women as passive in love and men as active.

Act I

🏵 SCENE I 🏵

[Early afternoon, in a street where the facade and windows of the noble VALIER *family's house face those of* ANGELA's *house]*

GIULIO and ORIA

GIULIO: [*Alone*] Thank God that I, a young man on my own with little money, have come to this noble and distinguished city. Here I'm recognized and respected more than my circumstances warrant, and even better, I've fallen in love with a fascinating young woman, well mannered and noble.[3] How happy I'd be if I were accepted at such a level! Or if I could just speak with her for a moment, perhaps my sweet talk would have some effect. O God, Prime Mover and cause of all good, help me reach my goal! I promise you that if she comes to love me, I'll take her back to my homeland as my wife—with her dowry, of course—and enjoy her beauty, nobility, and wealth all together.

But here comes one of her servants. [ORIA *enters*] Courage! I'll say a few friendly words to her and see if I can begin to try my fortune. [*To* ORIA] May God bless you, young lady. You have the fine manners of a wise young bride.[4]

ORIA: Why, I thank you, Your Magnificence.

GIULIO: Please, I beg you, stop here a moment so that I may say a few words to you. And forgive me if I'm presumptuous, but your gentle ways give me the confidence to address you.

ORIA: At your pleasure, sir.

GIULIO: I am a foreign gentleman, come to see the nobility of this distinguished place and the uniqueness of Venice. But above and beyond everything else that I have found pleasing in this city, nothing was more so than its most beautiful noblewomen, and among all of them none more so than your young mistress—she has stolen my heart and made me an eternal slave to her beauty and gentle ways. Please tell her for me that I am hers, and please commend me to her.

3. It is interesting that manners are associated with nobility even here in republican Venice, with its strong emphasis on merchant values. Manners were a newer marker of social status more associated with courts and cities ruled by nobles.

4. A heavy emphasis on manners is evident in Giulio's compliment and in the extremely deferential "Your Magnificence" in Oria's reply. The emphasis on courteous forms of address and behavior throughout the comedy might suggest a later date than the mid-1530s suggested by Padoan.

ORIA: Forgive me, sir, have patience; I don't want to be the ambassador of your love.

GIULIO: Please, I beg you!

ORIA: Go on, now, you seem too ready to trifle with me.

[*Intermission*]⁵

๛ SCENE II ๛

[VALIERA's *room*]

ORIA and VALIERA

ORIA: [*Rushing into the room*] Madonna Valiera, what will you pay me to hear the news?

VALIERA: What news, you little fool? Have you seen the first swallow of spring?

ORIA: I'm talking about something much better than swallows! This is really good.

VALIERA: What is it?

ORIA: I'm not going to tell you because you called me a little fool.

VALIERA: Don't get all worked up, my dear child. Go ahead, speak up.

ORIA: I don't know who the man was who spoke to me in the street about you. I don't know who . . . about you . . .

VALIERA: What are you saying? About me? What silly story is this?

ORIA: As God is my witness, I didn't want to listen to a word he said!

VALIERA: Who was this man? Who spoke with you?

ORIA: A foreigner dressed like a dandy, with a sword, a feather in his cap, and a short velvet jacket.

VALIERA: Was he a young foreigner with black hair?

ORIA: Yes, Madonna: black and in braids.

VALIERA: What did he say?

ORIA: Me, I refused to listen.

---

5. At this point in the manuscript there is inserted a short song attributed to Andrea Navagero and published in *Rime diverse di molti eccellentissimi auttori nuovamente raccolte. Libro primo* (Venice: Giolito de'Ferrari, 1545), 97–98. Padoan notes that this song is also attributed to Francesco Molza. Songs and dances were often inserted between the scenes of Renaissance comedies. It is unlikely that these songs were written for this comedy.

VALIERA: Oh, these damn people who are deaf at precisely the moment when they need to listen!

ORIA: Why, I refused to listen so that you wouldn't bawl me out for it or have me beaten by the master, your husband.

VALIERA: You're wise to be afraid! But don't you know when to keep your mouth shut about these things?

ORIA: I refused to listen so that I wouldn't have to keep my mouth shut.

VALIERA: Are you so forgetful that you don't remember a word?

ORIA: At least one, by this cross! The last one.

VALIERA: Tell me what you remember.

ORIA: He said, "Commend me to the Madonna."

VALIERA: You're teasing me.

ORIA: If you don't want to believe me, it's your loss!

VALIERA: What did you say to him?

ORIA: Nothing, absolutely nothing.

VALIERA: You shouldn't be so impolite. If you see him again, bow and say, "The Madonna thanks you." All right?

ORIA: I don't want the master to bawl me out afterwards.

VALIERA: Forget about the master. You do what I tell you and keep your mouth shut. Do you understand?

ORIA: Yes, madam.

[*Intermission*][6]

SCENE III

[*Night, in Nena's bedroom*][7]

ANGELA and (in bed) NENA

ANGELA: Nena, sweet, dear Nena, are you sleeping, my child?

6. Inserted here is a second song, a madrigal, which is attributed to Pietro Barignan (and is published in *Rime diverse*, 28) but which Padoan attributes to Niccolò Tiepolo.

7. There are very few indoor scenes in Italian comedies of the early sixteenth century, and scenes in the private spaces of homes like bedrooms are extremely rare, making this comedy quite unusual. Given the movement between rooms required by the dialogue, it is difficult to imagine how this comedy could have been performed during the Renaissance, or even how the author imagined it being performed.

NENA: I was hoping to drop off for a bit—I'm tired of tossing and turning in this godforsaken bed.

ANGELA: You're in the bed, and I'm in the fire, and it's burning me up!

NENA: What? What fire?

ANGELA: My flesh is burning up. The pain is killing me!

NENA: Do you have a fever? Let me feel.

ANGELA: The fever is here inside, in my heart.

NENA: We'll call our doctor, Master Antonio, first thing in the morning.

ANGELA: There's no doctor in all of Venice except one who knows how to treat Angela.

NENA: No, I'm afraid anyone who has balls would do.

ANGELA: You don't understand; I say there's only one man.

NENA: Are you thinking about some big, handsome, forceful type?

ANGELA: No, just a man who has a face of an angel, delicate golden features, straight from heaven.[8]

NENA: Madonna, they are all only men.

ANGELA: Yes, but this one is the best of any in Venice, in the Levant, on the mainland, in the whole world.

NENA: You believe that because you love him.

ANGELA: What, love?! He is my treasure, my jewels, my God!

NENA: Bring him here, if you want him so badly.

ANGELA: It wouldn't be good for him to see me dressed in my widow's clothes. He'll think I'm old. And worse yet, he's in love with Valiera who lives across the way.

NENA: Heavens! Is it that sweet boy? What do you want with that little sprig?

ANGELA: What do you mean, "heavens"? What a fool! You really don't know?

NENA: Go ahead, tell me a bit about what you want to do with him.

ANGELA: I want to take him in my arms like this [*lying down with* NENA *and taking her in her arms*] and taste his lips and hold him tight, very tight.

---

8. These contrasting ideals of masculine beauty will remain in play throughout this scene: the lower-class Nena is attracted to large, forceful men, the upper-class Angela to more delicate types. Angela's feelings recall Isabella's attraction to Fabio/Lelia in *Gl'ingannati*, also denigrated by the comedy's lower-class characters. It may be that the delicate youthful look became popular with upper-class women as courtly values that stressed manners and grace over physical prowess and force gained ground with the upper classes in the sixteenth century. Because Giulio claims to be a soldier and regularly appears armed, some critics conclude that he is a Renaissance example of that stock character of ancient Roman comedy, the *miles gloriosus*, or braggart soldier, but he is far too young, pretty, delicate, and well mannered to be related to that blustering character. See the parody of the *miles gloriosus* in the Prologue of *Il marescalco* (at n. 19).

NENA: And then? That's it?

ANGELA: Then the tongue in the mouth.

NENA: I could do it better than he could.

ANGELA: His sweet little mouth, I want it for myself always like this, always! [*Kissing her*][9]

NENA: Enough, you're suffocating me!

ANGELA: Dear boy, sweet, sweeter than sugar!

NENA: You're forgetting that I'm a woman.

ANGELA: I'm about to faint away. I'm all hot and bothered!

NENA: What do you expect, with all the crazy things you're doing?

ANGELA: This night too will pass, and morning will come.

NENA: And in the morning? What will you do in the morning?

ANGELA: I want that young man, I do!

NENA: How are you going to get him?

ANGELA: By means of money and presents.

NENA: Right, using someone who knows how to be a go-between.

ANGELA: And using you to do all that he tells you.

NENA: All right, but go back to your own bed now and sleep.

ANGELA: I want to stay here. And if you want me to be able to sleep, take me in your arms like this, and I'll close my eyes and make believe that you're that boy.

NENA: Like this? [*Taking her in her arms*]

ANGELA: Yes, my dear child.

NENA: Do you believe that I am he?

ANGELA: Not quite yet. After a little more.

NENA: I want to sleep. Take it easy—don't squeeze me so hard!

ANGELA: Do you want to do me a favor?

NENA: What?

ANGELA: Dear sweet, stay like this for a little; and then begin to swear, so that I can pretend that you're a man.

NENA: I don't know what to say!

---

9. Here and elsewhere we have added stage directions to the very minimal ones of the original manuscript to make it easier to follow the action. We have tried to avoid adding directions that are not implied (or demanded) by the dialogue. That Angela and Nena are in bed together hugging is clearly implied by "I want to take him in my arms like this," and the kissing may have begun when Angela states her desire to "taste his lips." To avoid this bed scene altogether, some critics suggest that Nena gets out of bed for the hugging and kissing—a reading that seems highly unlikely, given what follows.

ANGELA: Swear on the body of Christ, say dirty words like men do.

NENA: What words?

ANGELA: Oh, those dirty things they say in the bordello—you know.

NENA: If I don't fall asleep, I'll say them; but if I do fall asleep, I won't.

ANGELA: Sweet Nena, play the pretty boy a little, for my love!

Act II

❧ SCENE I ☙

[The next morning, in the street]

NENA and BERNARDO

NENA: *[Alone]* Everything that the Madonna dreams up during the night I have to run around to arrange during the day to make her happy. Now she wants a young lad called Giulio—a foreigner who is staying at the Ostaria del Pavon— who she says is the lover of Madonna Valier. But I don't know what to do. It'll be hard to bring him to her and keep it secret. And it's not a job for a woman. I need to speak with Bernardo, the porter; he's street-wise, knows how to keep his mouth shut, and has the trust of our house. I'll work this out with him and have him find the young man. [BERNARDO *enters*] There he is now; I'd better seize the moment. [*To* BERNARDO] Brother Bernardo, where are you off to in such a rush?

BERNARDO: I'm going to the warehouse on the Calle di Gallipoli, to load up some things.[10]

NENA: Wait up a minute. Come over here, I want to speak with you.

BERNARDO: I don't have time for chatter now. We can chat later, on some holiday.

NENA: I need you now! Listen up, because you may well earn more from this than from hard work.

BERNARDO: Well, it's certainly better to earn money and have fun by riding on someone else's back than by breaking one's own.

NENA: I'm going to tell you a secret, but you must keep it quiet, dear brother, so the whole city doesn't hear about it. Then I want you to do me a great favor.

BERNARDO: Don't you know me? Why, there's not a man in our city who's closer to a confessor than I. Your secret couldn't be safer!

---

10. Perhaps wine. According to Padoan, this street was noted for its wine shops.

NENA: My mistress is in love with a young foreigner who is called Giulio and is staying over at the Pavon. Do you know him?

BERNARDO: That's good news; she's right to seek out a little consolation.

NENA: Dear Bernardo, she's really hot for this boy; she can't sleep or eat anything more than an egg or a bit of something sweet.

BERNARDO: Bah! This is typical of the battles of Love: first comes the suffering, then the pleasures.

NENA: Do you know what she wants?

BERNARDO: I don't know exactly, but I have a good idea.

NENA: If you're brave enough to find him and speak with him—

BERNARDO: [*Interrupting*] Why, I'm brave enough to speak with the doge[11] himself!

NENA: Of course. That's why I want you to bring him to our house, but in such a way that he doesn't know how he got there. I don't know how to do it myself.

BERNARDO: If he lets me, I'll see that he arrives like smuggled goods—unknown to anyone.

NENA: I don't know if he'll be willing.

BERNARDO: Every man is ready to enjoy the *vita dulcedo*.[12]

NENA: Right! What will you tell him, dear brother?

BERNARDO: Um, well . . . shit! I'll just tell him that a woman wants him to pen her a letter.

NENA: No, not that. Tell him that a woman wants him to go to bed with her.

BERNARDO: The type of letter I'm talking about is written with another pen than the type you dip only in ink.

NENA: Oh, is that it? Well, will he believe you if you say it like that?

BERNARDO: If he doesn't, I'll give him a pledge, myself.

NENA: You know, my good man, you're going to make money on this deal. Do you know how much money my mistress wants to give you? Ten ducats safely tucked away in a pouch!

BERNARDO: That much? Well, who would refuse such a job bringing her a little pleasure at home. Shit, this is better than hauling around pepper or cinnamon, even better than sugar from Crete! Why, I'd say this is sugar from heaven itself.

---

11. The chief official of the Venetian government, elected for life and surrounded with great pomp and ceremony to create an aura of authority and distance from the populace—precisely the perception of superiority that Bernardo's boast reflects.

12. "Sweet life." Even a porter can throw around a word or two of Latin.

NENA: You make me laugh. I've nothing more to ask.

BERNARDO: But we aren't going to accomplish anything more either unless you give me a little down payment for my services.

NENA: I don't have any money. But if you want to take this ring, take it until the Madonna pays you. Go ahead, take it, but keep quiet!

BERNARDO: Hell! Me, keep quiet? Mum's the word.

NENA: Do you want anything else? Because I need to get back to the Madonna.

BERNARDO: Tell me, what does this guy look like?

NENA: He's a young fellow still without a beard, with a rosy face and black hair, dressed in silk and very finely.

BERNARDO: God damn! It's perfect—I know him already!

NENA: Dear Bernardo, speak to him today—I beg you, dear brother.

BERNARDO: I'll take care of it this evening and let you know what he says. Keep an eye out for me.

SCENE II

[In the street]

ORIA and GIULIO

ORIA: *[Alone]* Madonna is already in love with that gentleman, and she has sent me to find him so that I can speak with him. That's fine with me; if this is what she wants, I do too. *[GIULIO enters]* But here he is now.

GIULIO: Good day to you, my sister.

ORIA: And to you, Your Magnificence.

GIULIO: Did you give the Madonna my greetings?

ORIA: Yes, sir.

GIULIO: Thank you. Would you be so kind as to give me her reply?

ORIA: She thanks Your Magnificence, and she commends herself to you.

GIULIO: What happiness! Giulio, you are blessed that such a woman deigns to commend herself to you, her servant and slave!

ORIA: Your Magnificence is a real gentleman, not a slave!

GIULIO: I live only to die for her, and I pledge this sword and my life to her service.

ORIA: A thousand thanks to Your Magnificence.

GIULIO: Dear sister, tell me: might I be so blessed as to have a few words with your lady? Then I could call myself truly blessed.

ORIA: What, sir? Do you want her husband to kill her? She's still a newlywed.

GIULIO: Better that he kill me than her! I want no more than a quarter of an hour to let her know that I am her servant—nothing else.

ORIA: Oh well! For such a little thing I think the Madonna will consent, because she is courteous.[13]

GIULIO: To you, sister, I want to pledge all my goods and to reward you not with some small gift but with a great one: to see that you are married so well that you are always rich.

ORIA: Thank you so much, Your Magnificence!

GIULIO: Would you be willing to say a couple of words about my desire to speak with her to the Madonna, for love of me?

ORIA: Yes, sir.

GIULIO: But how will I know her answer?

ORIA: This evening at about nine[14] Your Magnificence should come by. If the Madonna has agreed to talk with you, the door will be slightly ajar. If not, just go about your business as if nothing had happened.

GIULIO: I don't know how I can ever thank you enough for your kindness. I'll do as you say, and I'll be here at nine.

ORIA: Be off, now. I mustn't stay out here any longer. Peace be with you.

SCENE III

[ANGELA's room]

NENA and ANGELA

NENA: I found your man[15] Bernardo, and I begged him so hard that he has agreed to speak with our friend.

ANGELA: Heavens, will he keep it quiet?

---

13. *Cortese* (literally, "courtly").

14. Actually, three. But as Renaissance time was told on a twelve-hour schedule that began with sundown and sunup, "three" at the time of carnival (when this comedy was presumably to be performed) would be approximately nine, three hours after sundown.

15. *Santolo.* Padoan takes this dialect term in its literal sense as "godfather." Venetian noble families often secured client-like relationships with those close to them by allowing them to serve as godparents. But *santolo* has the more general sense of someone who is close or helpful, and there is little other indication that Bernardo is Angela's godfather; he makes no reference to the fact. Throughout the comedy (as in everyday life), terms suggesting family relationships are regularly used to express ordinary closeness.

NENA: If you pay him well, he'll know how to keep quiet.

ANGELA: What did you promise him?

NENA: Ten ducats.

ANGELA: Why, I'll give him fifteen!

NENA: Oh my, just for that? He hardly deserves three. I did much more than he did.

ANGELA: I intend to give you one hundred,[16] when I arrange your marriage.

NENA: This evening you'll find out everything.

ANGELA: Let's not wait any longer. Get the mezzanine room and its wall hangings ready; put the canopy on the bed; take out the incense to burn.[17] All right, sweet daughter?

NENA: All right, I'll hurry.

SCENE IV

[Afternoon, in the street]

BERNARDO and GIULIO

BERNARDO: *[Alone]* I've been to the Pavon, but I haven't been able to find him, even after going to the Rialto and San Marco. Maybe the crows have eaten him. If I'd been intending to do him some harm, I'd have found him immediately. But I'll wait for him here, since this is the street he'll have to take to get back home. *[GIULIO enters, unseen by BERNARDO]*

GIULIO: O happy house that keeps my lady closed inside![18] Well might I praise you, along with this noble city, for a certain gentlewoman will have me as her true love.

BERNARDO: *[Noticing GIULIO]* Is this him? Well, let's see: his hair is in braids, and he has that feminine air of a dandy. Shit, it has to be him.

---

16. I.e., for a dowry.

17. Padoan points out that in the winter months, Venetian nobles preferred to sleep on the mezzanine level of their palaces because the ceilings were lower and the rooms easier to heat.

18. Although it was a general Renaissance ideal to keep upper-class women locked up in their houses, Venice appears to have been one of the places where this ideal was followed more rigorously. There is much evidence to suggest that Venetian women of the upper classes did get out of their houses occasionally, but in this comedy none of them do, and they must depend on others to act as their go-betweens.

GIULIO: It must be about time for the promenade in Piazza San Marco.[19] I wonder what time it is. [*To* BERNARDO] My good man, could you tell me the hour?

BERNARDO: My lord, did you ask me the time? It seems to be about four, more or less.

GIULIO: Thank you very much.

BERNARDO: There's no need to thank me, because I'm here to do something much better for you than tell you the time. Let me explain.

GIULIO: What are you saying?

BERNARDO: I'm saying that I'm here to do you a favor.

GIULIO: I hope to God it's a good one.

BERNARDO: Pay no attention to the fact that I'm a porter. I'm still capable of doing you a favor,[20] yes indeed!

GIULIO: I don't need favors; I'm a soldier.

BERNARDO: I mean a favor worthy of a gentleman, and one who knows how to enjoy a good time.

GIULIO: The best favor you could do me would be to show me a good place where I could indulge my youthful desires and have some fun—that's what I came to Venice for.

BERNARDO: And that's exactly what I'm talking about. Even the birds and the bees want that.

GIULIO: Come this way a bit. What are you trying to say?

BERNARDO: Look, if you're willing to give me your word as a gentleman and do as I say, tonight I'll send you to *gloria in excelsis!*[21]

GIULIO: My, my! An angel's voice! If that's all you want, I put myself at your service as well as my goods, my servants, and my person, and what's more, I'm your slave.

BERNARDO: I'm not asking for that much; only you.

GIULIO: Here I am, alone, if it's only me you want.

BERNARDO: Not now; tonight.

GIULIO: After nine I have an engagement; I have to meet some friends. Before that I'll go wherever you want.

19. The famed *passeggiata*, when people walk through Saint Mark's Square to see and be seen, a practice still followed.

20. *Benefizii:* a favor, but also an ecclesiastical office, a benefice—hence Giulio's reply that he does not need one because he is a soldier.

21. "The glories of heaven."

BERNARDO: No, no! If you want something really good, brother, don't go looking for friends then, not even the devil.

GIULIO: What do you want me to do?

BERNARDO: Just follow my lead.

GIULIO: Tell me, please, where you want me to go.

BERNARDO: To heaven to visit God, who's in love with you.

GIULIO: I don't know the way very well. And besides, even armed I'm not sure how safe I'd be.

BERNARDO: I'll take you by gondola so you won't be in any danger, and I'll take you right to the room. Could you ask for anything better?

GIULIO: Let me see if you have the face of an honest man, or if you're making up tales and trying to take advantage of me.

BERNARDO: Take a good look at me, and you'll see written all over my face that I'm a Ghibelline, just like you who come from the duchy of Milan.

GIULIO: It's amazing that you know I'm from Milan!

BERNARDO: It's nothing, really. Me, I can tell a good man at first sight.

GIULIO: All right. You give me your word, then, as a true Ghibelline?

BERNARDO: Yes, on the Gospels of the Savior.

GIULIO: What time should I expect you?

BERNARDO: At about ten.

GIULIO: Should I trust you?

BERNARDO: Don't worry—as a gentleman.

GIULIO: I'm staying at the Pavon.

BERNARDO: I know even better than you do where you're staying.

GIULIO: All right, I'll be waiting.

BERNARDO: Me, I'm off now to firm up the affair. [*He leaves*]

GIULIO: How strange life is! Yesterday and all my days in Venice I've been complaining because I haven't caught the eye of any woman. Now I'm complaining because I've caught too many. This morning that servant gave me the promise of a meeting—or if not a promise, at least she gave me good reason to hope; now this porter has invited me to a tryst. Heavens, I don't know what to do, I really don't know—for if I don't keep my appointment with that gentlewoman I'll lose much honor, but if I pass up this business with the porter, I'll always regret it.

For the moment I want to go with the porter, because deeds are better than words. The first affair is uncertain; this one seems certain. With the first, I'm begging; with this one, someone's begging me.

And maybe they're both the same woman: maybe she didn't trust her servant, so she sent the porter. Why, he's the type of man who would even shed blood if paid to do so—you can count on it! Fine, I'll wait for him, but I'll have my arms ready, with my brocade jacket, cap, sword, and shield, and I'll try my luck. As far as the other one is concerned, if she's not the same woman, I'll ask her forgiveness, as she won't know why I didn't come anyway. And then by tomorrow evening, with God's help, I'll be able to come up with some excuse.

It's already evening. I'd better get back to the inn. I'll dine lightly because I don't want to weigh down my stallion here, who will have many jousts to run this evening.

SCENE V

[Angela's room]

BERNARDO and ANGELA

BERNARDO: Good evening to Your Magnificence.

ANGELA: My dear Bernardo, welcome.

BERNARDO: I never come to see you without bringing good news.

ANGELA: That's the way good friends of the house behave.

BERNARDO: What kind of reward will you give me if I bring you a message that says something you'll like?

ANGELA: Whatever you want: any goods . . . and money.

BERNARDO: Above and beyond the money, I'd like a pair of scarlet tights.[22]

ANGELA: Here's a ducat—take it, it's yours. But tell me what you know.

BERNARDO: The affair is going exactly as you wished.

ANGELA: What? Is that so, dear brother? You spoke with him?

BERNARDO: Did I speak with him? Why, I looked all over for him, just as if he were a beautiful girl.

ANGELA: What did you say to him?

BERNARDO: I didn't say anything beyond that I wanted to take him this evening to a place where he could sleep the night.

ANGELA: What did he say?

BERNARDO: He didn't trust me, and he didn't want to come.

22. Padoan notes that scarlet tights were the proverbial gift given to servants. Such tights, which were quite revealing of legs and bottoms and often sported elaborate codpieces, were especially popular among younger men. As Bernardo was well past his prime, his request may have seemed comical to a Renaissance audience.

ANGELA: So, what did you do?

BERNARDO: So, I let him know the kind of man I am.

ANGELA: And he wants to come?

BERNARDO: Of course! At ten I'll bring the prisoner myself. I want you to treat him well.

ANGELA: Oh, heavens! Don't say another word.

BERNARDO: He's the spitting image of an angel.

ANGELA: He's too good-looking for me.

BERNARDO: Don't be silly. Give me something to drink. And be ready for me at ten. And prepare a bit of supper.

ANGELA: Whatever you want.

BERNARDO: Do you need anything else, then?

ANGELA: Only that you keep this secret, Bernardo, brother. You know I wouldn't have trusted my nearest relative here in Venice.[23]

BERNARDO: Don't worry. Once I'm paid, I'll immediately forget everything.

ANGELA: I intend to give you mocenighi fresh from the mint.[24]

BERNARDO: Damn! You're really eager to have me row that little gondola here tonight! I'd better get going. Goodbye.

Act III

☙ SCENE I ❧

[*After dark, inside* VALIERA*'s house near the street door*]

VALIERA and ORIA

VALIERA: It's already past nine, and he hasn't arrived. You weren't clear enough with him, Oria.

---

23. I.e., I wouldn't have trusted my nearest relative as I've trusted you. This comparison with relatives and Angela's use of the term "brother" should again be taken not as an indication of actual kinship but as a metaphor for the closeness of their relationship (a reading underlined by the fact that both are agreed that Bernardo will be paid for his services).

24. The mocenigo was a silver coin first minted in 1475 and named after the Venetian doge, Pietro Mocenigo. It was worth twenty soldi until 1525, when its value was officially recognized as twenty-four soldi. During the Renaissance coins were regularly shaved in order to steal a bit of precious metal from the governments that produced them. Although this crime carried heavy penalties, coins in circulation rapidly lost weight and value. As a result, "mocenighi fresh from the mint" were of assured value.

ORIA: I was perfectly clear. Maybe something happened that kept him from coming.

VALIERA: You know what I'm thinking?

ORIA: What? Tell me.

VALIERA: Some woman in love with him who wanted to sleep with him . . .

ORIA: Sure, dream on![25]

VALIERA: Boys like this who look like angels are manna from heaven that you don't come upon every day. And then he's a foreigner, which means that you can take your pleasure with him, and afterwards he'll leave town and no longer be underfoot.

ORIA: I'm afraid he's not going to come. It'll soon be ten.

VALIERA: You should have told him that I loved him!

ORIA: If you had told me to say it, I would have.

VALIERA: Don't you know that you mustn't say no to a boy like that?

ORIA: I don't know when I'm supposed to keep quiet!

VALIERA: Don't you understand that everyone wants what's beautiful and wants to eat what's good?

ORIA: But I didn't understand those things.

VALIERA: Don't you see? Another woman is going to be much happier than I tonight!

ORIA: If he doesn't come tonight, he'll come tomorrow. Let's close the door and not wait any longer.

VALIERA: Let's wait a little longer, but not much.

ORIA: I say he's not coming. [*The bells ring the hour*] Hear how late the hour is![26]

VALIERA: Oh no! It *is* late. Come on, let's go.

[*Intermission*][27]

25. *Sì, oxelle.* Padoan reads *oxelle* as *oselle*, the medal the doge gave every year to every member of the Great Council, and supposes that these medals were so rare that receiving one would have been an unlikely event; hence Oria is saying that Angela's fear is unlikely. But in dialect, *oxelle* read as *oselà* was commonly used to mean that someone had been misled—a much simpler reading. In either case the sense would be much the same.

26. One "heard" the time because the bells of the city rang the hours, then as now.

27. Here there was a sung intermission, attributed to Girolamo Fracastoro, published in *Ariosto, Castiglione, Fracastoro, Sannazaro, Casa. Canzonieri del secolo XVI*, in *Parnaso italiano*, vol. 26 (Venice: Zatta, 1787), 98.

ᐁ SCENE II ᐅ

[Angela's house]

BERNARDO, GIULIO, NENA, and ANGELA

BERNARDO: *[In a gondola at the boat landing outside the house]* Here we are. Jump out there. I'll get out on my own.

GIULIO: This is a beautiful palace.[28] Who does it belong to?

BERNARDO: As they say, "Don't worry about whether the clothes belong to the person wearing them."

GIULIO: I'm satisfied not to know any more than you want me to. If I've put my life in your hands, I can certainly leave the rest to you.

BERNARDO: Enough talk. Follow me. *[They enter the house]*

ᐁ ᐅ

NENA: *[Meeting them at the door]* Good evening to this gentleman, and to our good and gentle Bernardo.

BERNARDO: Good evening. Where do we go now—through this way?

NENA: Go into the mezzanine bedroom over there. *[They go as directed, and NENA goes to get ANGELA in the room next to the bedroom]*

ᐁ ᐅ

GIULIO: *[In the bedroom]* This is the house of a god! What a rich and richly decorated house! What a beautiful place!

BERNARDO: Didn't I tell you it was heaven?

GIULIO: Gentle people deserve such things and more.

BERNARDO: *[Helping himself to sweets and wine]* Eat some of these sweets, and have a bit of this fortified wine from Crete!

GIULIO: Really, I'm not hungry or thirsty, but I'll have some with you to keep you company.

28. Padoan believes this was the Palazzo Barbarigo at the Toletta.

꙳

NENA: [*Entering the room next to the bedroom*] Madonna, the gentleman has arrived, and he's the most elegant man in the world, all decked out in arms like Saint George.[29]

ANGELA: No need to go on, I saw him come in. What do you think: should I go like this with this black scarf so that he won't know me?

NENA: You look good like that. But hurry up so that he doesn't have to wait there alone too long.

ANGELA: Bernardo's still there with him.

꙳

BERNARDO: [*In the bedroom*] I'll leave you here as a prisoner for a while. Have fun!

GIULIO: Where are you going?

BERNARDO: I'm going upstairs to visit the kitchen for a bit.

GIULIO: Be well. [BERNARDO *leaves*]

꙳

NENA: [*In the room next to the bedroom*] That's Bernardo leaving. Did you hear that sweet voice?

ANGELA: Yes. Come on, I want to get going. You keep track of Bernardo and make sure the door is locked from the upstairs, all right?

NENA: Don't worry about a thing.

꙳

ANGELA: [*Entering the bedroom*] Welcome, my dear gentleman.

GIULIO: The same to you, Your Ladyship, so gentle and courteous.[30]

ANGELA: Sweet son of mine, I have longed for you so much! I can't think of a thing more dear to me than to have you here as my prisoner.

GIULIO: I'm more fortunate yet, thanks to Your Ladyship, for you've deigned to accept me as your servant. And my fortune is all the greater because you've done so out of your own kindness and not because of my merits.

29. One of the oldest patron saints of Venice, and one having a particular military connotation.

30. The language of this meeting is highly influenced by courtly forms, illustrating the close connection between the concepts of courtship and court that existed at least for the upper classes in late Renaissance Italy.

ANGELA: My heart, please forgive me if I've brought you here so directly and immodestly or if I speak too presumptuously or act in a way that seems incorrect. It's because my love for you burns so strongly that I'm aflame like a torch.

GIULIO: My lady, your beauty and your nobility are so great that everything you do seems absolutely polite. There's no need to apologize, as I give you my body, my soul, and from this moment on I'm totally yours.

ANGELA: I accept your gift, my soul. And in return take my soul, which is completely yours.

GIULIO: I'll take it along with your body, and I'll worship you as my lady and my God.

ANGELA: Doing so, you make me melt with pleasure. Take off your weapons. Have a little wine, and then we'll get comfortable.

GIULIO: I'm completely in Your Ladyship's hands. But I've already drunk a little and don't really need any more.

ANGELA: Have just a little, for my love.

GIULIO: For your love, if it were acid or arsenic, I would drink it.

ANGELA: How beautiful you are! Blessed are the parents who gave birth to you!

GIULIO: They're truly blessed, for they've made something that pleases Your Ladyship, who is truly worthy.

ANGELA: I must kiss you right now for those sweet words. [*She kisses him*]

GIULIO: Your mouth is far sweeter than the words from my lips.

ANGELA: Come here so that I can help you.[31]

GIULIO: That I won't allow. Let me help Your Ladyship undress.

ANGELA: Can't I do anything for you? Don't worry, just tell me.

GIULIO: No, Madonna, Your Ladyship doesn't need to be concerned about me, your most devoted servant.

ANGELA: Concerned? Don't you understand that you are my dear, sweet child? If you loved me half as much as I love you, I'd be content.

GIULIO: My love for Your Ladyship has just begun, but it will last until this Venice sees me as an old man.

ANGELA: Come, sit here by me—a little closer.

GIULIO: Your Ladyship needn't worry. For now that I'm yours, your wish is my command.

---

31. I.e., help you undress. Although some commentators have taken Giulio's reply as a sign of modesty or as a momentary rejection of Angela, it is more likely an expression of courtesy. Because undressing a gentleman is the task of a servant, not a lady, he refuses her offer and then offers to undress her as a sign of his servitude as her lover.

ANGELA: Ah, Angela this is your happiness! Now you are with your love and your every desire.

GIULIO: It's the same for me, Madonna, my desire, my lady.

ANGELA: Now that you are mine, I want to guard you so that no one will steal you. So I'll hold you like this, tightly in my arms. [*She embraces him*]

[*Intermission*]³²

ANGELA: [*A while later in the bedroom, in bed with* GIULIO] My sweetheart, I thought that you'd bring me water to quench the fire in my breast, but instead you've brought me wood and coal to make it burn more fiercely.

GIULIO: I came to visit Your Ladyship a free man, but now I'm chained more tightly than a criminal in your prison—the prison of these sweet breasts.

ANGELA: Ah, my sweet little thief, you kiss them, eh? Don't squeeze them too hard, or they'll cry out!

GIULIO: This sweet little apple I want to keep for myself. The other one you can keep.

ANGELA: That's good, because it's the one over my heart.

GIULIO: May I say a few words to my sweet little breast?

ANGELA: Yes, say whatever you want. Oh, oh, you're breaking my heart! Wait a second, I want you to feel the same sweet pain.

GIULIO: Do you know what my little apple says? That she's happy.

ANGELA: Tell me what you asked her.

GIULIO: If that was sweet for her and if she wanted to do it again.

ANGELA: She is sure she does, my sweet treasure.

GIULIO: Madonna, you've embraced me; let me embrace you, and we'll light our own fire.

ANGELA: Yes, but kiss me with your tongue.

GIULIO: I want the sweet breast that you gave me.

ANGELA: Not unless you kiss me with your tongue. I swear I'll bite you!

GIULIO: Do you like it like this?

ANGELA: Yes, everything, everything.

---

32. Here there is another sung intermission, a love song, by Jacopo Sannazaro, published in his *Opere volgari*, ed. Alfredo Mauro (Bari: G. Laterza, 1961), 162.

⁓᠔ ᠔⁓

BERNARDO: [*In the upstairs room*] The bells are ringing, ringing . . . it's two o'clock. But they don't hear them. I can tell you, they've got the stallion well closed up in the stall.

NENA: What are you going on about, you fool? Shut up.

BERNARDO: Can't you hear? Why, I'd do the same, as old as I am, if I could just get it up.

NENA: Have you no shame, you blockhead?

BERNARDO: But didn't you hear those big kisses? Oh, shit, they even smelled irresistible.

NENA: Leave that sort of thing to the young, and concentrate on making some money.

BERNARDO: Don't you realize that that's what I'm doing?

NENA: I do believe God Himself sent you to me so that everyone would be happy: the Madonna is happy, the young lad is happy, you're happy, and so am I.

BERNARDO: I go every day to mass to pray to the Savior that he watch out for this poor man.

NENA: Be quiet now. Listen to what they're saying downstairs.

⁓᠔ ᠔⁓

ANGELA: [*In the bedroom, in bed with* GIULIO] Can't you give me just a little more of your love? Come on, my dear sweet boy.

GIULIO: Madonna, I don't know how to give you more unless I cut out my heart with a dagger.

ANGELA: Tomorrow you'll have completely forgotten your love for me!

GIULIO: Tomorrow? Why, not even a hundred years after my death.

ANGELA: I want you to pledge on the Bible here to answer my questions truthfully.

GIULIO: [*Putting his hand on the Bible*] So I swear to Your Ladyship.

ANGELA: Do you have a lover here in Venice?

GIULIO: I'll tell you everything. Every now and then a noblewoman has made friendly gestures to me from her window, but I've never spoken to her.

ANGELA: Where does she live?

GIULIO: In San Barnaba, I think. But I'm not sure.

ANGELA: Listen, if I thought that you were touching another woman, I'd die of pain right in your arms!

GIULIO: Ever since the moment Your Ladyship deigned to love me, I want only you, and all my love and happiness I've placed in your hands.

ANGELA: I want you to pledge this as well.

GIULIO: So I swear, and I give my pledge.

ANGELA: I want all your body for me: your mouth, your eyes, your nose, your legs, your arms, and all the rest. And I'm sorry that you're not a little vial of perfume that I could carry here between my breasts, always, always!

GIULIO: Does Your Ladyship doubt my love? I don't know how it would be possible to find another like you, so loving, courteous, and kind. Your eyes shine with love, your face with grace, your mouth with sweetness. And I won't say anything more about my sweet breast, because it's more precious than gold or silver.

ANGELA: Tell me the truth, do you love your little breast?

GIULIO: More than my life.

ANGELA: Do you know what she will do if you don't come to visit her? She'll become ill with anger and grief.

GIULIO: I'll visit her often. I don't want her to become ill, no!

ANGELA: Do you want me to kiss you some more? Are you tired?

GIULIO: You don't have to ask for what is yours, Your Ladyship. You'll never find me tired when it comes to giving you pleasure.

ANGELA: Sleep, close your eyes, because I want to do it my way.

GIULIO: As long as I live, I'm here for you.

ANGELA: Put your arms like this.

GIULIO: Your Ladyship will be uncomfortable.

ANGELA: Be quiet and sleep. I want to do it my way.

꧁ ꧂

BERNARDO: [*In the upstairs room*] Enough! I don't have any more time to stand around with my hands in my pockets. They're never going to finish stirring the polenta.[33] I'll call them myself.

NENA: Give them a little more time. [*The bells ring the hour*]

BERNARDO: Hell! Did you hear that? It's already four. It's almost morning! Open the window a bit.

NENA: [*Opening the window*] Oh my! It's later than I thought.

---

33. A cornmeal mush that became a staple of the Venetian diet, especially for the poor, after corn was introduced into Italy. Before that the dish was made with barley and other grains. Whatever was used to make it, it required long stirring with a wooden spoon (about forty-five minutes) and thus was an apt metaphor for an extended period of lovemaking.

BERNARDO: Right! I'm going to call them, if it's all right with you. But God damn it, can't they attend to these things themselves? [*He goes downstairs, and* NENA *follows*]

⁊ ℰ

NENA: [*At the bedroom door*] Knock quietly at the door.

BERNARDO: Just leave it to me. [*He knocks*]

ANGELA: [*In the bedroom*] Oh, what sweet exhaustion! Are you asleep, my son?

GIULIO: I slept like this just for a moment.

ANGELA: And I've ridden a long way, and I'm weary.

BERNARDO: [*Knocking*] Hello! I'm beginning to think you're not in there.

ANGELA: Who's that knocking? Nena?

BERNARDO: Madonna, she's here as well. It's time to get going.

ANGELA: Oh dear! Is it morning already? He's mad. It seems like barely an hour that we've been here together.

BERNARDO: There's no time for rambling on; time flies. Break it up, get a grip on yourselves!

ANGELA: I want to see. [*Getting out of bed and opening the window to look out*] Jesus, it *is* late!

GIULIO: Don't worry, Your Ladyship, we'll be ready in a flash.

ANGELA: Don't move—wait a second. I want to say a few words to you in bed.

GIULIO: Come over here to this side, here.

ANGELA: [*Getting back into bed*] Dear child, sweet, handsome, golden boy, from the first moment that I gave you my body and life, I wanted to give you this small gift—this little golden chain that has always been the companion of your little breast, and this small emerald: the golden chain so that you're bound to me always, the emerald so that you know that my love requires that you not touch any other woman. And I beg you to accept these gifts with the same love with which I give them to you. And in return, all I ask is one last kiss from you.

GIULIO: If I were to refuse anything that Your Ladyship were to give me, I would be acting like a rude peasant who didn't have anything to give in return. But I accept these gifts, because you wish me to. My love for you doesn't require any more words, because in life and in death, Giulio is yours. And then you ask for a kiss? I'll give you one, if you give me one in return.

꙳ ᚯ ꙳

NENA: [*Outside the bedroom door*] Did you hear that?

BERNARDO: Oh yes! Now they've started kissing again.

NENA: Stay calm.

BERNARDO: I'll leave the problems to them. Me, I'm going to sit down here.

NENA: Is the gondola all shipshape?

BERNARDO: I wish I were that shipshape, because then I would have given your field a good plowing last night.[34]

NENA: Can't you talk about anything except your own manliness?

BERNARDO: Thank God it can still be talked about. [*The bedroom door opens, and* ANGELA *and* GIULIO *come out*]

ANGELA: Bernardo, I'm returning your prisoner to you safe and sound. Here he is.

BERNARDO: He must have lost quite a bit of weight; it looks to me like he's walking on air.

GIULIO: Madonna, he's in a bad mood because he was a widower last night.

NENA: You're right, because although he tried to do some knitting, his needle was limp.

BERNARDO: Do you know why? They worked him so hard when I was young that now he demands his sleep.

ANGELA: Be that as it may, must you leave, Giulio?

GIULIO: As you wish, Your Ladyship.

BERNARDO: God damn it! Aren't you ready to let him leave yet? It's not as if I were about to take him off to Cyprus.

ANGELA: Bernardo, take great care of my heart.

BERNARDO: I'll take care of the gondola so that it doesn't turn over, and he can take care of himself. Let's get going.

GIULIO: My lady and Madonna, I may be taking my body away, but I'm leaving you my soul. Is there anything else that Your Ladyship desires?

ANGELA: Just one thing: think well of Angela and remember what you promised.

GIULIO: [*Showing the chain*] I will carry this with me as an eternal reminder.

ANGELA: I commend myself to you.

GIULIO: Be happy and content, Your Ladyship, for you have me as your most loyal servant. [*He and* BERNARDO *leave the house and go to the boat landing, where the gondola waits*]

---

34. The actual metaphor refers to the back-and-forth motion of winnowing.

᷍᷍ ᪲

BERNARDO: All the lovey-dovey chatter is finally finished. Hop in and tell me, man to man, how was the tumble?

GIULIO: You really did take me to where my heart and soul were consumed by love. But tell me, what's her family name?

BERNARDO: That's what's neat about an ax: without the handle, you have nothing. I'll tell you tomorrow; right now I don't remember a thing.

GIULIO: If you don't want to tell me, I don't want to know.

Act IV

᪲ SCENE I ᪲

[Morning, in the street]

ORIA, alone

ORIA: So she has no peace—yesterday Madonna was modesty itself, but now she's all over me. Because the young fellow didn't come, she's sent me to the inn to find out what he has to say. I'd like to tell him what a disaster it was when he didn't come and beg him to come this evening. Maybe he thought that I was lying earlier. But this time I'll speak to him clearly so that he understands.

[Intermission][35]

᷍᷍ ᪲

[Afternoon, in the street]

GIULIO, alone

GIULIO: O Venice, kind to strangers and courteous to young men, how can you have produced women of such beauty and loveliness? Because of it, I'm now in the difficult position of having to decide which game is better. That older woman—handsome, rich, and passionate—gave me her heart and soul, but she didn't want to tell me her name. And how clever she was, enjoying me without my knowing or being able to find out her address, her family, or her neighbor-

---

35. The original stage directions suggest here that "after a little while" another sung intermission is to be performed using a song by Girolamo Verità. The song is printed in *Girolamo Verità: filosofo e poeta veronese del secolo XVI*, ed. Lamberto Borlini (Verona: G. Franchini, 1905), 6.

hood! Moreover, she took me as her only lover, once I gave her a firm pledge that I'd be faithful to her. And maybe she did all this for a good reason—because she's a noble widow or a wife of the highest rank.

Now after all that, this other woman who up to now has been so hesitant has sent for me with great fervor.

O Fortune, you're always so perverse: sometimes you're too stingy, sometimes too kind. It's difficult to satisfy one woman, and impossible to satisfy two. I don't know which game to play, but it seems clear to me that I ought to keep the faith that I pledged to the first woman—I should give my soul only to her, considering how openly she offered herself, sought me out, embraced me, gave me gifts, loved and adored me.

But really, this other one has only asked to talk with me. Well, Giulio, you were never impolite. Go to her, speak with her, and, being as boring as possible, get her to send you away. Break things off, forget it, don't get involved with her. Still, if she should be more beautiful, what will I do? But really, she could hardly be as kind and courteous!

All right, I've decided: I'll go to her, and when the moment is right I'll gently reject her plans and focus on my diva. Ah, here's her emerald—her love—and the chain that reminds me that I'm her servant. I'll remember all this and not break my pledge.

❧ SCENE II ☙

[Evening, in Valiera's room]

VALIERA and ORIA

VALIERA: Will Giulio come, as you said? Tell me again, dear, sweet Oria.

ORIA: Didn't you hear me? At nine.

VALIERA: You should have convinced him that he wouldn't have to worry about a thing.

ORIA: He said he'd come for sure, and I didn't know what else to say.

VALIERA: All right. What time is it now?

ORIA: The bells have just sounded eight.

VALIERA: Let's go wait downstairs.

ORIA: So soon?

VALIERA: Don't you know the proverb: "The person who has time to wait, can't wait"?

ORIA: I don't want to stay with you two the whole time. When you've been together for a bit, I'll come back up here.

VALIERA: Do you think I just want to chat with him? I don't want to know anything more than if he loves me; then I'll tell him what to do.

ORIA: Do you want me to bring a candle?

VALIERA: Bring it, and leave it hidden behind the door. Let's go right now.

❦ SCENE III ❧

[*In the street*]

GIULIO, alone

GIULIO: [*Walking in front of* VALIERA*'s house*] This is a worse way to arrive than last night. Last night was secure, tonight is dangerous. Last night was unexpectedly great, tonight I expect will finish badly—that is, unless some great kindness or a very warm welcome doesn't make me change my mind. Trying new experiences is really intriguing, because it offers so many possibilities to discover new things.

I'm going, and where there's pleasure. . . . Maybe, why not? . . . Enough.

Here's the corner that the servant pointed out to me; the door is open. I'll have to enter forcefully so that if there's some evil afoot, I'll see it immediately. [*He rushes in*]

❦ ❧

[*Inside the door of* VALIERA*'s house*]

VALIERA, GIULIO, and ORIA

VALIERA: It's clear who has little love and trust: from the first I dreamed to give him my trust, yet he has so little trust in me that he comes armed!

GIULIO: Madam, arms are necessary for a young man, especially a foreigner, for a host of reasons.

VALIERA: Only a person who is not a lover needs to watch out for enemies in a home!

GIULIO: If Your Ladyship is not my friend and I learn that she is my enemy, well—

VALIERA: [*Interrupting*] Tell me, why didn't you deign to come last night?

GIULIO: I was a little indisposed, and I didn't think it was wise to go out.

VALIERA: Oh, what a lover! Even a little indisposition keeps him at home.

GIULIO: That doesn't mean for a moment that I'm not the servant of Your Ladyship or that I don't love you more than myself.

VALIERA: So you say, and God is your witness. What led you to start looking at me that way in the beginning?

GIULIO: Your beauty and your kindness, they bound me to you as your eternal prisoner the first time I saw you.

VALIERA: Where did you see me?

GIULIO: In the church of those nuns, where there was a party.[36]

VALIERA: Didn't you know that I was a newlywed?

GIULIO: I thought about nothing but the grace and beauty of Your Ladyship.

VALIERA: What is this that you have around your neck under your collar? Let me see it, please.

GIULIO: It's a golden chain.

VALIERA: Let me have a look at it.

GIULIO: Take it, Your Ladyship, and it's yours if you like.

VALIERA: [*Taking the chain and looking it over*] This chain was made in Venice.

GIULIO: Madam, I bought it here.

ORIA: Magnificent Madonna, do you know what chain this reminds me of? The one that Madonna Angela wore before her husband passed away.

VALIERA: Yes, by my faith, I'd say that this is it.

GIULIO: It could be, Madam, that she had it sold.

VALIERA: Something is rotten here. Enough! I understand.

GIULIO: If Your Ladyship wishes, I'll give it to you.

VALIERA: For heaven's sake, this chain wasn't bought, it was a gift!

GIULIO: Your Ladyship has little faith in me if you can't trust me about a little thing like this.

VALIERA: Messer Giulio, if you had been as faithful to me as I've been to you, you wouldn't have this chain. Do you understand me?

GIULIO: Your Ladyship has already formed a bad opinion, and I don't even know about what!

VALIERA: The indisposition of last night is clearly a big fat lie!

GIULIO: Forgive me, Your Ladyship, but no one has been lied to.

---

36. The convents of Venice were noted for their entertainments and were an important gathering place for visitors and local nobility.

VALIERA: Angela would do better to behave herself and not go running after things she should leave alone.

GIULIO: You're all worked up, and you don't even know the reason.

VALIERA: Enough! It's not right to deceive anyone, do you understand that, Messer Giulio? No, it's not right to take advantage this way of a poor young noblewoman. I'm every bit as good as Angela.

GIULIO: I don't understand.

VALIERA: Messer Giulio, I didn't deserve this. Oh well! Angela was more fortunate than I.

GIULIO: It saddens me that I've come here only to make you unhappy, Your Ladyship.

VALIERA: But I say that you've done well to come, because God wanted me to see that you don't love me the least little bit so that I wouldn't think about you ever again.

GIULIO: I don't know what to say to Your Ladyship.

VALIERA: Say whatever you wish; you have wronged me greatly.

GIULIO: If you want it that way, I'll confess.

VALIERA: If Angela is yours, keep her. I have nothing more to say, and I'll keep quiet.

GIULIO: I don't know Angela, on my word as a gentleman.

VALIERA: Come, now, enough is enough! Do you really think that I would abide such an insult? Well, I won't tolerate this at all.

GIULIO: Your Ladyship should not do anything rash or unjust.

VALIERA: Justice is what I want above all else. You can be sure that if I wished it and if I thought it touched my honor, I'd take it all the way to the Avogadori di Comun,[37] by the holy cross!

GIULIO: Neither your honor or your property has been offended by me, as far as I know.

VALIERA: Messer, you'll be judged, and if you've behaved badly, you will be punished.

GIULIO: Your Ladyship may give me whatever punishment you choose.

VALIERA: Do you know what someone like you who tricks others deserves? To be banished.

---

37. Venetian high state officials who among other things acted much like prosecuting attorneys. Valiera's threat is largely a bluff, since taking the matter to court would merely expose her dishonorable behavior to her husband and Venetian upper-class society at large. Padoan suggests that Valiera was in fact Valiera Valier, wife of Giacomo Semitecolo, whom he identifies as an actual Avogador di Comun at the time.

GIULIO: But I'm a foreigner!

VALIERA: Enough! Angela and you have destroyed me.

GIULIO: Not as far as I know.

VALIERA: The chain that you're wearing proves it.

GIULIO: I don't know what to say.

VALIERA: Messer, leave. And in the future, take care not to treat noblewomen this way. And tell Angela that Valiera will pay her back in time.

GIULIO: I commend myself to Your Ladyship.

VALIERA: Commend yourself to Angela, not to me. [*He leaves*]

ᯓ SCENE IV ᠅

[*In the street*]

GIULIO, alone

GIULIO: Well I'll be damned! She recognized that chain in a heartbeat! And she says that Angela is a widow. They know each other well. I was totally out of my league.

Well, if she doesn't love me anymore, I'll be that much more appreciated by the other. And because Angela is a suspicious type, it would be a good idea to let her know that Valiera hates her. If she loves me now, she'll love me even more when she hears that.

Things have worked out just as I wished; I'll have only one burden. Two women are too much for any man—not just for me, but even for a giant, even if he were much stronger than Atlas.

[*Intermission*][38]

---

38. There is a sung intermission here by Fracastoro; it is published in *Ariosto, Castiglione, Fracastoro, Sannazaro, Casa,* 91.

ᵔᵔᵔ SCENE V ᵔᵔᵔ

[The next morning, in the street]

ORIA

ORIA: *[Walking]* My God! Could anybody, even a smooth-tongued preacher, ever be wise enough to understand how to please a noblewoman? Last night Madonna was furious with Messer Giulio and didn't want to have anything to do with him. Now she's all worked up and wants him dead or alive. And she doesn't want to talk anymore about Madonna Angela or her Messer Angel, Giulio. She's sent me to give him this letter, which she wrote with tears in her eyes during the night, and she wants me to beg him to come back this evening so that she can make peace with him. She can't think or speak of anything but him. She didn't let me sleep a wink the whole night. It was constantly "Oria, daughter, I'm dead because Giulio is angry with me and doesn't want to see me ever again." And I said, "Why did you throw him out, then?" And she said, "Because I was so jealous." And so she kept me up the whole night. Give me patience! "Do you know what you have to say to Messer Giulio? That he must come and that he shouldn't pay any attention to what was said to him, that Madonna needs him more than food and that as soon as he arrives he should go to bed with her to make peace." I'll tell him that, on my word, and then all the problems will be solved.

Act V

ᵔᵔᵔ SCENE I ᵔᵔᵔ

[Morning, in the street]

BERNARDO, GIULIO, and ORIA

BERNARDO: Good day to my honored young patron.
GIULIO: Good day to you, my brother. What good news do you have?
BERNARDO: What do you think? More of the same music as the other day.
GIULIO: Have you come, then, from that noblewoman who is your patron and my lady?
BERNARDO: I'm not sure where I'm coming from, myself; but for now it's enough that I've come back about that music.
GIULIO: Well, you're welcome and more than welcome.

BERNARDO: You understand, right?

GIULIO: I understand. There's no need to go on so that I'll keep quiet; I got it.

BERNARDO: I'm saying that I want to take you to a person who'll give you more caresses than Bernardo.

GIULIO: [*Laughing*] You're both taking care of me!

ORIA: [*Entering, but staying apart*] Goodness! There's a man with him. Oh dear, I don't know what to do; I'm unsure. But wait, he's leaving.

BERNARDO: [*Speaking to* ORIA *as he leaves* GIULIO] Hello, what are you up to? Are you looking for some meat of your own?

ORIA: Go away, I don't want anything from porters.

BERNARDO: Come on, you don't have to look any farther. [*She turns away*] All right, keep looking, then. Eventually you'll find a man who knows how to handle you. [*He leaves*]

ORIA: [*Approaching* GIULIO] Messer Giulio, may I have a couple of words with Your Magnificence?

GIULIO: Madam . . . ? Oh, Madonna Oria! Forgive me, my sister, I didn't recognize you. What can I do for you?

ORIA: Messer Giulio, the moment you left Madonna Valiera last night, unhappy and upset, she fell apart and has been a wreck ever since. She's been constantly in tears. Why, she's half dead! You must come this evening to comfort her, otherwise she'll die of grief. Dear handsome Messer Giulio, come back, for you'll bring great happiness to both yourself and her!

GIULIO: I'm very sorry that Madonna Valiera found a reason to be sad— really I am, as God is my witness—because I'm a good servant of hers. And I'm even more sorry that I can't relieve her suffering, which I'd do willingly.

ORIA: What? What do you mean, you can't do it? Why, you're the only one who can cure her! If you come at once she'll be cured.

GIULIO: I don't want to add to her suffering by going to see her. She's easily upset, and she doesn't trust me. When she sees me she'll get so worked up that it will do her harm.

ORIA: Don't say that. The truth is that she's suffering because she got angry with you, and she's been devastated about it ever since. She doesn't want to quarrel about anything with you anymore, as long as you're content, and she wants you to be her honor and her soul.

GIULIO: Please thank Her Ladyship, but I don't know what I can do, because I need to go to Padua tonight to meet some of my relatives who're coming to the university there.

ORIA: Messer, the time has come to stop fooling around. Look, it's absolutely necessary that you come, and then after you've been with her, you can go wherever you like.

GIULIO: What's all this "absolutely necessary" all of a sudden?

ORIA: What's the use of all this talk? She's going to die if she can't make peace with you!

GIULIO: Give me your hand, and I'll make peace with you in her name.

ORIA: I can tell you that that's not worth anything—she needs to touch your hand herself. And then if you'll listen, I can tell you that for every angry word you exchanged, she wants to give you a kiss. [*She hands* GIULIO VALIERA's *letter, which he quickly reads*]

GIULIO: Do you want me to come, then?

ORIA: Yes, sweet, dear, golden Messer Giulio.

GIULIO: At what time?

ORIA: At the same time as the other unhappy night.

GIULIO: I hope to God that tonight won't be like last time.

ORIA: I promise that this time it will be heavenly.

GIULIO: All right, I agree. Wait for me and greet the Madonna for me and commend me to her until I arrive.

ORIA: Peace be with you. [*She leaves*]

GIULIO: Again I'm starting the Via Crucis.[39] My adventures are coming in pairs, and things aren't going to be simple. Look, even the porter and the servant make a pair! How can I resolve this mess so that I don't get in trouble somehow? I swear, by the holy faith! . . . Hmmm, unless. . . . When the porter comes, I could refuse to get into the gondola unless he tells me the name of his mistress. He'll certainly refuse, and then, pretending to be angry, I'll send him away and go to Valiera to try a new dish.

[*Intermission*][40]

---

39. Literally, the way of the cross. One of the more popular expressions of religious enthusiasm in renaissance Italy was the imaginative reenactment of Christ's sufferings on the way to His crucifixion, the Via Crucis, as it was described in the Bible. One could do this privately or by following a prescribed itinerary in a church or other holy place.

40. The sung intermission that appears here is attributed only to "P.A.," and according to Padoan it is otherwise unknown. The initials may refer to Pietro Aretino.

❧ SCENE II ❧

[Evening, in the street, facing a canal]

BERNARDO and GIULIO

BERNARDO: *[Calling from his gondola]* Hey there, you on the land, what are you waiting for? I whistled six times. Didn't you hear me?

GIULIO: Bernardo! You're here already?

BERNARDO: Don't you see me here? Come on, hop aboard. It's time.

GIULIO: All right. But before I come aboard, I want you to tell me the name of our friend and where she lives, because I don't want to go crazy trying to remember every twist and turn of our trip.

BERNARDO: What's bothering you now? I don't know, and even if I knew I wouldn't tell you.

GIULIO: If you won't tell me, I won't come.

BERNARDO: I do believe that you've lost your mind. Don't you know where I want to take you?

GIULIO: I know, but I want to know better.

BERNARDO: Now I get it! Your stallion must be all tired out, if your ass is dragging like this.

GIULIO: Whether I'm tired out or ready to go, you get my point.

BERNARDO: Things go badly when the rose loses its blush.

GIULIO: I'm not coming. I've decided.

BERNARDO: I understand you perfectly: you want to put this off until tomorrow.

GIULIO: Go and tell Madonna that I don't want to come again until I know her name.

BERNARDO: By God, I'll do just that! I'll tell her. You'll not learn anything from me unless she agrees.

GIULIO: That's fine. Go talk with her.

BERNARDO: Don't think for a minute that I'll wait for tomorrow; I'll go to her right now, at once. *[He rows off]*

GIULIO: Great, my plan worked! Now for Oria! Giulio, get going, time flies. If Bernardo should return he won't find me here, and he'll have no way to bother me this evening.

❧ SCENE III ❧

[Inside VALIERA*'s house, near the street door]*

ORIA, VALIERA, and GIULIO

ORIA: Madonna Valiera, what would you give if this man coming along making so much noise was Messer Giulio?

VALIERA: Do you know what I'd give? Why, I'd give as much as this ring on my finger is worth!

ORIA: Quiet! It's surely him.

VALIERA: If you're right, I love you more than my sister Laurina.

ORIA: I wish! Be quiet and listen a little. Is it really him? *[Coming out the door into the street, followed by* VALIERA*]* Good evening, sir.

GIULIO: Who's this? Oh, good evening.

ORIA: Messer Giulio, you've earned me all Madonna's love by coming now.

GIULIO: I'm glad, and I'm also earning it.

VALIERA: You have earned a body and soul that would have been lost if you hadn't come.

GIULIO: My lady, I don't want to earn a thing beyond the respect of Your Ladyship so that you'll deign to have me as your servant.

VALIERA: No, I want you to be my master. You know very well how much pain you caused me because I wanted to be the master. But from this moment on I want to be your servant in every way.

GIULIO: Don't say that, Your Ladyship. I don't deserve it.

ORIA: Magnificent Madonna, it's time for Messer Giulio to make that peace with you that I didn't want him to make with me in your place.

VALIERA: Messer Giulio, my heart, why have you been so cruel to me?

GIULIO: Cruel to you, Your Ladyship? God forbid! Really, my only desire is to be most gentle with my goddess.

VALIERA: If that's the case, I want you to be mine, and forgive me if I upset you the other day.

GIULIO: Forgive me, Your Ladyship, if I caused you sadness. But now I'm all yours and ready to turn all your suffering into pleasure.

ORIA: What sweet, golden words!

VALIERA: Dear Messer Giulio, we often say that it's foolish to speak like this in the street, because the walls have ears and eyes. Come inside, and give me the pleasure of looking at you in the light. *[They all go into the house]*

GIULIO: Your Ladyship doesn't need to discuss anything with me. Just order me, saying "I want this," for I'm yours.

VALIERA: I'll do just that, Messer Giulio, my handsome, sweet child.

ORIA: Madonna, do you intend to make peace so quickly?!

GIULIO: Peace, Madonna, is written on your beautiful face, which bound me to you from the first time I saw it.

VALIERA: Oria, my dear, close the door to this room and go upstairs to keep track of the old lord so that he doesn't get worked up about anything. And if he should ask for me, tell him that I'm not feeling well and that I don't want anyone bothering me this evening.

ORIA: Leave it to me. I'll take care of it thoroughly and at once.

"This is not a fable or a comedy but a true story."[41]

41. There appears in the manuscript a later addition of a few lines in Latin questioning why the comedy was written and instructing the reader to "read, learn, and keep silent" about the events here narrated.

LAURA GIANNETTI, formerly a professor of Italian literature and history at the Istituto Magistrale "Duca degli Abruzzi" in Treviso, is now an associate professor in the Department of Modern Languages and Literatures at the University of Miami. In addition to several articles on Renaissance comedy, she has recently published *Lelia's Kiss: Imagining Gender, Sex and Marriage in Italian Renaissance Comedies*.

GUIDO RUGGIERO is a professor of history and chair of the department of history at the University of Miami. His books include *The Boundaries of Eros: Sex Crime and Sexuality in Renaissance Venice, Binding Passions: Tales of Magic, Marriage, and Power at the End of the Renaissance*, and *Machiavelli in Love: Self, Sex, and Society in the Italian Renaissance*.

Guido Ruggiero and Laura Giannetti spend summers at their home in Treviso, Italy, just north of Venice, where they often hike in the nearby Dolomites and enjoy exploring the local restaurants and wineries. They continue to research and write on sex and sexual identity in the Renaissance (Ruggiero) and the culture of food in Renaissance literature (Giannetti).